# VOICES FROM THE GRAVE

*by the same author*

THE SECRET HISTORY OF THE IRA
PAISLEY: FROM DEMAGOGUE TO DEMOCRAT?

# VOICES FROM THE GRAVE

## Two Men's War in Ireland

### ED MOLONEY

The publishers would like to acknowledge that any
interview material used in *Voices from the Grave* has been
provided by kind permission from the Boston College Center
for Irish Programs IRA/UVF project that is archived at the
Burns Library on the Chestnut Hill campus of Boston College.

PublicAffairs
New York

This book is dedicated to all those
who shared their memories
with the researchers from Boston College.

# CONTENTS

# ILLUSTRATIONS

Catholic families in Belfast flee their burning homes in the wake of Loyalist attacks. © *Belfast Telegraph*

Curfew on the Falls Road, 1970. © Victor Patterson

Seamus Twomey confronts British troops at Lenadoon.
© Victor Patterson

British troops patrol Divis Street. © *Belfast Telegraph*

'Bloody Friday', July 1972. © Pacemaker Press International

Jean McConville with three of her children.
© Pacemaker Press International

Gerry Adams photographed by British military intelligence after his arrest. © Victor Patterson

Ivor Bell photographed by British military intelligence after his arrest. © Victor Patterson

Brendan Hughes photographed by British military intelligence after his arrest. © Victor Patterson

Mass card for Paddy Joe Crawford. Reproduced with kind permission of Gerry McCann.

Robert 'Basher' Bates, one of the Shankill Butchers.
© Pacemaker Press International

Brendan Hughes in prison hospital during the failed 1980 hunger strike. © Pacemaker Press International

Brendan Hughes comforts a woman wounded in the Milltown cemetery attack, 1988. © Derek Speirs

Brendan Hughes in his Divis Tower flat with Anthony McIntyre.
© Kelvin Boyes

Gerry Adams carrying Brendan Hughes's coffin. © Kelvin Boyes

McGurk's Bar, December 1971. © *Belfast Telegraph*

Explosion on Talbot Street in Dublin, 1974. © *Belfast Telegraph*

David Ervine poses with Gusty Spence and fellow UVF internees
in Long Kesh. From the Bobbie Hanvey Photographic Archives,
John J. Burns Library, Boston College, presented to Hanvey by
Gusty Spence, and used with the permission of Gusty Spence,
though photographer uncertain.

Gusty Spence reviewing UVF internees on parade in Long Kesh.
From the Bobbie Hanvey Photographic Archives, John J. Burns
Library, Boston College, presented to Hanvey by Gusty Spence,
and used with the permission of Gusty Spence, though
photographer uncertain.

Gusty Spence with 'Buck Alec' Robinson. From the Bobbie
Hanvey Photographic Archives, John J. Burns Library, Boston
College, presented to Hanvey by Gusty Spence, and used with the
permission of Gusty Spence, though photographer uncertain.

David Ervine and Billy Hutchinson after their election to the new
Northern Ireland Assembly, 1998.
© Pacemaker Press International

Gerry Adams comforts David Ervine's widow, Jeanette.
© Kelvin Boyes

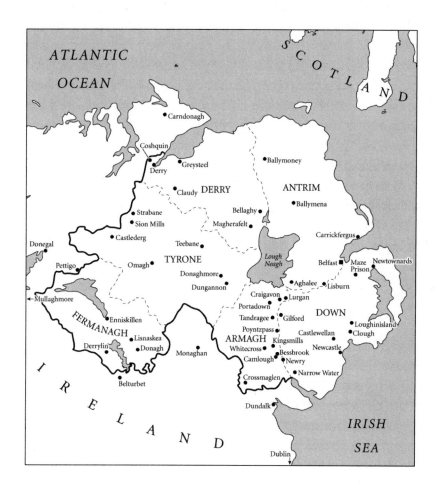

Map of Northern Ireland showing some of the places
referred to in the book

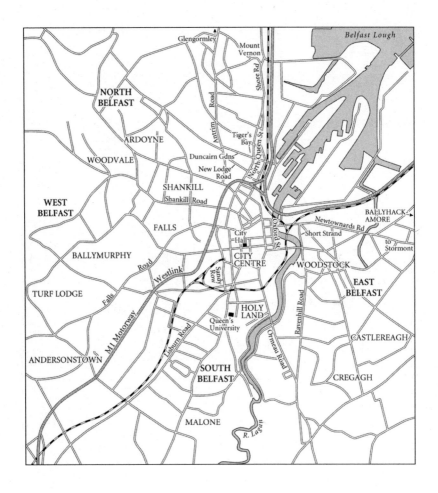

Map of Belfast showing some of the places referred to in the book

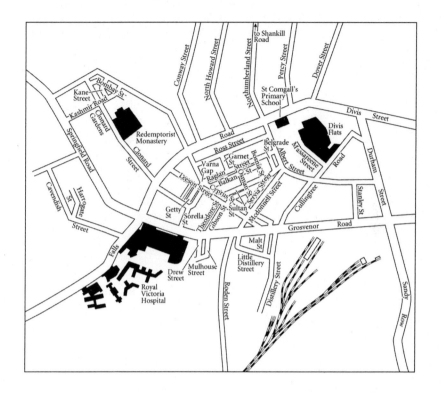

Map of the Lower Falls Road area, *c.* 1969, showing some
of the places referred to in the book

# PREFACE

This book represents the inaugural volume of a planned series of publications drawn from the Boston College Oral History Archive on the Troubles in Northern Ireland. The transcripts of interviews with Irish Republican Army and Ulster Volunteer Force veterans, most of whom were operationally active, are housed at the University's Burns Library and are subject to prescriptive limitations governing access. Boston College is contractually committed to sequestering the taped transcriptions unless otherwise given a full release, in writing, by the interviewees, or until the demise of the latter.

With the production of this initial book in the projected series, the General Editors wish to acknowledge the tireless and fruitful work of the project coordinator, Ed Moloney, whose personal contacts, professional skills, and established reputation as an accomplished journalist and historian were an incalculable asset in this undertaking. Profound thanks are also owed to Anthony McIntyre and Wilson McArthur, formerly activists from opposing sides who each took degrees at Queen's University, Belfast, and whose contacts among IRA and UVF paramilitary veterans helped make this oral history a reality.

Paul Bew, politics professor and senior political adviser to a Northern Ireland first minister, together with two historians who remain anonymous, assisted in an assessment of the information contained in the recorded interviews. Lord Bew strongly encouraged Boston College to document and archive the stories of paramilitaries who fought on both sides of that sectarian divide, known more popularly as the Troubles, because it was such a natural fit. Boston College has had a long interest in Ireland and offered a welcoming and neutral venue in which participants felt a sense of security and confidentiality that made it possible for them to be candid and forthcoming. What Bew perceived as the real value of the IRA/UVF accounts was in what they revealed about the motives and mind sets of participants in the conflict, a resource of inestimable value for future studies attempting better to understand the phenomenology of societal violence.

Ed Moloney's succinct and instructive introduction further underscores the scope and significance of the extraordinary archive on which this seminal account is based. What may not be as readily apparent to many people is why Boston College was seen as a familiar and trusted institution by all parties participating in this programme. Not only has the Irish Studies Faculty participated in faculty exchanges and appointments at Ulster universities over the past two decades, with professors from those institutions also serving as visiting scholars at Boston College; the University awarded an honorary degree to Irish nationalist leader John Hume of the Social Democratic Labour Party in 1995 and to British Unionist David Trimble of the Ulster Unionist Party in 1999.

Moreover, for a period of some twelve years the Irish Institute at Boston College has provided educational seminars for public officials, business leaders, policing authorities, etc., under a programme sponsored by the United States Congress, as a part of its effort to promote peace and reconciliation in Northern Ireland. Under the aegis of the Department of State, the Irish Institute has hosted seminars both at Boston College and at best-practice professional counterparts throughout the United States. The Irish participants come from the Republic and Northern Ireland, including some from both sectarian communities in the North. More than eight hundred people from various professions in Ireland have participated to date, and the seminars, especially those on community policing, cultural diversity and local-government management, have nurtured networking contacts among formerly adversarial groups in Northern Ireland who now perceive Boston College as their enabler.

It is the Burns Library, however, arguably the crown jewel of the

Boston College Centre for Irish Programmes, that provides the ideal repository for this unique archive. The extensive holdings of the Burns have long attracted researchers from all over the globe, including many of the most distinguished chair-holders throughout Britain and Ireland.

The John J. Burns Library of Boston College houses the largest, most comprehensive collection of Irish research materials in the United States, with more than 50,000 volumes, nearly 600,000 manuscript pieces, and significant holdings of photographs, artworks, recordings and ephemera documenting the history, life and culture of the Irish people. Material on Ireland since the Act of Union is particularly strong, including a superb collection of 138 late eighteenth-century pamphlets bound in nine volumes from the library of Daniel O'Connell dealing with the question of the Union; a rare collection of some 1,500 pamphlets bound in 105 volumes dating from the late 1700s to the mid-1800s, many dealing with the province of Ulster; the Canon Patrick Rogers Collection on the Troubles from 1916 to the 1980s, featuring many rare pamphlets and ephemeral pieces; the Thomas and Kathleen Clarke Papers; the Grand Orange Lodge of Ireland Collection; and the Bobbie Hanvey Photographic Archives, documenting many of the people, places and events in Northern Ireland in the time of the Troubles.

These collections were developed to further the academic mission of Boston College, founded in 1863 by the County Fermanagh-born Jesuit John McElroy to provide higher education to the children of refugees of the Irish Famine. Over the years Boston College has strengthened its ties with Ireland, North and South, establishing special relations through its various programmes with various institutions in Ireland and Northern Ireland. In 1999, for example, Boston College entered into an agreement of understanding with Linen Hall Library to share resources, enhance access to each other's library collections and promote knowledge and understanding. The Burns Library was the opening venue in 2003 for a nine-city North American tour of the award-winning exhibition *Troubled Images* from the Linen Hall Library, Belfast.

This unique paramilitary archive finds a proper place among the Burns Library's rich and diverse holdings of Irish books, collections of private papers, poetry, paintings and digitised music relating directly to Northern Ireland.

GENERAL EDITORS

Thomas E. Hachey
University Professor of History
and Executive Director, Center for Irish Programs

Robert K. O'Neill
Director, John J. Burns Library,
and Part-Time Faculty Member, Department of Political Science

# INTRODUCTION

There should have been more than one byline on the cover of this book but sadly it could not be. Thankfully the writing of this introduction provides an opportunity to remedy this deficit and to acknowledge that this book would never have seen the light of day but for the foresight, commitment and hard work of other people.

At the top of the list are the good people at Boston College who backed and funded this project when it was mooted back in 2000/2001. Professor Tom Hachey, the Executive Director of the Center for Irish Programs at the University, and Dr Bob O'Neill, Librarian at the John J. Burns Library, were both quick to recognise the potential of such an archive and they have thrown their weight behind it from the outset and throughout its life.

The notion of an archive devoted to Northern Ireland's paramilitaries was inspired by, if not modelled on, the Bureau of Military History established by the Irish government in 1947 and charged with compiling the history of the movement for independence between 1913 and 1921. While both projects had similar goals – collecting the life stories of those who fought in an Irish conflict – the Bureau had certain advantages denied to this enterprise, and it is to Boston College's credit that, despite these, the decision was made to support it.

The Bureau started its work some twenty-five years after the Anglo-Irish War had ended, when many of those active in those years were still alive and enough time had passed to cool the passions that earlier had almost certainly helped to seal lips. But time was not on the side of anyone seeking to replicate the Bureau's work in Northern Ireland. It was a case of doing it now, in less than perfect circumstances but while some key participants were still living, or allowing their untold stories to go to the grave.

5

Another advantage enjoyed by the Bureau of Military History was that the Irish taxpayer was footing the bill. That was not the case in Boston. This was not an inexpensive project and while some private funding was forthcoming, the bulk of the finance was provided by Boston College. Not only did Tom Hachey and Bob O'Neill happily canvass funds on our behalf when necessary, but they, and the readers of this book, were fortunate to have, as the target of their lobbying effort, Dr Patrick Keating, Executive Vice-President of Boston College, who understood and appreciated the historical value of this project and invariably received their financial overtures positively. Without his help none of this would have been possible.

One disadvantage, however, could not be as easily overcome. When this proposal was made, the Good Friday Agreement had not taken root; paramilitary weapons remained available for use, and the IRA and Loyalist ceasefires were still highly conditional. Not only were many passions still inflamed but no one could even say that the 'war' in Northern Ireland was over. None the less, it was our collective view that the conflict was on an irresistible course towards an ending.

The key consideration in going ahead was the willingness of interviewees, even before the smoke of battle had cleared from the field, to open up candidly and comprehensively not only about their own lives and activities but about others' as well. It seemed unlikely that they would be receptive to the traditional academic researcher – or, in the case of the Bureau of Military History, soldier researcher – and so to maximise trust, and the value of the interviews, it was decided that the interviewers should be people the interviewees could trust, who broadly came from the same communities while being academically qualified individuals with a record of research.

The other missing bylines on this book therefore are of Anthony McIntyre, a Ballymurphy Republican and Ph.D. who handled interviews with IRA and INLA activists and Wilson McArthur, a Shankill Road, former PUP activist and a political science graduate of Queen's University, Belfast, who interviewed UVF and PUP members. Their contribution went beyond researching and conducting the interviews; they took on extra research for this book and for that and their comments and analysis, I am grateful. Their work for Boston College was overseen by myself and I can testify to their individual objectivity and commitment to the truth. The fault for any deficiency in the final product therefore lies at my door while the credit for what is good resides mostly at theirs.

A defining rule of the project was that no material could be used until and unless the interviewee consented or had died. As fate would have it, among the first of our interviewees to pass away were two of the most fascinating figures of the Troubles, the Provisional IRA's Brendan Hughes and David Ervine of the UVF and PUP. Both men had ringside seats at the making of history and were either close associates of leaders or were leaders themselves who helped shape and determine events during this most extraordinary time in Irish history.

Their stories overlapped at crucial moments. Brendan Hughes commanded the IRA teams that ferried car bombs into Belfast on the day that would become known as 'Bloody Friday' while the death and destruction caused that afternoon pushed David Ervine into the arms of the UVF. Their lives wouldn't directly cross again until their deaths over thirty years later when their funerals symbolised how differently they had seen the ending of a conflict that had moulded their narratives.

Hughes died believing the struggle he had waged had been lost and betrayed while Ervine considered that his side, the UVF, had won most of what it had fought for, not least a more secure Union with Britain. Ervine died a successful, respectable politician, welcome in Downing Street and the White House, and fêted as a peacemaker wherever he went. Hughes died amid failure and recrimination, distrusting many of those he had fought alongside in the IRA's war and mourning the role played in facilitating the endgame by Gerry Adams, the closest of his one-time comrades but at the end the Michael Collins to his Harry Boland. Gerry

Adams's presence at both men's funerals was the last occasion that the two men's stories crossed and his appearance provided the metaphor for how their lives had ended: a welcome at David Ervine's service but a cold shoulder at Brendan Hughes's.

The purpose of the Boston College–Burns Library Archive was to collect a story of the Troubles that otherwise would be lost, distorted or rewritten, deliberately by those with a vested interest, or otherwise by the passage of time or the distortion wrought in the retelling. The resulting archive, while small in comparison to that compiled by the Bureau of Military History, provides a rare and valuable resource for historians seeking to explain and understand the Troubles. This book is the first fruit of the project. The stories of Brendan Hughes and David Ervine are very different but between them a captivating and valuable insight into a hitherto hidden world becomes visible. One thing is certain; there is more to come.

Editing the many thousands of words in the transcripts of the two men's interviews was not an easy task. The spoken word rarely transcribes perfectly or follows the rules of grammar with exactitude and is, believe me, much more prone to repetition. Oral-history purists will again object but in places the editing has been heavy when necessary but non-existent when not. Occasionally sentences have been rewritten to restore the intended meaning more elegantly but great care has been taken to ensure fidelity to the thoughts being expressed. Ultimately, though, this book was written to be read and enjoyed.

David Ervine was interviewed between May and October 2004; Brendan Hughes between March 2001 and August 2002. The interviews were recorded on broadcast-quality digital tape and were patiently and painstakingly transcribed by Michelle Millar in Crumlin, County Antrim. The interviews were then sent by encrypted email to the author and, after editing and indexing, the tapes and transcripts were shipped by the researchers to the Burns Library in Boston for storage.

*Introduction*

In addition to Tom Hachey, Bob O'Neill, Patrick Keating, Anthony McIntyre and Wilson McArthur, I would like to thank and credit a number of other people for their help in making this book possible: Jonathan Williams, my agent in Dublin, who once again produced the goods; my editor, Neil Belton, who was shrewd enough to recognise the value of this book, and his endlessly helpful assistant, Katherine Armstrong of Faber and Faber; Professor, now Lord, Bew, whose support at the very outset of the project was crucial; Resham Naqvi and Kate Murray-Browne of Faber and Faber; former Boston College Librarian, Jerome Yavarkovsky; Francis, Colette and Giselle Keenan for their hospitality in Belfast; Stephen Maxwell, Forensic Handwriting Expert, Northern Ireland; David McKittrick for his advice on the UVF; the Hughes and Ervine families in Belfast; Gerry McCann and Father Matt Wallace; the family of Joe Linskey; Frank Costello in Belfast for his encouragement; the Poor Sisters of Nazareth; Paddy Joe Rice; Alastair Gordon of the Linenhall Library; Professor Bob White of Indiana University who began the work of collecting the IRA's oral history and was generous with his advice; Ciaran and Stephanie for their love and support, and finally my wife, Joan, whose summer in the Catskills was again dominated by events from another existence and who carried the burden with patience, love and understanding.

Ed Moloney
Deer Lake, New York
August 2009

# BRENDAN HUGHES

1

Brendan Hughes was there at the very beginning, at one of the places where the Provisional IRA first saw the light of day. Republican mythology has it that there was only one birthplace, Bombay Street on 15 August 1969, a narrow terrace of small mill-workers' homes crouched, as if for protection, under the tower of a Redemptorist monastery set right in the heart of the Clonard district of West Belfast. There is a lot of truth to that, but what happened in Bombay Street on that late summer afternoon some forty years ago is only part of the story, only a partial explanation of what the Provisional IRA was and why it came into being.

Bombay Street was at the very borderline between the Catholic–Nationalist Falls Road and the Protestant–Loyalist Shankill Road, two of the largest of Belfast's many divided ghettos and the scene over the previous century or so of intermittent and often vicious sectarian violence. The date, 15 August, was the Feast of the Assumption in the Catholic Church's calendar, the equivalent in the Northern Nationalist community of the Orangemen's 'Twelfth of July', and the growing tension and violence that had spread like wildfire from Derry to Belfast in the previous few days spilled once more onto the streets of Clonard.

In the afternoon, a mob of angry Protestants from the Shankill area surged through the district determined to burn down the monastery and much of the surrounding area. There was a widely held conviction among the Loyalists that IRA gunmen in the past had used the monastery's spires as a sniper's platform from where they could pick off people in the Shankill at will. There was hand-to-hand fighting, many petrol bombs were tossed into Catholic homes and some of the Protestants were armed. Shots rang out and a fifteen-year-old boy, Gerald McAuley, fell fatally wounded. A member of the IRA's youth wing, the Fianna, he was the first Republican activist to be killed in what would soon become known as the Troubles.[1] There was minimal resistance though from Clonard's traditional defenders, the IRA. For some time now in the hands of a largely Marxist leadership in far-off Dublin, the IRA high command favoured political methods over the gun and the military side of the organisation had been run down. It was widely believed, for instance, that much of the IRA's weaponry had been sold to the Free Wales Army and while this explanation was probably apocryphal, it was beyond doubt that the IRA had next to no guns to defend areas such as Clonard. The Protestant mob had virtually a free hand and soon Bombay Street was on fire from one end to the other. By the next morning all that was left was a series of charred, blackened shells.

Within a few months the IRA would split into an Official and a Provisional IRA, names that were more the invention of the media than the choice of their leaders, and while there were significant political and ideological differences between the two factions – Republicans in the rural West and South of Ireland as well as many in the North were far more conservative than the Dublin Marxists – there was little doubt that the IRA's failure to defend Catholic areas such as Bombay Street had been the catalyst to bring long-simmering internal discord to the surface. The militant Provisional wing that emerged from the split chose as its icon a phoenix rising from the ashes of Bombay Street, picked deliberately to symbolise a determination that such a thing would never happen again.

While the burning of Bombay Street embodied the vulnerability of many Catholics in places such as West Belfast and was a symbol of victimhood that made marvellous propaganda for the new Provisional IRA, it was not true to say that the IRA in Belfast had been entirely inoperative during those turbulent and violent days. A day or so before Loyalist petrol bombs had razed Bombay Street, in an incident that Lord Scarman, the British judge chosen to probe the violent events of August 1969, would call, 'the only clear evidence of IRA participation'[2] in the events, a shooting took place that would herald another, more central characteristic of the new Provisional IRA: its determination to repay Unionist, and later British, violence in the same coinage or more. And Brendan Hughes helped make it happen.

Hughes was not a member of the IRA at the time, although in his interviews with Boston College he talked almost as if he were, possibly because the incident would be long remembered in Republican lore as one of the few examples of IRA defiance during those unsettled and brutal days. A seaman in the Merchant Navy, Hughes was back in his native West Belfast on a break between voyages when the trouble began – and what would happen in the following days meant he would never go back to sea. His return to his native city came at one of those moments when history turns.

A year or so of civil rights agitation by Catholic Nationalists seeking an end to Unionist-imposed discrimination in jobs and housing, the scrapping of gerrymandering and the restoration of equal voting rights had galvanised hardline Protestant and Loyalist opposition, much of it mobilised by a young, fiery preacher by the name of Ian Paisley. In the eyes of Paisley and his followers the civil rights campaign was merely cunning camouflage for an IRA plot to take Northern Ireland out of the United Kingdom and into a Catholic-dominated all-Ireland state and they were pledged to oppose it at every opportunity. Throughout 1969, clashes between civil rights marchers and the North's police force, the Royal Ulster Constabulary (RUC) on the one hand, and on the other between civil rights marchers and the Paisleyites, had grown in number and violent intensity. By the time the Orange marching season reached its height, in July and August 1969, Northern Ireland was on the edge of a dangerous precipice. On 12 August, during the annual parade of the Protestant Apprentice Boys of Derry, the tinderbox exploded into flames. Serious rioting between the Loyalist marchers and Nationalists from the Bogside, a Catholic slum that lay like a besieging army encamped under the walls of Derry, soon turned into a vicious clash between the Bogsiders and the RUC.

As the skies of Derry were darkened by volleys of stones and petrol bombs tossed at the RUC, and CS gas fired by the police enveloped the Bogside in a toxic fog, civil rights leaders acted to relieve the pressure on the Bogsiders. Orders went out to mobilise their followers in Belfast, Dungannon, Coalisland, Dungiven, Newry and Armagh, where protests and pickets were staged outside police stations. The decision to deploy civil rights supporters outside Derry was intended to draw the RUC away from the Bogside, to relieve pressure on the exhausted rioters, but its effect was like pouring petrol on a bonfire, and the consequences were predictable – the flames spread wildly.

The violence that followed was worst in West Belfast on the night of 14 August. Earlier that day, a company of the British Army, the Prince of Wales's Own Regiment, had replaced the RUC on the streets of Derry, an admission that the police there had lost control of the situation. The arrival of the troops brought scenes rarely witnessed in Irish history: Catholics welcomed the British soldiers as their saviours and celebrated the withdrawal of the RUC as a famous victory over Unionist rule. But the decision unnerved Protestants and that night in Belfast the guns came out. Protestant mobs surged onto the streets, their anger at events in Derry fuelled by alcohol. One of Ian Paisley's lieutenants, John McKeague, a Loyalist zealot, had formed the Shankill Defence Association, an early forerunner of the Protestant paramilitaries that would soon sprout everywhere, and he was active mobilising the mobs.

There were clashes in Ardoyne, in North Belfast and on the Falls Road where, in the Conway Street area, Catholic homes were petrol-bombed by Loyalist mobs as the police stood by, either powerless or unwilling to intervene. At one stage a huge Loyalist crowd advanced down Dover Street, at the point where the Catholic Falls Road and the Protestant Shankill Road are closest, at a place called Divis Street, and shots were fired from the Catholic side killing a Protestant rioter. Assuming the IRA was responsible, the RUC opened fire, using heavy-calibre Browning machine guns mounted atop Shorland armoured vehicles. Rounds the officers fired bounced off the tarmac outside Donegall Pass RUC station two miles away, adding to a police perception of a wide-scale Republican attack. Almost immediately a nine-year-old Catholic schoolboy, Patrick Rooney, was killed by a police tracer round which pierced his bedroom wall in Divis Tower, the tallest building in a large public-housing complex, and hit him in the head as he lay in bed.[3] When the violence finally subsided, four Catholics had been killed by police fire and one Protestant had been shot dead by someone on the Catholic side. The following day, 15 August, saw the Protestant assault on Clonard and the firebombing of Bombay Street and, by that evening, the British Army was on the streets of West Belfast, as well as in Derry. The Troubles were under way.

The extent of IRA involvement in all this was far from clear. The identity or allegiance of the gunman who fired the shot that killed the Protestant rioter in Dover Street is not known. But the IRA had very few weapons, and it is possible an armed civilian was responsible: 'There was a couple of .303s,* a couple of revolvers, and one Thompson sub-machine gun' in the IRA's arsenal that night, Hughes would later recall, hardly enough to protect Catholic Belfast from the rampaging Loyalist mobs. But the IRA's one Thompson machine gun, a veteran of a previous age, was put to use that night in Divis Street, as Hughes recalled:

*. . . when the Loyalist mobs came down off the Shankill [they] were attacking St Comgall's school with petrol bombs, stones and everything. I mean, they just wrecked the whole front of the school. I knew the school, I had gone there as a child and I showed ——, the IRA guy who had the Thompson, how to go through the school, through the classrooms [and] up onto the roof. I remember that McKeague, I think it was McKeague[†] . . . was leading [the crowds]. I was on top of the roof with —— [and the Protestants] were firing*

---

* A .303 is a .303-calibre Lee Enfield breech-loading rifle, which until the 1960s was British Army standard issue and a popular IRA weapon in the 1950s and 1960s.
† John McKeague, Loyalist activist and at the time Chairman of the Shankill Defence Association. He was shot dead by the INLA (Irish National Liberation Army) in January 1982.

*petrol bombs, a massive mob of people, right onto the Falls Road. I
was trying to encourage —— to shoot into the crowd [but] he was
under orders from Jimmy Sullivan, the O/C [Officer Commanding]
of the IRA at that time in the Falls area, not to shoot into the crowd,
[but] to fire over their heads. So, he emptied a magazine over their
heads which did break the crowd up. They retreated back into the
Shankill and we retreated off the roof.*

Those were the first authorised shots fired by the IRA in the
Troubles, or at least the first that can be authenticated, and the
incident at St Comgall's school illustrated key features of the soon-
to-be-born Provisional IRA. In the eyes of its founders, the Provisional IRA was first and foremost a defensive force, created to
protect working-class Catholic streets from Unionist assaults,
whether these be the work of drunken Loyalist mobs or of official
forces, either the police or the part-time Protestant militia, the B
Specials. From the orgy of anti-Catholic violence that accompanied
the birth of Northern Ireland in 1921 onwards that, much more
than fighting to 'free' Ireland, was what the IRA in Belfast was primarily supposed to be about. The second feature of the new IRA
was a distinct readiness on the part of its early members to meet
Loyalist violence on equal terms. The IRA man who refrained from
firing 'into the crowd' of Protestants from the roof of St Comgall's
school was a role model to few of the new recruits, not least among
them Brendan Hughes himself. In August 1969, sectarian fevers
were raging and Hughes, somewhat shamefacedly, discovered that
the virus had infected his bloodstream:

*[In] 1969, when whole streets were burnt out, I found myself in a
sort of a conflict . . . Most of my friends were Protestants. And here
Protestants were burning out Catholics. I mean, at one period, one
of my friends – a guy called Eddie Dawson – would go to Gaelic
football matches with me in Casement Park and would stand for 'The
Soldier's Song' which was a big thing for me; he was able to do it
and found no problem with it. So, in 1969, when the rioting started*

18

*on the Grosvenor Road where I lived and homes were attacked, I was conflicted. Protestant homes were attacked around Malt Street and so forth. Now, the [IRA] split had not taken place [at that point]. The Official IRA were on the ground around the Leeson Street area, trying to contain the riots. And I remember coming off the Falls Road and [joining] a gang [that was] headed along Cullingtree Road towards Malt Street which was seen as the centre of Loyalism at that period. People's blood was up; they were angry and it was decided that Protestant homes should be attacked. Around a hundred to a hundred and fifty men were heading towards Malt Street, when we were stopped by the IRA – the Official IRA at the time – and stopped from going in to burn the houses out. But there was a conflict within me at that time – I was with the mob, OK, [but] I was sort of relieved when we were stopped because I knew all the families there and in Little Grosvenor Street near by, although [it would be] true to say there were bigots there who would have cheered the burning of Bombay Street and the other burnings that were taking place. But, as the days passed, a lot of the Protestants in that area began to move out . . . and within a week or ten days, the whole of the area that I grew up in was totally deso-lated. I mean whole streets, rows of houses were lying empty, wrecked. And what houses were not wrecked Catholics began to move into . . . Almost all of the Protestants had moved out.*

These were the impulses, sectarian and Defenderist, that helped propel the IRA of 1969 to the most serious schism in the organisa-tion's recent history. The split took several months to develop, beginning in Belfast where the city's IRA Brigade assumed a semi-autonomous status, and then spreading southwards as rural and conservative Southern Republicans who had long been bitterly opposed to the left-wing, mostly Dublin leadership, rallied around the disgruntled Belfast men to make common cause. That Decem-ber, an IRA Army Convention met to discuss the organisation's political future and when the leadership's critics were defeated they walked out to form the Provisional IRA. The new leaders had been quietly recruiting in Belfast for weeks, anticipating the coming division, and Brendan Hughes had been talent-spotted early on. Around the time the rift became formal, he decided to join the new group.

*. . . by this stage I had a bit of a reputation of being a hard nut; I was able to fight. The split was about to take place and I was approached by John Joe Magee,\* who was an ex-paratrooper [in the British Army], about joining . . . Then my cousin, Charlie Hughes, who I didn't know was in the IRA, set in motion the procedure of joining up . . . there was a probation period before you were accepted . . . I think there was twelve of us at the time [and] we all went to this house on the other side of the Grosvenor Road – it was actually close to where Gusty Spence† had once lived, and we were brought in, sat down and Joe Cahill‡ came in and advised us of what the whole process of joining the IRA meant, the dangers we would [face] . . . It was a hard, hard session, and there was an obvious attempt to frighten away the people who could not – or Joe Cahill believed could not – hold the line. So he was pretty hard on the options of what was going to happen and basically it boiled down to: 'Either you're going to jail or you're going to die; that's what you can look forward to.' Now, there were two or three of these sessions . . . and constantly that was the message that was pumped across. By the end of all this, after the third session, there were just five left out of the twelve and we then went through the procedure of being sworn in and we took the oath, your right hand up to God, and you swore to abide by the rules and regulations of the Irish Republican Army. So, then, I then became a Volunteer in D Company, Second Battalion, Belfast Brigade.*

---

\* Later head of the IRA's spy-catchers, the Internal Security Unit; now deceased.
† Founder and leader of the modern Ulster Volunteer Force (UVF), a major Loyalist para-military group.
‡ Later the Belfast Commander of IRA and Chief of Staff; now deceased.

## 2

Winston Churchill's famous observation that not even the Great War of 1914–18 could diminish the integrity of Ireland's quarrel, much less make 'the dreary steeples of Fermanagh and Tyrone' less intrusive, could have been applied just as easily to Ireland in the years immediately after the end of the Second World War and, especially, to the city of Belfast where, in June 1948, Brendan Hughes was born.

Superficially, Ireland seemed to be more at peace, North and South, than for many years; but appearances were deceptive. It was a peace born more of exhaustion and defeat than anything else. For the Nationalist minority in the North and a rump of uncompromising Republicans – the detritus of two traumatic and violent splits in the IRA's ranks – there had been no rapprochement with the dispensation imposed after the Anglo-Irish War of 1919–21. Rather, each had, in their different ways, been suppressed and contained: the Nationalists both corralled and confined by the Unionist government of Northern Ireland and seemingly abandoned by their Southern compatriots, and the IRA's irreconcilables undone by their own incompetence and fiercely put down by successive Dublin governments.

In the Southern state – known first as the Free State but since Eamon de Valera's first term in government as 'Eire' – acceptance of the institutions created by the 1921 Treaty was at a wider level than ever. In Ireland's long search for independence the favoured approach had always swung back and forth between politics and violence and by the mid-1940s, the pendulum had moved decisively away from the gun, marking the end of a turbulent chapter in Ireland's stormy history. The Easter Rising of 1916 had been put down with such force by the British that its defeat became merely the prelude to another bloodstained effort to end Britain's control of Ireland's affairs, just as its authors had intended. The subsequent war between the British and the new Irish Republican Army had been brutal but, by the standards of what was to happen during Brendan Hughes's life, mercifully short. It began in 1919, not long after Sinn Fein's demand for an independent Irish Republic had been endorsed by the Irish electorate, and ended in 1921, first with a truce and then in negotiations in London, the Irish side led by the IRA's military genius, Michael Collins, and the British by the wily and deceitful Welshman, David Lloyd George. The result was a treaty that gave Ireland dominion-style independence within the Commonwealth but retained the British monarch as head of state. One aspect stuck in Republican throats: an oath of loyalty to the Crown that the Irish government and members of the new parliament in Dublin would have to swear. Prodded by military hardliners, de Valera reluctantly led a substantial section of the IRA and Sinn Fein in opposition to the Treaty and a vicious civil war followed. But after less than a year of fighting, the anti-Treaty IRA was defeated. De Valera led the rump, 'The Legion of the Rearguard', into a new, non-violent party, Fianna Fail, and eventually, by 1936, into government.

What was left of the IRA on the eve of the Second World War regarded both states in Ireland as illegal entities, imposed by British and 'Free State' violence in defiance of the democratic will of the people of Ireland, expressed twice, in the elections of 1918 and in 1921. But by the outbreak of European hostilities in 1939, the IRA had begun to turn its guns away from the Southern state towards the other entity spawned by the Treaty, Northern Ireland. Partition was already a de-facto reality by the time the Treaty negotiations commenced. The 1920 Government of Ireland Act had created two partitioned states in Ireland and the Treaty had given the North the choice of opting out of the new Irish state and choosing instead the version of local Home Rule envisaged in the 1920 Act, which it had done instantly. The pill had been sweetened for the Irish side by a promise given by Lloyd George to the Irish delegation. A Boundary

Commission set up to draw Northern Ireland's borders would, the Irish were led to believe, so dismember the new state that it could not be viable and would eventually fall, no matter what the Unionist leaders tried to do, like a ripe apple into the arms of the South. The Commission was supposed to take into account the feelings of local communities when drawing lines on the map and this surely would mean, Nationalists believed, the exclusion of large slices of Catholic Ulster from the Northern state. Partition thus barely figured in the quarrel between Republicans in the wake of the Treaty or the ensuing civil war.

But Lloyd George had spoken weasel words and the Boundary Commission did nothing of the sort. Its report was never published but the contents were leaked. Northern Ireland would consist of six of the nine counties of Ulster: Antrim, Down, Londonderry, Tyrone, Fermanagh and Armagh – but the prize offered to the Unionists came at a price. Tyrone and Fermanagh, as well as Derry, Northern Ireland's second-largest city, had substantial Catholic majorities, while Londonderry and Armagh had significant Catholic minorities. Catholics would constitute at least a third of Northern Ireland's population; in Unionist eyes, a serpent had been placed within the bosom of the new state. The Protestants of Ulster had initially opposed partition, preferring to remain an integral, undevolved part of the United Kingdom. Their leader, Edward Carson, had rejected partition a decade earlier, declaring that there could be 'no permanent resting place between total union and total separation' from Britain. But a separate parliament had been proposed for Belfast as a compromise between the Unionist and Republican positions, in the belief, or even hope, that one day Irish reunification would be eased.

There was, however, only one way that Unionists could hope to ensure that such a day would never dawn and that was to maintain their political, economic and demographic domination over their Catholic, Nationalist neighbours. To do this, the Unionists resorted to the most readily available and trusted ways of doing so: by encouraging discrimination in jobs and public housing, the gerrymandering of electoral boundaries in places such as Derry, restricting the franchise at council level and by putting in place a harsh system of law and order, complete with heavily armed Protestant militias, with ready access to a panoply of draconian laws, which ranged from internment without trial and floggings through to the banning of political parties, meetings and demonstrations. The seeds of future conflict were sown at the outset and the soil in which they had been planted was fertile and rarely left unwatered.

For their part, the North's Catholic and Nationalist population felt trapped in this new state, abandoned by their Southern compatriots and surrounded by a hostile Protestant and Unionist community whose attitude towards them was never better expressed than by Sir Basil Brooke, a Unionist cabinet minister at the time, but prime minister of Northern Ireland when Brendan Hughes first gazed upon the world. Addressing Orangemen on the Twelfth in 1933, he chose as his subject the vexed matter of Catholic employment: 'Many in this audience employ Catholics', he preached, 'but I have not one about my place. Catholics are out to destroy Ulster . . . If we in Ulster allow Roman Catholics to work on our farms we are traitors to Ulster . . . I would appeal to Loyalists, therefore, wherever possible, to employ good Protestant lads and lassies.'[4] When the North's then prime minister, Lord Craigavon, was asked to dissociate himself from these and subsequent similar remarks, he responded, 'There is not one of my colleagues who does not entirely agree with him . . .'[5]

Bigotry and discrimination of this sort worsened the economic plight of Catholics as the world depression intensified in the 1930s, and to the poverty and misery of life in the Catholic ghettos of Belfast were added regular and terrifying bouts of murder and destruction. Anti-Catholic, sectarian violence had been a recurring feature of life in the North throughout much of the nineteenth century and it continued unabated into the next one. During the Anglo-Irish War, IRA activity was often the occasion for murderous reprisals against vulnerable Catholics carried out by Loyalist mobs, at times assisted by RUC officers or members of full- and part-time Protestant militias such as the Ulster Special Constabulary, the B Specials. The burning of Catholic homes and mass expulsions from workplaces such as the Belfast shipyard became commonplace. The declaration by the IRA of a truce in July 1920 was the prelude to an especially grisly carnival of death; in the following three days, twenty people were shot dead as Loyalist gunmen and police rampaged through Catholic districts in the York Street area of North Belfast. Such violent outbursts continued even into the 1930s, sometimes spreading far out of Belfast to rural towns and villages and often without the excuse of IRA activity as justification.

In a possible reflection of their vulnerable state, Northern Catholics had in large measure eschewed the Republicanism of Sinn Fein at the polling booths, preferring instead to vote for the Nationalists, a conservative and moderate party, closely aligned to the Catholic hierarchy, whose origins lay in the pro-Home Rule, Irish Parliamentary Party of John Redmond. After partition, the Nationalists vacillated between boycotting and participating in the Stormont parliament. But they were never made welcome; Craigavon, after all, had defined the prevailing ethos in 1934: 'We are a Protestant parliament and a Protestant state.'[6] The IRA, however, was in little doubt as to what had to be done. A flirtation with de Valera's Fianna Fail ended abruptly in 1936 and three years later, as Europe prepared for war, the IRA launched a brief but ill-fated bombing campaign in England, with partition the declared *casus belli*. It was an important juncture in the development of physical-force Irish Republicanism, signalling that from thereon the IRA's guns would be ranged against the Northern state, not the Southern one. The English bombing campaign was a catastrophe for the IRA; frightened that the organisation's flirtations with Nazi Germany might threaten Eire's neutrality in the European war, de Valera cracked down on the organisation, while in Britain police activity kept the IRA on the run. The campaign petered out in 1940 but in 1942 Northern units, now organised in a separate Northern Command, launched their own assault on the Unionist state.

Disaster overtook the Northern IRA almost immediately. A diversionary attack on the RUC, intended to draw them away from a banned Easter commemoration march in West Belfast, ended with the death of a policeman and the arrest of the entire IRA unit. All six members of the team were tried, convicted of murder and sentenced to hang in Belfast's Crumlin Road jail. The episode would feature IRA figures who would play parts, some incidental, some seminal, in Hughes's own IRA career and provide evidence of just how small and essentially incestuous the pre-Provisional Republican movement in Belfast really was.

In the face of an international campaign to commute the death sentences, the Unionist Government reprieved five of the unit but hanged Tom Williams, their Commander, who offered to take responsibility for the attack. Although he claimed otherwise, Williams had not fired the fatal shot but one of those spared, twenty-two-year-old Joe Cahill, was reputed in some Republican circles to be the real culprit. Two decades later Cahill would swear Brendan Hughes into the IRA. When Tom Williams was hanged, the IRA decided on a series of retaliatory attacks and in one of them a sixteen-year-old Volunteer, a member of the IRA's famed D Company in West Belfast by the name of Gerry Adams, was shot and wounded by the police. Sentenced to eight years' imprisonment, Gerry Adams was released in 1946. A year later he married Annie Hannaway, one of whose brothers, Alfie, had recruited Tom Williams into the IRA, and in October 1948 she gave birth to the couple's first son, whom they christened Gerry after his father.[7] Four months younger than Brendan Hughes, Gerry Adams junior would arguably become the most important and influential figure in Hughes's life.

By 1948 the IRA was virtually defunct but the mission it had come into being to carry out, the business of securing a thirty-two-county Irish Republic, remained unfinished. And in the North the Catholic minority still laboured under the Unionist whip, as it were, discriminated against and deprived of social, economic and political equality. These two elements of Irish society – one a dream of what could be, the other more a nightmare of what was – had given birth to Irish Republicanism a century and a half before and the same forces were still in place. Mixed together in the right way they could combine to produce political gunpowder. A mere spark could cause the concoction to explode.

The roots of Irish separatism can be traced to a flowering of radical, democratic ideas at the end of the eighteenth century that had been shaped in large measure by the French and American Revolutions. The Society of United Irishmen, founded and led by the likes of Wolfe Tone, was the first to promulgate the notion of independence from England, but when the time came to assert these ideas on the battlefield, it was the Northern Catholics, organised in a secret agrarian society called the Defenders, created to resist Protestant land aggression in the 1780s and 1790s, who provided the manpower and the muscle to make the rebellion of 1798 possible.

As the twentieth century approached its halfway mark, these two component parts of Republicanism appeared in retreat: the IRA was quiescent and the Northern Catholics had been cowed into passivity – but all that would change. Events in Britain, not in Ireland, would see to that. The democratisation of secondary education, the provision of free health care and a massive expansion of the welfare state by the post-war Labour government in London would slowly but surely transform the lives of many Northern Catholics as nothing before, and create an educated, aware generation whose expectations and impatience would shake all of Ireland.

Brendan Hughes, however, was to share in few of those gains. The benefits of the British welfare state would eventually filter down to those on the lowest rungs of the social ladder but for him and many others in the poorer parts of West Belfast, it would not happen soon enough and life would be much the same as it had been for their parents: minimal schooling up to the age of fifteen, followed by a search for whatever work was available.

*. . . there was no secondary school at that period for people like me. We got minimal education – I went only to primary school, St Comgall's – and it was why I refer to it as 'training you for the building sites', training you for labouring jobs. The best thing that could have happened to you was that you got a job that got you out of the country, away somewhere else, and you made it . . . somewhere abroad. When I say 'abroad', I mean England, America or Australia. Actually two of my brothers emigrated to Australia. It was the only way that people could make it. In 1963 I left school and was employed in the abattoir, the slaughterhouse, as a tripe-dresser. After that, I drifted from job to job [and] eventually joined the Merchant Navy and I went to sea for over two years until 1969.*

*Most Catholics from the Lower Falls area were looking for a way out. I mean, if you stayed in Belfast, you were on the building sites or in a factory – on the building sites, labouring jobs, bricklaying jobs, plastering jobs were all done by Catholics. Even to this day you will not find many tradesmen in the building industry like plasterers, bricklayers, who are not Catholic. So, most people wanted out, and the way out was to join the Merchant Navy or to go and work in England, and many, many, many people from the Lower Falls did that. In fact, I don't know a family that hadn't got one member working in England or in the Merchant Navy. The Merchant Navy was a very common, very popular job in the Falls area. I had an uncle, my Uncle Bobbie, who was a chief mate in the Merchant Navy, and he had been promising me for years to get me on the boats. Eventually, I got fed up waiting, and I went myself and applied to the sea school and this meant going to England, to a place called Sharpness. I went when I was sixteen, and it was like a British Army camp . . . it was based on military training, long hours, up in the morning, big Nissen huts. I was the only Belfast man there at the time; most were Welshmen or Englishmen. So we did our training there for three months. You wore a uniform, a navy-blue uniform with beret and boots and all the rest. You drilled, but mostly it was navigational training, how to tie knots. So, I served three months there and I remember being really glad to get the hell out of it . . .*

*you were instructed on leaving the camp that you must arrive at your home with your uniform on. And I remember getting off the boat, getting the bus up to the Grosvenor Road and rushing like hell to my own house to get that bloody uniform off. I refused to wear the beret . . . on the side of it was stamped 'Merchant Navy', but to me it was a uniform, and a British uniform at that . . .*

Hughes's later travels in the Merchant Navy would complete his political education and confirm his radical views, but the formative, early influences in his life, his ex-IRA father, the family's poverty, the anti-Catholic sectarianism of the day and the central place of Republicanism in the surrounding community were already pushing him towards dissent and rebellion.

*My mother died when she was very young; she was thirty-one years of age. My father was left with six children, five boys and one girl. He was a tile-carrier, a hodsman, and he brought us all up; he made sure that the family was never broken up and kept us all together. He worked very, very hard, and he was a Republican; he was interned in the 1940s. After my mother died he lapsed from the Republican Movement to concentrate on his family . . . my father was a Republican, but I think, foremost, he was a socialist. At that period in the 1960s, up to 1969, Republican socialists did not have a great deal going for them, and so my father was a constant British Labour voter. He was always voting for the Labour Party because there wasn't any alternative, but, when we talk about socialism and socialists and the ideology of socialism, I think Catholic Nationalist people at that time were largely socialists at heart. They could not, did not, read Marx; could not quote Marx or Engels or anyone else, but by and large they were working-class socialists. There was a socialist mentality about at that period. My father's great hero was a Republican called Liam Mellows, but again, my father would never have read Liam Mellows's writings – it was just through the influences of other people, being in prison and so forth, that and the natural working-class socialism that was there.*

*

*During that time in Belfast, you were either Protestant or Catholic
and the alternatives weren't great. That's how my father finished up
voting for the Labour Party. But the breakdown of the six-county
state at that time meant that Catholics were largely discriminated
against. The old adage of 'a Protestant country for a Protestant
people' was very much in vogue and I remember the job adverts in
the* Belfast Telegraph *at night were quite blatant: 'Catholics need
not apply.' And if you went for a job interview you were asked what
school you went to. Catholics were identified by what school they
went to and by their names. I mean, you never heard of a Protestant
in the North of Ireland called Brendan or Kevin, Barry or Seamus,
so you were identified by your name and your school and, Belfast at
that time, as it is today, was made up of ghettos, Catholic ghettos,
Protestant ghettos, and the Protestant people at that time were made
to feel superior. They weren't any better off than most working-class
Catholics; they lived in the same type of accommodation, terraced
houses . . . the better jobs, certainly, went to the Protestant people.
And there was an exclusive Protestant middle class, and, by 1969–70,
a developing Catholic middle class. But, I was brought up in a
Protestant area. My father – my grandmother was pretty well off,
she and my grandfather had been dealers, and my grandmother
actually owned the house that I was born in, Blackwater Street on
the Grosvenor Road, which was exclusively Protestant. When we
moved in my father was constantly fighting. The neighbours used
to put an Orange arch up, celebrating the Twelfth of July and my
father was in constant fights with the Orange Order who would
insist every year on putting the arch up outside our house, the only
Catholic house in the street, and on one occasion my father actually
pulled the whole thing down and we were all evacuated out of the
house over to the other side of the road which was the Catholic
enclave. Over the years, we kids were in constant fights with our
Protestant neighbours. Eventually we were accepted, until the
marching season would come round, the July period. I never had
any friends during that period, no Protestant friends. They would*

*all go off to beat the Orange drums and so forth. So reluctantly we were accepted, but, it wasn't easy. I remember one particular day having to fight this person three times on the one day – he was the local Protestant hard man and his mother just could not accept the fact that he was beaten by a Taig and kept sending him back. There was one old woman, she was in her nineties, Mrs McKissick, and every time I walked past her door she would spit on me; every Sunday she would shout – this is a woman sitting outside her front door, bigoted old woman – 'Did you bless yourself with the Pope's piss this morning?' But around the July period that got worse. There was always a real tension, not so much in the lead-up to it – actually, I used to collect wood for the bonfire on the Eleventh night – they would celebrate the victory of King William over King James and put an effigy of the Pope on top of the bonfire . . . But the next morning that was it. The Twelfth, Thirteenth, Fourteenth, all my Protestant friends disappeared; the bigotry really got bad, but up until the Eleventh night, it was OK.*

*I remember my father, after a hard day's work; carrying tiles on his head was very hard work, and . . . I remember him at night putting us all to bed and we only had an old tiled floor. My father was a very proud man; if he had wanted to, he could have asked [for] money from my grandmother, or my grandfather or my Uncle Joe, but he never did. The only thing he ever asked my Uncle Joe for were caps, because carrying tiles on your head meant the caps wore out pretty quickly. My father used to get down on his knees twice a week and scrub the floor with the scrubbing brush and a bucket of soapy water. We didn't have much furniture, there was one soft chair in the house which was my father's chair. Because my mother died we had to take our turns at household work. One week it would be my turn to light the fire and make the dinner when my father was at work. The next week it was my turn to make the beds and someone else's turn to light the fire and make the dinner . . . we had a rota system. We had two bedrooms, a sitting room downstairs and what we called the parlour, where my mother actually died. But we had* *the most basic of facilities, the most basic. I remember my father every Friday night, he would come in and put the wage packet on the mantelpiece and it was £11 and my job every Friday night was to go round and get what we called the 'rations'. I remember it as well, three-quarter pound of tea, three pound of butter, a pound and a half of margarine, a bottle of HP sauce, six pound of sugar, and two shillings' worth of broken biscuits, and that was my job every Friday. Every Friday we had our choice of what to eat for supper. In the summer we always got a bit of fruit, or fish out of Fusco's,\* but during the week, you took what was going. I remember one midweek, we had no money whatsoever; we hadn't even a loaf of bread. We had an outside toilet with a lead pipe coming from the cistern and my father got a hacksaw and went out and sawed the lead pipe off the cistern in the toilet and sent me over to the scrap-yard and we got enough money for two shillings' worth of chips, a loaf and a block of margarine, and we had chips and bread for our tea that night. I had an uncle who worked in the slaughterhouse, and every Friday, he used to leave us meat from the butcher's; there would be a liver, an oxtail, sometimes sweetbreads and bits and pieces of other meats, what you called 'skirting', which you made stew with. But even if you were starving on a Friday, you weren't allowed to eat that meat, because my father was a practising Catholic and Friday was a fast day. No matter how hungry you were, you did not eat meat on a Friday! But, most of that meat my father would give away, and one of my chores on a Friday night was to bring some of this meat to other people in the street who were just as bad off as us. There was actually one family at the bottom of the street, it was a mixed family, the father was a Protestant and the mother a Catholic, and the kids were never practising Catholics. But there were twenty-one people in that house, a two-bedroom house – twenty-one people living in it at the one time, twenty-one people. Often the meat would have gone down to them. It was unbelievable, I mean, when I think back on it now . . . there were three of us in*

---

\* A local fish-and-chip takeaway.

*one bed, four of us sometimes. My father had his own room, and my young sister was in a cot. She was only a child, eighteen months old when my mother died. Initially she slept in my father's room, in the cot. Looking back on it now, I mean, one soft chair! All the rest were bamboo chairs or just wooden chairs. But – now this is the major contradiction – my grandmother was pretty well off; she was one of the few people I knew on the Falls Road who had an indoor toilet, an indoor bathroom, with a bath. For us to get a bath we went to the Falls Road public baths, sometimes once a week, maybe once a fortnight, where we could have a bath. But my grandmother had all the facilities, she had a bath, a shower, everything indoors, and she owned the house that we lived in. As I say, we had the most basic of furniture. My grandmother decided one time that the outside of the house needed done up and she employed this builder to put in French doors and French windows. They were the 'in thing' at the time. We were the only house on the street with French doors and French windows! That was an image thing. It didn't matter what was going on inside the house, it was the appearance from the outside that mattered. She's putting French doors and French windows in and we're cutting the drainpipe off the toilet to get food. When she died most of her money went to the Catholic Church. She went to Lourdes every year, religiously every year, and I don't know to this day just how much money was left to the Catholic Church. But certainly none of it was left to my father . . . my father and his mother did not get on very well together.*

*I think all my life, my father has been my hero . . . if you look at the life that my father had after my mother died. He was only a young man himself, and yet he gave up everything. He devoted his whole life to bringing his children up as best he could. And I believe he did a pretty good job. When we all began to leave, for instance to England or Australia, I had a great desire to do something to pay back all the years that my father spent in bringing us up. He never had another woman in his life. He could easily have sorted us out, or separated us, which was suggested at one time by an aunt of mine* *and my father threw her out of the house! . . . So, there was a great strength there, a great love, a bond there with his kids. And right up until the day he died. I remember when I was on hunger strike, my father and Tim Pat Coogan\* came to me [on a prison visit] and Tim Pat Coogan asked the question, as a journalist would, a direct question to me: did I think I was going to die? And I felt the tension in the visiting box at that moment. My father just froze and it seemed like an eternity before I could answer, and by that time my father had broken down, had got up and walked out of the visiting box, crying. Crying! I think it was the first time in my life I ever saw my father crying except for the time when my mother died. It must have been like a knife piercing his heart and I felt it for him. I remember thinking, during the hunger strike, the love I had for my father was great, and the love he had for me was great. I remember feeling totally confused at one period [during the hunger strike] when I feared for my father's life and I remember thinking that 'I hope I die before my father does', because I couldn't bear to see him die. And then the thought occurred to me that 'I hope that does not happen, I hope my father dies before I do', because if I died before my father did then it would break his heart.*

Both of Brendan Hughes's parents and one set of grandparents had been involved in the IRA. He grew up hearing all the stories of the terror Belfast Catholics had experienced in the 1920s and how sometimes the IRA could strike back, although such incidents would pale in comparison to the activities of the IRA units of 1972 that he would lead. One famous action, 'The Raglan Street Ambush', took place in West Belfast on 10 July 1921, just a day before a truce between the British and the IRA was to come into effect, and two days before the annual Orange 'Twelfth' celebrations when Protestant emotions usually ran high. The timing was unfortunate. A large force of policemen, known then as the Royal Irish Constabulary (RIC), and Specials – an exclusively Protestant auxiliary

---

\* Former editor of the *Irish Press* and author.

police force established by the new Northern Ireland government – were on a mission to raid homes in the Lower Falls Road area when they were ambushed by the local IRA. One policeman was killed and two were wounded in the fierce gun battle that followed. Already angered by the truce with the IRA, which proved to be a prelude to the Treaty negotiations, lorry loads of Specials went on the rampage in Catholic parts of Belfast shooting wildly. In the following few days twenty people were killed, scores wounded and over a hundred and fifty Catholic homes were torched.[8]

Four months before, in March 1921, a great-uncle, Eoin Hughes, was taken off a tram in the York Street area of North Belfast and shot dead. His killer is believed to have been a notorious Loyalist gunman known as 'Buck Alec' Robinson, a petty criminal who had been inducted, despite his lengthy criminal record, into the Specials. 'Buck Alec' was a member of one of several murder gangs made up of RIC officers and Specials that carried out unofficial reprisals during these turbulent years, activity that in his case did not deter the Lord Lieutenant of Ireland, Lord French, commending him 'for his good police work'.[9] Hughes's father, Kevin Hughes, better known as 'Kevie', was active again in the 1930s and in the early 1940s he was interned, ending up in Belfast's Crumlin Road jail alongside Gerry Adams's father. Growing up, Brendan Hughes rubbed shoulders with men who were IRA heroes in the local community, none more celebrated than Billy McKee, later a founder member of the Provisional IRA in 1969 and its first Belfast Commander. Ironically Hughes and McKee would eventually find themselves on opposite sides during Gerry Adams's bid to gain control of the IRA.

*. . . my mother was involved in the 1930s, my grandmother was involved, my grandfather was involved . . . my father, as I say, was an old Republican; he did time in prison but very seldom would he tell us any stories about his involvement. He never ever talked about any operation that he was on, even though I know he was on operations. He was interned in 1942, during the war years. My father's*

35

*great friend was a man called Billy McKee; my father would have spoken more about Billy McKee than about himself. And Billy was a person that I admired and looked up to even though I didn't know him. He lived in McDonnell Street just across the street from where I lived. We're talking about the 1960s. My father would bring us all to Mass and we'd walk past Billy McKee's house on McDonnell Street and we almost felt like genuflecting because my father thought so much of him. Billy McKee was one of those people who spent his whole life in the Republican movement, in and out of jail, hunger strikes, being shot, and I remember picturing Billy McKee with a .45 stuck on his belt . . . one of my memories of him was in a house in the Falls Road, Belgrade Street – a friend of my father's, John O'Rawe, his mother had died, and we were all in the back room, in the scullery where the tea was being made, and Billy was there. And I remember purposely bumping up against Billy to find out if he had a .45 stuck in his belt and, yes, he did, he had a .45 automatic stuck in his belt, and I remember asking him could I look at it. I don't know what age I was; I was young. But later on, in years to come, I saw Billy with more than a .45 in his hand. I was so enchanted by him, and admired him so much, and my father was there as well. I was so sort of romantically involved with the IRA, even before I joined it. It was just something that I believe I was destined to be, and I don't think my father actually directed me towards this, consciously directed me towards this, [but] he probably unconsciously directed me towards the movement. Well, it was not so much the IRA as the resistance to what was going on; a resistance to, and a resentfulness towards, the way life in the six-county state that I lived in, the way that it was treating my family, treating my father. The stories of the B Specials, of the shootings and of the oppression and of all that was all consciously ingrained. I remember the story of my uncle, my uncle Eoin Hughes. He was on a tram in the 1920s going down to York Street and he was taken off the tram and shot dead in the middle of the street. One of the names mentioned at the time [as being responsible] was a famous Loyalist from down there, 'Buck Alec'. It was hard to differentiate a B Special from a Loyalist assassin;*

*they were one and the same. And, I mean, we heard all the stories –
my grandmother used to tell me stories about the 1920s and of the
shootings and the murders and so forth, and I remember being
really scared about the B Specials . . . stories about my Uncle Eoin
and of my great-grandfather during the War of Independence,
losing his arm, throwing a hand grenade at an armoured car somewhere in County Louth. The grenade went off and blew his arm off.
I believe my [grand]father was involved in Raglan Street, even
though he never told me that, but I know he was there and abouts.
It was one of the famous ambushes in the Falls area, and, I mean,
Raglan Street has drifted into oblivion because of all the other gun
battles that have taken place since. The Raglan Street Ambush was
small fry compared to some of the stuff that happened afterwards.*

These were the influences that shaped Brendan Hughes as he
reached adulthood, and in that regard he was not very different
from hundreds of other young working-class Catholics in Belfast at
that time whose parents and grandparents could tell equally chilling stories about the violence of the 1920s and 1930s. In his and their
lives the IRA was an organic part of their community, even if not
all would approve or adopt their methods. The IRA was made up
of neighbours, friends and even relatives, people they knew and
respected and to whom they would naturally turn for protection
from the worst excesses of Orange extremists. Distrust and dislike
of the police, a feature of working-class life the world over, was so
much more intense in such communities because, for Republicans
and Nationalists, the RUC was seen as the political enemy, the force
that imposed their second-class status and upheld Unionist rule
and with whom co-operation was frowned upon.

*. . . we never had money to buy bikes when we were growing up so
we would go to the scrapyard and buy scrap pieces and so forth to
build an old bike and ride about the place. Four or five times I was
arrested, for not having brakes, for not having lights, for playing
football on the street . . . We used to play cards at the bottom of the*

*street which was illegal as well . . . we'd have people out watching for the cops coming. But, as a Catholic family in the area, we were constantly singled out for special attention. I mean, I was arrested, God knows how many times, taken to court and fined five shillings or ten shillings for not having lights on the bike, for not having brakes on the bike, for playing cards on the street, for playing football on the street. But there was one time, we were playing cards on the street and the cops came and everybody bolted, but I was caught, and I was taken to the barracks and I was interrogated. I think I must have been thirteen, maybe fourteen. And I gave the names of the people who were in the card school with me and the cops brought me back to the house and left me there. They then came back and gave me a summons to go to court. My father asked me what did I say, and I told him and I got a powerful smack on the face, not for playing cards but for giving the names of the other people who were involved with me . . . Right through my early years, I had plenty of run-ins with the RUC, over petty little things, but I can't remember anyone else, any of my other Protestant friends, being arrested as often as I was. And I think there was a great understanding there with my father, that he knew that there was a certain amount of discrimination going on here and that I was being picked on.*

Going to sea with the Merchant Navy was the next major influence on Brendan Hughes's political journey. In South Africa he witnessed the cruel consequences of apartheid for that country's black population and it hardened his hatred of injustice. His travels away from Belfast also brought his first brush with the British Army, albeit in very different circumstances than would be the case a few years later – although the reason for that encounter, his swarthy looks, would later give him his IRA nickname, 'The Dark'. British troops first gave him that soubriquet, and it was later adopted by all who knew him, because they had no photographs of him, just an idea of what he looked like and the nickname stuck. His father had destroyed any pictures there were and even earlier, when Hughes went to sea, he seemed to anticipate the turn his son's life would take when he told him never to get a tattoo because it was a sure way of identifying someone.

*My first job was bringing a ship from Belfast to Southampton. It was a scrap ship, and it was probably the best job I ever had because there was no cleaning . . . and it was pretty basic and simple. I then signed on to a British Petroleum boat,* British Courage, *a tanker going to the Middle East for oil. I sailed out of Belfast on that and it's probably [the source of] some of my fondest memories, although the fondest of all was sailing back . . . after three or four months at sea with a brilliant tan, well dressed, plenty of money in my pocket, looking forward to getting home. On that trip, we went to a place called Aden in the Persian Gulf and, at the time, the British occupied Aden. We were not allowed to go into the town, so, if we wanted a drink, we had to go to a British Army camp, which we all did. And me being the only Irish one there! But there was no hostility between the people I went to sea with; most of them were English and Scottish . . . We had been drinking all night in this British Army camp. I got detached from the crowd I was with, and was walking across an open field outside the camp when I was attacked and pushed to the ground and a rifle put to my head. It was the British Army. Luckily, I had a Merchant Navy ID card with my photograph and name in it. I was thrown into the back of a jeep and roughly treated, initially, until they found out that I wasn't an Arab terrorist. At that time I was very, very dark and could easily have been mistaken for an Arab . . . But I was brought back to the ship [and let go].*

    *The British Army in Belfast [later] . . . called me 'Darkie'. They didn't have any photographs of me, but they knew of me . . . and the reason they never had a photograph is, when I went on the run in 1970, my father destroyed every photograph of me in the house, so any time the British Army raided my home, which was often, there was never a photograph of me there to be found. For all the years I was on the run, the British Army never had a photograph of me.*

*There were times when I was one of the most wanted men in the North, walking past a British Army foot patrol . . . I don't know whether my father had a premonition of this, but when I joined the Merchant Navy, my father insisted that I didn't get any tattoos. It was a common thing for seamen to have tattoos and many a time I sat in a tattooist's in Europe or the Far East, with other people [but] I never ever got one because I always remembered my father telling me, 'Never get a tattoo, because it's an identifiable mark', and this is long before I went on the run. That's why I'm saying he must have had a premonition that I was going to be on the run. And I don't know where that came from, whether my father knew the road I was going to be taking or he suspected I was going to be taking. But anyway I never got tattoos, and they never had a photograph of me until I was arrested in 1973.*

*After the British tanker, I came back to Belfast, was at home for six weeks and then re-signed on to a fruit boat, the* Carrigan Head, *which went to South Africa. We sailed from Southampton to South Africa, down to Durban, and that was the first time that I saw the deprivation and the squalor and the slavery [of apartheid]. When we [sailed] into Durban, to load with oranges, there was possibly a hundred and fifty men or so, black men, all labouring, all [the loading] done by hand . . . I worked in the galley at that time and I remember looking out the porthole at lunchtime, all these guys sat along at the deck of the ship with milk bottles full of cold tea and whatever food they had; it was mostly bread and cold tea. And I remember feeling angry, the way these people were treated . . . if I was never a socialist [before] I certainly became a socialist during that period in South Africa. I went to the galley and I got milk, cheese and whatever else out of the freezer and brought it out, and the first guy I went to, a black guy sitting there, drinking a bottle of cold tea, he says, 'No.' He wouldn't take it, he was so proud, and I suppose I was being naively charitable, but I felt compassion for them and, in my naive way, I was trying to help. I was told to go away, which was good. These people . . . didn't want my charity. It affected me so much. And as soon as these guys finished work, the beer was there, in a massive big barn. And . . . as soon as they got paid, [they went] into the beer hall, and I've no doubt, the people that owned the fruit going on that boat also owned the beer hall. And they wondered where the drink problem in Cape Town [came from]? You were allowed ashore, obviously when you were in dock, especially me being a deck hand. We were all lined up and told that there were certain areas that we were not allowed to go to. One of these areas was called District Six in Cape Town. We were told to stay away from it or we'd be killed . . . But being curious, as I was, I went to District Six. Cape Town was a sprawling big city, all the amenities were there for the white man. I searched out District Six which was a massive area of cardboard-box houses. I remember the cornflake boxes, vividly, in this field where people were living and I was really affected by that . . . in the city centre of Cape Town, where there was anything you wanted there [and] just a mile or so outside the city here was a sprawling slum, where people survived, didn't live! They survived there. This had a bigger impact on my thinking as a socialist than reading books, or studying revolutionary tactics. That had a deep effect on me as regards fair play and social- ism. When we left there and went to Mozambique, and it was even worse. The Portuguese were there at the time, in a place called Lourenço Marques [now Maputo]. I'm not sure if the conditions have changed in Mozambique, but then it was total and utter depravity, poverty and oppression. Going back onto the ship you realised just how lucky you were. Yet we weren't supposed to experi- ence that; we were to stay in our wee cosy, white shells, in the city, where we were safe. I just didn't become a rebel in 1970. I didn't become a gunman in 1970. I didn't become a revolutionary in 1970. That process was being built up over the years, and years of seeing privation, years of seeing exploitation, years of hunger and sadness and love.*

## 3

The IRA's failure or inability to defend Nationalist Belfast from Loyalist assaults in August 1969 was only part of the story why, in the winter of 1969–70, the organisation fractured into two rival, bitterly divided factions. A more comprehensive explanation can be found in the twists and turns that the IRA's journey took in the two decades or so that followed the end of the war in Europe. After the debacle of the English campaign of 1939 and the Northern IRA's disastrous outing in 1942, the IRA had painfully and slowly reorganised. By 1956, it was ready once again to resume armed struggle against the Northern Ireland state but the campaign that followed was largely confined to the border counties and, for reasons that have yet to be adequately explained, never took off in Belfast. The absence of IRA activity in Northern Ireland's major city was a fatal weakness, but what really doomed the Border Campaign, as it was called, was the Northern Catholic population's lack of enthusiasm for the IRA's methods and war aims. Politically isolated and geographically confined, the IRA was easily suppressed by the Belfast and Dublin governments, which interned scores of activists on either side of the border. By 1962, after six years of desultory, often bungled attacks, which had barely dented the Northern security forces, the campaign fizzled to halt.

In the 1960s the Republican pendulum swung once again towards political and constitutional methods. Under the leadership of a new Chief of Staff, a Dublin veteran and contemporary of Brendan Behan called Cathal Goulding, the policies of the organisation moved distinctly leftwards, with the goal now a republic that was socialist in nature. Economic and social agitation replaced armed struggle as the favoured modus operandi and the military side of the IRA was run down. The organisation also moved

towards accepting the hated Dublin and Belfast parliaments, which traditional Republicans had deemed to be illegal, and pressure grew, mostly from the top, to abandon the policy of refusing to take seats in the two assemblies if elected – an unlikely eventuality but one to which the Goulding leadership aspired. Ending abstentionism was the logical outcome of broadening the movement's support base, but for traditional and doctrinaire Republicans this was the road to hell. The IRA leadership also modified its stance on partition, or rather how to end it. While once the accepted goal was to force British withdrawal, now the aim was to reform the North, to democratise it in preparation for the sort of working-class unity necessary for the transition to socialism.[10] Again this was anathema to conventional Republicans even if many of them happily participated in the civil rights marches and demonstrations that were the principal manifestation of the change in emphasis.

The IRA leadership, based almost entirely in or near Dublin, badly misjudged the North's capacity for reform. For as long as most people could remember, the Unionist establishment had resisted any rapprochement with Catholics and Nationalists, viewing them as a fifth column in league with the Irish government or the IRA to end Northern Ireland's link to Britain. The Nationalist rejection of the IRA's 1956–62 campaign was an opportunity to reach out to Catholics but it seems not even to have been considered by the government of the day. Nevertheless, social, political and economic changes were under way that demanded that a different, more cordial approach be taken to the Catholic minority. The crusty, unbending Brookeborough had been replaced as prime minister by Captain Terence O'Neill, who inherited an economy whose best years were behind it. The decline of traditional industries such as shipbuilding and linen created a need for foreign investent but luring such companies to Belfast and Derry required more than generous grants and tax breaks; any shortfall in political stability could be a great deterrent and so O'Neill extended a hand of friendship, albeit tentatively, to Catholics. He was a mildly reforming, if sometimes patronising, moderniser, whose modest overtures to Nationalists and diplomacy with the government in Dublin drove O'Neill's hardliners from a state of unease to alarm and then to virtual rebellion. When impatient Nationalists launched the civil rights agitation in late 1968, up stepped a figure from another century, the Reverend Ian Paisley, a fundamentalist preacher and determined foe of all and any religious or political ecumenism, to lead and voice opposition to all this. As 1969 unfolded, the opposition to civil rights became increasingly violent; slowly but surely, O'Neill's political base crumbled and the North inched towards the edge.

So it was that by the time the Orange marching season reached its climax in July and August 1969, Northern Ireland was set to explode. The IRA leadership in Dublin, its faith in the theory of working-class unity unfazed by the growing sectarian reality on the streets, had failed to prepare for the eruption. When it came, and the Loyalist mobs, B Specials and RUC went on the rampage in Catholic Belfast, there was little or no resistance. The IRA had few weapons and minimal planning had been made for such an eventuality. This for sure was the catalyst for the split in the IRA that followed but Goulding's real mistake was that he had made one more enemy than he and his allies could handle. Goulding's move to the left made sense in Dublin and one or two other urban areas where there was a recognisable working class but not in the rural heartlands of Republicanism. In those areas, the West and South-West in particular, the IRA's activists and supporters were more likely to be small farmers, shopkeepers, small businessmen, schoolteachers and the like. The leadership's Marxism, the accompanying dismantling of the IRA's essentially Catholic rituals, the threat to ditch abstentionism and the gradual abandonment of armed struggle were not just an abomination to such people. Together they spelled another impending betrayal, just like that of Michael Collins and Eamon de Valera. The Southern conservatives had support in Belfast for sure, but essentially the group that emerged from the split, the Provisional IRA, was an alliance of rural, Southern conservatives and Northerners, angry and ashamed at the failure of August 1969.

The events of that summer persuaded a group of former IRA stalwarts to mobilise against the Goulding leadership. They were men who had been involved in the 1940s and the 1956–62 campaign but who had quit in disgust over the direction Goulding had taken or had been expelled when they protested. In the autumn of 1969 they rejoined the IRA and then met to discuss what should be done about the Belfast Command, then headed by Goulding acolytes Billy McMillen and Jim Sullivan, and to formulate a plan of action. They were led by Brendan Hughes's boyhood hero Billy McKee and included figures whose names had been legend in bygone years: Jimmy Steele, Joe Cahill, John and Billy Kelly, Jimmy Drumm and Seamus Twomey. They were joined by a Southern Republican, Daithi O Connail (Dave O'Connell), who had been imprisoned in Belfast's Crumlin Road jail during the Border Campaign and had got to know many of the Belfast men, and by Gerry Adams junior, the only serving member of the Belfast IRA at the meeting. Adams had a foot in both camps; he admired Goulding's politics and favoured dropping abstentionism but disagreed with the leadership's sanguine view of Unionism. Although he took part in the rebels' meeting, it would be quite a while before Adams decisively plumped for the anti-Goulding side.[11]

A month later, the dissidents forced McMillen to separate the Belfast IRA from the parent body until the larger argument was settled. The various divisions in the IRA were distilled into a single issue: whether or not to recognise and participate in the parliaments established by the Treaty settlement. An IRA Convention, a delegate conference of the IRA's grassroots, was called for December 1969 to discuss the matter and as is often the case with such events, the leadership had ensured beforehand that the bulk of the chosen delegates would be on their side of the argument. The dissenting minority, led by another veteran of the 1956–62 campaign, Sean MacStiofain, walked out to form a separate, rival IRA. The legal niceties dictated that the new IRA's ruling bodies, an Executive and an Army Council appointed by the Executive, could be chosen only at a Convention and until the new IRA convened one of its own Conventions, a provisional Executive and Army Council would fill the gap. When news of the split was leaked, the Irish media, searching for something to call the rebels, seized on the term 'provisional' and so the Provisional IRA was born. The IRA from which they had parted became known, just as predictably, as the Official IRA.

The Provisional IRA was conceived in the angry, charred back streets of Catholic Belfast and that bestowed on the new group a puissance that had been denied its predecessor during the Border Campaign. But it would mean that the engine of the IRA, which would drive it for the next three decades or so, was the city's unrelenting sectarian politics, itself a metaphor for the state. Right from the outset, the North's politics would shape and colour the Provisionals' violence and ideological direction until, eventually, the North and Northerners would dominate the entire organisation. From its Belfast core, the Provisionals would expand outwards, outgrowing and replacing the Officials in Counties Armagh and Tyrone and in Derry City, areas that would be among the IRA's key battlegrounds in the coming years. But what is striking from Brendan Hughes's account of these first months is just how fragile the infant Provisional movement was and how it could easily have been swallowed up and destroyed by the much larger Official IRA, had the cards fallen the other way. To describe the politics and motivation of its founder members as undeveloped and unsophisticated would be an understatement, while another key feature of the early IRA was that its leadership, North and South, was drawn overwhelmingly from the IRA of the late 1930s through to the 1956–62 campaign. It was older, more conservative or Catholic in social outlook, was wedded completely to the primacy of the gun and had an immovable view that politics, that is parliamentary and electoral politics, were the refuge of the scoundrel and the traitor.

The first Belfast Commander was Billy McKee, a veteran and former Commander of the Belfast Brigade's D Company in the 1940s. He was famous for his Catholic piety and was said to attend Mass daily. A contemporary once joked that in those early days he would allow only 'altar boys' into the IRA, an exaggeration for sure, but a comment that captured the centrality of his Catholic faith in all aspects of his life. His deputy, the Belfast Adjutant, was Proinsias MacAirt, or Frank Card as the British Army insisted on calling him, a veteran of the 1940s and the Border Campaign. Alongside them in the city were other famous names, people such as Jimmy Steele who had escaped from Belfast jail in 1943 and would soon launch the Belfast Brigade weekly newspaper, *Republican News*, the Drumms, Jimmy and Maire, the politically active members of the Hannaway and Burns families, activists who had drifted away or been purged during the Goulding years. The first Provisional Army Council was peppered with similar figures. Three stood out: MacStiofain, who was the new IRA's first Chief of Staff, had been arrested and jailed along with Goulding during an ill-fated arms raid at Felsted, Essex, in 1953; Ruairi O Bradaigh, a County Roscommon schoolteacher who had been Chief of Staff during part of the Border Campaign and was interned at the Curragh Camp, in County Kildare; and Daithi O Connail, a County Cork school-teacher, who had taken part in a famous raid on Brookeborough RUC station during that campaign and was later shot and wounded in County Fermanagh by the RUC.

The recruits at rank-and-file level were a different matter:

*. . . most of us at that time did not have a great deal of political ideology. It wasn't until later that we really began to learn what Republicanism meant. We were motivated by the fact that Catholic homes and streets had been burned down, [that] Catholics had been forced out of their homes. People like me, who joined what was later called the Provisional IRA, were the people who had been rioting for over a year, who burned lorries, who had come under fire from the Shankill Road, who had seen people shot. They had been fighting with petrol bombs and stones and whatever else they could lay their hands on. These were the people who were defending the areas, the people who were defending the Catholic Church, who were defend-ing against the B Specials. They were like I was, the night —— fired*

*his Thompson over the head of the Loyalist mob from the roof of
St Comgall's school; they would have wanted to fire into the crowd
instead. So most of us would have been – reactionary might be the
wrong word – but I mean, that would be close enough. The older
Republicans, like McKee, MacAirt and the rest, saw all this as an
opportunity for another war against England. The British were now
on the streets, and this was an opportunity to take them on – on our
terms, on Republican terms, on the Irish people's terms. But, at the
same time, for a lot of us, it was a big adventure.*

Hughes joined D Company of the IRA in Belfast, a unit that
historically had played a central role in the city's past disturbances
and which it would again do during the modern Troubles. D Company's operational area embraced most of the Lower Falls Road
district which, until the construction of modern public-housing
estates in Ballymurphy, Andersonstown and Turf Lodge in the
post-war years, was where most of the city's Catholic population
had always lived. At first the Provisionals were dwarfed by the
Official IRA and there were sufficient members and new recruits
to fill only one battalion in the Brigade area. Only later, when
Catholics flocked to its ranks, did the Provisionals expand to three,
and at one point four, battalions in Belfast. D Company was eventually put under the control of the Second Battalion and became
not just the largest single IRA unit in that area but in all of Belfast.
Such was its record of ambushes and bombings that it was dubbed
'the dogs of war' or just 'the dogs'. But at the start, and for many
months, D Company was tiny – only twelve members – and it
shared its base of operations with the headquarters of the Official
IRA, a recipe for bloody rivalry. At the beginning there was training and very little military activity but efforts were made to demonstrate to ordinary Catholics that the protection that had been
missing in August 1969 was now available.

*When I joined, the Official IRA was still the largest of the organisa-
tions. But, in saying that, we began training with whatever weapons*

*there were, [mostly] Second World War weapons. A lot of these were old and rusted but they were sufficient to be trained on. We would be sent to a house, a secret location where someone, a training officer, would come along with a particular type of weapon, be it a Thompson sub-machine gun or a Garrand rifle, a .303, .45 auto-matics, .45 revolvers, that type of small-calibre weapon. And an hour or so of training, of getting the feel of the weapon, being able to strip the weapon blindfolded . . . the whole idea was to know the ins and outs of a weapon. These lectures would have taken place in kitchen houses and families would have left the house free for a couple of hours. Within a short period I became the Training Officer of D Company and . . . began giving these lectures myself. Occasion-ally, camps were organised where weapons could be fired [and] explosives set off. Most, in fact all, of these training camps were in the South, in the twenty-six counties . . . We would be picked up at a rendezvous, taken away in a minibus or [in] cars and met at a central point in Dublin. We were then escorted at night time to a location, usually a farm . . . and never did we know where we were, not even which part of the country we were in. We would stay there for maybe three days, possibly a week, sometimes ten days, and we were trained on revolvers, semi-automatics, rifles, explosives. Most of it was indoors initially, and then you were taken outdoors to the firing range. But very seldom was there much firing . . . You were restricted in the amount of ammunition that could be used because at that time it was very, very scarce. A lot of the ammunition and weapons . . . were not reliable . . . you would have misfires, or you would have damp ammunition or it was just burnt out, too rusty . . . But this [was] early 1970, and there wasn't a great deal of oper-ational activity.*

*. . . the barricades were still up around where I lived, round the Grosvenor Road. When I say the barricades, the whole [of] what was known as the Lower Falls was sealed off by barricades, built by the people themselves to keep the British forces out and to protect ordinary Catholics from attacks by the B Specials and the RUC . . .*

*the barricades were ten foot high, with ramps so we could walk across them . . . they were pretty extensive, solid structures. And in behind this particular barricade where I was stationed, there was an old paint factory, Garvey's paint factory, which became almost the headquarters [of D Company, and was] known as the 'Dirty Dozen area', because there was twelve men in D Company at that period. In 1970–71, a lot of time was spent on standby, which meant that you were armed, you were sent to a particular house and told to wait there for further instructions – either an operation was going to take place or you were to patrol the streets with weapons to let the people of the area know that there was protection . . .*

The Provisional IRA was slow to get into gear. The strategy formulated by Chief of Staff Sean MacStiofain was a three-stage one. In the first phase, the emphasis was on recruiting new units, training them and providing them with weapons, so that the IRA in Belfast would be strong enough to defend Catholic areas. The second stage was to be a mixture of defensive and retaliatory actions, to strike back against the Loyalists or the RUC when the circumstances seemed to demand it. When the IRA was strong enough, the third part of the strategy would be launched, an offensive campaign against the British Army and other security forces with the aim of forcing the British to negotiate their withdrawal from Northern Ireland. It was an unsophisticated strategy, rather like its authors, with little evidence of any consideration, or concern, about Protestant and Unionist reaction to all this. In D Company's area, the first attacks were not against the British Army but were aimed at the area's many RUC stations, or barracks as they were more properly called in Belfast. In those early days, IRA activists such as Brendan Hughes still socialised and mixed with British soldiers, and even drank with them in bars. The first troops to arrive in West Belfast had been welcomed as knights in shining armour by Catholics who fêted them with pots of tea, sandwiches and plates of food. IRA old-timers knew, or hoped, that eventually this amity would wither, that the IRA would wage war against the military, and new recruits such as Hughes were eager for that fight. But in the meantime, the infant Provisional IRA's real enemy was the RUC, which in the view of Nationalists had allowed, or even assisted, the Loyalist mobs in burning down places such as Bombay Street. That would change though, very dramatically, in July 1970 during Belfast's most violent week since the arrival of British troops, when the entire D-Company area would be placed under a British military curfew. From the time of the Falls curfew onwards, the war would be between the IRA and the British. During this phoney-war period, as far as British troops were concerned, the IRA was astonishingly open and public about many of its activities, in a way that would be unthinkable just a few months later.

*. . . the headquarters of the Belfast IRA was in Kane Street [in] MacAirt's house. Everything happened around that house and everybody knew it – to the point that when the British Army moved in, they had a searchlight constantly [shining] on the house and we would [have to] use the back door. But it was always a hub of activity. There was always a group of people in the house. Old Jimmy Roe, Billy McKee, MacAirt, Liam Hannaway, all the old-timers, they were all there. And all the instructions came from that house . . . and everybody's movements were watched.*

*The* Republican News *was centred around that house as well – and one of the first jobs that we were given was to sell* Republican News . . . *There was nothing in Derry at the time, no [Provisional IRA] structure in Derry, so we would travel up to Derry going door to door. I remember the hills in Derry, selling* Republican News *round the doors was frustrating; it was something that had to be done, but after being trained in weaponry, trained in explosives, we were busting to start taking action.*

*McKee always said, 'This is our opportunity, the Brits are here, the Brits are on the streets', and the whole objective was [eventually] to take on the British Army . . . I saw myself as a soldier not a politician, naively so. And most of us did . . . we had been trained to be soldiers, we were trained to fight, and I wasn't really concerned about ideology, about where we were going [politically]. As far as I was concerned, the Brits were on the streets and we were going to go to war with them . . . at that time the soldiers would have been coming into pubs, sitting in pubs, and I remember in Dan Lane's pub, off Stanley Street, sitting in the pub and getting the British soldiers to give us a weapons lecture . . . how the SLR [self-loading rifle] worked, which they were quite happy to do . . . we mixed with them and it was quite normal to stand talking to a British soldier in the street, and here [we were] being told that we were going to go to war with them . . . They didn't know this, but we knew that we would be shooting each other within a short period . . . And there wasn't a great desire on our behalf to be shooting British soldiers. There was [for] people like McKee and MacAirt who had already fought a war with the British [and] the six-county state.*

*. . . the war, when it started in 1970, was geared towards bringing down Stormont and taking on the RUC and the B Specials. Military activity was aimed at the RUC initially . . . there was an RUC station on the Springfield Road, one on Cullingtree Road, and one on Roden Street. The first operations that were carried out were against these stations. These [usually] consisted of a five-pound charge of gelignite strapped onto a butcher's hook and four or five men, two men to give cover and two men to go to the barrack door with the charge; it was like a long sausage with cardboard wrapped around it and we'd walk up to the barrack door, which always had a big knocker; you rapped the door, hung the charge on the door, light the fuse and run like fuck! It was usually a ten-second fuse, so, you had that to get away. Roden Street was blown up maybe five, six times, in this way. Sometimes you'd walk round to the back of the station and throw the charge over the wall. One time there was a bit of a gun battle – we ran into an RUC man . . . he began to fire and [we're] only ten, fifteen feet apart . . . the charge went off and there was a massive bang! Most of the houses in Roden Street had their windows smashed, the slates blown off or whatever. But the gun battle between two of us and the RUC man resulted in no casualties*

*whatsoever. We both missed. No one was caught; we got away and*
*the RUC man got away as well . . . It got to the point where they*
*closed Roden Street RUC station and they closed Cullingtree RUC*
*station. My father was involved in the 1940s, blowing up Cullingtree*
*Road RUC station. When the troops moved in they took over an old*
*mill on Drew Street, on the Grosvenor Road, and they took over*
*another mill on Albert Street. So, when the RUC stations were*
*closed down you had this massive military presence still in the area.*
*We continued by targeting the [RUC] Special Branch. Some of the*
*Special Branch men who had been there in the 1950s were still there*
*in the 1970s. One famous cop was called Harry Taylor who was*
*responsible for the round-up in the 1950s when internment was*
*brought in – he was still there in the 1970s. He became a major*
*target. Cecil Patterson,\* who was shot, was another one of the old*
*school.*[12] *These people mixed freely during the 1950s and 1960s in*
*Nationalist areas . . . for instance, Harry Taylor was into boxing in*
*a big way and he used to drink on the Falls Road. A friend of mine*
*who finished up in jail with me – Fra McCullough – his name*
*was on a cup that Harry Taylor had won in the 1950s and Fra*
*McCullough had won in the 1960s. So you had Fra McCullough*
*who finished up being interned by Harry Taylor, their names on the*
*same cup for boxing.*

In retrospect, 1970 was the year of the Provos, the year when they
became a key player in the Troubles. Events played into their hands
without them really having to try very hard. In late 1969, a British-
appointed Commission, headed by Baron John Hunt, who had led
the team that first conquered Mount Everest in 1953, recommended
that the RUC should be disarmed and the B Specials disbanded.
Unionist reaction at these measures, especially to the loss of the
Specials, was violent. The 'B men' were regarded as the last and
most reliable line of defence against Irish Republicanism; their
disbandment was a disturbing portent. On the night that Hunt's

---

\* Detective Inspector Cecil Patterson, shot dead by IRA, 27 February 1971.

report was published Loyalist gunmen took on the British Army in the Shankill area of Belfast, losing two of their own but killing the first policeman of the Troubles. The political fallout was devastating. Terence O'Neill had been forced to resign earlier that year and was succeeded by his cousin, James Chichester-Clark, whose family, on both his and his wife's side, could trace their lineage back to the plantation aristocracy. Chichester-Clark faced a grassroots Unionist revolt in the wake of the Specials' disbandment. All this was grist to the mill of Ian Paisley, who had made it his speciality to sniff out the slightest odour of appeasement by the mainstream Unionist leadership. Desperate to fend off the Paisleyite challenge, which was echoed in his own party's ranks, Chichester-Clark won British Army support for forcing Orange marchers through sensitive Catholic districts in Belfast and elsewhere during the early months of 1970. Common sense suggested these marches should have been banned to avoid serious trouble but Chichester-Clark's political insecurity dictated otherwise. The result was major rioting, particularly in the mixed, but predominantly Catholic, Ballymurphy housing estate in West Belfast. None of this did Chichester-Clark much good, however. Ian Paisley romped home in a by-election to the Stormont parliament caused by Terence O'Neill's retirement from politics. Rattled by Paisley's victory, the Unionist government piled more and more pressure on the British Army to confront the IRA in its own backyard.

On 18 June 1970 a British general election saw Ian Paisley win a seat at Westminster, the defeat of the Labour Party and a new Conservative government, headed by Edward Heath, put into power in London. Harold Wilson's government had been sympathetic to the plight of Northern Nationalists and supported many of the reforms demanded by the civil rights movement. Unionists suspected, with good reason, that some in Wilson's cabinet favoured Irish reunification and independence. The loss of such a friend to Nationalism, along with Paisley's new stature, appears to have either emboldened the Unionist cabinet or terrified it into action. Pressure on the British Army to appease Protestant hardliners grew and, within a week of getting their way, Belfast was set ablaze.

In North Belfast, the military forced an Orange march through part of the Catholic Ardoyne area and the result was fierce rioting during which the Provisional IRA shot dead three Protestants, alleged Loyalist rioters. The trouble spread across the River Lagan, to the small Catholic enclave of Short Strand in East Belfast where stone-throwing following the return of bands and lodges from the North Belfast Orange parade deteriorated into a gun battle that would enter Provisional mythology. The 'Siege of St Matthew's' was, according to the IRA's account, a determined effort by Loyalist mobs and gunmen to burn down the area's sole Catholic church. All this, the version continues, was facilitated by the British Army, which stepped aside to give the Loyalists a free hand. Into the gap stepped a small group of IRA men led by Brigade Commander Billy McKee, who kept the mobs at bay and finally drove them off. Two Protestants and one Catholic were shot dead that night, and McKee was left badly wounded.

Loyalists strongly denied this version, saying they had been the victims of an IRA set-up, while there have been claims recently that the Catholic fatality was caused by an accidental IRA shooting and not by a Protestant bullet.[13] No matter what had really happened; there was little doubt that between the two incidents that weekend in Belfast, the Provisional IRA had convincingly validated its claim to be the Catholic defenders.

There was more to come. The following Friday, British troops raided a small cluster of homes in the Lower Falls Road area searching for weapons dumps. It was a puzzling raid for the troops had raided Official IRA homes and, since the split, the Officials had been reluctant to seek serious conflict with the British. The carnage of the previous weekend had left hardline Unionists angry, adding to the pressure on Chichester-Clark for a response. In those early days and for reasons more to do with British politics, the military regarded the Marxist Officials as the more dangerous of the two Republican groups, and that might have influenced the decision to mount the raid, or it might have been simply that the British knew more about the Officials who were the initial point of contact with areas such as the Lower Falls. Whatever the reason, the troops were stoned as they left; some were trapped and reinforcements were sent in to relieve them. Soon three thousand troops had occupied the district and the British Commander declared a curfew that lasted the weekend, during which scores of homes were searched, businesses wrecked and bars looted by soldiers. Four men were killed, three shot dead by troops and one deliberately run over by an armoured car. It was a turning point for the Provisionals, poisoning public opinion in this key Catholic area against the British Army and pushing sentiment towards the more militant Republican group. Brendan Hughes was in the thick of it.

*. . . during that whole day there was a continual gun battle, blast bombs being thrown at the British, petrol bombs and, later on that afternoon, a helicopter arrived and announced over loud hailers that the Lower Falls was under curfew and anyone found on the streets would be shot. Charlie Hughes was the O/C at that time and he assembled the whole of D Company at his house in Servia Street. The Falls had been surrounded by British troops and Charlie's house was right on the corner of Servia Street. At the other end was Albert Street . . . there was eleven of us at that time in D Company and we were informed that we were going to break the curfew, so we had to get out of the house. The first man out ran across Servia Street to the corner of Bosnia Street, with a .303 rifle. He was called John Joe Magee and he was an ex-British marine who was good with a rifle. He ran across and took up a firing position to give us cover . . . he fired up Servia Street towards Albert Street at the British. They obviously returned fire. One by one, we came out of Servia Street, out of Charlie's house, and made our way along as a foot patrol. John Joe continued firing at the Brits; they had not moved into the area at this time. They'd surrounded the whole area [but] they hadn't actually moved into it. So we moved along and, I mean, the weapons we had were old and there wasn't a great fire-power there. The .303 was probably the best rifle we had. By this*

*time the whole area had been cleared, we were the only ones on the street, people took the warning from the British seriously and got off the streets. We made our way to Cyprus Street and split up into two groups, one group went to the one side of Cyprus Street. I finished up on the right-hand side, four of us, but before we got to the top of Cyprus Street, the British had moved into the area and they opened up. We took cover in houses in Cyprus Street and continued to fire at the British who were in the corner of Varna Gap. The gun battle lasted five, maybe six, minutes. I had run out of ammunition and found myself in a house [owned by] a man called Giuseppe Conlon whose son was later convicted for bombing Guildford.\* That was Gerry Conlon; he and Paul Hill were convicted but they were not guilty. They were in England because of me . . . Gerry Conlon and Paul Hill were two young criminals. It was actually me who ordered the two of them out of the country. They were breaking into people's houses; they were totally uncontrollable. Actually, at one period both of them had spent a short time in the Fianna Eireann, the young IRA. But . . . when they were put out [of the Fianna] they were breaking into people's houses, breaking their [gas] meters open and stealing the money. So they were both ordered out of the country or they would be shot. And that was the last I heard of them until they were arrested for the bombings . . . Giuseppe would not have been a Republican; he was just a nice, typical practising Catholic man . . . He went over to visit his son, Gerry, was arrested and charged in connection with the Guildford bombs which was . . . totally untrue; the man was not involved in anything. But [on] the night of the curfew, 99 per cent of the people on the Falls Road would have been sympathetic to us. I mean the whole area had been saturated by British troops; they began to kick in doors . . . the person next door . . . was firing at the British as well . . . that was Hatchet Kerr† who*

---

\* Guildford pub bombings, October 1974, later admitted by Balcombe Street IRA unit. Giuseppe Conlon was convicted of supplying nitroglycerine to the IRA along with six other people, the 'Maguire Seven', mostly his in-laws. He died in jail in January 1980. The 'Guildford Four' and 'Maguire Seven' were cleared on appeal in 1989 and 1991 respectively. The Conlon story was the subject of the 1993 movie *In the Name of the Father*.
† Eamon Kerr, killed by an unknown gunman in March 1983.

*was one of the well-known Official IRA men of the area at the time and was later killed by the IPLO [Irish People's Liberation Organisation].*[14] *So I settled down in Giuseppe's. I had two hand grenades left and I asked Giuseppe was there anywhere I could hide them because all we could do now was sit and wait on the door getting kicked in. Giuseppe brought me out to the back and I hid the two hand grenades, two blast bombs they were, on the roof of Giuseppe's shed, came back in and we sat down. We worked out a plan and this is ironic . . . Giuseppe would claim to be my father and I would be Gerry Conlon. That was in the event of the Brits coming in. So, I took my coat off, washed my hands, cleaned up a bit and Giuseppe made tea. There was this eerie silence; the whole area was totally quiet, the only noise was a helicopter hovering overhead. Then we heard the doors getting kicked in. —— was in the house directly facing me and his door was kicked in. Coincidence again. —— was the man with the Thompson sub-machine gun that night on the roof of St Comgall's school. His house was picked out because that's where the machine gun was being fired from, so they had pinpointed the house, kicked in the door, and I could see the Brits trailing —— up the street, on his back. A few other doors were kicked in and I was just sitting waiting my turn. Fortunately for me, it didn't come. We sat up the whole night, myself and Giuseppe waiting and waiting. Then it went quiet again and we settled in for the night. We sat up the whole night and the next morning the curfew continued. But we didn't know what was going on. We couldn't communicate with anyone, there was no telephone in the house, so we just had to wait and listen to the radio . . . I think it lasted three days. On the third day, there was this total silence except I could hear the sound of people talking, an awful lot of people, and it got closer and closer and I could distinctly hear people shouting, 'The curfew's over, come out, the curfew's over.' I looked out the window and I saw hundreds of people passing the window with prams and children and there was this great sense of . . . 'it's over'. So I went out the back and recovered my weapon and two grenades and joined in with the crowd and there were women I knew with*

*prams and the weapons were handed over and put in the prams . . .*
*we just mingled . . . there were five of us left in Cyprus Street who*
*were not arrested that night. We made our way out of the area, and*
*up into Andersonstown . . . we were picked up in cars and brought*
*to a location, a school where there was a debriefing, what weapons*
*we had lost and what weapons we had gained and what casualties*
*and so forth. The Chief of Staff was there . . . he assembled us all,*
*lined us up and congratulated us for our stand. I did not expect*
*Sean MacStiofain to be there, but obviously he had made his way*
*into Belfast, during the curfew . . . Actually afterwards, when the*
*weapons were counted, we had five or six weapons more than we*
*went into the curfew with because the Officials had left their*
*weapons and we were able to recover them. So I think we had four*
*or five extra short arms and we lost a Thompson sub-machine gun.*

The year 1970 continued in the same vein. The British Army
responded to the growing street clashes in working-class Catholic
districts with a promise to shoot petrol-bombers dead, a promise
made good three weeks after the Falls curfew when a nineteen-year-
old youth was killed during a riot in North Belfast. The British
move caused the IRA problems. The rioting between the military
and Catholic youths had several benefits for the IRA. It invariably
alienated and radicalised communities and for many young people
was often the spur to join the IRA. It also gave a chance to blood
Fianna members and very often it was they who made and threw
the petrol bombs. But the prospect of being shot dead was clearly
a serious deterrent. How they solved that problem revealed a feature
of the IRA that would become the organisation's hallmark, an ability to improvise, invent and manufacture its own weaponry and
explosives.

*. . . at that period they were shooting petrol-bombers. Anybody, I*
*mean. They used to warn you during riots. A Brit would come out*
*with a big loud hailer: 'Petrol-bombers will be shot!' And they were*
*quite easy to identify, petrol-bombers, because you had to light the*

*petrol bomb before throwing it. One of our E/Os, Explosive Officers,
came up with this torch paper. It was a chemical mixture . . .
sodium chlorate was one [ingredient], sugar and something else and
you just got an* Irish News, *our daily newspaper, tore it into strips,
soaked it in this stuff and then hang the strips on the washing line
to dry . . . you then wrapped it round the bottle of petrol, and tied it.
You could throw it and once the liquid hit the torch paper it ignited
. . . which meant there was no need to light the thing . . . many a time
we'd have made torch paper and hung it out to dry. I'm sure people
were wondering, 'What the fuck are they doing drying paper?'*

In September 1970, Northern Ireland had its hundredth bombing
since August 1969; a month later the first killing was carried out by
a Loyalist paramilitary group called the Ulster Defence Association
(UDA); in January 1971, the IRA started policing Catholic areas,
tarring and feathering four men accused of criminal behaviour.
Early February saw the first British Army fatality of the Troubles,
Gunner Robert Curtis, who was shot dead by the IRA in North
Belfast, not far from where the Catholic petrol-bomber had been
killed, and the following day Unionist leader Chichester-Clark
declared, somewhat clumsily, that 'Northern Ireland is at war with
the Irish Republican Army, Provisionals.'[15]

By early 1971, hostility to the British Army in Belfast's working-
class Catholic communities was rising. The days when soldiers were
fêted with tea and biscuits were a distant memory and the Provisional IRA was reaping the benefit. It offered angry Catholic youths
an opportunity to hit back at the soldiers who harassed them on the
streets and fought with them during riots. Recruitment was up and
the Provos were beginning to establish a presence in Derry and in
some rural areas. But in the Lower Falls Road area, the Officials were
still the largest Republican group. This was an important matter,
for the Lower Falls was the historic and psychological heart of West
Belfast and thus of all Catholic Belfast. Whichever group held the
Lower Falls, held it all and unless and until the Provos wrested
domination of the Lower Falls from the Officials, their ambition to

bring the war to the British could not be realised. For their part, the Official IRA was determined that would never happen. The split in the IRA had come over weapons, or rather the lack of them, in the summer of 1969, and the first clashes between the Officials and the Provisionals were also about guns.

*When the Provisional IRA was formed, D Company only had twelve members so we became known as the Dirty Dozen . . . we had a few houses we could use, in Getty Street, Servia Street, my Aunt Bella's house and my cousin Charlie Hughes's house . . . the main street in the Lower Falls at that time was Leeson Street, the main Republican street and there were two pubs in it. One was the Bush Bar which the Official IRA owned and the other was the Long Bar, also with the Official IRA. We did not have any bases. The Officials also had a drinking club in Leeson Street called the Cracked Cup; they also had one in Servia Street, directly facing my cousin's house, called the Burning Embers. So, they had five [sic] drinking establishments under their control . . . every night we had to have people on standby to protect ourselves from the Official IRA, not from the RUC, not from the British Army, but from the Official IRA. We began to sell* the Republican News *round the areas [but] we were constantly put against the wall, the papers taken off us and burned. The Official IRA made an attempt to kill the Provisional IRA at birth. It happened pretty regularly that people like me would be put against the wall and searched for weapons. And soon there was conflict. Paddy McDermott was the QM [Quarter Master] of D Company before the split and Paddy went with the Provisional IRA. The Official IRA arrested Paddy, looking for their weapons dumps which only he knew about, and he was viciously beaten by them. But the dump that Paddy had control of was lifted by the Provisional IRA. That resulted in Tom Cahill being shot. Tom was a brother of Joe Cahill and he was a milkman in Ballymurphy. They just blew him away. He survived, was hit five or six times but survived. So you had this sort of conflict going on, the Official IRA trying to hold onto the weapons that they had, the Provisional IRA trying to get hold of them. So there was this constant tension all the time. Before most people had to go on the run, the D Company volunteers were all issued with handguns and a hand grenade, that is anybody who was staying in the [billet] house, and . . . if the Official IRA attacked or tried to get into the house, you were to throw the blast bomb, and when I say 'blast bomb' it was gelignite, strapped up with black tape with a four-second fuse, and if you believed that you were being attacked or the Official IRA were coming to arrest you, the blast bomb had to be thrown out the top window and you had to fight your way out of the house with whatever weapon you had, usually an old .45 Webley or a .45 automatic.*

*The Official IRA were negotiating with the British at the time. Almost every night a British colonel would be sitting in the Bush Bar talking to them. And as far as I was concerned, that was collusion. The Officials, that is the IRA pre-1969, had got rid of all the weapons and had adopted a non-military line. People felt let down by them because they did not protect them in 1969. Most of the people I'm talking about who were Official IRA were seen as drunken, 'bar IRA men'. The Provisional IRA was seen as a clean military organisation, not centred around drinking clubs and pubs. They [the Officials] were seen to be co-operating with the British. For instance when the barricades came down, they came down with the co-operation of the Official IRA. The Officials and the British negotiated that and I remember most of us being really angry; it was almost like a defeat – the IRA had surrendered. They tried to kill us at birth. That was the intention, to kill us at birth. And I don't know of any evidence that this was done with the encouragement of the British Army – it would not surprise me one bit if it was.*

*[The Officials] arrested a man called Alec Crowe from the Ballymurphy area and they brought him to the drinking club in Leeson Street. He was brought to the Cracked Cup and I was in a house directly facing, in Eileen Hickey's house, and saw Alec being taken out of a car and trailed in. I left the house, went round to Charlie's*

*house, my cousin, told him what I'd seen. Charlie ordered me then to mobilise the rest of the Volunteers, open up the dump and be on standby in his house. I got them together, got the weapons out, a couple of .303s, two M1 carbines, three revolvers, and a few hand grenades. Charlie went up to Kane Street, up to Frank Card's house, MacAirt as we called him, and I sat awaiting instructions . . . an hour, hour and a half later, Charlie came back and we were mobilised into one group. A squad was sent down from Andersonstown. They moved into a house in Balkan Street and we were under orders to burn down the two clubs. By this stage, Alec Crowe had been released by the Sticks\* [but he] had been badly beaten, pistol-whipped, and thrown out. After that – a silly, silly, silly operation it was – we moved out of Charlie's house, straight across the street, no more than thirty yards and took over the Burning Embers. Charlie sent me upstairs to empty the room. I went up and produced my weapon, a .45, and told them to get out but they wouldn't move, so I fired a couple of shots into the air. At the time there was a party in the bar for Paddy Devlin who was an MP at Stormont.† They were celebrating and he was sitting at the bar with Jimmy Sullivan. So I went down and told Charlie that they wouldn't move. We had cans of petrol and Charlie gave the order 'burn it'. So the petrol was laid and the match put to it. And only then did they start moving out. Paddy Devlin was one of the first out; his car was sitting outside, and he drove off. He arrived back in Leeson Street later, I believe, with weapons. So, the Burning Embers was burning. We then assembled outside and moved round along Balkan Street to the Cracked Cup to burn that as well. A group of us went up Cyprus Street, through Varna Gap, heading down into Leeson Street. Another group came along McDonnell Street in a pincer movement.*

---

\* The Official IRA was popularly known as the 'Sticks' in Nationalist areas, after the paper Easter lilies they wore on their jacket lapels to commemorate the 1916 Rising. The paper had a special adhesive backing that stuck to cloth.

† A former member of the IRA in the 1940s who was interned, Devlin joined the Northern Ireland Labour Party in the 1960s and won a Stormont seat in West Belfast. He later was a founder member of the SDLP (Social Democratic and Labour Party) and a minister in the 1974 power-sharing government. He died in 1999.

*As soon as we got to McDonnell Street we were opened up on. Two men [were] shot: Frank Gillen and Dipper Dempsey. A gun battle ensued [and] went on for twenty, twenty-five minutes, us firing at the Cracked Cup. We never got burning the Cracked Cup, but I remember lying at the corner of McDonnell Street firing up at the Cracked Cup and . . . the British Army driving past the bottom of Leeson Street. They never came into the area; they let us just shoot it out. Eventually we were ordered to pull back. Orders came from Kane Street for us to pull back into billets. I took my group over to a street off the Grosvenor Road into a safe house and we sat awaiting further orders. By one o'clock in the morning we'd had no communication whatsoever, and I left the house to find out what the situation was. I was QM at this time, which meant I was in charge of the weapons. So I walked up to Grosvenor Road and to Kane Street. And Kane Street was empty. I came back down and I was stopped by someone who told me that Charlie had been shot – in Cyprus Street. I didn't know what the hell was going on. I went back to the house and by the time I got back we got instructions to stand down. I told everyone to stay and I went out again and by this stage people had arrived at Kane Street and I discovered what had happened. A ceasefire had been called and a meeting was arranged in a house in Cyprus Street, Squire Maguire's house. It was decided that all weapons would be put away that night and talks would be resumed the next morning. On leaving the house after this agreement was made, Charlie went across the street to a lamp-post to give cover to McKee and MacAirt coming out of the house. —— was there as well with a Thompson. As McKee and MacAirt were coming out a shot was fired and Charlie was shot. —— opened up with the Thompson. Nothing – no shots returned. There was speculation going round at that time that it was Joe McCann, that it was Hatchet Kerr. But to this day I really don't know who shot him.*

*The next day there was another meeting held; obviously we were busting to go to town on these people but we were ordered not to. Charlie was brought home. And I remember well – sitting in the house at the wake, and there was a guard of honour [for him]. The day of the funeral, the British Army sealed the whole area off. We wanted to give Charlie a military funeral with the full regalia, the combat gear, berets and a firing party outside the house. It proved to be impossible. The British Army moved in, held up the funeral. They moved in heavy-handed and we were in a house two doors below Charlie's house with our combat gear on, our weapons and so forth, and McKee came down. I remember having my first fight with McKee, with Billy. The British Army Commander at that time said to McKee, 'If there's any military appearance of men', that he would move in. So McKee came to a compromise with the British that if we wore black Dexters [overcoats], would that be acceptable? It proved to be. And we did the guard of honour in black Dexters but no berets. I wanted to face them down; there was thousands of people there – we would have gone out in military uniform, firing the volley of shots over the coffin and saying to the British, 'Do what you want.' But that did not happen . . . it probably was the right decision that Billy made. He was thinking of a dignified funeral without loss of life. Anyway, it turned out to be one of the biggest funerals that Belfast had seen in many a year . . . The British soldiers saluted Charlie's cortège, British soldiers saluting another soldier, a gesture that we all respected . . . After Charlie's death, the Official IRA got a bad press. Charlie was well respected, a pioneer – he didn't drink, went to Mass, and was seen as a good Catholic. They took a hammering, publicly, and a lot of people withdrew their support for the Official IRA and threw their weight behind us. Things started to change. Before Charlie's death we were under heavy, heavy pressure from the Official IRA, but after Charlie's death, the Sticks knew they had made a mistake, and we got stronger. D Company began to get stronger. We began to get more weapons in.*

The recruits began to flood in as well. Soon D Company's numbers were around the hundred-and-twenty mark, making it the largest single unit in the Belfast Brigade.[16] As for the Officials, their days of dominance in the Lower Falls were over and with D Company triumphant, the last obstacle in the way of the Provisionals achieving supremacy in Belfast, and subsequently throughout Republican areas in the North, had been removed. The surge of support that followed Charlie Hughes's death also cemented the ties between the IRA in the Lower Falls and the local people, making the Provisionals an organic part of the Nationalist community and therefore much, much harder for the British to defeat. After the defeats of the 1940s and the 1956–62 campaign, the IRA in Belfast had turned in on itself, becoming an inbred, inter-married and diminishing clique which most Catholics shunned out of fear of official punishment or reprisal. Those days were ending.

*. . . after Charlie Hughes's death there was a major influx of younger recruits coming in . . . you had the Fianna at this time, young kids, from twelve to sixteen, [but] they had to be over fifteen to be trained in weapons, both Fianna and the Cumann na gCailini [girls' version]. They were potential recruits [to the adult IRA]; they did scouting work, for instance . . . on their way to school. We had call houses throughout the area, some abandoned houses, others occupied by supporters . . . Volunteers would meet at a different call house each day . . . weapons would have passed through the call house, explosives, men and women and plans. People would wait for instructions for whatever operation was coming next. And every area had two or three different call houses. You also had billets where volunteers could rest and sleep, and pretty often the house was occupied by civilians . . . many a time I would see myself going into a call house maybe late at night after a long standby or after an operation, and kids would be taken out of their beds to make room for you. You were dependent on people feeding you and a lot did. In most of the call houses we absolutely depended on the locals for our survival, for our food. I remember one particular week we had a call house in Sultan Street; it was a house occupied by a Volunteer, a female Volunteer. That house was used extensively, almost twenty-four hours a day. And other people in the street brought us food. One particular week we lived off tins of pilchards because the guy in the house worked in a factory producing the stuff and that's what he brought home for us*

*every night. There were other houses where you were really well fed. People were poor. People didn't have much to give, but what they had they shared. And unfortunately sometimes, while we didn't abuse it, we began to take people for granted. For instance, there was one house in Theodore Street, which we used constantly, morning, noon and night, far too often really; the woman of the house was a Republican herself, Annie Walsh . . . the mother of Roy Walsh, one of the people convicted of bombing London [in 1973]. Ninety-eight per cent of the doors [in the Lower Falls] were left open at nights; people did not feel in danger of being robbed, they did not feel in danger of being assassinated because they knew we were there. So most people co-operated with the IRA; they left their back doors open, or if they saw you jumping over the yard wall, they'd open the back door if it was closed. So you had that sort of relationship; we were the fish and the water was our local community.*

*I always had a very strict regime based on giving respect to the residents because I knew without them we wouldn't survive. I'll give you an example. One time we got a report of a British Army patrol in this particular backyard, and grenades were thrown into it. But there were no soldiers there and the back windows of the house had all been blown out. We had a system whereby any damage was immediately paid for and people were compensated . . . it happened pretty regularly. When the Brits raided a street, sealed off a whole street, we would have thrown blast bombs and nail bombs into the centre of the street, intending to kill and wound British soldiers . . . we were probably a wee bit too complacent doing that, and we took our own people for granted sometimes. I think it was youthful enthusiasm, but if I had to do it all over again, there are certain things I would not do and that would be one of them, putting our own supporters and civilians at risk. We did do it, and I admit it and I regret it. It's hard to explain what this was like; this was a liberated area, where people like me would walk past a door and some old lady would come out and throw holy water around you, or say prayers for you. At that period you would have times when women would say the rosary at street corners for peace. A lot of these people were our supporters or had houses that we stayed and slept in; they were people who held weapons for us and they were standing at street corners at night saying the rosary for peace. And that night we'd go to their houses and they'd make tea for us. The Brits and the media tried to put it across that these people were actively opposed to the IRA, and they were not. They wanted peace but, as I say, a lot of them were our supporters. I mean, auld Annie Walsh and auld Ma Hickey used to say the rosary at nights but we used their houses more than most.*

*We were all pretty much on the same level . . . we didn't have any-thing. There were no rich people in the IRA then; a massive differ-ence nowadays from the way things were then. We were all working class, we were all pretty poor . . . There may have been one or two who would be seen as well off, like Hugh Feeney,\* whose father owned a pub . . . but that was as wide as the wealth gap went. A pub owner would not be seen as a rich person any more and even then, they were still working people. There was no gap; we were all from the same working-class background, which is totally different from today. Most of us were out of work; and if you had no work, you were paid. For instance, if you were on the run, you got £5 a week to live on, which obviously you couldn't do. You therefore depended on people for food or cigarettes . . . there was a comradeship – I sometimes com-pare it to what it must have been like for the English people during the Blitz, you know, when they were getting bombed, this sense of neighbourliness, a bonding of comradeship. I experienced it again during the blanket and hunger-strike periods, that bonding, that comradeship and that love, that's there when you're all going through a hard time. You get exceptional sacrifices from unexceptional people during situations like that. And a lot of the people that I knew then were just ordinary people like myself. When they were thrown into a situation like that, they produced exceptional performances.*

\* Convicted for 1973 IRA bombing of London.

# 4

It had taken Gerry Adams some time to make up his mind finally about which side to join when the IRA split in December 1969 and the new Provisional IRA came into being. Although he had attended meetings prior to the split at which critics of the Goulding leadership had aired their grievances and began plotting a takeover of the Belfast Brigade, he clearly had divided loyalties; while sympathetic to much of the Goulding ideology and tactics, both his mother's and father's families and many of his and their friends had quickly switched over to the Provisionals. After all, his parents' generation and background were the same as Billy McKee's and it was no surprise that they saw the world, especially that little bit of it in the north of Ireland, through a similar lens.

In early January, Sinn Fein split on the same issue, abstentionism, as the IRA had two weeks earlier, but confusion surrounds Adams's disposition that weekend. He would later claim that he was barred entry to the Sinn Fein conference, or ard-fheis, because he didn't have the correct credentials, thus missing the divisive debate on abstentionism, and instead went off to join an anti-apartheid demonstration at the Ireland versus South African Springboks rugby international. But that version is undermined by the fact that the abstentionism debate happened on a Sunday while the rugby match was the day before.

One eyewitness, Official IRA Belfast Adjutant Jim Sullivan, an ardent supporter of the Goulding wing and admittedly a hostile witness, claims that Adams was in the hall, seated beside him when the crucial vote came and that he stayed in his seat when the anti-Goulding faction walked out in protest to set up Provisional Sinn Fein. The first President of Provisional Sinn Fein, Ruairi O Bradaigh, recalls that Adams was not at the meeting afterwards that formally launched the new party, which is where he would likely have been had he been part of the walk-out. While reluctance to break from what was once the mainstream IRA was fairly commonplace at the time – units in County Tyrone, for instance, who later provided some of the most militant Provisional activists, did not change sides until well into 1971 – all this was enough to feed speculation in the intervening years that Adams was waiting to see which of the two IRAs got most support in Belfast before casting his lot. Whatever the truth, the bulk of pre-split IRA units in Belfast, with the exception of the Lower Falls, had aligned with the Provisionals by the spring of 1970, fifteen out of sixteen companies according to one count, and by that time Adams had thrown his hat into the Provo ring.[17]

Brendan Hughes remembers meeting Gerry Adams for the first time in early 1970 and again shortly afterwards, and both times was impressed with what he saw.

*I met Gerry for the first time in Osman Street [in the Lower Falls area] during rioting and Gerry was at the corner of Osman Street directing the rioters . . . At that time, I didn't know who he was, but he certainly stuck out as a leader because he was able to control and he was able to direct. I can't remember if he threw anything but he certainly directed everybody else to do it. That was my first contact with Gerry. A few weeks later there were riots taking place in Ballymurphy and Billy McKee sent us up there with guns. We took a few short arms, a rifle, and we walked up the Falls Road into Ballymurphy. —— was with me and we were there to give back-up power [to the rioters] with weapons. But Gerry directed us to this house . . . and he ordered us not to leave it. So we sat there all night while the riots were going on. We were wearing holsters and, you know, we were busting to get into the action, to shoot British soldiers. But Gerry's attitude at that time was he wanted to keep the rioting going. He didn't want any gunfire. It was the first sign of conflict between Adams and McKee. Billy [McKee] was Belfast Commander and had ordered us to go there but Adams was the O/C in Bally-*

*murphy . . . If there had been any sort of contact there between
McKee and Adams, we wouldn't have been sent into Ballymurphy
in the first place.*

That incident took place in April 1970, after British troops had
bowed to pressure from the Unionist government and forced an
Orange parade through part of Ballymurphy. The estate, which is
quite close at one spot to the strongly Loyalist Shankill Road area,
had once been mixed, but since the violence of August 1969, Protestants had been moving out in growing numbers, some because of
intimidation, others because they expected it. Orangemen believed
that even though the area was no longer a Protestant district, they
still had the right to march along what once had been a traditional
route. Local Catholics objected and when troops escorted the
Orangemen into the estate, there was intense rioting that lasted
several days.

Eight weeks or so later, in June, Ballymurphy was caught up in
the city-wide disturbances that had followed the 'Siege of St
Matthew's' and the Ardoyne gun battles. This time, however, the
rioting in the estate lasted six months. Not once during that time,
however, did the Ballymurphy IRA fire a shot. Instead there were
long nights of fierce hand-to-hand fighting between locals and
British riot squads whose cumulative effect was to radicalise the
whole community and entice scores of young men and women into
the ranks of the IRA. The decision to stop Brendan Hughes and his
squad firing on the British military during the April riots was part
of the thinking that would, by the end of 1970, make the IRA an
integral, organic part of life in Ballymurphy and the IRA units
among the strongest in the North. It was an early example of Gerry
Adams's strategic talents, a characteristic that eventually would
make him the Provisional movement's dominating figure.

After a few months as a lowly Volunteer, Brendan Hughes began
climbing the ranks of D Company. First he was made its Training
Officer, or T/O, and by early 1971 he was promoted to Quarter Master, or QM, which meant he had to source weapons and explosives,

provide them for operations and then locate hiding places for the weaponry when it was not in use. No issue was more divisive in the IRA than weapons, the lack of them especially – and that did not change after the split. Inadequate weaponry had created decisive tensions between Belfast IRA activists and the Dublin leadership forcing a nasty split to the surface and it was much the same afterwards. The belief that the Dublin leaders never properly understood the military needs of the Northern units, and of Belfast in particular, persisted inside the Provos and deepened as the fighting in the North intensified, a reflection of a deeper resentment of all things Southern that had its roots in the belief that the North had been forsaken in the years after partition. Eventually this sentiment produced what was effectively a Northern takeover of the IRA in the late 1970s and early 1980s. In the Provisionals' early days, this grudge against the Dublin leadership sent Brendan Hughes on two missions abroad to find the guns that the Belfast IRA wanted and that Dublin either couldn't or wouldn't supply; one was a miserable failure, the other a spectacular, transformative success.

*. . . it was very rare for someone like me, a QM, to travel abroad to engage in arms procurement, but what I think needs to be made clear here is that even in the early days, 1970, 1971, there was a sort of resentment towards the Dublin leadership . . . we believed that they could have been doing a whole lot more in procuring weapons and stuff for us. We were quite prepared and willing to carry out the operations but we were very, very badly armed. Anyway, one time I got a contact in Glasgow, a person who told me that they could get explosives. So I travelled to Glasgow, this was in 1971, and I met this little old man in a pub. He was a peterman, a safe blower. He was introduced to me as: 'This wee man is the best peterman in Glasgow.' I was there for three or four days waiting for this meeting that we arranged, and eventually word came back that it was set up, so I bought a car in Glasgow to transport the stuff. I got into the car with the peterman. I was driving, and we drove to this estate in Glasgow. I'd been given this address but I hadn't told the peterman where we*

*were going. The other contact, one of the family members, brought*
*me. And as soon as we got to the street, the peterman says, 'Get the*
*fuck out of here'; apparently we had been dealing with Loyalists.*
*The peterman actually knew the house that we were going to, and*
*he believed it was a set-up. I got the hell out of the place, got rid of*
*the car and back to Belfast . . . a few weeks later, the pub that I had*
*met the peterman in was blown away.*

Using the contacts he had made as a merchant seaman, Hughes
had also set up an arms-smuggling route from New York, using the
Cunard Line's famous luxury flagship, the *Queen Elizabeth 2*, to
ferry weapons from the United States. The *QE2* had just begun
service between Southampton in England and New York in May
1969, only seven months before the Provisionals came into being.
The ship's crew was over a thousand strong and, thanks to West
Belfast's links to the Merchant Navy, quite a few of them had strong
ties to the IRA.

*We had people working on the QE2, and we had people in America.*
*The Lower Falls is well known [as] a catchment area for seamen;*
*a fair percentage of men from that area went to sea [and] I knew*
*a good few of them. Some were actually in the IRA, one or two of*
*them worked on the QE2. I went to Southampton, put together a*
*wee squad, all Belfast men. They weren't all members of the IRA but*
*supporters. Belfast men practically controlled Southampton [docks]*
*at the time. Gabriel Megahey\* was one of the main people there at*
*the time. He was later done for smuggling missiles from America.*[18]
*We had a line of communication from New York to Southampton*
*and Belfast via one phone. Phones were not common then in houses*
*in the Falls; very few people had one and the particular phone that*
*we used was Governor Ward's; the family [was] a notoriously hard-*
*fighting family. The messages were always in code, so, when we got*

---

\* Megahey was arrested in New York in 1982 by FBI agents posing as arms dealers ready to sell
the IRA surface-to-air missile launchers for use in South Armagh.

*word from America to the Guv's house, that the stuff was on board,
I would then go to Southampton and arrange for transport. I
would drive into the docks, all pre-arranged through contacts in
Southampton . . . and I would actually get onto the boat to take the
weapons off. Normally the shipments would have been five, six,
eight or ten weapons at the most, maybe a couple of hand grenades,
that sort of stuff. You're talking about seamen going ashore in New
York, carrying the stuff on board, hiding it in their lockers, or on
the boat somewhere, and then having it ready for us [to hide in] . . .
the panels of cars. We would have hired cars out of McCauslands
(a Belfast rental agency) . . . what's important here as well is that
D Company always had a special relationship with Belfast Brigade.
You might wonder how was D Company getting away with all this?
Well, D Company was the heart of things in Belfast; it was not on a
solo run. No, it was all above board, because it had to be financed.
But it was outside of the realm of GHQ [in Dublin]. Belfast was
attempting to up the war and GHQ were lagging well behind.*

It was unusual for a section of the IRA such the Belfast Brigade
to seek weapons in such an autonomous fashion. Opportunistic
acquisition of weapons was one thing, but well-planned and
resourced operations such as that set up in Southampton were a
different matter. Acquiring and supplying the IRA with weapons
and explosives was the responsibility of the Quarter Master General, a member of the IRA's General Headquarters staff (GHQ),
which was answerable to the organisation's military commander,
the Chief of Staff, who in turn reported to the policy-making,
seven-man Army Council. The GHQ also consisted of other
departments, such as Intelligence, Engineering, Operations and so
on, each one of which co-ordinated activity in their speciality
downwards to the grassroots. So, once the QMG had acquired
weapons they would be distributed, via Brigade, Battalion and
Company Quarter Masters such as Brendan Hughes, to the units on
the ground and hiding places found for them. That is the way it
was supposed to work and so the Southampton and Glasgow

operations represented a usurping of GHQ functions, effectively an act of defiance of the national leadership.

That such bravado was, by the middle of 1971, part of the way the Belfast Brigade behaved was due in no small measure to the removal of Billy McKee as Belfast Commander and his replacement by figures who would foreshadow the rise of Gerry Adams and his allies, first to the Belfast leadership and then to the national leadership of the IRA.

The sequence of events that led to this began with one of the most merciless and controversial killings of the Troubles. In March 1971 three young, off-duty Scottish soldiers, two of them brothers, were lured from a downtown Belfast bar, taken to a lonely hillside road overlooking the city and shot dead. The killings were so ruthless and cold-blooded that the IRA actually denied responsibility, a sense of shame that was also evident in its own official account of the campaign between 1970 and 1973, *Freedom Struggle*, which makes absolutely no mention of the incident. But there was little doubt in the public mind that the IRA had been responsible and the following days saw such an upsurge in Loyalist anger – at one point thousands of Protestant shipyard workers downed tools to march to Belfast City Hall to demand the internment of IRA suspects – that the Unionist Prime Minister, James Chichester-Clark, was obliged to resign.

With Unionists now demanding tough action against the IRA, the British moved against its Belfast leadership. McKee and his Adjutant, Proinsias MacAirt, were stopped by British soldiers, their car searched and a handgun found. The two men claimed, with some credibility, that they had been framed, that they would never have been so foolish as to carry weapons around so openly. Whatever the truth, they were jailed and Joe Cahill, the man who had sworn Hughes into the IRA, took over. Cahill had been Commander of the Second Battalion, effectively covering most of the Falls Road area, and Gerry Adams, previously Cahill's deputy, became the the new head of the Battalion. Seamus Twomey was made Cahill's Adjutant, or second in command, while Adams brought Hughes onto his Battalion staff, as Operations Officer (OO), and made Ivor Bell his deputy. Bell was a veteran of the 1956–62 campaign and had been interned in Crumlin Road jail for much of that time. He was one of those who rejoined the IRA after the violence of August 1969 and went with the Provisionals at the split. A Commander of C Company in the Second Battalion area, the district that encompasses Clonard and Bombay Street, Bell was a left-wing Republican and well read, unusual qualities in the IRA of those years, and was equipped with strategic talents to match those of Gerry Adams. Hughes's rise through D Company had been meteoric, a reflection of his skills and enthusiasm as an IRA activist; after a spell as Quarter Master, he was made Adjutant, or deputy commander, and then the Officer Commanding D Company before Adams transferred him to the Second Battalion staff. The trifecta of Adams, Bell and Hughes – two strategists and an operational specialist – would forge the Provisional IRA in Belfast into a fearsome killing machine.

The resolve of the Belfast Brigade to bypass GHQ in the search for modern weaponry strengthened in line with the three men's grip on the Belfast IRA. The next sortie for guns would involve a difficult mission to New York for Brendan Hughes – a mission that was ordered by Gerry Adams – and it would bring to the IRA a weapon with which it would become synonymous: the Armalite rifle.

*. . . before Charlie Hughes's death, it must have been late 1970, a seaman came off the* QE2 *with this booklet. It was about this weapon called the Armalite – the* AR15. *It folded, it could be dumped in water, and we were fascinated by this weapon. The* AR15 *came in first and then the* AR18, *the 18 had the folding butt. We all fell in love with this weapon. We were sitting in the [call] house [talking about this] and we decided that, 'We need to get these guns.' We pushed – or I certainly pushed – that this was the weapon we needed. We needed the Armalite because we were using Garrand rifles,* M1 *carbines and Thompsons . . . a lot of the ammunition and weapons came from the 1940s era and they'd been lying in dumps all the*

*years . . . I remember getting a big consignment of .303 bullets. And they were soaking wet. We got biscuit tins and put a layer of sand in the biscuit tin, a layer of ammunition, layer of sand, layer of ammunition, and put it in the oven to dry out the rounds. We would be sitting in a wee kitchen house and the oven full of biscuit tins drying out .303 ammunition or .45 ammunition or whatever. I mean, weapons were so scarce. You had to be careful that you didn't overheat them or they very easily could have exploded. The other problem was that very often you hit a dud round maybe in the middle of a gun battle, and you're constantly re-cocking . . . It was a daunting thought at the time . . . that we were going to take on the might of the British Army with the antiquated weapons that we had . . .*

*From my point of view, all I was concerned about was arming my Volunteers with the best weapons I could get. The problem and it's something I was never able to work out, was why the hell [the] people in GHQ were not doing their job right. Did they not know about Armalites or RPG rocket launchers? Why were they still supplying us with Garrand rifles, M1, M2 carbines, which were not the weapons we needed? The Armalite was much superior for street fighting than any of those weapons. The Garrand was a great weapon for heavy combat, but for the type of operations that we were talking about, for street fighting, the Armalite was perfect. And yet it took us from Belfast, not GHQ in Dublin, to get them in. I don't believe they had a clue, and that's the most innocent explanation I can come up with. The other explanation is that they didn't want us armed in Belfast, in D Company . . . I think we did push the war forward more than anyone else. And I think Gerry Adams was largely responsible for that . . . it was Gerry who sent me to America to get Armalites. To escalate the war. Same reason for the London bombings, to escalate the war, to bring the war to the British. The Gerry Adams I'm talking about then and the Gerry Adams I'm talking about now are two different people . . . [but] at that time, the most important thing was the war, keep the war going.*

*I went to Gerry, who was my O/C . . . [and] it was Gerry who sent me [to New York]. We had people in D Company who were on the QE2; we had the American connection. I left Belfast to make arrangements to go to the States and I stayed in Dublin with a guy called Harry White who was an old 1940s man who had been in jail with my father. And he was a pretty prominent guy, an uncle of Danny Morrison. He arranged for me to get . . . a bum passport, the plane ticket and the contact when I got to New York to pick me up – all the arrangements.*

*The Second Battalion decided I would be the best man to go because I was regarded as a good operator. So I went, as I said, down to Dublin . . . and eventually I got to New York. In New York, I met this contact called 'Bob', an ex-Vietnam War vet and he was to help me get the Armalites. We set up a meeting with Noraid; a guy called Martin Lyons [who] was head of Noraid at the time who lived in this big house, [with a] massive conference table. We sat around the table, and I said, 'We need these Armalites', and Martin Lyons replied, 'But we were told by Dublin that you want Garrands and M1 carbines', and I said back, 'Listen, I come from Belfast and we're fighting the war there, we want Armalites.' And then I was brought to this other house, to this other top Noraid man, and I went to sit in this chair and he told me, 'You can't sit there, that's Joe Cahill's chair.' I says, 'Right, right', so I moved. Again I had the same message: 'We want Armalites', and again he said, 'We have instructions from GHQ to send you back to Belfast.' Without the Armalites. I said, 'What do you mean?' He says, 'Well, we're under instructions from Joe Cahill [who was then Chief of Staff] that you have to go back to Belfast, that you're here unofficially.' I says, 'I'm here on the direction of the Belfast Brigade', and he says, 'But you're not here under the directions of the GHQ.' I replied, 'Well, I'm not fucking going without Armalites.' The Noraid people were so conservative, they had no understanding what the war was like in Belfast and they were controlled totally by Dublin . . . and Dublin thinking, to me, was very conservative, restrictive, and very: 'The war's OK but don't let it get out of hand; don't give them weapons that were too sophisticated.' That was my opinion of Dublin, that was my opinion of America, that was my opinion of Noraid. The Noraid contact I had, the ex-Vietnam vet, talked about 'gooks' . . . which I had a problem with, but at that time my main concern was getting Armalites, so I'd have dealt with anybody . . . So, I was ordered to leave New York. I refused and myself and Bob organised a group of people to buy Armalites for us. At that time you could go into a gun shop, and if you had a driving licence you could buy guns, so that's what we did. We set the group up, and . . . I think [we acquired] something like twenty-six or twenty-seven Armalites. You know the old John Wayne film about the Winchester rifle? Bob had a Winchester in his house and I said, 'Could I get that sent over as well?' 'No problem,' he said. So along with the Armalites came a Winchester rifle.*

*. . . this is where the Southampton thing and the QE2 came in again. We sent the cars over, some [with] a woman and a child, to pick up the stuff; it was hidden into the panels and sent back to Belfast. Whenever a car arrived, we would leave it sitting for an hour or so, and watch it to see if anybody else was watching and then drive it into the Falls, strip the car and get the weapons out. I remember the first time all the Armalites came in. They had just arrived the day before, and we were involved in a gun battle in the Falls, and actually the Sticks were still operating at that time, and I drove into Balkan Street; the Brits were at the top of Raglan Street and I had sixteen Armalites in the boot. I opened it and started handing out Armalites and I remember the Sticks looking at us . . . That was the start of the Armalites.*

*The Sticks got night sights in and that's what we needed badly. They got them in and there was a wee man who was a Stick who jumped over to the Provos, wee ——, who told us where the night sights were. So, we went and robbed their dumps and then we became effective at nights. The night sights fitted onto the Armalites lovely.*

*The Armalites made all the difference, not just in the Lower Falls,*
*but in Belfast, and I loved them. I loved the Armalite. They were so*
*compact, so easy to fire, so easy to maintain, not like the old rifles*
*like the Garrand, the .303 – they had to be oiled all the time.*
*Armalites were much easier to handle.*

Between them, the Armalite and growing support for the IRA in
Catholic working-class Belfast combined to give the Provisionals
in the Lower Falls almost unfettered control of their area during
the early 1970s. The British Army was now facing a well-armed and
determined force that had roots in a community whose alienation
from established authority was on the rise. These were ideal
circumstances for guerrilla warfare and difficult ones for the
British; and occasionally British *naïveté* would make things worse
for themselves.

*I remember that they used to drive down in Saracens with a Sacred*
*Heart picture tied to the front . . . thinking that we wouldn't fire at*
*it. I mean, that's silly. I wasn't one of those who went to Mass, even*
*though I was brought up in a strict Catholic household. We said the*
*rosary every night, went to Mass every Sunday morning and you'd*
*be asked the colour of the vestments when you got back in for your*
*breakfast! But these people obviously thought that we were such*
*devout Catholics that we wouldn't fire on a Saracen with a holy*
*picture on the front of it. They were sadly mistaken. It was only a*
*picture.*

*. . . there was constant activity from the different call houses that we*
*had. Every day there would be a different call house, every day the*
*weapons were being used, every day there were Volunteers out in*
*what was called the 'float' which meant you had a driver – you had*
*to steal a car – possibly one or two men in the back seat, just driving*
*around looking for targets. While that was taking place, it was quite*
*normal for another squad of men – and women – to go and rob a*
*bank, or carry out a bombing mission in the city centre . . . D Com-*

*pany was very active there as well . . . my only agenda in that period in the 1970s was to fight the war, to plant as many bombs as I could, to rob as many banks as I could, to kill as many Brits and RUC as I could, to develop the war to a higher level than it was . . .*

*. . . there wasn't a [British] regiment that came into the Falls area that didn't go out with casualties, and the reason for that was that we were on standby twenty-four hours a day. There was one particular day, we were all sitting in the call house and, for some strange reason, an open-back jeep came in through McDonnell Street, across Leeson Street and up Cyprus Street – now they [had] pulled open-back jeeps off the streets a year before. Whether it was an act of bravado or an act of stupidity I still do not know. At this time the British Army would never come in unless they [were] heavily armed and in armoured cars. This particular day we weren't expecting anything like this; we were in an area that was practically liberated. I had been over every yard wall in the Lower Falls area, through every back door, through most people's houses, everybody knew who we were. Here was something that just came out of the blue . . . It was a crazy fucking thing to do, because we walked round the area with weapons over our shoulders, just walking through the streets . . . I mean, it would be like sending an American open-back jeep into Viet Cong territory in Vietnam. It was just so unbelievable [that] actually we thought this could be a set-up. But we were so confident and in such control of the area at that time that instinct took over: 'There's a target' and 'Hit it.' By the time the jeep had got to Varna Gap, we had an ambush set up. I often wonder what the hell happened; were they doing it for a bet or was it a mistake? When I think back on it now, it frightens the life out of me. And them poor Brits, whoever they were, and for whatever the reason drove into Varna Gap and they were just wiped out!\* You know. There were three dead. I think one survived, but the jeep was just cut to pieces.*[19]

---

\* This would seem to be a reference to an ambush on 20 February 1973 in which two soldiers from the Coldstream Guards, on mobile patrol, were shot dead.

*I'd gone from Volunteer to Quarter Master, to Adjutant and at this stage I was O/C, and it was just an opportunity that could not be missed . . . but then it wasn't the first time that this had happened. Some months before, two soldiers had been sent into the area in the middle of the night under cover, and they were caught. The Official IRA got one and D Company got the other one. The one D Company got was shot in Sorella Street, just facing the Royal Victoria Hospital. The other one the Official IRA allowed to go free. I believed that the Official IRA were in contact at all times with the British Army, and that this had started back in 1969, 1970, when the British Army was based in Mulhouse Street Mill . . . they used to have meetings [with the British] in the Bush Bar and I believed that the Officials held their man there that night, and were in contact with the British in Mulhouse Street. Whether there was a deal or not, that they got something for releasing him, I do not know, but it would not surprise me. In the case of the soldier caught by D Company, he wasn't unarmed, he was armed, he was the enemy, and was seen as that. They were easily spotted and two IRA Volunteers apprehended them. The Sticks, the Officials, appeared at the same time and there was a bit of an argument between the Volunteers and the Officials but everyone backed off. The soldiers didn't offer any resistance at all, the Officials took one away and the one held by D Company was executed. I'm actually not 100 per cent sure but I think he might have survived, that he crawled to the Royal Victoria Hospital, but later he died. The Volunteers took his notebook from him, which had names and addresses; mine was one of the names he had in his book. He had photographs as well . . . but none of me.*

*. . . they were two young lads sent in on an undercover operation against D Company, in one of the most hostile areas you could send soldiers into, and yet it happened. And they were both caught . . . they weren't going to do any damage to the IRA, trying to gather information in the early hours of the morning. And they were spotted by a local resident coming into the area, as most activity in the area at the time was . . . everyone passed on information. Even the*

*Official IRA at this stage would have passed on information if they thought your life was in danger or if they thought there was a chance of you getting arrested; at least some of them would. Most residents would have done the same. There were times when [British Army] foot patrols would have come in – one from one end of the area, one from the other end of the area – and within seconds you knew exactly where they were; it would be passed from one resident to another: 'If you see any of the boys, tell them there's a foot patrol there, a foot patrol here.'*

Brendan Hughes's assertion that the IRA in the Lower Falls, D Company, exerted such a degree of control over the area during this time seems borne out by the security statistics. Only three IRA members were killed by the British Army in the Lower Falls between February 1971, when the IRA in Belfast took the offensive against the British, until Hughes's arrest in July 1973. As many were killed by their own bombs, which in those days were crude affairs, unequipped with the safety devices built into bombs in later years. In contrast twenty-two soldiers died in bomb and gun attacks mounted by D Company members during the same time.

Predictably, Hughes was in the thick of it when two of those IRA members were killed. The first was in late September 1972 and, not untypically of the time, one killing sparked many more. The first to die was a forty-eight-year-old Catholic waiter, Daniel McErlean, who was killed in a UVF bombing of a Nationalist social club in North Belfast, a random, no-warning attack which Loyalist para-military groups were at the time making their speciality.[20] Two days later, McErlean's funeral cortège was due to travel across North Belfast towards Milltown cemetery in the heart of West Belfast and the route would take it up Divis Street, at the very bottom of the Falls Road, into the heart of D Company's territory. It was not unusual on such occasions for the Provisional IRA to stake out the area in case of trouble. Loyalist snipers had in the past attacked funerals in this area, which is adjacent to the Shankill Road, and even without that threat funerals in those days were unpredictable events and often the cue for more violence, as it was that day. As the cortège made its way up the Falls Road, British soldiers opened fire and killed an eighteen-year-old youth, a member of D Company. The troops reported that they had seen him, armed with a rifle on the roof of a chemist's shop at the junction of Servia and Albert Streets, and shot him dead. Their target was Jimmy Quigley, one of D Company's youngest members who, local people later claimed, had not opened fire on the troops, although his subsequent inquest was told a Garrand rifle had been found near his body.[21] Local eye-witnesses claimed that the troops had tossed his lifeless body from an upstairs window on to the street, and this sent angry D Company members racing for their weapons, eager to avenge their fallen comrade. Soon a major gun battle was raging, as Hughes recalled: 'We brought the place to a standstill.' Almost immediately, the IRA drew blood. A member of the Royal Anglian Regiment, Ian Burt from Essex, with eighteen years' service, was shot dead by one of an estimated twelve IRA gunmen attacking the troops.[22] But the soldier was not the last person to die.

*. . . there was a wee girl, a wee Sticky girl, a member of the Official IRA, Patricia McKay you called her. She actually had an Armalite that the Officials had stolen from us, but the wee girl was only a kid. She was only nineteen and she was nervous. They were firing from all over the place and I took the Armalite off her. So I had two Armalites, one over my shoulder and one on my arm, and we were coming under fire from all over the place . . . and I ran out, and just fired like hell and got away but I told Patricia to stay where she was. Her daddy and mummy have asked me so many times about this. I just told her to stay, but she was scared, the child was scared. I said, 'Don't fucking move from here, stay here where you are.' And I went down the street and carried on with the gun battle which went on for the rest of the day. Obviously the Brits had seen me firing from the house and they pinpointed it . . . if only she had listened to what I had told her . . . well, anyway, she came out of the house and they shot her dead. A child. Lovely child. I know her mammy and daddy.*

*And, I remember going the next day to her home; I was on the run, and she lived in Divis Flats, and they put a big military funeral on for her, the Official IRA did. A Tricolour over her coffin and all the rest. I remember walking through them all. And it wasn't easy to do, you know, [walking] through the Sticks, right? And her mummy and daddy kept asking me, 'What happened?' What do you say? I took the weapon off the wee girl. And she just came out; they just pinpointed the house where the firing was coming from. She was game enough to come out and do it. I mean, I was used to gun battles at that time but not her . . . it was like going to work for me, right, going into a gun battle in the Falls, you know.*

The second D Company loss during Hughes's days in charge took place seven months later and the account he gave of the death of twenty-seven-year-old Edward O'Rawe, known as 'Mundo', is sharply at variance with the official version of events. The British Army's story was that O'Rawe was shot dead after firing at a patrol that was pursuing him and another man as he was climbing over an entry wall in Garnet Street in the Lower Falls. His inquest was told, however, that no weapons were found at the scene and that there was no forensic evidence to support the claim that he had been using a weapon.[23] Hughes's version is that his death was a cold-blooded execution, a fate he might have missed himself by just a few minutes.

*I remember when Mundo was killed, we were in a house off Raglan Street . . . It was the same house that we had organised the London bombs from. There was a whole crowd of us there, Lucas Quigley and all . . . he and myself had just left when the Brits hit the house. Big Mundo O'Rawe was still inside. Mundo tried to get over the backyard, that was always your escape but they were waiting for him. And I got out of the house, Lucas and me, just two fucking minutes before they hit the house. So I went and organised the boys and we started to hit back with Armalites. I was in Raglan Street where the 1920s ambush had taken place, and I actually saw Mundo*

*against the wall, and then I next saw him on the floor in an entry.*
*I believe he was executed in the entry of Garnet Street . . . and then*
*a major gun battle followed. At that time Mundo was QM for*
*D Company and he had a group of people around him, one in*
*particular, a girl called Moya. She and Mundo were very close and*
*after the gun battle had settled down and the British troops had*
*pulled out, we assembled back in the call house in Sultan Street.*
*Moya was really upset; she was crying uncontrollably, and I took*
*her by the shoulder, gave her a rifle – a Garrand rifle it was – and*
*brought her outside. And there was a helicopter hovering above and*
*I just ordered her to fire at the helicopter and while she was doing*
*this she was crying uncontrollably, but she kept firing at the*
*helicopter. Not that it was going to do any good, she wasn't going*
*to bring the helicopter down, but it helped her to control her*
*emotions . . .*

While D Company fatalities were relatively few during Brendan
Hughes's time, IRA members were often wounded or injured
during attacks, sometimes badly. Taking such casualties to a local
hospital such as the nearby Royal Victoria Hospital risked the victims being arrested and so, unless the injuries were life-threatening
and required urgent treatment, the IRA preferred to spirit such
people across the border to a hospital in the Republic. One early
attack on a British Army base in Mulhouse Street Mill in the
Grosvenor Road area would set the pattern for the future.

*We organised an ambush, throwing blast bombs and nail bombs*
*over [the walls] trying to pinpoint Brits coming out on patrols. So*
*five or six nail bombs were thrown. Bang! Bang! And ——, his nail*
*bomb bounced off the corrugated-iron wall onto the Grosvenor*
*Road, blew up, and one of the nails went into his spine. He was*
*lying in the middle of the Grosvenor Road but we had all bolted off.*
*Big Fra McCullough was driving one of the cars, he did a U-turn,*
*a handbraker, pulled up in the middle of the Grosvenor Road; the*
*Brits were firing at us now, and he pulls —— into the passenger*

*seat and we get him into the call house in Gibson Street. We put him on a mattress on the floor, under the windowsill; he couldn't move, he was in agony. Everything was quiet. The Brits were patrolling the areas. We could hear their voices over the radio. And ——'s lying under the windowsill in agony, and we're trying to keep him quiet. I went over the yard wall, over to Divis, made contact with his da. I thought he was going to die and I told him the situation. We kept him all night. There was a doctor's surgery at the corner of the street and the next morning I went in, held a gun to the doctor's head, and said, 'We need you down here', and the doctor says, 'There's no need for the gun, I'll come.' So I put the gun back in my belt and brought him down to ——. This is only a couple of hundred yards from the barracks we tried to blow up. The doctor examined him and said, 'If you move him, he's dead; get him to the Royal, phone an ambulance and get him there.' I said, 'What chance has he if we try to move him?' He replied, 'You're risking his life cause that nail can kill him.' So I sent for his da and I said to him, 'We can get him to the Royal, it's only across the street, or we can get him across the border. If we move him we may kill him, but if we send him to the Royal, he's going to jail for twenty years', and his father said he'd leave it up to me to make the decision. It was the last thing I wanted. So, I decided, 'Fuck it, I'm not giving the man up', and I organised a van with a mattress in the back and a medic out of the St John's Ambulance Brigade who was prepared to travel, and fair play to him, he did. So, the Brits had pulled out of the area by this time and remember we were only forty yards away at most from the place we tried to blow up. The van pulled up and we got a stretcher in and got —— onto the stretcher. I explained to —— what was happening and he agreed to go along with whatever I said. We'd already made contact with the South Armagh people, and they arranged a route for us. And we got him across the border and into Dundalk Hospital. I'd a contact in the hospital. —— was there for a year. And to this day he's in terrible agony most of the time. He lives now with his mother, he looks after her. It's only him and his mother in the house together now. He was only a kid, only a Fianna boy when I got to know him, then he came into the IRA. And he was a good Volunteer. He was a real good kid, a good wee operator.*

The British Army knew about Brendan Hughes from early on, but thanks to his father's foresight, it would be some time before Military Intelligence was able to acquire his photograph, to put a face on the IRA leader they knew only as 'Darkie'. They knew he was a leader of D Company, an organiser of many of the attacks that had claimed the lives of their soldiers, and that his elimination would badly hurt the IRA. He was a thorn in the flesh of the British Army and a priority target. One undercover effort mounted by the military very nearly succeeded in removing the thorn. It failed, only just, but it brought Hughes and Gerry Adams closer, helping to cement one of the IRA's most famous partnerships.

*One day, I was standing on the corner of Varna Gap; two or three other people were with me – we hadn't arranged a call house that day – and a van drove down Leeson Street. As the van passed I noticed there was something wrong with the driver – he was nervous. He drove past me and down McDonnell Street onto the Grosvenor Road. I crossed over to the other corner and saw the van going up the Grosvenor Road away from me. Five minutes later it came back down. At that time I always carried a weapon, a .45 automatic, but I'd given it to another Volunteer that morning to go and steal a car we needed, so I sent one of the runners to get a weapon. As the van approached, my eyes were on the driver the whole time, and the guy was really shitting himself. He drove about twenty yards past me, past Varna Gap, and the back doors flew open. Three guys with rifles jumped out and they immediately started firing at me. One had two .45s in his hands. They were wearing baseball boots and tracksuits . . . The bullets went whizzing off the wall, all over the place and there was nothing I could do, only run along Varna Gap, and they came after me firing. I turned round at Varna Gap into Cyprus Street and then I took a shortcut into Sultan Street which was where the call house and our weapons were.*

*I ran the whole length of that street, and they were running and firing after me. Later I worked it out that they knew who I was. There was a derelict house directly facing Varna Gap that the Brits had been using as an observation post and they had obviously identified me, whether it was a photograph or description I don't know, but they identified me obviously because they were trying to kill me. There was a baker's van delivering bread – it was early-morning time – to Willie Dark's shop at the corner of Sultan Street and the van was shot to pieces. I almost ran past the call house I was going so fast, so I grabbed the door as I was running and the momentum carried me right through the living-room window. But the weapons were there, and I grabbed an Armalite and I came out fucking firing. The next thing Saracens came from all over the place and the soldiers in the observation post, in the derelict house, were picked up; it pulled up outside and the two Brits jumped out onto the roof of the Saracen and into the back of it and the other ones who had been chasing me were picked up in another Saracen. They had been there all night. Why the Brits in the derelict house didn't fire I do not know. I was a sitting target for them; they didn't have to send the van down, I mean, they could have shot me from that window. The operation was aimed at assassinating me and whoever else I was with.*

*I didn't realise I was bleeding until afterwards and then I thought I had been hit but I had been badly cut in the arm by the glass when I crashed through the living-room window. I was taken to a house, my cousin's house, just a couple of hundred yards down the street. And the next thing Gerry [Adams] came into the district. The artery had been severed. But it was the 'Big Effort', Gerry, who organised the doctor, brought him into the area, fair play to him. I have to give that to him. It was ——, the heart surgeon. But he had no equipment with him so my cousin got a needle and thread and —— sewed me up. There's a wee lump still there where he inserted tweezers, pulled the artery down, tied it in a knot to stop the bleeding, and then he got a needle and thread and sewed it up. I didn't realise how much blood I had lost but it was an awful lot. Gerry may well have saved my life by bringing the surgeon in because the blood was pumping out. The Brits were still driving round, and I remember the doctor sewing it up while the Saracen was passing the door. You know, Gerry did that but he didn't have to. We were close at that time and I think there was a genuine thing there. He didn't have to come into the area, he could have sent someone else in, but he did come in. I didn't want to leave town – you know, 'the true soldier' – I didn't want to leave Belfast but Gerry insisted, he ordered me out. And I went to Dundalk and booked into a bed-and-breakfast for a week but I just couldn't wait to get back.*

Gerry Adams had talent-spotted Brendan Hughes, realising that he had great skills conceiving and planning operations. When Adams was made Commander of the Second Battalion, he persuaded Hughes to join him on the Battalion staff as his Operations Officer, and it was after this that the Second Battalion took the lead role in Belfast. Hughes didn't want to leave D Company, but he did. And he came to regret the close ties he was to forge with Gerry Adams.

*I didn't want to go, I didn't want to be promoted. I didn't want to leave the Dogs, no, I was quite happy there, I was content there. Every day there was something going on . . . three or four operations, maybe we were robbing a bank or putting a snipe out, putting a float out, planting bombs in the town. You were at that every day, seven days a week, you were on standby. It wasn't a romantic lifestyle, adventurous more than anything else, I would say . . . the D Company that I was O/C of was a very, very young crowd; there were kids there, fourteen, fifteen, sixteen, in the Fianna. They couldn't get into the IRA but they wanted into the IRA, really, really keen. And every one of them were used to their full potential. This was a rundown area. Try and picture it – derelict houses all over the place. We had to use different call houses but there were houses we did constantly use, 39 Theodore Street, for example, Annie Walsh's*

*house; 9 Gibson Street, Mrs Maguire's house, both constantly used.
Twenty-four hours a day we were in and out of their houses. They
were cooking for us, feeding us, letting us sleep there and moving out
when we needed them to. And many a time the houses were raided.
I remember one time, 9 Gibson Street, Mrs Maguire's house, the
Brits raided and the two twins were there, big George and Frank
Gillen, both twenty-seven, twenty-eight stone. Frank's dead; George
is still alive. The usual escape was out the back, over the yard wall.
This particular time, George couldn't get over the yard wall and I
was helping him – everybody else was gone and I was helping
George and he's up and away and over. A Brit charged into the
backyard armed with his SLR; he was an ordinary wee guy, only
eighteen or something, and he had the rifle pointed at me, just on
his own. And I was caught; I put my hands up and he came towards
me. He was really nervous and he knew who I was. I mean by that
stage they all had my photo and he was shitting himself, shouting,
'Sarge, sarge, sarge, sarge!' and he was really shaking. So I tried to
calm him down. I made a move towards him and I pushed him,
pushed the rifle and made a dash for the yard wall. Mrs Maguire
was there and the wee lad was in total panic. And he could have,
he should have shot me. Mrs Maguire jumped on him, lay on top
of him and saved my life and I was away again. Years later, after
I got out of prison, Annie Walsh died, and I gave the oration at the
funeral – the family asked me to do it. Same thing with Mrs Maguire.
I gave the oration at her funeral as well. I can't remember what I
said, but I probably said what I'm saying now, that I have a deep
appreciation of people like her. There's one clear image I have of
Annie Walsh before she died. She was on an oxygen tank in her bedroom. And I went in along with Gerry Adams to see her. I could
never understand where she was coming from, what she was thinking of because she threw Gerry Adams out of the house, asked him
to leave, and called him all sorts of names – 'Waster!' This is in 1986
just after my release. She had absolutely no time for him. And I
didn't know why. [But] I go back to a story that an old Republican
told me about relying on a woman's instinct. It might sound sexist*

*but I believe it. John Joe McGirl\* told me this. We used to be in and out of John Joe's house in County Leitrim and John Joe always relied on his wife's intuition, that if someone came into the house that she didn't like, John Joe had no time for them. And every time I think of that image of us standing in Annie Walsh's bedroom and her telling Gerry Adams to leave, I think of that.*

---

\* Veteran from the 1940s and the Border Campaign, a former Chief of Staff and founder member of the Provisional IRA.

# 5

Without doubt, 1972 was the year of the Provos. Never again would the IRA be as strong at it was that year and never again would it come as near to achieving its military goal, forcing the British out of Northern Ireland. In late June the British and the IRA negotiated a ceasefire and in early July the British government and the IRA leadership met in London, a secret but nonetheless significant rerun of history and the first official contact between the two since 1921 when Michael Collins and Lloyd George met to agree the Treaty. It was an extraordinary moment for the Provisional IRA. Their predecessors had spent the years since the civil war in the wasteland of Irish politics, defeated and increasingly marginalised by the governments in Dublin and Belfast, seemingly destined to be a quaint, occasionally troublesome but essentially irrelevant relic of a bygone era. Yet just two-and-a-half years after their birth the Provos had fought the British to the negotiating table. No wonder that, in Belfast, the IRA's Volunteers relaxed their guard and partied in the Falls Road's many bars, brandishing their weapons openly as grateful neighbours plied them with drink.

But the celebrations were premature. The 1972 ceasefire might well have been the high point of the Provisional IRA's short life but it was also the bend in the road. Not long after their historic meeting in London, the IRA in Belfast would carry out one of the most notorious botched bombings of the Troubles on a day known as 'Bloody Friday', and that would mark the beginning, first of its political isolation and then of its military decline. This would also be the year of Adams, Bell and Hughes, the 'Young Turks' of the Belfast IRA who would first elbow aside the old guard in the city and then set their sights on capturing the IRA's national leadership. For one of the trio, Gerry Adams, 1972 would be the year in which he would establish his credentials as the Provisionals' foremost strategist, in which capacity he would eventually take the IRA from war to peace, from isolation to seats in government. The other two, Bell and Hughes, would journey only part of the way with him before falling out with each other bitterly, like Michael Collins and Harry Boland had in the aftermath of the 1921 Treaty, in the way it always was with the IRA. But that year was also to be remembered for a darker chapter in the Provisional IRA's history, the year when it began 'disappearing' people, individuals whose activities would bring embarrassment or shame to the IRA had the world known them or because their deaths would cause political difficulties. Brendan Hughes was a witness, and a participant, in it all.

Gerry Adams very nearly missed out on the 1972 ceasefire. More than that, if it hadn't been for the solicitous concern of an IRA comrade and friend, it is possible that recent Irish history would almost certainly have charted a different course. Although it appears counter-intuitive to say the least, no one had striven harder to persuade the British to start interning IRA members than Adams, Bell and Hughes. The IRA in Belfast knew it was only a matter of time before the swoops would start and better that when they came in they did so on the IRA's terms. The Unionist Prime Minister, Brian Faulkner, was a big fan of the measure – he had helped implement it during the 1956–62 campaign when it had worked well – and his supporters were baying for it. But Gerry Adams and his allies knew that the Provisional IRA was more or less a blank page to British Intelligence. While the RUC Special Branch's offices held numerous files on the old men of the 1940s and the Border Campaign, some of them inches thick, the Provisional IRA was full of young recruits whose existence and life stories were completely unknown. It would not be long, however, before that changed and so the Second Battalion in Belfast, commanded by Adams, with Hughes still in charge at that time of D Company and Bell still heading C Company, set out to force internment onto the agenda before the British could improve their knowledge of the IRA's battle order. The escalation of rioting, bombings and shootings worked and the pressure for internment from Faulkner and his angry supporters increased. In August 1971, the British swooped, but it was a political and security disaster. Many of those arrested had little or no connection to the IRA and some were simply political activists. The operation was also one-sided; Nationalists were targeted while the increasingly violent Loyalists were left alone. Internment outraged even moderate Nationalist opinion and the SDLP led a Catholic walk-out from public life that effectively doomed the Stormont system of government. And with their ranks swelled by new recruits eager to settle scores with the British, the IRA grew in strength and capability, spreading out of Belfast into Derry, Armagh and Tyrone.

The Belfast Commander of the IRA, Joe Cahill, disappeared down to Dublin after internment and Seamus Twomey, another veteran of the 1950s, took his place. Gerry Adams eventually joined his Brigade staff while Ivor Bell took over the Second Battalion. Adams didn't last too long in his new job. On 14 March 1972, he was arrested and interned. Like most senior IRA figures of the day, Adams had gone on the run after internment was brought in and rarely slept more than one night in the same bed. He had married Colette McArdle, from a West Belfast Republican family, in July 1971 and without doubt his post-August 1971 lifestyle was hardly one that most typical newlyweds would wish to have. None the less, he arranged a house for Colette, now pregnant, in Harrogate Street in the Clonard district off the Falls Road where from time to time they could get together. During one overnight visit, British troops swooped, apprehended him and after he was positively identified he was interned, first on the *Maidstone* prison ship moored in Belfast docks and then in Long Kesh.

Adams would have remained in Long Kesh but for a sequence of events that began in Derry on Sunday, 30 January 1972, 'Bloody Sunday', when paratroopers opened fire during a civil rights march protesting against internment. Fourteen men and youths were killed that day and soon all Ireland was ablaze in anger. On the day of the funerals the British Embassy in Dublin was burned to the ground and in the face of escalating fears that the Northern instability could infect the entire island, Whitehall suspended the Stormont parliament and imposed Direct Rule. The atmosphere changed noticeably in the Nationalist community almost immediately. A women's peace movement surfaced in West Belfast and after Official IRA members kidnapped and killed nineteen-year-old William Best, a Derry Catholic who had joined one of the British Army's Irish regiments and was visiting his family, there was a wave of public protests by Derry Catholics and the Official IRA called off its offensive war against the British. The pressure on the Provos to follow suit intensified and after some back and forth with the British that was facilitated by SDLP leaders John Hume and Paddy Devlin, the IRA agreed a ceasefire while the British, led by the new Northern Ireland Secretary, William Whitelaw, accepted a proposal to hold talks with the IRA leadership.

There were two conditions set by the IRA. One was the conferral of non-criminal status on their prisoners – the IRA called it POW status, the British preferred the phrase 'special category' – which the British conceded. The other was the release of Gerry Adams. It was a seminal moment in his life for, had he not been freed, Adams would have stayed in Long Kesh, possibly for another three years, and by the time he got out of jail not only would the IRA's best years have been behind it, and an opportunity to make his name lost for ever, but it would be facing defeat. His big chance to lead the IRA in Belfast, and later in all of Ireland, would never have come, and it is possible that the peace process would never have happened, or that someone else would have led it. Brendan Hughes was not privy to the leadership's deliberations before the ceasefire, although he remembered Ivor Bell 'being totally arrogant, totally mischievous and planning to dress down' for the meeting with Whitelaw. He also recalled that it was Bell who insisted that his friend Gerry Adams be released for the meeting with the British.

*. . . one of the conditions of the ceasefire was that Gerry Adams had to be released and the person who pushed that was Ivor Bell. Ivor*

*had made it clear to Twomey: 'No fucking ceasefire unless Gerry is released.' I've since criticised Ivor for this, but that was one of the conditions that he made.*

Thanks to Ivor Bell, Gerry Adams was released from Long Kesh in time to leave his mark on the ceasefire episode, and if Hughes would later criticise Bell for arranging Adams's release it was because both men would in later years accuse Adams of betraying the cause they had all once fought for. Hughes's parting of the ways would not come until the 1990s, after a long spell in jail, but the spat between Ivor Bell and Gerry Adams came much earlier. By 1983 Bell was IRA Chief of Staff and as keen as he had been in 1972 to intensify the armed struggle. But by this stage the Provos had embraced the ballot box along with the Armalite, and with such enthusiasm that Bell's doubts and suspicions grew about where Adams was leading the movement. Briefly arrested on the word of an IRA 'supergrass' who later recanted, Bell lost his post as Chief of Staff but stayed on the Army Council from where he plotted Adams's overthrow. The ploy failed and in 1984 Bell was charged with undermining the IRA leadership, an offence that technically carried the death penalty. Instead he was court-martialled and dismissed from the IRA. There was an additional punishment; he was declared *persona non grata* and former IRA colleagues were told to shun his company. It had been less than a dozen years since he had extricated Adams from the clutches of internment but to both men it must have seemed more like a lifetime.

The 1972 ceasefire began at midnight on 26 June. Ten days later an IRA delegation consisting of Chief of Staff Sean MacStiofain; his Adjutant Daithi O Connail; the Belfast Commander, Seamus Twomey; Gerry Adams, Ivor Bell and Martin McGuinness was flown by the Royal Air Force to London where in a flat in Cheyne Walk, in Chelsea, they met the Northern Ireland Secretary, William Whitelaw; a junior minister, Paul Channon; a senior official from the Northern Ireland Office, Phillip Woodfield, and Frank Steele, an officer with the British Secret Service, MI6. Steele's presence marked the beginning of a long and tantalising interaction between IRA leaders and British Intelligence. The meeting achieved nothing in the way of bringing a settlement and peace closer. If afterwards the British declared themselves to have been disappointed by the IRA's inflexibility, they were naive to have anticipated anything else. There was no movement from the IRA's declared public position, nor any reason to expect it. The core demand, which MacStiofain read out to Whitelaw, was that Britain should declare its intention to withdraw from Northern Ireland by 1 January 1975, in just two-and-a-half years' time, and that the guarantee to Unionists that constitutional change could come about only with the agreement of the people of Northern Ireland, the so-called Unionist veto, should be discarded. These were demands that a victorious general would put to a vanquished enemy, and while the British had certainly been battered by the IRA, they were far from beaten. From the British viewpoint, these were impossible demands. The meeting ended inconclusively; it was not even clear if there would be a second one.

On Sunday, 6 July, the ceasefire ended. A dispute with Loyalists in the Lenadoon district of West Belfast over housing Catholics in vacant Protestant homes was the immediate cause, although it could have one of a half-dozen other reasons. At an interface in Lenadoon called Horn Drive, a number of Protestant families had abandoned their homes because of nightly violence and a large number of Catholic families that had been intimidated out of housing estates in Rathcoole in North Belfast moved to occupy them. But a new Loyalist paramilitary group, the Ulster Defence Association (UDA), which had already forced one British Army climb-down on the Shankill Road, had threatened mayhem if this happened. Faced with a choice between taking on two powerful forces at the same time rather than the one they were already fighting, the British opted for the latter, as they had done at other critical points in Irish history. That Sunday afternoon, Seamus Twomey led a crowd of three thousand Catholics through Lenadoon along with a cavalcade of lorries piled high with furniture destined for the abandoned homes. But the British Army had blocked the route to Horn Drive and soon fierce rioting broke out and, not long after, the IRA opened fire. Within an hour the violence had spread to Ballymurphy, where five local people were shot dead by British paratroopers. At 9 p.m. the IRA announced that the ceasefire had ended; it had lasted just over twelve days.

The conventional view then and ever since was that the ceasefire collapsed because the Belfast leadership wished it so. Not only was Whitelaw unwilling to discuss withdrawal but they suspected British trickery. Michael Collins had discovered in 1921 that nothing was worse for a guerrilla army than a ceasefire, an extended ceasefire especially so. The problem was not stopping the IRA; it was cranking it up into renewed action that was the hard part. Suspecting that the British knew this very well and would play for time and that the IRA in Belfast could force a more realistic response from the British by ratcheting up their violence, key Belfast Brigade figures took a hard line on the Lenadoon dispute. By contrast, the Dublin leaders, MacStiofain and O Connail, were thought to be keen to keep the truce alive in the hope that some political advantage could be extracted. Once again the views from Belfast and Dublin differed.

The British view of the IRA in Belfast, both at the time and later, chimed with this, except in the case of Gerry Adams. At a pre-truce get-together on the Derry–Donegal border held a few days after his release from Long Kesh, Adams and Daithi O Connail met two British officials, Phillip Woodfield of the Northern Ireland Office and Frank Steele of MI6, to discuss the arrangements for the cease-fire and the London meeting with Whitelaw. Woodfield wrote a report for Whitelaw, which was released in 2003, in which he made an assessment of the two IRA leaders:

Mr O'Connell is about forty and Mr Adams is twenty-three. There is no doubt whatsoever that these two at least genuinely want a ceasefire and a permanent end to violence. Whatever pressures in Northern Ireland have brought them to this frame of mind there is also little doubt that now that the prospect of peace is there they have a strong personal incentive to try and get it. They let drop several remarks showing that the life of the Provisional IRA man on the run is not a pleasant one.[24]

Many years later, in the mid-1990s, the BBC journalist Peter Taylor interviewed Frank Steele about his memory of the ceasefire meeting in Cheyne Walk and he confirmed this optimistic view of Gerry Adams. On their way back to Belfast, Steele recalled, he had attempted to talk sense to the IRA delegation, to tell them that persuasion more than violence could win Protestants over to Irish unity. 'Steele knew he was wasting his time', wrote Taylor, 'and felt that all Seamus Twomey and Ivor Bell in particular wanted to do was to get back to the IRA's simplistic doctrine of physical force in the belief that "one more heave and the Brits would be out". However, he sensed that Adams, who had said little, either at the meeting or during the journey (although he was taking everything in) felt that this was not enough. Steele believes that the experiences and discussions of that day and the meeting at Cheyne Walk increased Adams's recognition of the limitations of "armed struggle" and the need for the IRA to have a parallel political policy if it was ever to get anywhere'.[25] Twenty years later that is exactly what Adams did.

Brendan Hughes played only a marginal role in the preparations for the ceasefire talks but he was at the very centre of the breakdown in Lenadoon, an event that Seamus Twomey had helped to contrive. Twomey had ordered him and two other seasoned IRA men to occupy a position overlooking the scene and to begin firing at the British when he gave the signal. What struck Hughes about this was that normally it would be Adams who would have given such orders, not Twomey. Many years later he concluded that his long-held assumption that Adams shared Twomey's and Bell's hostility to the ceasefire was mistaken.

*Twomey ordered me, Jim Bryson\* and Tommy Tolan† to Lenadoon
. . . and gave me specific instructions that when he raised his hand
we were to open fire. We were supposed to be on the roof (of local
flats) but it was too dodgy, so we were inside a flat looking down
over this confrontation. We had a Lewis gun and two Armalites.
Twomey wanted to end the ceasefire . . . but the situation got out of
control so much that we couldn't; we'd have shot civilians. The Brits
were all lined up and when Twomey raised his arm, I think the
crowd thought that was the sign to move forward. We held back and
held back until we could get the crowd out of the way. We fired a
couple of shots in the air to get the crowd back. But when the crowd
pulled back, the Brits pulled back as well. Gerry's role [in all this]
was passive . . . I was taking my orders from Twomey . . . and it
was normally Gerry who would give me instructions . . . The talk
between Gerry and Ivor [about the Whitelaw meeting], and it was
mostly Ivor, was that 'This isn't serious, they're not serious, the Brits
are not serious.' I don't think Gerry wanted the ceasefire broken. I
think Twomey did. Ivor did. But not Gerry.*

If 1972 was the year that saw the IRA bring down Stormont and
force the British to the negotiating table, albeit briefly and to little
effect, it was also the year in which the IRA proved that it was
every bit as capable as the British Army of self-inflicted military
disasters. Civilian casualties, particularly killings, were not supposed to be part of the IRA's stock-in-trade. Not only did the
organisation claim to be a non-sectarian army which fought by the
rules of civilised warfare, but in practical terms the IRA operated
within well-understood boundaries set largely by its own community. One of the limits of acceptability was killing civilians,
especially when it looked deliberate or casually careless. It was
not that the Catholic community was especially tender-hearted
about the issue but rather that they knew the inevitable Loyalist

---

\* Ballymurphy IRA leader shot dead in disputed circumstances, 22 September 1973.
† Ballymurphy IRA leader shot dead during a feud with the Official IRA, 27 July 1977.

retribution would be directed randomly, like scatter shot, against them. It is one of the reasons why causing civilian casualties has consistently cost Republicans politically down through the years of the Troubles, right up to the carnage at Omagh in August 1998. The IRA had come close to causing large-scale civilian slaughter a few times in 1971, but got away relatively lightly. But in the spring of 1972 that changed utterly.

In early March, a small bomb, thought to have consisted of around five pounds of gelignite, exploded without warning in the Abercorn restaurant in downtown Belfast. It was late on a Saturday afternoon and the restaurant was packed with shoppers, mostly women and children, taking some refreshment before heading home. Two women were killed in the blast and 130 were terribly injured, some losing one or more limbs. The televised scenes of the aftermath were so shocking that the IRA chose to deny responsibility then and ever since, although IRA sources have confirmed unofficially that the Abercorn blast was its work. The bomb, which eyewitness accounts suggest was placed by two young girls, caused a public backlash against the IRA even in Republican areas of West Belfast, not least because the Abercorn was a popular venue for Catholics and the two female fatalities, a twenty-one-year-old and a twenty-two-year-old, were both Catholics. The IRA supposedly had guidelines for commercial bombings which said there had to be phone warnings both to the target or nearby, as well as either to the Samaritans or to the RUC. These were also supposed to be given in sufficient time to clear the area but in the case of the Abercorn there was no evidence that any of this had been followed. A phone warning was made but it actually came seven minutes after the blast and to many, not least the maimed survivors, it looked as if it was a deliberate atrocity. The second bombing disaster came just two weeks later and this time there were warnings but conflicting, contradictory ones that ensured the death and mayhem that followed. On 20 March, a North Belfast unit of the IRA, from the Third Battalion, drove a 200-pound car bomb into Donegall Street, just a few streets away from the Abercorn restaurant, and left it there.

The first warning gave an inaccurate location for the car, as did two or three subsequent calls, and when the police cleared people away from the area, they inadvertently moved them in the direction of the real car bomb, which exploded killing seven people, three of them binmen working in the area. This time the IRA did admit responsibility but gave an explanation for the bloodshed that would form a familiar script in the years to come: proper and adequate warnings had been given but the information had been 'changed and confused' by British security forces. In other words the Brits were to blame. A statement issued the next day said the IRA regretted the civilian casualties but claimed the British carried ultimate blame for all the bloodshed in Ireland. Despite the words of bravado, the Abercorn and Donegall Street bombs were disasters for the IRA. They turned some Catholics against the IRA and emboldened others to speak out. Nationalist opinion had been fairly united up to then in opposition to the Unionist government and the British military and even though many had qualms about IRA violence they found it easier to stay silent as long as the British continued to behave as they had done in Derry on 'Bloody Sunday'. That started to change in the spring of 1972 and then in July, in a way that ensured the reverberations would be profound and long-lasting.

The Abercorn and Donegall Street bombings would be dwarfed by what happened just two weeks after the ceasefire collapsed. On the afternoon of Friday, 21 July, between nineteen and twenty-two car bombs – the exact number varies in the different accounts – exploded throughout Belfast in the space of just over an hour; nine of them in an eighteen-minute period, six within three minutes. Nine people were killed and a hundred and thirty injured, some very badly. The greatest loss of life occurred at the Oxford Street bus station in the city centre where the car bomb exploded as the security forces were clearing the area, killing two soldiers and four employees of the Ulsterbus company. On the Cavehill Road in North Belfast a car bomb exploded outside a row of shops, killing two women and a fourteen-year-old schoolboy. No warning had been received in that case. As television news programmes that night showed horrifying images of policemen shovelling the mutilated remains of torsos into plastic bags, the day was already being called 'Bloody Friday', the IRA's answer to 'Bloody Sunday'.

'Bloody Friday' was the Belfast Brigade's response to the ceasefire breakdown, a message to the British government that the IRA could and would make a commercial desert of the city unless its demands were met. But the IRA leaders had miscalculated terribly and had badly overestimated the ability of the police, the British military and the emergency services to respond to so many warnings and devices in such a short space of time. The consequences for the IRA were devastating. Politically, 'Bloody Friday' placed the IRA 'outside the pale of political negotiation', as one account put it, and turned moderate Nationalist opinion on both sides of the border firmly against the Provos.[26] It widened the gulf between constitutional Nationalism and those who favoured the ways of physical force, and set a pattern of mutual hostility that would last until the peace process, two decades later. The IRA's difficulty was also Britain's opportunity, militarily speaking. Ten days later thousands of British troops moved into 'Free Derry' and dismantled the barricades behind which the IRA had, since 1969, been able to move and organise freely while in Belfast soldiers constructed imposing military forts deep inside the IRA's strongest areas from where they could launch patrols and conduct surveillance and intelligence-gathering operations against the Provos more or less at will. Operation Motorman, as the exercise was called, was the largest deployment of British military since the Suez crisis of 1956 and it marked the point at which the IRA lost the initiative in its war against the British and was forced on the defensive.

Brendan Hughes commanded the 'Bloody Friday' operation on behalf of the Belfast Brigade and had assembled the bombing teams from all over Belfast. But almost as soon as the first bombs exploded, he knew a disaster was in the making. There were too many bombs for the British to cope with and casualties were inevitable.

*Well, I was one of the key figures involved in organising 'Bloody Friday'. It wasn't directly my decision to do it but I was the person who organised it from the First, Second and Third Battalions. I was the operational commander of the 'Bloody Friday' operation. I remember when the bombs started to go off, I was in Leeson Street, and I thought, 'There's too much here.' The boom, boom, boom, boom, boom of the explosions! A lot of the Volunteers – remember at that time we practically controlled the Lower Falls – were cheering, —— and others like him. I remember his face in particular cheering and cheering and I got angry at them and shouted at them to get off the streets. I sort of knew that there were going to be casualties, either the Brits could not handle so many bombs or they would allow some to go off because it suited them to have casualties . . . And I knew . . . that there were going to be casualties. It was a major, major operation, but we never intended to kill people. I feel a bit guilty about it because as I say there was no intention to kill anyone that day. I think we were over-zealous . . . I mean, if I could reverse the situation I would . . . it was a major undertaking to put so many bombs like that into the town. I wouldn't do it again . . . the risks were far too high, and even if there wasn't any collusion or deceit on the part of the British, I don't believe they were capable of handling so many bombs at one time. I was responsible for a fair number of the bombs that had gone into the town up to then and never once was a bomb put into that town [deliberately] to kill civilians. There were bombs put out, booby traps placed to kill military targets. And I have no guilt about them whatsoever [but] I have a fair deal of regret that 'Bloody Friday' took place . . . a great deal of regret . . . As I say, if I could do it over again I wouldn't do it. [But] I don't accept full responsibility for what took place. It was an organisational decision. But the fact of the matter is [that] I was the person on the ground and if I had . . . said, 'No', the operation wouldn't have gone ahead . . . I don't believe I have any more responsibility for what happened than Twomey, Adams or Bell. [But] the point I'm trying to make is that I was the person who sent . . . these bombs in that day. I was standing at the corner of Leeson*

*Street with an Armalite to give cover to the men coming back. Now, it's all right for others to moralise over it; the fact of the matter is that I was the person on the ground, I was the person who went into Ardoyne, the New Lodge, Beechmount, and the Lower Falls, and everywhere else, to organise 'Bloody Friday'. I don't hold myself personally responsible for all that took place there . . . but certainly I take some of the responsibility.*

'Bloody Friday' was not, as he told Boston College, solely the work of Brendan Hughes. The bombings were planned and approved by the then entire Belfast Brigade staff, including Seamus Twomey, the Brigade Commander; Gerry Adams, his Adjutant, and Ivor Bell, the Brigade Operations Officer. Since 1983, around the time he was first elected as the MP for West Belfast, Gerry Adams has had a policy of denying that he was ever a member of the IRA. By so doing he is also denying that he shares any responsibility for operations such as 'Bloody Friday', implying that whatever blood was shed on that or other days stained only the hands of others. IRA members would usually never admit the truth of their status for a good reason: it could lead to a jail term. But neither would they deny membership in any explicit way. The customary response would be either an evasive one, or a straight 'no comment'. Adams's outright denial has infuriated very many of his colleagues from those and later days and Brendan Hughes was no exception. His view of the events of 'Bloody Friday' was that the entire Belfast Brigade staff was responsible, including Gerry Adams, not just because of his rank in the Brigade but because he was, in Hughes's eyes, the de facto Belfast Commander by virtue of the fact that Seamus Twomey invariably deferred to his strategic judgements.

*Gerry Adams was largely responsible and has to accept responsibility for a lot of these things . . . Gerry was the [real] O/C. Twomey was practically out of it by that stage, to the extent that eventually we sent him down to Dublin. Gerry was always the O/C. Even if he was not the O/C in name, Gerry was the man who made the decisions.*

*[Adams and Bell] could have stopped everything; they could have stopped every bullet being fired. If they had wanted to they could have stopped 'Bloody Friday' . . . [When Adams denies IRA membership] it means that people like myself and Ivor have to carry the responsibility for all those deaths, for sending men out to die and sending women out to die, and Gerry was sitting there . . . trying to stop us from doing it? . . . I'm disgusted by it because it's so untrue and everybody knows it. The British know it, the people . . . know it, the dogs in the street know it. And yet he's standing there denying it [all] . . . The fact of the matter is that we fought a war for thirty years; we [even] brought the war to England. Many Volunteers died in carrying out this war. Gerry was a major, major player in the war, not just in Ireland, but in the decision to send Volunteers and bombs to England. I'm totally disgusted. I mean, there are things that you can say and things you can't say. I'm not going to stand up on a platform and say I was involved in the shooting of a soldier or involved in the planning of operations in England. But I'm certainly not going to stand up and deny it. And to hear people who I would have died for – and almost did on a few occasions – stand up and deny the part in history that he has played, the part in the war that he has played, the part in the war that he directed, and deny it, is totally disgusting and a disgrace to all the people who have died.*

It wouldn't be long before Gerry Adams was the *de jure* IRA Commander in Belfast. Seamus Twomey was persuaded to move to Dublin where initially he had a job on GHQ staff. In March 1973 he succeeded Joe Cahill as Chief of Staff when Cahill was arrested on board the *Claudia*, a 300-tonne cargo vessel intercepted off the County Waterford coast as it ferried some five tonnes of weapons in from Libya, a gift from that country's unpredictable leader, Colonel Gaddafi. Twomey's departure was the moment Adams and Bell had been waiting for as the Belfast IRA, the cockpit of the armed struggle, fell into their hands. Adams was made Commander; Bell became Adams's deputy, the Brigade Adjutant, and Hughes was the new Brigade Operations Officer, the 'double O'.

His recollection of the changeover suggests that the new leadership was full of contempt for Twomey and the brand of old-style Republicanism that he and his generation represented.

*People like Billy McKee, Seamus Twomey, that sort of leadership were all . . . taken off the scene or demoted to GHQ. That was an old saying: 'Demote them to GHQ.' In Twomey's case that's the remark that was made. Twomey was seen as one of the old brigade, someone with the old traditional Republican ideals. And so the whole Belfast leadership changed and people like myself, Ivor Bell, Gerry Adams, Tom Cahill took control of the Belfast situation.*

Twomey is the only Provisional IRA leader to have served twice as Chief of Staff. His first stint ended with his arrest in Dublin in October 1973 but at the end of that month he and two other prominent IRA figures, both veterans of previous IRA campaigns, J. B. O'Hagan from County Armagh and Kevin Mallon from County Tyrone, made one of the most famous prison escapes of the Troubles when a helicopter hijacked by the IRA landed in the exercise yard of Mountjoy prison and whisked them to freedom. Twomey resumed his tenure as Chief of Staff and lasted until December 1977, when the Irish police, the Gardai Siochana, discovered his hideout in south Dublin. Gerry Adams replaced him as Chief of Staff and Hughes claims that Twomey's removal and that of other Army Council figures who were regarded as obstacles was deliberately planned by Adams and his allies. Hughes had a complicated relationship with Seamus Twomey. On one of the very first times they met, he threatened to get Twomey court-martialled for 'loose talk' as it was called, drunkenly discussing IRA operations in a bar, but afterwards they reconciled. In later years, when his own disillusionment with the IRA was setting in, Hughes befriended Twomey and grew angry at the way he had been discarded – 'thrown on the scrap heap' – by the Adams leadership. Twomey died in Dublin in September 1989.

*In 1970 I had become Quarter Master of D Company and QMs at
that period were not supposed to operate, but I did. Their only role
was to procure weapons, secure them and supply them. I broke all
the rules and that's how I came to the attention of people like
Charlie Hughes and Seamus Twomey. My reputation was made the
day I put Seamus Twomey on a charge for loose talking. I was trying
in my capacity as a QM to get more and better weapons, so I went
up to Casement Park [a social and drinking club attached to a
Gaelic Athletic Association club] to talk about this with Twomey,
the O/C of the Belfast Brigade at the time. What I wanted was to go
to Scotland. I had a contact in Scotland who could get me gelignite
but I couldn't get talking to Twomey about this so I got up and
walked out – he was half cut! And he treated me almost with contempt: 'Who was this wee shit?' And they were talking away and his
wife was sitting there, a whole crowd of them all sitting there talking
about weapons and operations and so forth. I got annoyed and I
said to him, 'I'm charging you with loose talk' . . . He went totally
quiet and I walked out. Brian Keenan actually was there that night
. . . and walked out behind me [and] encouraged me to carry on
with the charge. That was my first contact with Keenan. He was
Quarter Master with GHQ at that time . . . he'd an old uncle, Yank
Campbell, who lived facing one of my call houses and he used to
appear in Belfast every now and again. I can't remember if Keenan
ever fired a shot; I'm sure he did, round the border . . . but never in
Belfast . . . anyway, the next morning, Twomey came to me . . .
apologised and promised that it would not happen again. Now here
was the Belfast Brigade O/C coming down to me, the QM in D
Company, to apologise . . . his nickname was Thumper because he
always thumped the table when making a point. But he never ever
did that with me. He knew my father, he was in jail with my father,
and he knew my da was a real upfront man and I think . . . when
Twomey found out who I was he gave me respect . . . I had great
time for Seamus Twomey afterwards. First of all he was man
enough to come and apologise to me and promise it wouldn't
happen again, if I dropped the charges, which I did. And remember*

*this, I was only a young man, while Twomey was a contemporary of my father in the 1940s and 1950s IRA – and here's me putting him on a charge.*

*After we brought the Armalites in we had two call houses, one in 9 Gibson Street and one directly facing it. One day we were all called over to get something to eat; Mrs Maguire had made us something . . . and . . . three or four of us went over and Twomey arrived at the house to find the weapons and no sign of us . . . he could have court-martialled me, but he didn't. He shouted at me, for leaving the weapons unattended, which was an offence . . . he could have done me that time but he didn't. Me and Twomey had a funny relationship.*

*[Eventually] there was a takeover [of the IRA leadership], directed, controlled, manipulated and achieved by Gerry Adams. He was the person who removed the old Army Council. Now at that time I agreed [with all this] . . . I saw them as conservative, as right-wing and as people who were not going anywhere. So I was in agreement. I didn't oppose what Adams was doing. I was part of it – I was one of the tools used by Gerry to remove that Army Council . . . [But later] I started to get concerns at the way Seamus Twomey was treated and at that stage my concerns were more humanitarian . . . When I got out of prison in 1986, he had been thrown on the scrap heap. I remember going in and out of Parnell Square in Dublin, Sinn Fein headquarters, and Twomey would be sitting there, down and out; he would sit in a chair in Parnell Square all day. Joe Cahill was downstairs counting his money and Twomey didn't have enough for a pint. He had a small flat in Dublin which was really run down. This is a man who had spent his whole life in the IRA. And then he took bad, and I would visit him in hospital . . . he died a sad, lonely man. I remember bringing his coffin back to Belfast and when we got to his house after driving the whole way from Dublin there was nobody there, only his wife. It was so sad, so sad. And even . . . when he lay in hospital, he got very few visitors.*

While the military setbacks the IRA would suffer would not really be evident for some time, the political isolation caused by 'Bloody Friday' would quickly become apparent. By the end of 1972, the British had outlined the parameters of any future settlement, limits that would never change in the years that followed. Executive power would have to be shared between Unionists and Nationalists and a mechanism created to accommodate the cross-border relationship with Dublin, something to give expression to the so-called Irish dimension. On the security front, the British made the first moves to 'criminalise' the IRA's armed struggle and to make it easier to obtain convictions in court. A government commission recommended the creation of no-jury trials, with the power to accept confession evidence, to deal with terrorist-type offences. The noose was tightening around the IRA. Meanwhile the violence that year would be the worst of the entire Troubles: 496 deaths, nearly three people killed every two days. The IRA was responsible for almost half of the deaths and for most of the 151 soldiers and policemen who perished. But Northern Ireland would never see as violent a year again.

In later years, not long after the formal beginning of the peace process, 1972 would be remembered for a more notorious reason. This was the year in which the IRA began 'disappearing' people it had killed. By the standards of Chile, Argentina or Peru, the IRA's use of this practice was mild, but many would argue that it is not the scale of the practice that matters as much as the fact that it happens at all. The IRA has admitted killing nine people and burying them in secret graves between 1972 and 1978, a tiny number compared to the hundreds disappeared by General Pinochet or the Argentinian junta. Most of those killed in Ireland were allegedly spies or informers working for the British. The IRA regards itself as an army at war, and during wartime spies are shot dead when they are caught – so it believes such killings are permissible. But letting the world know what had happened was usually seen by the IRA as a vital part of the process, generally by leaving the body in a public place along with a press release explaining the reasons for the killing. Spies and informers were dealt with in this way as a warning to others and to discourage anyone tempted to follow their example, an especially important factor for the IRA since most informers would be recruited either from within its own ranks or from the community within which it operated. So killing and then secretly burying the victim runs counter to the IRA's stated traditions, values and interests and the practice has left the organisation, or at least those who ordered such disappearances, open to the charge that it was done only to avoid embarrassment or shame. That the only other known example of the IRA disappearing people was the cause of huge controversy at the time confirms the point. In April 1922, after the Treaty but before the civil war, the IRA in West Cork allegedly disappeared three local Protestants who had been accused of spying for the British. The killings brought accusations of sectarian bigotry in their wake and both sides in the Treaty debate, those for and those against, united to condemn the deaths and to distance themselves from the perpetrators. A measure of the scale of the controversy is that those far-off events in County Cork continue to reverberate to this day in often bitter exchanges between rival historians about what really happened.

Disappearing people is also a war or human rights crime. In April 2009 the former president of Peru, Alberto Fujimori, was convicted of a number of human rights violations, among which was the 'enforced disappearance' of nine students and a university professor by virtue of the fact that he had effective command of those who actually committed the crimes, a secret military squad.[27] The seventy-year-old faces a lengthy jail term for disappearing around the same number of victims that the IRA has admitted treating in the same way. In Northern Ireland, the issue assumed huge significance during the peace-process negotiations. Relatives of the disappeared had been campaigning for the truth and the recovery of their relatives' remains for years and the issue had become a festering sore that needed resolution if the wider settlement was to take root. So in the wake of the Good Friday Agreement of 1998, the British and Irish governments established an Independent Commission to co-ordinate the search for those still missing. In March 1999, the IRA finally admitted that it had deliberately disappeared those people who had gone missing and furnished a list of the victims to the new commission.

The IRA began disappearing people in the summer and autumn of 1972, not long after Gerry Adams was released from Long Kesh internment camp and around the time that he became the Belfast Brigade Commander. The IRA has procedures for dealing with alleged informers. The accused would face a court martial and, however imperfect the process, the procedure and verdict would have to be ratified by GHQ and eventually by the Army Council, which would also confirm the sentence, normally death in such cases. However, the manner of execution, whether the victim would be acknowledged or their death covered up, was often a matter to be determined locally and by the circumstances of the case. This latter feature of the process is what made the Belfast Brigade's behaviour during this time so controversial. Brendan Hughes was a witness and participant in some of the events that led to these disappearances and in his interviews with Boston College, he confirmed that a special unit called 'the Unknowns', several of whose members were active in the bombing campaign in Britain, took some of these victims to their deaths, and that the unit was established by and, ultimately, was responsible to Gerry Adams.

Another startling assertion made by Hughes is that the IRA has been lying about just how many people were disappeared over the years. One of the names omitted from the list of victims handed over to the authorities, according to Hughes's interviews, is the very first person killed in this way by the IRA. An IRA member like most of the disappeared, the first victim's 'crime' was not treachery but the attempted murder of an IRA colleague for reasons of love or lust. The IRA man at the centre of the story was a senior figure called Joe Linskey, the Belfast Brigade's Intelligence Officer (I/O) at the time he vanished. Joe Linskey, who spelled his name 'Lynsky' for IRA purposes so as to confuse the police and army, was court-martialled and then, Hughes believed, shot dead and buried in a secret grave after it was discovered that he tried to kill a fellow IRA member so that he could have the man's wife to himself. Linskey had been conducting a lengthy affair with the woman and apparently decided that only her husband's death could ensure the survival of the liaison. One warm evening in June 1972, the cuckolded husband answered a knock at his door and was shot in the doorway as he held a child in his arms; and, probably because of that, the shot was poorly aimed and not fatal.

Although badly wounded, he managed to make his way down to the Lower Falls where he told Brendan Hughes that he thought his attacker had been a member of the Official IRA whom he knew. That sparked a feud between the Provisionals and the Officials in the Lower Falls area, in the course of which Desmond Mackin, a member of a family closely linked to the Officials, was shot dead. Only later did Provisional IRA leaders discover that Joe Linskey had attempted to use his position in the IRA to remove a rival for his lover's affection. Hughes said he cannot give first-hand confirmation that Linskey was killed and disappeared but he knew that he had been taken away by 'the Unknowns' – as was at least one other of the disappeared – and he believes that he was shot dead and secretly buried. The betrayed IRA husband was wounded and Mackin killed on the night of 18–19 June 1972. Gerry Adams had just been released from Long Kesh as part of the ceasefire deal when all this happened. On 20 June, he and Daithi O Connail met the British on the Derry–Donegal border to arrange the terms of the ceasefire and, by the time Linskey was dealt with – arrested by the IRA and condemned to die – Adams had been restored to his place on the staff of the Belfast Brigade.

Joe Linskey was one of the founder members of the Provisional IRA in Belfast, a personal friend and associate of Gerry Adams and was in his late thirties or early forties when all this happened. In his younger days, he had been a Cistercian monk – his nickname, predictably, was 'the mad monk' – but he left the order around the mid-1950s and became involved in Republican politics well before the events of 1969. According to those who knew him, Linskey's

IRA hero and role model was Michael Collins, from whose many exploits he derived his interest in intelligence. When he joined the Provisionals he ensured, like Collins and Brendan Hughes's father, that the British would not know what he looked like by destroying all photographs of himself.

Members of Joe Linskey's family have been trying for the best part of thirty-five years to find out what happened to him, but without success. As they told the author last summer, they have made repeated efforts to persuade senior Republicans, including Gerry Adams, to tell them what happened but each time hit a brick wall of silence. His mother and only brother went to their graves not knowing what had become of him, or whether he was alive or dead, while others in the family worried that their uncle had been killed for informing or had been hiding in fear the IRA would catch up with him, an offence that would cast a shadow over the entire family. In the last four years, with the peace process firmly embedded, family members intensified their inquiries but again with no result. As one of them put it: 'It was perhaps understandable that no one would tell us when the war was on, but now that there is peace, his family should be told the truth.'[28] Whether the IRA leadership – or what remains of it – now comes clean about Joe Linskey's fate and reveals what happened to him, whether he was killed or not and if so where his body might be found, remains to be seen. In the meantime Brendan Hughes's testimony is, for the moment, the only clue as to what happened to Joe Linskey.

*That night [18–19 June 1972] I was at the corner of Varna Gap when a Volunteer came and told me that —— had been shot. He was a Volunteer from the Kashmir Road area and he had made his way after being shot to a drinking club called the Rapid Metal Club on Osman Street, directly facing the Raglan Street School where the famous ambush had taken place. I went and saw him and he'd a bullet wound . . . the bullet was still lodged in his stomach so we arranged to get —— away. He was taken across the border which was the normal practice where there were no questions asked.*

—— *told me that it was the Sticks shot him. So, I then went and mobilised the Volunteers in D Company and we went into the Cracked Cup (an Official IRA drinking club). I fired a couple of shots into the air to get their attention and arrested eight or nine Officials. Hatchet [Eamon Kerr, a well-known OIRA gunman] was one of them, —— who was the brother of Jim Sullivan, the O/C of the Officials, —— and I can't remember the other names. They were the three most prominent ones in the area. A man died that night as well because of this incident . . . a man called Dessie Mackin resisted . . . [and] he was shot. He was actually shot by ——. He bled to death; it was an accidental death, if it can be called that. We brought them to a house in Gibson Street and held them in the house and threatened to execute them unless the person who shot —— was handed over. We held them for most of the night until the next morning. They denied shooting ——, but the Officials organised a picket outside the house. Fifty or sixty women came around – everybody in the area knew we had them in that house; so to cut a long story short we were forced to release them, otherwise the attention that it was bringing could have brought the Brits in. As it turned out later that day we found out that it wasn't the Official IRA who shot ——. It was one of our Volunteers – a man called Joe Linskey. And Joe Linskey was having an affair with ——'s wife. He was a strange fella. I believe he was at one time a Christian Brother, but he was a Volunteer in the IRA and he was the man that shot ——. That's the way it happened but what I have since learned [is that] he was taken away, Joe Linskey was taken away by the IRA for interrogation and has never been seen again. I believe he was executed and buried. I believe he was the first to be disappeared by the IRA. I can't confirm it, [but] I believe it . . . I know he was taken away by 'the Unknowns' – [as] they were called at that time. Wee Pat McClure\* ran the squad . . . anyone that needed to be taken away, it was Pat's squad that normally did it. Its members were ——, ——, ——, ——; they were the main ones in this squad. There were obviously*

---

\* Former Brigade Intelligence Officer from Turf Lodge in West Belfast.

*other ones, at times, who drifted in and out . . . They were always Gerry's squad . . . I had no control over this squad, as O/C of the Second Battalion even. Gerry had control over it . . .*

Q. *Did they not sort of double up as a type of Irish Republican Brotherhood, a group within a group which was loyal to Gerry Adams in that sense?*

A. *I think that's probably the best description of them . . .*

Q. *Were they not his own personal squad, something like Michael Collins had, a personal squad?*

A. *By and large, that's what it was, that's exactly what it was . . . that's what they were . . . a flying column type thing . . . they could move into any area [and] they finished up as the nucleus of the team the first time London was bombed. But because of the situation . . . at the time, the Brigade, the Battalion, Company structures, if they were coming into an area to do a particular operation, there was always a tie-in with the local Company. Pat McClure was an ex-British soldier, a very good organiser and very capable of leading a squad like that. He died in Canada, Pat did . . . I never got talking to Pat before he left and it was a surprise to me [that he left] because I always saw Pat as a very dedicated IRA man. I don't know the personal circumstances that made him leave . . . whether he got disillusioned or whatever . . . Pat would have been in his thirties when I knew him in the 1971, 1972 period; he would have been one of the older ones. When I say older ones, he'd have been older than most of us. As I say . . . plenty of military experience behind him. I think he'd served in the Middle East.*

Q. *Why did Gerry Adams need a particular personal team? A squad? A personal squad?*

A. *I think it was for effectiveness, right, and I think that it was a naive attempt possibly to introduce the cell system into the IRA.*

\*   \*   \*

No single event in the annals of the IRA during 1972 more firmly established the Belfast Brigade's name for military daring, or the mastery that its Commander, Gerry Adams, seemed to exercise over the dark world of counter-intelligence, than the so-called Four Square Laundry operation. It was a strike against British Military Intelligence that evoked comparisons with Michael Collins whose famous 'squad' had wiped out the bulk of Britain's secret agents in Dublin in one violent day, the first 'Bloody Sunday', nearly fifty-two years earlier. Adams, whose 'Unknowns' were very possibly an attempt to replicate Collins's squad, was not shy in making the comparison in his autobiography *Before the Dawn*: 'It was a devastating blow, on a par with Michael Collins's action against British Intelligence in November 1920,' he wrote.[29]

In 1972, the British Army dominated the security offensive against the IRA and that included the intelligence war. In those days the level of distrust and hostility between the Army and the RUC, including the Special Branch, was quite intense. The British Army's own analysis of its three-and-a-half-decade-long campaign in Northern Ireland reflected this frosty relationship, describing the RUC of those days as 'secretive and mistrustful of outsiders'[30] and the Special Branch 'as mediocre and . . . hugely overworked'.[31] Reluctant to share responsibility with the RUC for gathering intelligence on the IRA, the Army created its own network which operated at a number of levels, from the foot patrols that daily criss-crossed the Catholic working-class districts of Belfast hoovering up street-level information through to specialist units whose main task was to penetrate the IRA and to recruit and run double agents. In 1972, the foremost of these outfits was an organisation known as the Military Reaction Force (MRF), which was partly an under-cover unit that spied on and attempted to disrupt the IRA and partly a pseudo-gang cum dirty-tricks operation, not beyond making assassination attempts on IRA suspects, of the sort that Brendan Hughes had survived. A parliamentary written question put by the Labour MP Chris Mullin to the Junior Defence Minister in March 1994 drew out this official, if somewhat understated, description of the MRF: 'The Military Reaction Force was a small military unit which, during the period 1971 to 1973, was responsible for carrying out essential surveillance tasks in Northern Ireland in those circumstances where soldiers in uniform and with Army vehicles would be too easily recognised.'[32]

Some time in early 1972, the MRF devised an operation to discover, via forensics evidence, where the IRA's bomb-making factories in Belfast were and who was involved, or at least that is what the British told their American counterparts some thirty-five years later, as the US Military attempted to quell an insurgency in Iraq that made the violence in Northern Ireland seem pretty tame. The story was told in 2008 by a US Special Operations officer to Tom Ricks, the military correspondent of the *Washington Post*:

I attended a briefing at the CI [Counter-Intelligence] Center a year ago and one of the speakers was a former British SAS officer who worked Belfast for ten years. He provided some fascinating insights into their operations and, specifically, some of the 'out-of-the-box' methods they utilised to collect and target the IRA, PIRA [Provisional Irish Republican Army], Gerry Adams and their sympathizers. One of the most interesting operations was the laundromat. Having lost many troops and civilians to bombings, the Brits decided they needed to determine who was making the bombs and where they were being manufactured.

One bright fellow recommended they operate a laundry and when asked 'what the hell he was talking about', he explained the plan and it was incorporated – to much success. The plan was simple: build a laundry and staff it with locals and a few of their own. The laundry would then send out 'color-coded' special discount tickets, to the effect of 'get two loads for the price of one', etc. The color coding was matched to specific streets and thus when someone brought in their laundry, it was easy to determine the general location from which a city map was coded.

While the laundry was indeed being washed, pressed and dry-cleaned, it had one additional cycle – every garment, sheet, glove, pair of pants, was first sent through an analyzer, located in the basement, that checked for bomb-making residue. The analyzer was disguised as just another piece of the laundry equipment; good OPSEC [operational security]. Within a few weeks, multiple positives had shown up, indicating the ingredients of bomb residue, and Intelligence had determined which areas of the city were involved. To narrow their target list, [the laundry] simply sent out more specific coupons [numbered] to all houses in the area, and before long they had good addresses.[33]

The British account, delivered courtesy of America's premier daily newspaper, concluded: 'During the entire operation, no one was injured or killed.' Whatever was claimed about the alleged success of the 'laundromat' operation or the accuracy of some details, this last statement was certainly not true. The laundry described was in fact the Four Square Laundry which operated from premises in the heart of Loyalist South Belfast. Customers did not bring their dirty clothes into the laundry to be washed but rather vans bearing the Four Square Laundry logo would tour Nationalist districts of the city offering a cut-price service, collecting dirty laundry and returning clean clothes door to door. Colour-coded coupons would therefore not be needed to identify customers. Whether gathering forensic evidence was the principal activity of the Four Square operation is also questionable. The van had a hidden compartment in the roof, large enough to accommodate two people and was used, the IRA discovered, to facilitate surveillance of IRA suspects.

The Four Square Laundry operation was, the IRA later claimed, the tip of a large intelligence-gathering iceberg created by the MRF. On 2 October 1972, after a painstaking counter-intelligence operation that had lasted some six months or more, the IRA struck. The outcome of the IRA attack is disputed to this day. Only one British fatality has ever been acknowledged by the military and the IRA's claim that it dealt a much larger blow to the MRF remains unproven. The one admitted death occurred as the Four Square van made calls in the Twinbrook area of West Belfast that midmorning. Another van drew alongside and at least one gunman raked the vehicle, and its roof space, with automatic fire, killing Sapper Edward Stuart.[34] A colleague, a female soldier called 'Jane', escaped and was helped by local people who thought the van had been attacked by Loyalists. 'Jane' was from Coleraine in County Derry and her local accent enabled her to chat safely to women in housing estates such as Twinbrook and to pick up local gossip and possibly valuable snippets of information. The IRA claimed that four other MRF operatives were shot dead that day, two of whom were killed when its members attacked a massage parlour on the Antrim Road in North Belfast that was staffed by English prostitutes and used as an MRF front. A city-centre office allegedly maintained by the MRF was also raided but found to be empty. None of these deaths has ever been conceded by the British, a failure the IRA has always put down to their unwillingness to admit such a bloody setback.

Brendan Hughes was responsible for the downfall of the Four Square Laundry. His suspicions about a missing Volunteer from D Company, Seamus Wright, slowly unravelled the MRF plot, uncovering in the process another IRA double agent, Kevin McKee from Ballymurphy. He won the two men's confidence and persuaded them to tell all they knew about what the MRF was doing. Hughes was then on the staff of D Company but by the time the investigation began to get serious, in the weeks after the 1972 ceasefire and 'Bloody Friday', he had moved on to the staff of the Second Battalion while Gerry Adams was now Belfast Commander and took charge of the counter-assault against the MRF. Hughes wanted to move against the laundry operation straight away but Adams overruled him, saying that a cautious, careful probe would reveal much more about the British operation.

In the wake of the attack on the MRF, Wright and McKee were killed and their bodies dumped in secret graves, probably somewhere in South Armagh. Until now, and Brendan Hughes's dis--closure about the killing of Joe Linskey, it was thought they were the IRA's first such victims. They were disappeared ostensibly to spare their families embarrassment and shame. Having an informer in the family carries a special stigma in Ireland and all the more so when the victims' families were as well known for their Republican fervour and involvement, as were the immediate Wright and McKee families. While sparing the families this ordeal was perhaps an understandable motive in 1972, that attitude gave way to what was arguably a much greater cruelty: keeping the truth from the families for decades, long after it was necessary. It was not until March 1999, twenty-seven years later, that the IRA admitted not only that Wright and McKee had been killed but that they had been disappeared as well. If it had not been for the pressures brought about by the peace process it is feasible the IRA would never have come clean about the disappeared. There is another possible reason why Wright and McKee were disappeared. Erasing Seamus Wright and Kevin McKee from the Four Square Laundry story kept hidden the British success in penetrating the Belfast IRA, while enhancing the triumph and achievement of those who had dealt the MRF such a heavy blow.

As for Brendan Hughes, it is clear from his interviews with Boston College that he carried a burden of guilt about the fate meted out to Wright and McKee. They had told him all they knew about the MRF because he had given them his word that they would not be killed. When they were shot and dumped in a secret hole, both they and he were betrayed.

*Seamy Wright was a D Company Volunteer . . . One of the Dogs . . . he went missing and we knew he must have been involved in something. He was married into the Hickey family who were central to . . . D Company. Patsy [Hickey] was involved, the whole family was involved and so were Mary and Eileen – they were a major Republican family in the Lower Falls. Eileen became O/C of Armagh [women's] jail and Patsy served a life sentence for something he did not do. So when Seamy Wright went missing he sent for his wife. It turned out that he was in England and his wife went over, met him there, came back and I met her in the Hickey household in Leeson*

*Street. Seamy wanted out of the situation he was in. He was under the control of British Intelligence and they had him in a house, I believe, outside London but he wanted guarantees that [if he came back] he'd be OK. I gave the guarantee to his wife and he escaped his handlers and got out of England. That was his story. We met him in a house in Bombay Street, talked to him and convinced him that he was [going to be] OK. We then formally interrogated him and got the whole rundown on the Four Square Laundry situation, that it was a British Intelligence network [they had] set up. They had a base on the Donegall Road, a laundry . . . in the Village area, the Protestant part of the Donegall Road. They would travel round the areas, going to specific houses to pick up laundry and what they did was do forensics tests on the clothes. Seamy Wright was able to tell us about this whole network. They had an office – you can actually see it from here [Hughes's flat in Divis Tower] – in College Square and a massage parlour on the Antrim Road. He gave us a list of names of those who were involved with him in this undercover operation, three of them were IRA Volunteers; two from Bally-murphy – it was mainly a Belfast set-up. The IRA had been heavily penetrated – they had Seamy Wright who was in D Company, prob-ably the most active company in the North. They had infiltrated Ballymurphy, another very active company – they had Kevin 'Beaky' McKee and another Volunteer as well.\* Wright was able to tell us about how much 'Beaky' loved his involvement with this undercover squad. They carried their own weapons. They had shoulder-holsters. They trained in Holywood Barracks where they had firing ranges and they were trained in anti-interrogation tech-niques and so forth. So the Seamy Wright thing expanded into a Belfast operation which brought in Gerry, and Gerry took control of the whole operation. I mean, I was prepared to move right away against the van itself . . . but his attitude was 'hold back, hold back,*

---

\* On 1 July 1976, a thirty-nine-year-old Catholic, Brian Palmer, was shot dead in a bar by the IRA, which claimed that he was working for the MRF. By 1976, the MRF had ceased operations in Northern Ireland for three years, meaning that if Mr Palmer had worked for the MRF, it would have been in the same era as the Four Square Laundry operation.

*hold back – more information, more information, more information', you know. So 'Beaky' McKee was pulled in and we interrogated him as well. It had started off as a D Company operation but became a Brigade operation . . . and after getting as much intelligence as we thought we could get, we moved against it. You have to understand that McKee and Wright believed they had been given immunity and [afterwards] they were taken away across the border where they were held for weeks and weeks. The order was given for them to be put down. I didn't give the order and I felt betrayed . . . There was no purpose in killing them; it was pure revenge . . . I don't know who gave the order for them to be executed . . . I can't say for sure who took the decision. I know they were supposed to be dead and weeks later we found out they were not dead and the order was reinforced. Apparently the people who were holding them, now this is hearsay on my behalf . . . the people who were holding them liked them and couldn't kill them and so people were sent from Belfast to do the actual execution. Seamy Wright's sister was a very prominent Republican and the sad thing about it is that for years I knew the two of them were dead but I couldn't tell anybody. I was in prison in Long Kesh when Eileen came to visit me; her sister was Seamy Wright's wife. They hadn't been told a thing so I took it upon myself to tell Eileen that Seamy was dead. The same thing with the McKee family . . . they came to me to ask what had happened and although I genuinely could not say for definite that they were dead, I believed that both of them were.*

In the hierarchy of the disappeared, there is little doubt that the most disturbing, controversial and poignant killing of this type carried out by the Belfast IRA during this time was that of Jean McConville, who went to her secret grave some time in December 1972, very possibly around the same time as Seamus Wright and Kevin McKee. The disappearance of Jean McConville has assumed such a dark status because of her wretched circumstances. She was a widow struggling by herself to bring up ten children, the oldest a sick, hospitalised daughter of twenty, who herself died not long after her mother's disappearance, and the youngest six-year-old twin boys. She was a Protestant who had married a Catholic ex-soldier, converted to his religion, lived in East Belfast until Loyalists intimidated the family out of their home and ended up in Divis Flats, perhaps the most squalid and dangerous public-housing estate in all of Europe at the time. One night, some time between the last two days of November 1972 and 7 December, masked men and women took her away from her flat in St Jude's Walk, delivered her to a crowd of up to twenty people, who were armed and wearing balaclavas, and she vanished, never to be seen alive again. Her surviving nine children were separated and six were admitted to care. That such a woman had gone missing in circumstances as disturbing as these, and a family destroyed, would be enough to make the Jean McConville case a cause célèbre but there has also been great controversy over why she was killed in such a way.

In March 1999 the IRA admitted that it had killed and secretly buried nine people during the course of the Troubles, all in the 1970s, and offered to help locate their graves. The statement came during a moment of crisis in the peace process. The Good Friday Agreement had been successfully negotiated the previous year but a number of obstacles still stood in the way of implementing the power-sharing government that lay at the centre of the deal, most notably the refusal of the IRA to begin decommissioning its weapons. Towards the end of March, the deadline for devolution was extended and crisis talks with British premier Tony Blair and his Irish counterpart, Bertie Ahern, were convened in Northern Ireland, during which the IRA's statement on the disappeared was made public. Some saw the move as an effort to deflect pressure on the weapons issue but on the day it was released the British and Irish governments granted immunity to anyone providing information about the whereabouts of the disappeareds' remains, a sign that the Provos and the governments were co-ordinating their approach to the issue in the face of growing pressure. Families of the missing had been campaigning for the truth for some time and when President Clinton gave them his support, signalling what the

United States, a partner in the peace process, wished to see happen, the satisfactory resolution of the issue was thus elevated to something of a test of the IRA's peace-process bona fides.

In that, and a subsequent statement, the IRA said that Jean McConville was killed because she was an informer and that she had admitted so at the time. This was an allegation that her family, especially her daughter Helen, who was fifteen when her mother disappeared, and her husband Seamus McKendry angrily denied. They maintained that she had been killed because she had gone to the aid of a British soldier who had been shot near her flat in Divis by the IRA, that her crime was to show compassion to a fellow human being who happened to be wearing a British uniform. Their narrative depicted the IRA in the worst possible light and created even more sympathy for the family.

Although the IRA had given the impression that it knew where the bodies of the missing had been hidden, this was far from the case. A cross-border commission established to co-ordinate efforts to find the bodies had, by 2003, been able to locate just three of the nine victims. In Jean McConville's case, the IRA had given a location that was not precise: a beach near Carlingford Lough in County Louth in the Irish Republic, a picturesque spot at the southern foot of the Mourne mountains. Repeated searches of the area had produced nothing. Then, in August 2003, a walker discovered her remains on Shelling Hill beach some distance from the spot identified by the IRA. A storm the previous spring had washed away part of a car park and roadway constructed on top of her unmarked grave and eventually erosion exposed her body.[35] An autopsy established that she had been killed by a single gunshot fired into the back of her head, the classic hallmark of an IRA execution.

Confirmation that Jean McConville had been killed and disappeared by the IRA, together with growing public disquiet about the case, was the spur for an official British inquiry carried out by the new Police Ombudsman for Northern Ireland, Nuala O'Loan, at the behest of two of McConville's children. In July and again in August 2006, O'Loan pronounced her verdict. While her inquiry centred on whether the police had properly investigated McConville's disappearance at the time – she concluded that they hadn't – O'Loan also dealt with the vexed question of the reason for her death. Her conclusion left the matter unresolved, vindicating neither the IRA nor her family. 'As part of our investigation', O'Loan pronounced, 'we have looked very extensively at all the intelligence available at the time. There is no evidence that Mrs McConville gave information to the police, the military or the Security Service. She was not an informant.' But O'Loan also discounted the family's explanation, that she had been killed after she had helped a wounded soldier; the only soldier shot around the time she disappeared was wounded after she had been abducted. Some of her children had a memory of her aiding a wounded soldier, she said, but that had been in January 1972, ten months before she was taken away by the IRA. If this had angered the IRA, it had taken an inordinately long time, ten months or so, for them to take their revenge.

Gerry Adams had by this stage become enmeshed in the Jean McConville saga, formally by virtue of the fact that at the time of her disappearance he had been Brigade Commander of the IRA, the figure at whose metaphorical desk the buck stopped. Under pressure to respond to demands that Republicans should come clean about the affair, Adams met McConville's daughter Helen and her husband, Seamus McKendry, in 2000 and denied all knowledge to them about her disappearance. During one exchange with McKendry, Adams had told the couple that he could not have been involved as he had been interned at the time. According to McKendry, 'He told Helen and I: "Thank God I was in prison when she disappeared."'[36] In fact Adams was very much at large when Jean McConville was abducted and was not arrested and interned until July 1973, more than six months after her death. None the less, the efforts by Gerry Adams and his colleagues to distance the Sinn Fein leader from the McConville scandal have been largely successful because no other participant in Jean McConville's abduction and disappearance has come forward publicly to say what actually did happen. Until now.

Brendan Hughes was deeply involved in the affair – he handled McConville's initial questioning by the IRA and took the first decisions on how to deal with her case. When the IRA was told that Jean McConville had a radio transmitter in her apartment, they searched her flat and discovered it. Hughes said he confiscated the transmitter – given to her by a British Army handler – and she was taken away to be interrogated. Hughes said that she had admitted working for the Army but, because she was a woman, she was set free with a warning not to do it again. Shortly afterwards, the IRA in the area discovered she had resumed working for the military and this time she was taken away and killed. On the vexed questions of who decided to disappear her and why, Hughes confirmed there was a dispute between Adams and his deputy, Ivor Bell, about whether to hide her body or to leave it in a public place, with Adams advocating her disappearance. The reason for hiding her body, he said, was because she was a woman – the same reason Hughes gave for releasing her the first time. Adams prevailed and, Hughes alleged, gave the order for her to be taken away and buried. It is evident that Hughes decided to reveal what he knew about the Jean McConville affair because of his anger at Adams's own efforts to distance himself from the IRA and the various decisions that caused the loss of human life. When the Jean McConville scandal worsened in the peace-process years, Hughes confirmed, Gerry Adams attempted internally to place the blame for her disappearance on Bell. Hughes's testimony from the grave brings the Jean McConville case to a new level.

*At that time Divis Flats still existed\* and it was a major source of recruitment and activity by the IRA . . . I'm not sure how it originally started, how she became . . . an informer [but] she was an informer; she had a transmitter in her house. The British supplied the transmitter into her flat. ——, watching the movements of IRA*

---

\* In 1993 most of Divis Flats was demolished. Only Divis Tower, where Brendan Hughes lived at the time of his death, remained standing.

*volunteers around Divis Flats at that time . . . the unit that was in . . . Divis Flats at the time was a pretty active unit. A few of them, one of them in particular, young ——, received information from —— that —— had something in the house. I sent . . . a squad over to the house to check it out and there was a transmitter in the house. We retrieved the transmitter, arrested her, took her away, interrogated her, and she told [us] what she was doing. We actually knew what she was doing because we had the transmitter . . . if I can get the hold of this other wee man he can tell you more about it because I wasn't actually on the scene at the time. And because she was a woman . . . we let her go with a warning [and] confiscated the transmitter. A few weeks later, I'm not sure again how the information came about . . . another transmitter was put into her house . . . she was still co-operating with the British; she was getting paid by the British to pass on information. That information came to our attention. The special squad was brought into operation then. And she was arrested again and taken away . . .*

Q. *Arrested by the IRA?*

A. *By the IRA.*

Q. *For the second time?*

A. *Yeah. Second time, and that was as much as I knew. I knew she was being executed. I didn't know she was going to be buried . . . or 'disappeared' as they call it now. I know one particular person on the Belfast Brigade at the time, Ivor [Bell], argued for [her] to be shot, yes, but to be left on the street. Because to take her away and bury her . . . would serve no purpose, people wouldn't know. So looking back on it now, what happened to her . . . was wrong. I mean, she deserved to be executed, I believe, because she was an informer and she put other people's lives at risk . . . There was only one man who gave the order for that woman to be executed. That . . . man is now the head of Sinn Fein. He went to this family's house and promised an investigation into the woman's disappearance. That man is the man who gave the . . . order for that woman to be executed. Now tell me the morality in that . . . I wasn't involved in the execution of the woman . . . but she was an informer, and . . . I warned her the first time. I took a device out of her house . . . and warned her. She'd a load of kids. She carried on doing it. I did not give the order to execute that woman – he did. And yet he went to see them kids – they are not kids any more, they are grown up – to promise an investigation into her death . . . [Ivor Bell] argued, 'If you are going to kill her, put her on the street. What's the sense of killing her and burying her if no one knows what she was killed for? It's pure revenge if you kill someone and bury them. What's the point of it?'*

Q. *And he, Adams, rejected this logic?*

A. *He rejected it.*

Q. *And ordered her to be disappeared?*

A. *To be buried. She was an informer.*

Q. *. . . with all her kids and the way the family was left, in hind-sight, do you still feel as strongly about executing her?*

A. *Not really, no, not now . . . at that time, certainly . . . but not now because as everything has turned out, not one death was worth it.*

Q. *. . . after the event, did you never discuss the issue with Gerry as to why it happened, what was the purpose of it, given that you had a different attitude?*

A. *. . . there was a never great deal of [that sort of] conversation; certainly we talked about it but the war was so intense and, I mean, you might have had twelve, fourteen operations taking place on the one day, and I never got a great deal of time to sit down and think about [anything] except organising operations and getting opera-tions out and getting kills and getting bombs in the town and so forth . . . you never thought about it too much because you were so intent on carrying out the war. I lived from operation to operation*

*. . . you were robbing banks, robbing post offices, robbing trains, planting bombs, shooting Brits, trying to stay alive yourself, trying not to be arrested.*

Q. *Well, you know in recent years that Gerry has been trying to blame Ivor?*

A. *Hmm.*

Q. *And has actually been telling people like Bobby Storey to go and ask Ivor Bell questions because Ivor Bell would know the circum-stances of Jean McConville. And Ivor Bell when asked is obviously denying it, and saying, 'Well, go and ask Gerry, coz he's the man.'*

A. *Hmm.*

Q. *It seems very machiavellian, I mean, you worked with all these people.*

A. *. . . I just can't believe, well, I do believe but I find it so difficult to come to terms [with] the fact that this man has turned his back on everything that we ever did . . . I never carried out a major oper-ation without the OK or the order from Gerry. And for him to sit in his plush office in Westminster or Stormont or wherever and deny it, I mean, it's like Hitler denying that there was ever a Holocaust . . . I don't know where it ends, once you get onto [a] position where you . . . start denying that you ever were what you were. It's a lie and . . . to continue telling lies and to deny his whole life. I just cannot accept that it's so, I mean, did he not go and talk to Willie Whitelaw as an IRA representative? Of course he did.*

Q. *So was he lying when he denied any involvement in 'Bloody Friday'; was he lying when he denied any involvement in the killing and disappearing of Jean McConville?*

A. *He was lying.*

Q. *Does he just lie about his whole life in the IRA?*

A. *It . . . appears that way, that he has just denied and lied about everything that ever took place. And to do that gives me the impression that the man cannot be trusted.*

*Q. Although you agreed with the informer executions, do you think the reason for the disappeared was that there was an element of embarrassment at the Belfast Brigade – which was supposed to be a lean, mean, fighting machine, striking terror and fear into the heart of the enemy [but] had actually itself been extensively penetrated, and he didn't want this known?*

*A. I don't believe that is the case . . . As regards McConville . . . I think the reason why she [was] disappeared was because she was a woman. The reason why Seamy Wright [was] disappeared is because of the Republican family that Seamy Wright came from . . . McKee was the same . . . he came from a Republican family and that was the reason there . . . to protect the family . . . that was the reason as well for Eamon Molloy's\* disappearance, because of the Republican family connection, because of his wife, Kate. I don't know where the logic came from. I don't, well, obviously it came from Adams; he was the person that was largely responsible for the disappeared . . . But looking back on it now . . . it was totally, totally wrong.*

\*   \*   \*

On Sunday, 3 June 1973, IRA internees housed in Cage 5 of Long Kesh made a gruesome discovery: from a wall heater in the woodworking room of the hut used for recreation hung the lifeless body of one of their comrades, twenty-two-year-old Patrick Crawford from West Belfast, known to everyone as Paddy Joe. His death was regarded then, and ever since, as a suicide, thanks in no small way to the prison authorities' speedy assertion, issued that same afternoon, that 'foul play was not suspected'[37] in the death. That Sunday, IRA internees had taken part in a march and parade to commemorate comrades who had been killed in the Troubles, and so the huts in Cage 5 had seemingly been emptied of their occupants at

---

\* Former Belfast Brigade Quarter Master shot dead as an informer in July 1975. His body was the first of the disappeared to be produced by the IRA in May 1999.

the time of Crawford's death. When the parade ended, Crawford's body was discovered by other internees, or at least that is what the story was. One of the first on the scene, within 'five or ten minutes'[38] of the grim find, was Father Denis Faul, the Dungannon-based priest who celebrated Mass weekly in the camp for IRA detainees and was a popular figure with the prisoners, thanks to his staunch critique of British security policy and his sympathy for the Republican cause. Some two weeks later, the IRA staff at Long Kesh issued a statement that said that the dead man had been found by two internees immediately after the parade and attempts to revive him were made by prisoners, prison officers and Father Faul. After twenty or thirty minutes these were abandoned and Crawford was declared dead. Paddy Joe, the statement said, was 'one of the most liked [internees] by all men'.[39]

The suicide theory was widely accepted and Nationalist politicians lined up to blame prison conditions, internment and the British for Crawford's untimely end. A group of nine priests, led by Father Faul, said the 'inhuman and degrading conditions of Long Kesh' had driven Crawford to suicide, adding, 'Death was his hopeless protest against the whole situation of which Long Kesh is the symbol.'[40] SDLP leader Gerry Fitt and his colleague Paddy Devlin called on the International Red Cross to investigate the reasons for his 'suicide' – although later Fitt, alone of all the Nationalists, would accuse the IRA of hounding Crawford to death – while the Mid-Ulster MP, Bernadette McAliskey, called for the closure of the prison.[41] The Fermanagh-South Tyrone MP, Frank McManus, said of Long Kesh, 'The entire camp is a torture chamber.'[42]

But Paddy Joe Crawford did not take his own life. In his interviews with Boston College, Brendan Hughes revealed that the IRA killed Crawford by hanging him, supposedly because he was working as an informer for the British. But Hughes was convinced that his only crime was to break during police interrogation, like countless other young IRA activists who were never punished as harshly. It was, he said, 'a brutal, brutal murder'.

Hughes's belief was that the order to kill Crawford had come into the jail from Gerry Adams, who was still Belfast Commander at the time. Hughes was not present, he admitted, at the Brigade staff meeting that discussed Crawford's fate and at the time of the hanging he believed that Ivor Bell had sent in the order. But when he discussed the matter with Bell some years later Bell told him that it was Adams who had issued the order, not him. Boston College's researcher, Anthony McIntyre, interviewed former IRA internees held in Long Kesh at this time in an effort to confirm Hughes's account and they corroborate his claim that Crawford was hanged. But they say that Adams's role in the affair was to refer Crawford's case to GHQ in Dublin which then ordered his death. If true this would mean that, ultimately, permission for the killing was probably given by the then Chief of Staff, Seamus Twomey, the most senior figure on GHQ.

According to this account, the usual IRA procedures for handling accusations of informing were ignored both inside and outside Long Kesh. Although the IRA's justice system was inherently flawed, Crawford should none the less have been court-martialled and given a chance to defend himself from charges that, *inter alia*, alleged that he had led British troops to arms dumps and IRA safe houses, and had identified fellow IRA members, admissions he had purportedly made when he was debriefed in Long Kesh by IRA intelligence officers. But he was not court-martialled; instead his life was ended on an improvised gallows by fiat of an IRA leader, whether in Belfast or Dublin it is not certain, and the decision made to lie about what had happened. Whatever the truth about who ordered Paddy Joe Crawford's execution, it is clear that the Belfast Brigade leadership and the IRA's GHQ were both fully complicit in his wretched death.

The former IRA members interviewed by McIntyre, who spoke on condition of anonymity, added disconcerting detail to the story. The hanging was accompanied by a macabre ceremonial: a black cloth was draped over the improvised steps from which young Crawford was pitched into eternity and his wrists were taped behind his back. Afterwards the cloth, a vital piece of evidence, was removed. They also say that he went meekly to his death. Paddy Joe Crawford was a strong young man and could have fought his executioners – and by so doing could have created enough forensic evidence to cast doubt on the suicide theory – but for reasons still unfathomable, he chose not to resist. Four men helped to hang Crawford. One of them was Harry Burns, known as 'Big Harry' to his friends, a prominent Belfast IRA man who was related by marriage to Gerry Adams. During the hanging a group of internees inadvertently burst into the hut and saw everything. Afterwards the word spread among other inmates. 'Prisoners were simply told he had taken his own life. But people knew, although they did not talk,'[43] one of the sources told McIntyre.

Paddy Joe Crawford's death was in one essential respect no different from the deaths of those who had been disappeared before him by the Belfast IRA: Joe Linskey, Seamus Wright, Kevin McKee and Jean McConville. While his body, unlike theirs, was not hidden in a secret grave, the truth about his death was buried just as securely. And he has been disappeared from the death lists of the Troubles as well, made a non-victim by those who ordered and arranged his hanging. Neither *Lost Lives* nor the *Sutton Index of Deaths*,[44] the two most extensive and reliable records of Northern Ireland's death toll, list him among those who were killed in the conflict. Paddy Joe Crawford has simply been forgotten, his story erased from the narrative of the Troubles and, for over three decades, lies told about why and how he died.

Paddy Joe Crawford rightly belongs in the list of the IRA's disappeared victims because, other than wreaking vengeance on him for his alleged treachery, his death, like theirs, was pointless. Fabricating his suicide meant that killing him could never have a deterrent effect on other IRA members who might have been tempted to work for the British, since only a very small number of people would know the real facts of his death.

It is difficult not to wonder if the reason why Patrick Crawford was chosen to die, rather than other IRA members who had broken during interrogation, was that no one would kick up a fuss afterwards, or ask awkward questions about what had happened, much less campaign for years for the truth. Others who were disappeared, such as Jean McConville, left behind relatives to fight for them and, eventually, they persuaded powerful politicians to back their efforts. Apart from one childhood friend, Paddy Joe Crawford really had no one to fight for him afterwards; he was an ideal candidate to be disappeared in the way he was.

Paddy Joe Crawford was an orphan, brought up by nuns in Nazareth House in South Belfast after he was abandoned by his mother. According to records kept by the orphanage, Crawford was born on 5 March 1951 and admitted into care just eleven days later, on 16 March.[45] The Poor Sisters of Nazareth, to give them their formal title, no longer look after children. Nowadays they care for the elderly but in the Belfast of the 1950s and 1960s their convent on the Ravenhill Road was home to scores of rejected waifs. Founded in Hammersmith in London in the mid-nineteenth century, the Poor Sisters built a veritable empire of children's homes in England, Scotland, Wales and Ireland. The Order spread to America, to Australia, Canada and New Zealand, where more homes were built. Paddy Joe Crawford stayed with the Poor Sisters until he reached the age of eleven, when he was transferred to the De La Salle boys' home run by the Christian Brothers at Kircubbin on the picturesque eastern shore of Strangford Lough in County Down. He stayed at Kircubbin until he was fifteen years old, the school-leaving age, when he was transferred to digs in West Belfast and a job found for him. He lived with a family in Broadway in the heart of the Falls Road and became a builder's labourer. He and other orphans from the Nazareth and De La Salle homes were members of St Augustine's Boys Club, run since the early 1970s by Father Matt Wallace, a Wexford-born priest and one of the most loved and popular clerics in West Belfast. Father Wallace helped Paddy Joe Crawford get a job, gave him the last rites an hour after he died and officiated at his funeral, during which his coffin was carried by members of the youth club. To this day Father Wallace tends his grave in Milltown cemetery and that of other Nazareth and De La Salle boys killed in the Troubles.

Like other Catholic religious orders in Ireland and around the world, the Poor Sisters of Nazareth and the De La Salle Christian Brothers in Kircubbin have both been embroiled in scandals arising out of allegations from former residents of physical and mental cruelty, of neglect and sexual molestation. Legal suits against the Poor Sisters have been filed as far apart as Aberdeen in Scotland and San Diego in California, where in 2007 former Nazareth residents won part of a $198 million settlement against the local Catholic hierarchy. One elderly Poor Sister from Scotland was convicted in 2000 of cruelty, and former inmates of the Scottish homes have been financially compensated for their ordeals. Former residents of the Belfast home are similarly seeking redress for alleged ill-treatment through the courts. The De La Salle Order in Kircubbin has similarly been caught up in scandal. The home was extensively investigated by the RUC in the mid-1980s after allegations surfaced of physical and sexual abuse and a government report published in 1984 strongly criticised management at the home for employing abusers. In 2001 two former residents were awarded £15,000 each in out-of-court compensation for sexual abuse committed when they were sixteen years old and charges were filed but dropped against a former principal at the home alleging buggery and other offences.[46]

Frances Reilly was two years old when her mother left her and her two sisters with the Poor Sisters in Belfast and ran off to England. That was in 1956 and many years afterwards, when she read about the court case in Scotland, she decided to write her life story, a heart-rending account of physical, mental and sexual abuse, which was published in January 2009.[47] It was a story, she claims, no Catholics in Belfast at the time would believe. What makes her story relevant to events in Cage 5 of Long Kesh in 1973 is that she and Patrick Crawford would have been residents at the Belfast home at around the same time – albeit in segregated sections. There is no evidence that Patrick Crawford experienced the sort of physical and sexual abuse that Frances Reilly claims happened to her – nor that he was ever abused at Kircubbin – but it is impossible to read her book and not wonder if he did.

As it is, the story of his life and death has to be one of the saddest of the Troubles: abandoned at just eleven days old, he was destined never to know a mother's love. Instead he was brought up by nuns and brothers, some of whom allegedly ill-treated those in their care, and when he reached twenty-two, his life was brutally ended, hanged in jail by the IRA on disputed charges, and then the truth about his death covered up for over three decades.

How or why Patrick Crawford joined the IRA are questions that cannot now be answered, but it seems that he may have become a member not long before he was interned. He and seven or eight other young men were stopped on the border near Newry by British paratroopers as they attempted to cross to the Republic in a van in April 1973. Their story was that they were on a fishing trip but when the soldiers searched their vehicle they could find only one fishing rod. It looked as if they were really en route to an IRA training camp, and if so this suggests that Crawford was a relatively new recruit. He was arrested, questioned and then sent to Long Kesh.

After Crawford's death, the IRA in Long Kesh had described him as one of the most liked of prison comrades but it seemed this feeling was not shared by the organisation outside the prison. Although an IRA member, he was not given a Republican funeral. There was no Tricolour on his coffin or guard of honour around his cortège and there were no crowds lining the streets around Milltown cemetery to pay respects to or merely gawk in curiosity at this man whom the British had allegedly driven to suicide in Long Kesh. An eyewitness account of the event, given recently to the author by a Sinn Fein member who attended the burial, described a funeral that had been shunned by West Belfast Republicans:

There were just a few people [there], a couple of Nazareth nuns at it, a hearse followed by a single car, that was all. Just members of the family who had taken him in and perhaps one or two of their neighbours and friends. There was nobody from the organisation at all, not one single person. I thought it would be a Republican funeral. None of the general public who come out to look at Republican funerals turned out. There wasn't a soul when I went down. It was really a sad funeral, it was so small. I'll never forget it. I was the only Republican who went. I was the only one there I knew.

Years later, this Sinn Fein activist was told the truth about Patrick Crawford's death by a former IRA prisoner: 'I must have been the only one in West Belfast who didn't know,' the source now says.[48]

Inquests on victims of the Troubles have often been the occasion for controversy and further conflict. Juries are limited in the verdicts they can deliver, something Nationalists have long believed is intended to spare the police and military authorities deserved scrutiny. They cannot make a finding such as 'unlawful killing', while inquests into some high-profile victims, such as people killed in disputed circumstances by the police or Army or where security-force collusion with paramilitaries has been alleged, have still to be held years after the deaths occurred. The inquest on Paddy Joe Crawford happened with remarkable speed. On Friday, 15 June 1973, just twelve days after his lifeless body had been discovered in Cage 5, a jury sitting in Hillsborough courthouse, a few miles from Long Kesh, delivered a verdict in the Coroner's Court saying that Crawford had 'died by his own act', echoing the prison service's statement hours after his hanging. His inquest file, provided to the author on foot of a Freedom of Information request, contains no evidence that the authorities harboured suspicions about the way he died or that anything approaching a vigorous investigation of the death had taken place.

Crawford was, his autopsy report said, a young man of 'strong, muscular build' and was six feet tall and healthy. He was wearing a blue T-shirt, a green V-necked pullover and a pair of denims, in the back pocket of which was a plastic comb. An RUC Inspector called

James Black said that his body was hanging by a linen rope, apparently torn from a mattress cover lying on the floor near by, fixed to an iron strut which was attached to the wall of the hut, some ten feet from the floor. Directly underneath the strut were two plastic chairs with boot marks on one of them and near by a steel locker lying on its side. Inspector Black surmised that Crawford had placed one of the chairs on top of the locker and climbed up to secure the linen rope to the strut. A pair of boots, thought to be Crawford's, were sitting in the centre of the floor and his coat was draped over one of the chairs. There is nothing in the policeman's deposition to suggest that any check was made on the boots to determine if they were Crawford's or if they matched the marks on one of the plastic chairs. Nor were any of Crawford's fellow prisoners questioned.

The IRA Commander of Cage 5, whose name has been redacted in the released documents, refused to give evidence at the inquest but on the evening of the hanging he provided a handwritten statement to a senior prison officer which purported to explain why Crawford might have taken his own life. Along with this, the IRA leader handed over a note found in Crawford's personal belongings which could be read as a suicide letter. The IRA Commander's account is peppered with anecdotes that reinforced the view that Crawford was behaving irrationally before his death, including a suggestion that he might have killed himself to put a spotlight on conditions in Long Kesh. There is no evidence in the inquest documents, however, that the police attempted to interview the IRA Commander about his statement or any of the inmates mentioned by him, while the question of why the IRA had possession of Crawford's personal effects instead of the detectives investigating the death was left unasked.

The IRA Commander's statement read:

The day before his death he made a number of gestures to his friends in Hut 28 that he might be leaving them soon. The first gesture he made was when he gave his pipe to a friend and told him to keep it as he would not need it any more. Then in a conversation with his friends he started talking about Long Kesh not getting enough publicity and what it needed was a death to highlight the place. Later on that night he was walking round the cage with a friend and told him that nobody in the cage would talk to him and that they were all against him. This of course is wrong as he got on well with everyone. According to some of the men in Hut 28 he was acting very strange over the past few days, but at no time did anyone think he was about to hang himself. At about 9.00 o'clock that night he went round to the workshop to work on a plaque and he was the last one to leave that night. According to a number of other men he was in the workshop every day for a week before his death and spent long hours in it for reasons unknown. On the morning of his death the Hut O/C woke him up at the normal rising time of 12.00 o'clock and he told the Hut O/C that today would be the last time he would be wakening him. When the O/C asked him what he was talking about, he told him to forget about it. The last time he was seen alive was about 1.55 that day when he was seen walking towards the workshop. At about 2.30 two men went to the workshop to learn music and they found him hanging by a rope from the first heater on the left when you enter the workshop. They then informed me and I ran round and found him hanging there. I then ran to the gate and told the Officer to get a Doctor as a man had hanged himself. When I got back the men and the Officers in the cage had him cut down and tried to help him but it was to [sic] late as he was dead. In his personal belongings he left a note that read, 'When I lay me down to sleep I pray the Lord my soul to keep and if I die before I wake I pray the Lord my soul to take. God bless everybody. P. J. A. Crawford'. This is all the information I can find. Signed —— O/C Cage 5.[49]

In the context of all that was said in the IRA statement, the two-page note found in Patrick Crawford's belongings could be regarded as the last words of someone who is about to kill himself.

Except that the part quoted by the IRA Commander, which has the word 'POET' written beside it, is actually a well-known bedtime prayer said by Catholics, something that he would almost certainly have been taught by the nuns in Nazareth House, and evidence only of a Catholic upbringing, certainly not of suicidal tendencies. It is written at the top of the first page, which is headlined 'Notes', and underneath the prayer is listed the sort of information that might be given out during a geography or general studies class: a list of the counties of Ireland, its provinces, the two capital cities and some historical sites in Dublin. On the second page Crawford had made a list of precious stones and the countries whose soccer teams played in the 1970 World Cup tournament. All this prompts a question: why would Crawford add all this to a suicide note? It is of course the signature that makes it look as if self-destruction was on Paddy Joe Crawford's mind when the poem cum prayer was written. After all, suicide notes are always signed, or at least that is what many people believe. But there are problems with this as well. The signature is written at the side of the prayer, not directly underneath, which is where it should have been placed. The line immediately underneath the prayer is where the list of Irish counties begins and the signature seems to have been written by a different pen, as if it was added later. The question is by whom: Paddy Joe Crawford or one of those who hanged him?

It has proved impossible to answer that question and the authenticity or otherwise of Paddy Joe Crawford's signature remains undecided. To determine properly whether the same or a different hand wrote his name, the original note would have to be examined and the signature expertly compared to other writing on the paper. The inquest file released by the Northern Ireland Court Service is a photocopy and, according to one forensic expert consulted by the author, is useless for this purpose. Only the original copy, which lies in the Court Service's archive, can tell the full story and permission to release the document to the NI Forensic Laboratory in Carrickfergus was denied. For the moment, the truth remains locked away in the file.

The real story of Patrick Crawford's sad and miserable death was for decades an open but never admitted secret among many in the Provo community. His hanging was witnessed by several prisoners and, through them, Paddy Joe Crawford's murder was known about widely, albeit only by Republican activists. Yet for some thirty-five years they kept it hidden from the rest of the world. Now, thanks to Brendan Hughes, a member of the Belfast leadership when the order to kill him was sent into the jail, the truth about Patrick Crawford's harrowing end can be told.

*Patrick Crawford was, well, I don't even believe he was a tout. He broke during interrogation and then gave intelligence and information to his interrogators. He was then interned and he was put in Cage 5. He was executed by the IRA in the prison; he was hanged. And the order was given by Gerry Adams . . . I believed for a long time that it was Ivor [Bell] but it wasn't . . . There was no purpose to it. The only reason that you execute someone is [to make] an example and [create] a deterrent to others. To hang someone who broke and then deny it and say he hanged himself was brutal, brutal murder. [During] that period I remember so many . . . going into the cages, kids who had broken . . . When other people broke they were just sent to Coventry. No one spoke to them. They were put in a small hut of their own. It was a brutal regime. And that's the sort of mentality that brought about the death of Crawford. [If he had lived] Pat Crawford probably would have been on the blanket\* as well. I mean, I know so many of them who are grown men now. They were brought into the IRA, they were given a weapon, they were given a bomb, they went out and they did the job well. When they were arrested by the RUC, the Special Branch, or whatever, [and] brought into a room, beaten, interrogated and tortured . . . some of them broke. What do you expect? You don't hang someone who is going through a war. I mean, if every American soldier or British soldier was hanged for breaking during interrogation by the*

\* IRA prison protest to restore political status.

*Japanese or by the Nazis, there'd [have been] an awful lot of deaths.*
*I had this understanding because I recruited so many of these young*
*lads. They went out and they did what they were told to do, but they*
*were never trained in anti-interrogation [techniques] or how not to*
*break when they were caught. So I had a lot of sympathy for people*
*like Pat Crawford, and others. And I know so many others, like*
*—— and so forth, who was ostracised in the jail, who was recruited*
*into the IRA when he was fourteen, and was very, very good at*
*operations. There were loads of others, young ones, and some of*
*them broke.*

Two people, both of them close to Paddy Joe Crawford, have for
years harboured doubts and suspicions about his death. One of
them is Father Matt Wallace, who told the author, 'I remember
going to the inquest and it was a routine thing, that he died by his
own hand. I was so young and stupid I didn't even question it at
that time but I was never satisfied that Paddy Joe did take his own
life. I argued that he was in an institution all his life so Long Kesh
would have been easier for him than for other young men at the
time because he . . . knew nothing else except institutional life.'[50]

The other is Gerry McCann, a fellow orphan and resident at the
same time in both the Nazareth and De La Salle homes, although
McCann was six years younger: 'Paddy Joe was one of the older
boys and he would be like a protector for me. If you were being
bullied as a five-year-old Paddy Joe would have been there for me
and I always got on well with him. He was a bubbly, outgoing person, out for a bit of craic but a soft, gentle person. His very presence
would lift the atmosphere, full of spontaneous laughter and a teller
of jokes. He was a tower of strength to those who knew him well.'
Gerry McCann had suspicions 'from day one' that Paddy Joe had
been killed in Long Kesh: 'My gut feeling was that he had been taken
out,' he told the author. But for over thirty years he kept his doubts
to himself: 'I was afraid of going into something that would burn
my hands. I was a wee bit gullible [back in 1973] and only later did
I realise that this was a minefield.' McCann made a success of his life

and now manages a golf club in Belfast. He got married and had a son and as his boy approached his thirtieth year, Gerry McCann felt the need to tell his life story and so he began writing a book which he hopes one day will be published. It was then that he decided to try to find out what really happened to Paddy Joe Crawford, a mission that would send him knocking at Sinn Fein's door.

In January 2008, Gerry McCann contacted Gerry Adams via the Sinn Fein website to ask for a meeting and, on 7 March, he and the Sinn Fein President got together at the party's offices on the Falls Road to discuss Paddy Joe Crawford's untimely death. While Adams's role in ordering Crawford's killing is open to question, there seems little doubt that the Belfast Brigade staff, of which Adams was the leading member, did play a central part in the events. But like Jean McConville's family before him, Gerry McCann met a wall of denial from Gerry Adams. 'The meeting was very cordial,' recalled Gerry McCann. 'I gave him a working document with questions. Was Paddy Joe an IRA Volunteer, which I knew he was, and Adams said he wasn't. I didn't believe he took his own life at the time and I still believe that he didn't take his own life and I told Gerry that. His reply was that under no circumstances was he killed by his own people.' Adams told McCann that he wasn't in Long Kesh at that time and had no personal experience of the event but he would try to contact people who were and they might be able to tell him more.

The matter rested there but nothing happened for five months until McCann contacted Sinn Fein to ask when Adams would deliver on his promise. After that he got his second meeting, not with Gerry Adams but with Bobby Storey, who was a seventeen-year-old internee in Cage 6, next door to Paddy Joe Crawford's cage in June 1973. Bobby Storey is, as Gerry McCann put it, 'Gerry Adams's right-hand man', named in the House of Commons by the former Unionist MP David Burnside as the then Director of IRA Intelligence and the alleged moving force behind some of the IRA's more spectacular operations in the last years of the peace process.[51] Among the many tasks Storey has undertaken for the Sinn Fein leadership was handling the delicate issue of the disappeared, in particular the potentially explosive case of Jean McConville. As Adams had done, Bobby Storey denied any IRA hand in Crawford's death: 'I asked him', recalled McCann, 'was Paddy Joe taken out by his own people and Bobby's response was decisive and direct: "Under no circumstances could this tragedy be attached to the movement or any inmates."' Gerry Adams had told Gerry McCann that Paddy Joe Crawford wasn't an IRA Volunteer but the Sinn Fein President's right-hand man had a different answer: 'Storey said he was,' Gerry McCann recalled, 'which raises the question why there were no Republican trappings at his funeral if he had committed suicide. It beggars belief.'[52]

\* \* \*

By the spring of 1973, the Provisional IRA had been at war with the British for the best part of two years. Yet remarkably, given the IRA's history, there had been no attempt to take the war to English soil as Michael Collins had in the 1919–21 period or as had happened on the eve of the Second World War. That all changed in London on 8 March 1973 when two IRA car bombs exploded, one in White-hall, the bureaucratic heart of the British government, and the second near the Old Bailey, England's Central Criminal Court. Two other car bombs, one outside Scotland Yard, the headquarters of the London police force, and the other in Dean Stanley Street, just down the road from the Westminster parliament, were discovered and their explosive contents neutralised. Two hundred people were injured in the blasts and one man, Frederick Milton, a sixty-year-old caretaker from Surrey, who was caught up in the Old Bailey explosion, died of a heart attack. Like Patrick Crawford, he does not appear in any of the death lists of the Troubles, although arguably he would not have suffered a fatal coronary that day but for the bombing. The explosions happened on the same day that in Northern Ireland people were voting in a British-sponsored refer-endum on the state's constitutional status – asking whether its people would prefer to stay British or not. Nationalists of all stripes had agreed to boycott the poll and the results (58.7 per cent turnout and 98.9 per cent supporting the British link) suggested that most Catholics had ignored the referendum. The high level of Nationalist opposition to the poll added to the immediate suspicion of IRA culpability.

Confirmation that the IRA was involved came later that day when seven men and three women were arrested at Heathrow airport as they were about to board a flight to Belfast – they were all Belfast IRA members and several of them had strong associations with Gerry Adams. Two of the women were Dolours and Marion Price, members of a renowned Republican family – their aunt, Bridie Nolan, was an tragic figure, a member of the women's branch of the IRA, the Cumann na mBan; she had been blinded and lost both hands when a bomb she was carrying exploded prematurely in 1938. One of the sisters, Dolours, had been sent to collect Gerry Adams from Long Kesh internment camp when he was released as part of the 1972 ceasefire deal and drove him back to the city where he was reunited with the Belfast leadership. Another person arrested at Heathrow was Gerry Kelly, a member of Adams's Ballymurphy unit, B Company, who later in his Republican career was variously a hunger striker, prison escaper and eventually a junior minister in the power-sharing government set up by the peace process. He remained a loyal ally of Adams throughout his political life, while the Price sisters angrily broke with Adams.

All those caught at Heathrow airport were convicted and sentenced to between twenty years in jail and life imprisonment. In subsequent years there have been allegations from members of the team that the mission had been betrayed by someone in Belfast, although others dispute this. The Price sisters, Gerry Kelly and another member of the team, Hugh Feeney, went on hunger strike almost immediately after they were sentenced, demanding they be repatriated to a jail in Northern Ireland, nearer their families. The protest lasted over two hundred days, largely because the authorities force-fed them, but eventually they secured their return to Belfast.

The striking aspect of the 1973 London bombings is how completely they were a Belfast Brigade operation. They were conceived in Belfast, planned in Belfast and carried out by Belfast members. The IRA Chief of Staff, Sean MacStiofain, gave the final go-ahead to be sure but in a sense that was a technicality and an acknowledgement that Belfast was the powerhouse of the IRA's war. The dominating role of the Belfast Brigade in this operation was another sign of the tensions that had existed almost since the outset between Dublin and Belfast, South and North, tensions that had led the Belfast IRA to seek out Armalite rifles in New York and which much later would lead to the creation of a separate Northern Command. And the bombing of London also did little to harm the growing reputation the Brigade Commander, Gerry Adams, was building for strategic skills. As Brendan Hughes told Boston College, Adams was deeply involved in planning the first bombing of London.

*... up till 1973 we had been fighting the war within Ireland, within the six counties. But there were constant suggestions that we could be much more effective if we hit England, where the occupation forces had come from. They were raiding our houses, killing our people ... And myself and Adams and the rest of the Belfast Brigade – and I must stress this as well – it was a Belfast Brigade initiative that brought about the London bombings. It was ourselves who planned, organised and recruited for the London bombings ... the initial idea was discussed at Belfast Brigade meetings with myself, Gerry Adams, Ivor Bell, Pat McClure, Tom Cahill, basically that group of people. We would have been the main people in the Belfast Brigade at the time ... No one dissented. At that particular period, everyone knew we had to step up the war and bring the war to England, and I can't remember anybody dissenting from that ... I can't remember anyone.*

*Once the decision was made, the next thing was to pick who would go ... we ordered people from different units within Belfast to come to a call house in the Lower Falls ... Myself and Gerry*

*Adams were there and it was put to these Volunteers that there was a job planned; it was a very dangerous job . . . [it] would mean being away from home for a while; [it] would mean being out of Belfast for a while. They were not told that they were going to England [and] after the talk people were invited to either stay or leave. Twelve or so did. Those who remained were the two Price sisters, Hugh Feeney, Gerry Kelly, Gerry Armstrong and Roy Walsh. It was put forcefully to them that the operation was extremely dangerous, [there was] a possibility of their being killed, arrested and not returning to their homes. Then they were told what the operation was.*

*They were then sent across the border for intensive training in explosives . . . weapons and so forth, for about three weeks. Then the cars had to be acquired – there was a special squad put together. Pat McClure was in charge of that, taking them across the border. After that, I had no contact with them because the operation was starting from across the border. I was [Brigade] Operations Officer at that time and once the people were picked, once they were moved across the border, Pat McClure took over . . .*

*We didn't intend to kill people in London. The intention was to strike at the heart of the British Establishment . . . if the intention had been to kill people in London, it would have been quite easy to do so, quite simple, but our intentions were not to kill people . . . what we should have done was to bury the team in England [after- wards]. When I say 'bury the team', we should have arranged hiding places for them there. The mistake we made was to get the bombs in and get the people out as quickly as possible. Unfortunately the British got onto the bombs too quickly and arrested our people coming back. Our idea was a simple one, get the people in, get the explosives in and get our Volunteers out . . . It was like that with the bombing campaign in Belfast or Derry or wherever: put the bomb in, run back, always plan your run back. And we went with that simple idea. In hindsight it was obviously the wrong one. [Maybe] if the British hadn't got onto the bombs so quickly it would have been the right idea. But I think it was bad logistics. I don't think that the operation was compromised. I have never come across any proof or evidence to say otherwise. There possibly may have been, but I've always put it down to the fact that one of the bombs went off prematurely and the British authorities automatically closed down the airports and the ports . . . But after saying that I would not be shocked if the operation was compromised. There's always that possibility . . . But I've heard this so often before when jobs went wrong, that there must have been a tout. And that's not always the case. I mean, the British have intelligence sources as well and they watch, they record intelligence, that's their job. And operations can go wrong sometimes thanks to simple mistakes. And I have always believed that the simple mistake we made was that we tried to get the people out of England too quickly.*

*The operation took weeks, months to set up. It was not set up to coincide with the Border Poll, to my knowledge. I can't remember the bombs going off that day for that particular reason . . . To me it was just a military operation that went drastically wrong . . .*

*There was always from the early 1970s a confrontation between the Dublin leadership and the Belfast leadership. There was confrontation to the point that we believed, and this might have been an elitist thing, that we knew how to run the war, not those people sitting in Dublin in their safe houses; people like Daithi O Connail, Ruairi O Bradaigh, who were never in any danger. Daithi O Connail had not visited Belfast except during the [1972] ceasefire. I remember having arguments with him, that we knew how to run the war, and they didn't . . . there was always that conflict between Belfast and the Dublin leadership especially with Daithi. He was a tall, good-looking, dashing figure who saw himself as – and he was – very articulate. But he was not involved in the war, not involved in places like Derry or Belfast or Armagh. He was sitting in Dublin directing. And there was a fair deal of resentment, not just from me, but from people like Adams and Ivor Bell and the rest of the leadership in Belfast at the time. And that developed into Northern Command, with people like Martin McGuinness also arguing for it. Before the Northern Command came into existence, there was just the Belfast Brigade, the Derry*

*Brigade, the GHQ staff and the Army Council. Once the Northern Command came into existence that changed and the Dublin leadership faded into the background; they were more figures for the media than [people] running a war. They became the public face of the movement. I mean, Ruairi and Daithi were, as I say, very articulate, they were good on television and they could go on television and be safe.*

By July 1973, Gerry Adams had been out of Long Kesh for just shy of a year, while Brendan Hughes and Ivor Bell were well into their fourth year of uninterrupted but exhausting active service with the Provisional IRA. All three men had risen rapidly in the ranks of the IRA and it would not be an exaggeration to say that, thanks to their track record, they were, by the end of 1972, candidates for national leadership of the Provos. Adams had been arrested once already while Hughes had narrowly escaped both arrest and death. Bell, too, had avoided ending up in Long Kesh but in July 1973 luck ran out for two of them. Or rather, to be accurate, the British bested them. The Belfast Brigade's strike at the MRF in November 1972 had proved to be just a temporary setback for British Intelligence. Within a few months the British were beginning to get the edge on the IRA thanks to the recruitment of high-level figures such as Eamon Molloy, the Belfast Brigade's Quarter Master. Molloy would reveal the location of huge numbers of IRA weapons dumps in 1973 and 1974 and it is strongly believed in IRA circles that Molloy was responsible for divulging the location of a meeting of the Belfast Brigade staff on 19 July 1973, in a house in the Iveagh area off the Falls Road. Whatever the truth, it was a disastrous day for the Belfast IRA. British Army swoops netted Gerry Adams, Brendan Hughes and Tom Cahill at the Belfast Brigade meeting while in North Belfast virtually the entire staff of the Third Battalion was arrested. In all, seventeen senior IRA members were put out of action that day.

*. . . basically it was what we did every day, a meeting of the Brigade staff. Gerry was O/C, Tom was Finance Officer, I was Operations*

*Officer. And the rest of the Brigade was there as well, but most of them had left by this stage; there was only the three of us left. We met every day, to plan what operations were going to take place, what robberies we were going to do; we basically pooled our ideas about where we were going; it was simply a military planning meeting to decide our next step in the war. That's what we were doing the day we were arrested in 1973. Actually I believe the intention that day was to execute us because I was sitting in the house and I looked out the window and I saw a suspicious car. I left the house, went over to Beechmount, got hold of a Volunteer and told him to get a squad together and go and pull this car in. But one guy had got out of it with a briefcase, and walked down the street behind where we were. As I looked out the window I saw [our] two guys approaching the car and [then] the car speeding off. Now the two Volunteers didn't know that we were sitting in the house directly facing them . . . what I didn't know until later was that the guy in the car threatened them with a machine gun and when the Volunteers approached the car they didn't have a weapon with them. And, as I say, the guy in the car was obviously in touch with . . . the other agent who had got out of the car and moved down the street behind us. Within seconds the house was surrounded and the three of us were arrested. They charged into the house, the British Army, arrested us, brought us to Springfield Road police station and basically . . . tortured us. I was tied to a chair and beaten with small hammers, and punched, kicked, interrogated. They were looking for information on dumps, other Volunteers, safe houses. They had me in one Portakabin and Gerry Adams in another and Tom Cahill in another. Tom had been pretty badly shot up a few years before and he was handicapped. So Tom wasn't beaten. He was interrogated but they really went to town on me and Adams. Adams passed out, I think three times, and they revived him with buckets of water. Me, they just beat the crap out of. And then afterwards they put me into another Portakabin. The guys who interrogated us were in plain clothes; they weren't uniformed. The interrogations . . . lasted about eight hours or so. I remember one particular guy walking in. He* *was a very tall, distinguished-looking character in a pinstriped suit, collar and tie, and a .45 in his belt. And he put the .45 to my head and cocked it and said he was going to kill me and throw me up onto the Black Mountain and put a statement out saying the Orangees\* had killed me. He could have done it, only for the crowd outside the police station, protesting. Gerry's wife, Colette, was one of them. I was brought into another Portakabin and sat down beside uniformed British soldiers. They had rifles and I was handcuffed . . . but the soldiers were just curious and they took photographs of me handcuffed to a different soldier. I've never come across one of the photographs but I wouldn't mind doing so. They asked me . . . what I was going to do. I was a trophy for them and I just said to them, 'I'm going to escape.'*

*. . . after the interrogation ended we were marched out, put into a Saracen, taken to Castlereagh [RUC station], put in a helicopter and flown to Long Kesh. And it was one of the great experiences, getting out of that helicopter and walking into Long Kesh. All the boys could see us, getting marched in, handcuffed to the British Army. All the boys were cheering. It was such a relief to get there . . . I was under so much pressure, it was an actual relief to get into Long Kesh. But as soon as I got there I started to plan my escape.*

---

\* 'Orangees' is Belfast Catholic slang for hardline Protestants or Loyalists, as in members of the Orange Order.

## 6

All three Belfast leaders, Gerry Adams, Ivor Bell and Brendan
Hughes, would try to escape from Long Kesh over the next few
years but only two of them ever did. Adams had the most dismal
performance – two tries, two failures – whereas Hughes and Bell
succeeded first time and, of the two, Brendan Hughes stayed free
the longest. Adams's first effort was on Christmas Eve 1973 as the
other inmates were attending Midnight Mass. He and three IRA
men from his old Ballymurphy unit had acquired wire-cutters and,
as darkness fell, they tried to creep towards what they thought was,
from the vantage of the prison guards, a blind spot in the wire fence
and the plan was to cut their way through. But a light fog descended
on the camp and, far from assisting the would-be escapers, this persuaded the British to increase their patrolling. They were caught. In
July 1974, Adams tried again, and this time the results were almost
comic. A 'look-alike' had agreed to make a visit to the jail and to
swap places with Adams, who had arranged his own visitor for the
same time. But the 'look-alike' turned out to be several inches
shorter and the former Brigade Commander was, as he put it himself, 'copped' by an alert warder as he tried to walk past him out of
the jail.[53] After the arrest of Adams and Hughes, Ivor Bell had taken
over as Belfast Commander and he lasted for another seven months
until February 1974, when he too was arrested, caught during a
sweep of Andersonstown by British soldiers. Within two months
Bell had broken out of Long Kesh using a variant of Adams's plan
to make good his escape. Another internee who resembled Bell had
been given parole to attend his own wedding but Bell took his place.
He lasted just eleven days on the outside and by the end of April
he was back in British hands, betrayed, it seems, by a girlfriend.
Brendan Hughes's escape was in a league of its own, a getaway that

was both ingenious and clichéd. Offered to a Hollywood screen-writer, the story line might well have been rejected on 'I'm-sure-I've-seen-that-in-another-movie' grounds. But that's probably why it worked.

It is a measure of how hurried the British decision to introduce internment without trial was in August 1971 that few preparations worthy of the name were made to accommodate the hundreds of people who were on the lists to be arrested. Operation Demetrius, as the British called it, scooped up 342 men, all Nationalists, in the early hours of 9 August but only a small number – one estimate suggests around eighty[54] – were Provisional IRA activists. The IRA had been tipped off and had ordered its members to go on the run to avoid arrest. The rest were mostly peaceful political opponents of the Unionist government or elderly, long-retired IRA veterans. Even so, the internees had to be housed somewhere. C Wing of Crumlin Road jail in North Belfast was emptied of its criminal inmates to make room for the new prisoners while HMS *Maidstone,* a former submarine depot ship of the Royal Navy, initially commissioned in 1937 and used first to house British troops in October 1969, was turned into a floating jail. Eventually, the British improved their knowledge of the IRA and starting arresting the right people in larger numbers. By 1972, the number interned had risen to over nine hundred and that is when the need for a place such as Long Kesh arose. Situated on the outskirts of Lisburn, County Antrim, about nine miles from Belfast, Long Kesh had been an RAF base during the Second World War; in August 1969 it was used to house British troops sent over when the riots in Derry and Belfast broke out. It was the perfect site for an internment camp and that's what it was reopened as in early 1972. Complete with barbed-wire fences and watchtowers, it could have been the set for *The Great Escape,* except both jailers and inmates, who certainly regarded themselves as prisoners of war, spoke the same language, at least most of the time.

Prisoners were housed in distinctive RAF-style Nissen huts grouped in compounds – the IRA called them cages for obvious reasons – that were spread across a large area. As many as twenty-two cages, each holding up to a hundred and twenty men, were constructed. It was a damp, miserable place with too few facilities for too many people. John McGuffin described living conditions in his 1973 book *Internment*:

> Overcrowding was, perhaps, the worst feature. Each cage . . . measured 70 yards by 30, and was surrounded by a 12-foot-high wire fence with coils of meshed barbed-wire on top. Each cage had four Nissen huts and one washroom. Three huts acted as sleeping quarters, the fourth as a canteen. Each hut was 120 feet by 24 feet and had to house 40 men. There was not an inch of space between the bunk beds, the roofs leaked, the wind whistled in and everyone spent the nights huddled in heavy pullovers beneath the two thin blankets. The 'central heating' was a small electric heater, fixed high up on the wall. Those fortunate enough to be within two yards of it got some heat. Everyone else froze. Rats appeared. The separate 'wash hut' contained ten wash-hand basins, eight toilets, and eight showers. It had to serve 120 men, and because of the length of the queues many just gave up shaving. Besides, traditionally, 'revolutionaries' are bearded. The other hut served as canteen, workshop, 'library' . . . recreation room . . . writing room, classroom, place of worship and music room. For all 120 men.[55]

Thanks to its geography, and the distance from what the IRA would regard as safe territory, Long Kesh was a difficult place to escape from. If anyone managed to cut through the wire fences or burrow a tunnel under them and actually got outside the perimeter, they would find themselves in strongly Protestant countryside where no friendly doors would be opened to a Republican, least of all an escaped IRA man. Any decent escape plan therefore needed outside help and pre-arranged transport to pick up the fugitive, which added to the danger of the enterprise. By the end of 1973, the prisoners in Hughes's section had identified the bin or garbage lorry as a weak link in security. The lorry made two daily runs through the camp picking up rubbish which it would deliver to a dump outside the jail. If a prisoner could somehow hitch a lift on the lorry and stay undetected, he might make it out. The first idea was to attach a harness to the underside of the lorry which would hold the escaper until he was outside the main gate. Hughes practised under his bunk bed to see how long he could hold on for, but he discovered that he was too weak from the beating he had received at the time of his arrest and gave up that idea. Another prisoner called Mark Graham was in better condition and volunteered to go in his place. When the lorry hit a ramp on the way out, Graham was crushed and broke his back. Then someone had the idea of sewing Hughes into an old mattress and then tossing the mattress into the lorry.

*. . . we had a person working with the lorry, Wee Buck Valliday, who helped in the escape. He was what they called an ODC, an Ordinary Decent Criminal. And he was a trusted orderly. The arrangements were made for me to be put into the mattress and left at the gate of the cage. Wee Buck would lift me and just throw me into the back of the lorry, which is what happened. Our Intelligence Officers had told us that before the lorry left the prison the back would be speared by British soldiers. But our information was that they had stopped doing this. So Wee Buck threw me into the back of the lorry; off it went and then it stopped. He was able to whisper to me that the lorry wasn't leaving the prison straight away, that the workers were going for their lunch . . . up into the sentenced end of the jail [where non-internees, the tried and convicted were held], and he advised me to get out of the lorry; he didn't think I could stay in it that long. But I decided to stay . . . I couldn't see what was going on but I could hear all the voices of the British soldiers all around the lorry. About an hour later they came back to the lorry and Wee Buck again said to me that there's loads more rubbish going on top of me. I told him, 'Just try and keep as much off me as you can', whispering to him, which he did. And the lorry went back into the jail, so I was right back where I started from, only at a*

*different end of the camp. At this stage we were actually in the British Army compound. Back in and more rubbish came on top of me. Wee Buck tried his best to keep as much away as possible. Eventually they finished the run and the lorry was heading out and I knew the routine – it went over two sets of ramps and then it turned right out of the camp. Well, once that happened, I was out of the camp. The lorry stopped and – fuck I/O officers who didn't do their intelligence – the spear came. I heard the soldiers and I knew exactly what was coming, I had a picture in my mind of what they were doing . . . I was on the point of jumping up because if the spear had hit me, it would have gone right through me but, by pure chance, it missed me, both sides of me, once up the left, once up the right, and that was it, and I was a split second away from jumping up and surrendering, but I didn't. And the lorry went over the next two sets of ramps and turned right and I knew I was out of the camp.*

*. . . I had a penknife in my hand the whole time and an orange slice stuck in my mouth, just for fluid. I tried to cut the mattress but the knife was small and just bent back, so I began to panic. I was covered in rubbish, all sorts of stuff, and I started to kick the mattress cover open. I got my head out and I'll never forget that breath of fresh air. I looked back and saw that thanks to my struggling with the mattress, rubbish was falling on the road, the old Hillsborough Road. I thought the driver would have stopped when he saw this, but he didn't. I knew at the top of the Hillsborough Road there's a sharp right turn, then a sharp left turn and I jumped out just before it turned left, onto the footpath, stood up and the lorry was driving away up the Hillsborough Road. I was covered in dirt and sawdust, one of my eyes had closed up. I didn't know it at the time [but] someone had seen me jumping out of the lorry and had reported it. I was in a terrible state, mucky and dirty. Gerry had organised a car to meet me but the lorry had taken so long to leave the camp it had gone. So I started walking. I had some money. I had the equipment to steal a car, jump wires, and immediately I began to look for a car. I was nervous, I was scared. I was stuck in the middle of Hillsborough, a predominantly Loyalist town. No one there to pick me*

up, so I just started walking. I tried to thumb a lift but, because of
the state I was in, nobody was stopping. There was a garage just on
the other side of Hillsborough and a van parked there. I went over
. . . and they were travelling people, Gypsies. I asked them for a lift,
but they said no. So I hit the road again and I started to thumb a lift
again; the travelling people came by and picked me up. They were
only going as far as Dromore. So they dropped me there and I began
to hitchhike again. As I was walking along the road thumbing a lift
I turned round and there was a British Army jeep coming and I
thought the game was up, but they drove on by. I was still thumbing
a lift and another car pulled up and an Englishman was in the
driving seat, and a child sleeping in the back. I got into the back of
the car beside the child who slept on. I believe to this day that the
driver was a screw, a prison officer, but he drove me to Newry. I
talked away to him and told him I worked in a sawmill and I was
heading back to Newry, back home early, because of the injury to my
eye. So he dropped me in Newry and I thanked him and he drove off.

. . . I knew I had about a half an hour before the alarm was
sounded. The head count took place at four o'clock. This bit is a little
complicated but I could not get to the bin lorry from the cage I was
being held in. I was in what they called the 'Generals' Cage', and
there was more security there. Davy Long* was the PO [prison
officer] on the cage. At that time you were allowed cage visits and
so I left Cage 6 to visit Cage 9 which was less secure than Cage 6. So,
I put my name down that morning for a cage visit to Cage 9 as
Brendan Hughes. There was a guy in the cage who resembled me. At
twelve o'clock, Brendan Hughes had to be back in his own cage. So
when I got to Cage 9, I took my clothes off, gave them to this guy who
had the same big moustache as me and black hair. And at twelve
o'clock the screws came to Cage 9, to take 'Brendan Hughes' back to
Cage 6. This guy went back as me, wearing my clothes . . . and I was
wearing a cap that morning as well. He went back into Cage 6 as
Brendan Hughes, and the screws never caught on. At four o'clock,

---

* A tough warder who was disliked by most IRA inmates.

*the screws would do a head count and he would have to be back in his own cage. His name was Piggy O'Neill from the New Lodge Road.*

*So he's back in his own cage, I'm sitting in Newry and it's coming up to four o'clock when they would discover that I had escaped so I went to a taxi rank, jumped into a cab and asked the driver to take me to Dundalk. All the while I'm counting the minutes before the alarm bells go off. At that time there was a twenty-four-hour-a-day roadblock on the Newry to Dundalk road. And this guy is driving me along and we're stopped. The British Army halts us at the roadblock, which I expected anyway, and asked him for ID and he had no problem. He had his licence. Then they came round and asked me. It was dark by this time so the soldier shone the torch in my face. All I had was a receipt for the leather that was brought into the jail, you know, for handiwork. I had a receipt for that with the name of the supplier on it. And I gave him that and I says, 'That's all I have, I was at work there and my eye . . .', pointing to the closed eye, I says, 'I'm going home, I was working in the wood factory.' And he shone and had another look at me and I thought, 'They know damn well, they've got me.' But they waved us on and I was waiting, just waiting for one in the back of the head. I was pretty sure that they were going to take me out. From that roadblock to the other side of the border was the longest couple of minutes of my life. I was just waiting on the shots; well, you don't hear a shot, if you're dead, but I was just sitting waiting and this poor taxi driver hadn't a clue . . . the hairs on the back of my head were standing. I didn't know whether we were across the border or not, it was pitch black on that stretch of road, and I asked the taxi driver, 'Are we across the border yet?' And he says, 'Yeah, we just crossed, just passed that garage there, that's us, we're in the twenty-six counties now.' I says, 'Have you a smoke? Give us a smoke.' And he says, 'What's wrong with you?' So I told him, 'I just escaped from Long Kesh and I need a smoke.' 'Oh fuck!' he shouts. He lifted his hands off the wheel and started to thump me on the back, he was so excited. But ten seconds later, we hit another roadblock, the Gardai [Irish police], and this guy is now shitting himself, he's really nervous. He was more nervous*

*than I was by this stage. Once I knew I was across the border, I knew
I was OK. They let us through. It was no problem. They just asked
for his ID, and didn't ask for mine, and he drove on. And all he kept
talking about – and this is the God's honest truth – he says to me,
'There's people in Newry that keep hijacking my car. Can you do
anything about it?' I said, 'No problem, aye, just give me the names.'
And he gave the name of the people in Newry, two IRA men.*

    *. . . I didn't want him to know where I was headed. I was going
to a pub called the Jolly Ploughboy in Greenore; it's a place I used
pretty regularly. An old IRA man, a friend of my father, owned this
pub, called the Jolly Ploughboy, so I asked the taxi man to drop me
at the top of the road. I had money on me, about £10 which we had
smuggled into the jail and I tried to pay him but he wouldn't take it.
I gave him the money anyway, and we parted company . . . I was
jubilant. I had done it, I was across the border, I had escaped. So I
trekked the half-mile to the Jolly Ploughboy, walked into the bar and
there [are] two guys standing at the bar. One of them was an auld
fella called Gerry McCrudden who actually lives in this building
[Divis Tower] now and the other was a guy called Patsy Brown who
was a barman. I'll never forget the expressions on their faces when
I walked in. I was well known round the bar and around that area.
Patsy immediately set me up with a double whiskey. And I then
went round the back and someone made me something to eat;
they'd a big kitchen there. It was a very popular bar for Republicans,
for bus runs and so forth. By this time the news had broken that I
had escaped from the jail, and Joe Kearney, who owned the bar,
cooked a massive steak to celebrate. I got cleaned up, had a bath;
they got me new clothes. My eye was still closed and they worked on
that to get the sawdust out. The problem was there was a bus run
that night to the bar, for traditional music, a bus full of Republicans
from Portadown. And I asked Joe not to say that I was in the bar.
And, of course, once the music started and Joe got a few drinks in
him, it came on the news again that I had escaped and a big cheer
went up. And Joe got up on the stage after the cheering had died
down and announced that I was here and brought me out of the*

*kitchen. It was a fantastic feeling. But now the whole fucking country knew where I was. So I slept on a settee in the bar and when I woke up I knew I had to get out of the place. Joe made a couple of phone calls. The next morning, Brian Keenan turned up and took me away, brought me to Dublin, to a guy called Harry White's house. Harry was a well-known IRA man. We went to his house; his daughter was a hairdresser . . . and she dyed my hair a shade of auburn.*

Hughes had escaped on 8 December 1973 and by Christmas he was back in West Belfast and had teamed up with Adams's replacement as Belfast Commander, Ivor Bell, as his Operations Officer. When Bell was arrested in February 1974, Hughes became Commander in his place until his arrest in May. Gerry Adams had urged Hughes to escape in a bid to counter the negative consequences of their arrest, which along with other setbacks had demoralised both the rank and file and the Provo supporters throughout the city. Hughes had been a skilled Operations Officer and Adams made his return to the fight a priority.

*The Brigade's operational capacity had been diminished by the arrests, very much so. There was a big demoralising factor in it. I mean, it was all over the newspapers, the Brits built it up like hell; here was the Belfast Brigade wiped out. Morale did suffer. There was myself, Gerry and Tom [Cahill] scooped but it wasn't just us. There was another major operation that day, almost the whole of the Third Battalion was wiped out, Ardoyne, New Lodge and so forth . . . Many men were lost that day; it was a major coup for the Brits. And this escape of mine was meant to be a major morale booster to the rank and file. That was part of the reason. The thinking behind choosing me was simple: operations, operations, operations. I had been Operations Officer before I was arrested and that was the reason for getting me out, to build up and intensify the operational capacity of Belfast Brigade, that was my job . . . Gerry, to me, was the key factor in the war and he was the key strategist, yes, he was . . . And I had great, great respect for him at that time.*

*If Gerry had told me that tomorrow was Sunday when I knew it was Monday I would have thought twice, that maybe it was Sunday, because he said it. Now, if he told me today was Friday, even though it was Friday . . . I'd call him a fucking liar, you know. But Gerry wouldn't have had the ability to put operations together in the manner that I could. He could maybe devise a strategy but in terms of getting it done, it required a person like myself. I came from D Company, and I was an operative, so I'd been in every tight corner, every operation, and one of the main things I always pushed was that I wouldn't ever ask anyone to do something I wouldn't do myself. And the people on the ground knew that. They didn't know that about Gerry, because Gerry was never regarded as an operator. Gerry was seen as a strategist, right, not an operator. So, therefore, I had much more weight than Gerry would have had on the ground. I was much more capable of organising and putting operations together. So, from that point of view, it was the right move to make, to get someone like me out first. The point was that strategy could be devised from inside the jail but implementing it was another matter . . . the reason for getting me out was to enhance and intensify the war.*

A day after Brendan Hughes escaped from Long Kesh, at around 8 p.m., 9 December, a ten-page communiqué was issued by the British and Irish governments announcing that a four-day-long political conference at the Civil Service Staff College at Sunningdale, in Berkshire, England, had reached agreement on how relations between the two parts of Ireland would be conducted in a new power-sharing settlement that had been in the making for almost all of 1973. The British government and three major parties, the Unionists, the SDLP and the Alliance party, had already agreed to set up a power-sharing executive but before the new government could take office there had to be agreement on cross-border arrangements.

In March that year, the British had outlined the essential ingredients for any new settlement. The first, power-sharing, had been agreed. In May, elections had been held to a new Stormont assembly and they had produced what seemed to be a solid 52-to-26-vote majority in favour of the new arrangement. The second precondition was a loosely defined 'Irish dimension', which would be there to cater for Nationalist aspirations. The Sunningdale Conference, chaired by British Prime Minister Edward Heath, had been convened to hammer out the details of what it would mean. The centrepiece of the cross-border deal was a Council of Ireland, which would have harmonising and executive functions on a range of issues that affected both states. When agreement was announced, hardline Unionists and Loyalists, of whom there was no shortage, immediately denounced Sunningdale as a sell-out, and a prelude to a united Ireland. Which meant, by the iron rule of Northern Ireland politics, that most Nationalists were pleased with it.

Although Republicans then and now would argue that Sunningdale was achieved on the back of IRA violence, the deal was constitutional Nationalism's answer to the tactic of armed struggle. By this stage the SDLP had established itself as the sole and unchallenged political voice of Nationalism by dint of its success in two Northern Ireland-wide elections. The IRA's political wing, Sinn Fein, was an illegal party at this time but that hardly made a difference. It produced policies, acted as cheerleader for the IRA and was a convenient front for some of its leaders, but otherwise Sinn Fein was really a small solidarity group that showed no inclination to participate in Northern politics in the ways a normal party would, least of all by taking part in elections. Sunningdale thus reinforced the SDLP's domination of Nationalist politics and made the Provos that bit less relevant, if not to the conflict then to its ending. When Hugh Logue, a rising SDLP star, told a student debate at Trinity College, Dublin, that the Council of Ireland was 'the vehicle that would trundle Unionists into a united Ireland', he was really declaring ideological victory over the Provos' violent ways. The howl of outrage from Loyalists that met Logue's claim served only to reinforce the point.

But Sunningdale was too heady a brew for Northern Unionists. They could live with power-sharing, perhaps, but not something that looked like, and was claimed to be, a slow but sure mono-directional walkway towards an all-Ireland republic. A February 1974 Westminster election brought a stunning victory for anti-Sunningdale Unionists in Northern Ireland and suddenly the pro-settlement majority in the Stormont assembly looked vulnerable. In mid-May, leading Unionist political opponents of Sunningdale, people such as Ian Paisley and Bill Craig, and their counterparts in the Loyalist paramilitaries, the UDA and the UVF, joined forces in the Ulster Workers' Council and declared a general strike aimed at bringing down Sunningdale. The strike was supported widely and the disruptive effects were significant. During the strike, Ireland also saw what was then the single worst day for violence in the Troubles. In an effort to diminish enthusiasm for Sunningdale in the South, Loyalists bombed Dublin and Monaghan, killing thirty-three people. Two weeks after it started, on 28 May, the strikers won. The power-sharing government collapsed when its Chief Executive, former Unionist Prime Minister Brian Faulkner, resigned. It was back to the drawing board and to Direct Rule.

Britain's principal political strategy had failed but it soon became evident that ministers and officials had a separate initiative under way, on which they had been working equally hard, which could transform the situation on the ground and improve the chances that another effort to reach a political deal might have a better chance. Alongside Sunningdale, the British had begun an ambitious attempt to draw the IRA into a long, enervating cease-fire, whose aim was to weaken the IRA in a significant way and even defeat it. Or at least, thanks to what Brendan Hughes learned during his five months of freedom, that is what Gerry Adams and Ivor Bell concluded the British were up to when Hughes told them his story. Secret meetings between senior Republicans and the British were taking place, Hughes learned, and there was evidence of duplicity on the part of Dublin-based IRA leaders. These were some of the secret manifestations of the ceasefire initiative but things were happening in public as well to back up Hughes's suspicions. The new Labour Secretary of State for Northern Ireland, Merlyn

Rees, had announced on 24 April 1974 that the legal prohibition on Sinn Fein would be lifted and the party would be able to function openly. Three days later the IRA leadership told the German magazine *Der Spiegel* that it was ready for negotiations with the British at any time and would call a ceasefire if the British Army withdrew to barracks pending withdrawal. On the same day an interview with Sinn Fein President, Ruairi O Bradaigh, was screened by the influential current affairs TV programme *Weekend World*, in which he warned against a precipitous British withdrawal in case the violence that had devastated the Congo after Belgium's hasty withdrawal was repeated in Northern Ireland. He would prefer, he told the programme, 'some kind of phased and orderly and planned getting-out of British forces'. Between this and the secret diplomacy, it was evident that conversations had taken place between the IRA and the British.

What Hughes had to say about all of this planted the seeds of conflict in the IRA, between the Adams camp and those associated with Ruairi O Bradaigh and Daithi O Connail, and created the conditions for Adams's later takeover of the IRA leadership. Alongside these secret machinatons, the Belfast IRA was beginning to experience life on the back foot by the time Hughes assumed command. He had escaped to a situation that had, since he last walked its streets, become distinctly more difficult for the IRA and dangerous for people such as him who were well known. Even so, when Hughes took over as Brigade Commander, the tempo of IRA activity in the city noticeably quickened. Five days after Bell had been picked up, the Belfast IRA set off twelve bombs in the city, six of them substantial car bombs, and followed these up with two large bombs, one in a van and the other in a lorry, exploding outside the British Army's Belfast HQ, at the former Grand Central Hotel on Royal Avenue, causing entensive damage to surrounding shops. These bombs had to be smuggled through the security cordon of fencing and armed checkpoints that now surrounded the city centre. The IRA's violent ingenuity was again demonstrated later in March 1974 when two bombs badly damaged the Europa Hotel in downtown

Belfast, one of them planted near a water tank on the fourteenth floor. Despite these successes, the reality for the IRA in Belfast was that the British had vastly improved their knowledge of the organisation and the net was tightening. Well-placed informers had been recruited and their intelligence had become so good, and their penetration of the IRA sufficiently deep, that the British were not just arresting key players and scooping up arms caches; they had begun to manipulate and play mind games with its members.

*I escaped from Long Kesh to operate in the areas that I was used to, over yard walls and through back doors and so forth. But there came a point in 1973 and 1974 when that was no longer feasible for people like me. For operators on the ground, yes, but not people like me who were on the run, who were wanted. So we had to move into middle-class areas, to acquire property, garages, houses, flats and so on, to operate from. And we had to take on new identities. Until I was arrested in 1973, I was 'Darkie' Hughes on the street. Everybody knew who I was. Every time I saw a Brit, I was over a yard wall and through someone's hall. After my escape in 1974, the situation had changed and we acquired property like the house I was eventually arrested in, Myrtlefield Park.\* I moved in there and operated around that area, around the Malone area, around the Ormeau Road area, and I would go into our own areas as well because, you know, it was important that someone like myself who was well known be seen by the Volunteers on the ground. And so, I had to go into our areas every day. I took on the identity of Arthur McAllister, a travelling salesman, I had my hair dyed and I dressed like a businessman and carried a briefcase, but I still travelled in and out of all the areas.*

*. . . Belfast Brigade was under massive pressure. Dumps were being caught and people were being arrested and the whole thing looked like it was falling apart, [but] still people were being released from internment. One of those released was a man called Seamus*

---

\* A large detached and expensive home in the affluent Malone area of South Belfast.

*Loughran.\* The first I heard he had been released was when I walked into a room in Dublin with Daithi O Connail and Ruairi O Bradaigh and the whole Army Council was sitting there, including Seamus Loughran, and I immediately said, 'What the fuck is he doing here? He didn't report back to me in Belfast.' And they said that he was on a special mission for GHQ. I went back to Belfast after that, very, very suspicious that something was going on. My Intelligence Officer, Belfast Brigade Intelligence Officer, wee John Kelly, then told me that Jimmy Drumm† was having meetings with the British . . . I immediately sent for Jimmy Drumm. He was arrested by the Intelligence Squad and brought to a house in the Holy Land [a section of South Belfast]. He was shitting himself. I interrogated Drumm, who informed me that he wasn't meeting the British, but he was meeting some professor or surgeon from the Royal Victoria Hospital. And I asked, 'In what capacity?' 'Just as a Republican,' he replied . . . That's what he said. I didn't believe him. I believed there were other people involved, British reps or . . . the surgeon obviously was not doing it on his own bat. He obviously had other people involved . . . He wasn't talking with a surgeon about medical problems, obviously not.*

*I was very,very angry at what was going on; Seamus Loughran had reported directly to GHQ and Jimmy Drumm was meeting people over my head . . . This is why Jimmy Drumm was chosen to read the keynote speech at Bodenstown in 1977 which was critical of the ceasefire. That was purposely done. Jimmy Drumm was not happy about doing that, but he did it. But you've got to understand my position here as well. So much was happening around me. I was on the run; I could see the whole thing falling around me. I didn't know who was friend and who was foe. I suspected when I first met Seamus Loughran in Dublin that something was going on, that what happened with Jimmy Drumm meant something big was*

---

\* Belfast Republican who met Protestant clergymen in December 1974 to arrange a ceasefire.
† Founder member of the Provos and IRA representative at talks with British Intelligence in 1975.

*happening . . . I knew there was a conspiracy but I just couldn't pin it down because I was trying to keep the war going; that was my main objective. And here I was coming across people who were . . . conspiring behind my back. Obviously if Seamus Loughran was in Dublin with GHQ personnel then someone in GHQ was involved as well. I don't know who it was – all I know was that Seamus Loughran was involved and Jimmy Drumm was involved. Internment was ending at this time; people were getting out, but they were hand-picked people. The British had complete control of who they let out and who they kept in and they kept in the ones they saw as a danger and allowed out those who they thought they could deal with. It was shortly after this that I was arrested . . .*

Brendan Hughes had come across evidence of the opening moves towards what would evolve into an IRA ceasefire by the end of 1974 and early weeks of 1975, a ceasefire that he, Adams and Bell would come to regard, and decry, as a plot to enfeeble and possibly destroy the IRA. The plan, they believed, might have been hatched by the British but it was made possible by their own leadership in Dublin. When the ceasefire began their doubts grew. The British promise of withdrawal never came, while the cessation was endlessly extended, eroding the IRA's military capabilities with every day that it lasted. The British could not be blamed for furthering their own interests but what the Dublin leadership had done, they averred, was unforgivable in its stupidity and *naïveté*. The three became convinced that the British had taken advantage of their improved intelligence on the IRA to remove people such as themselves who would be obstacles in the way of this plan, and replace them, via internee releases, with more pliable leadership candidates. Seamus Loughran and Jimmy Drumm were examples and so was Billy McKee who was freed from Long Kesh in 1974. But there was more to the British strategy than that. The British Secret Service MI6 and the IRA had maintained contact after the 1972 ceasefire. A 'pipeline', as it was called, had been created to assist communication and, occasionally, to sort out misunderstandings. Well-intentioned individuals, trusted by both sides, would from time to time carry messages or signals from one to the other. After the collapse of Sunningdale, Republicans detected 'vibrations' from the British, as Ruairi O Bradaigh's biographer put it, that they were now inclined to consider withdrawing from Northern Ireland.[56] Withdrawal sentiment had also become more evident in public-opinion polls carried out in Britain and, in this context, a ceasefire began to look like a good idea.

Against this background and with an intensified bombing campaign in England that included one of the worst atrocities of the Troubles, the death of twenty-one people in two Birmingham pub bombs, the IRA and Sinn Fein leadership met a group of Protestant clergymen near the County Clare village of Feakle on 10 December 1974. The meeting was at the request of the clerics to discuss whether a basis existed for an IRA ceasefire. The Republican delegation consisted of Ruairi O Bradaigh; Daithi O Connail; Seamus Twomey, the Chief of Staff; Billy McKee, who had also been made Chairman of the Army Council by this stage; J. B. O'Hagan from Lurgan, County Armagh; Kevin Mallon from Tyrone; Maire Drumm, the head of the women's IRA, Cumman na mBan, and wife of the evasive Jimmy Drumm; and Seamus Loughran, by now the new Belfast IRA Commander. Brendan Hughes's suspicion that Drumm and Loughran were up to something was well founded. Although the meeting was interrupted by the Garda Special Branch and had to be dramatically curtailed, the clerics were suitably impressed by the people they had met. The Army Council drafted a formal response to the clerics' ceasefire proposal – talks were possible as long as they led to a British declaration of intent to withdraw, the details of which were negotiable – and the clerics showed the document to the new Labour Secretary of State in Belfast, Merlyn Rees. Ruairi O Bradaigh was at his home in Roscommon on Christmas Day 1974 when he spotted one of the 'pipeline' intermediaries, a Derry businessman called Brendan Duddy, walking up the pathway to his front door. Duddy carried a message, a letter written in the handwriting of Michael Oatley,

MI6's man, seeking a meeting to 'establish structures for British withdrawal' from Northern Ireland.[57]

What Michael Oatley and his political masters meant by withdrawal was then, and still is, a matter of considerable controversy and debate. The IRA leadership of 1974 and 1975 became convinced it meant political and physical withdrawal of British sovereignty – even if the British could not admit as much publicly – whereas the British, now if not then, insisted the dialogue was merely about withdrawing troops from the North, not Britain's political authority. The language and the contacts were sufficiently ambiguous to accommodate both meanings, but the proof was in the outcome. A first ceasefire petered out in January 1975 but was renewed in February. It lasted, if such a word could be used to describe what happened, for nearly a year but in reality it had petered out by August or September 1975 as one by one IRA units went back to war. Incident centres were set up so Sinn Fein could monitor the ceasefire and smooth any wrinkles that developed with the British but that was about the most concrete result of the truce. Of British withdrawal there was no convincing evidence nor any sign it was on the horizon.

In the first week of February 1975, just before the ceasefire was renewed, Merlyn Rees announced that new H-blocks would be built at Long Kesh as an interim measure. It was the first manifestation of a change of gear by the British in their war against the IRA. Within a year the special-category status given to IRA prisoners in 1972 would be phased out and newly convicted IRA men would be sent to the H-blocks, not to the huts and cages of Long Kesh. To symbolise the change the prison was renamed 'The Maze'. Within a year the British Army would gradually be replaced on the front line of the struggle against the IRA by the RUC. IRA suspects would be arrested and questioned in new police holding centres where a remarkably high number would sign confessions sufficiently credible for them to be convicted in new single-judge, juryless courts. The IRA's struggle against the British was being criminalised.

The charge levelled by Adams, Bell and Hughes against the IRA leadership of that time is that their foolishness gave the British a breathing space within which to develop and implement their new security approach. The ceasefire also encouraged the IRA on the ground to drop its guard – as ceasefires invariably do – and allowed the British further to improve their intelligence in preparation for processing suspects through the holding centres. Their alleged crime, in other words, was at worst to create the conditions for the IRA's defeat and at best to allow the British to redefine the struggle in their own terms. The ceasefire had meanwhile set alarm bells ringing in the world of Loyalist paramilitarism and the response of the UDA and especially the UVF in 1975 and 1976 was an unprecedented surge in killings. Gangs of Loyalist killers scoured the streets of North and West Belfast at night to abduct, torture and kill any Catholic unfortunate enough to fall into their hands, while during the day no-warning bombs would be tossed into Catholic bars. The IRA's response, particularly in Belfast, was to retaliate by killing Protestants, sometimes on the pretext of targeting Loyalist activists but often on the same indiscriminate basis as the Loyalists chose their victims. The IRA in some areas of Belfast, notably Ardoyne, were notorious for their sectarianism and this period allowed them to indulge their prejudices virtually unchallenged. Adams, Bell and Hughes were incensed by this, not just because the IRA claimed to operate by much higher standards but because in their view the IRA was helping to legitimise Britain's claim that it was involved in Northern Ireland only to keep the irrational, murderous Irish from each other's throats, that they were playing the part of 'piggy in the middle' in a ferocious sectarian war. The IRA presented the war in a very different way, as a fight to eject a neo-colonial power whose meddling in Ireland over the centuries was the major cause of sectarian conflict and division. Those who led the IRA in 1975 and 1976, who sent out Volunteers to take Protestant lives in this way, were, the trio angrily charged, playing straight into the hands of the British.

This, in essence, was the case developed by the deposed Belfast leadership confined inside Long Kesh against the 1975 IRA leadership. It was the start of a rift that would fuel the later Adams–Bell takeover of the IRA and pave the way, ultimately, for the Adams–McGuinness partnership, which brought Republicans to the peace process. The internal IRA conflict has often been inaccurately depicted as another example of the North–South rivalry that was otherwise pervasive in the IRA. Nothing could be further from the truth, although it sometimes suited the Adams camp to portray things that way. Of the eight-strong delegation at Feakle only O Bradaigh and O Connail were Southerners. The divisions were really based on other factors, such as age, politics, outlook and ambition.

On 10 May 1974 Brendan Hughes's luck ran out. An informer – a strong candidate is the Belfast QM, Eamon Molloy – told the British about Hughes's hideout in Myrtlefield Park and he was arrested. A search of the house revealed a cache of weapons – a sub-machine gun, four rifles, two pistols and several thousand rounds – as well as a sum of stolen money. For this and because of his escape in December *1973*, Hughes would receive a fifteen-year jail term. During Brendan Hughes's five months of freedom the IRA was pushed increasingly on the defensive, although there were some notable successes. IRA engineers had been able to tap the phone used by the British Army's Commander, the GoC, in Thiepval barracks, its Lisburn headquarters, and to acquire the technology to unscramble the recordings. But the story otherwise was of a seemingly endless series of arms seizures and arrests, many the result, it seems, of Molloy's treachery. When first Bell was arrested, escaped and then re-arrested and then Hughes was caught in Myrtlefield Park, the Belfast IRA's best years were at an end. When the ceasefire came it was at a point of great IRA weakness.

Hughes was dispatched to Crumlin Road prison, to the remand wing to await trial. But the British were not far behind. The IRA was about to be edged into a long and debilitating ceasefire and British Intelligence had plans to sow distrust and conflict in the ranks of the IRA's prison community. It might have been the British intention to distract, confuse and possibly dilute opposition to the planned cessation from inside the jails or it might have been an attempt just to cause as much damage and turmoil as possible. Either way it demonstrated that the British had recovered well from the Four Square Laundry setback. The extraordinary story of the Heatherington–McGrogan psy-op affair began not long after Brendan Hughes fell back into the hands of the British.

*When I was arrested, I was wearing a grey checked suit. I was taken to Castlereagh, interrogated for a few days, and then put into a prison van and driven to Crumlin Road jail. There were other people in the van, young lads who thought I was a Special Branch man because of the way I was dressed . . . it got a wee bit uncomfortable. But when we got to the Crum, I was asked was I claiming political status, and I says yes, of course I was. There was little or no hostility at the time from the prison regime. I was led to A Wing and in A Wing there was one cell left aside, left empty for debriefing. The IRA controlled the wing, so anyone entering it had to first pass through the Intelligence Officer who would question you. Who were you, where were you coming from, what were you in for? And only when they were convinced that you were who you said you were, only then were you allowed to stay in the wing. It made no difference who you were, whether you were Chief of Staff or Belfast Brigade O/C or whatever, you had to go through this. Obviously I was pretty well known at the time so I didn't have any problem getting through the debriefing and I was allowed entry . . . I was allocated a cell, not by the prison regime but by the command structure of the IRA in A Wing. Quite soon afterwards I was appointed Officer Commanding of the Wing. Tommy Roberts had been the O/C; he was up for trial, and wanted to stand down so he asked would I take over, and he became my Adjutant. There were roughly, I think, between two hundred and fifty and three hundred men in A Wing at that time; it was practically full, I believe. But there was a constant flow of people going from remand to court, being sentenced and then moving on to Long Kesh. So it was a place for passing through. Being O/C consisted mainly of debriefing people when they came into the jail. So a squad of Intelligence Officers was set up to question people coming in, people who were arrested with guns, with bombs and so forth and our job was to find out as quickly as possible and to get word to the outside if a man had broken under interrogation and had given information . . . on other Volunteers or about weapons . . . The idea was to get word out as quickly as possible so as the weapons could be removed. Or if the dump or the men were in jeopardy . . . to make sure they got offside as quickly as possible . . . A good few would break. I think the age of the average IRA prisoner at that time was eighteen or nineteen. I was an old hand, and I was twenty-five or twenty-six. A lot of these young lads did break under interrogation. There's a difference between someone breaking and someone being an informer. That had to be investigated and we had to decide whether the person had just broken or whether they were working for the British. If the Intelligence Officers doing the interrogations believed that something was seriously wrong, then I would move in and take over . . . Or some of the other higher-ranking staff would, and there were a few of them: Junior Fitzsimmons; ———, who had an assistant from Newry, whose name passes me.*

*. . . what you have to remember here, as well, is that people were always passing through. You might have had an Intelligence Officer one week and the next he would have been taken away to court, sentenced and you didn't see him again. So someone else took his place. So there was a continual flow of staff, Adjutants, Intelligence Officers and so forth. And so our intelligence was here, there and everywhere. But there was always that line of communication from Crumlin Road jail to Long Kesh, which was the main holding centre for sentenced prisoners. This was a passing-through period and you would have spent from six months to a year, sometimes eighteen months, on remand, depending on the case, [and] how much evidence they had and so forth. The average was a year to eighteen months . . .*

\*    \*    \*

Four days after Brendan Hughes was arrested in Myrtlefield Park, the Ulster Workers' Council strike began. The trigger was a motion supporting Sunningdale that was passed in the new assembly. Anti-Sunningdale Unionists were defeated by 44 votes to 28 but the balance of Unionist politics had changed radically since the assembly was elected and there was little doubt by the spring of 1974 that anti-Sunningdale Unionists reflected majority Protestant opinion. After all, their candidates had outpolled Brian Faulkner's pro-Sunningdale Unionists by four to one in the February 1974 general election. On the evening of 14 May, workers at the Bally-lumford power station in ultra-Loyalist Larne, County Antrim, reduced electricity output by nearly half, a signal that Protestant Ulster had begun an extraordinary rebellion against British authority. It soon became clear that the Protestant middle class was backing the strike and after that it was just a matter of time before the UWC won. Loyalism had been in a ferment ever since the February election and sectarian tensions were rising alarmingly. Protestant crowds had rioted against the British Army in East Belfast and there had been gun battles in which one Loyalist was shot dead. Respectable anti-Sunningdale Unionists were cosying up to the hard men; in April the UDA, the largest of the Loyalist paramilitaries, was invited to attend the anti-Agreement Unionists' conference to plan the way ahead. There were marches at which Unionist leaders mingled happily with men wearing masks and combat gear. In such an atmosphere predictions of a civil war, or a serious bloodbath, did not seem outlandish and the IRA was making plans for the worst. Documents outlining one such plan had been discovered in Myrtlefield Park, and the Labour Prime Minister, Harold Wilson, claimed they were evidence of a plot by the IRA to 'foment inter-sectarian hatred' so that they could take and occupy large parts of Belfast. But, according to Brendan Hughes, the documents were really a proposal to defend Catholic districts in the event of a Loyalist uprising against Sunningdale. He was working on the plan when he was arrested.

*When I came into Crumlin Road jail, the IRA outside had great fear that Unionists would declare UDI, a unilateral declaration of independence, and the reason why I was caught [in Myrtlefield Park] was that we were drawing up plans for defence of Nationalist areas in the event of this happening. So I carried all that in my head into the prison with me, that there was a possibility of a major blow-up in the six counties; that the Loyalists, especially Paisley, believed that the British were withdrawing. I didn't believe that, but precautions had to be taken within the prison and we began to organise defence preparations in the event that something developed inside the jail. I was quite conscious of the fact that if UDI was declared by the Unionists – the militant Unionists – we would be in grave danger.*

*That worry became quite acute when eight men arrived onto A Wing. On the day I was arrested two policemen were shot dead\* and some of these people had been charged as a result.*[58] *Now I should have known these people, at least some of them . . . but I didn't. So . . . interrogations started under Tommy Dougan and his assistant. Within a short period it became clear that these people were not involved in shooting the policemen. Tommy was interrogating a guy called Vinty [Vincent] Heatherington who was put into a cell just two away [from] me. Tommy asked me would I take over, that there was something wrong. So I began to interrogate Heatherington. He told me that he was in the Fianna but he couldn't understand why he had [been] arrested for [killing] the two cops; he hadn't been involved. I then left and went up to interrogate McGrogan, Myles McGrogan, and he insisted that he wasn't involved either. And he didn't know why he had been arrested. The other people who came in with them were also being investigated but the interrogations centred round these two people, Heatherington and McGrogan, because the intelligence I was getting said that they were two hoods. People who knew them and were from the same area told us this. It was so crazy that they had been arrested because they were not even Republican. Heatherington had a short*

---

\* Constables Malcolm Ross and Brian Bell, shot dead at Finaghy, South Belfast, on 10 May 1974.

*history of involvement in the Fianna, but had been dismissed because of his criminal activities. Heatherington was, I think, about eighteen or nineteen. So I started the interrogation and initially I talked to him in a very friendly way, to try and tease him out. And he told me that a few years before he had been arrested by the [RUC] Special Branch and taken up to Hannahstown Hill\* – it was a Sunday. There was a Gaelic match being played . . . and the Special Branch fired a burst of automatic fire at the people playing football. They then handed the rifle to Heatherington and took it back off him and said, 'Your prints are now on this gun; you can be charged with this shooting.' So I put the question to him: 'Did you start working for them?' He says, 'No.' He denied it. And I says, 'What did you do?' 'I went on the run,' he said. I was soon able to break that down. I went and made tea and sandwiches for him and came back and talked to him in a fatherly way. He then admitted that he was working for them, at a low level, passing on information, watching people, their movements, and passing that on to his handler. He told me he used to meet his handler in different places. He had a code name, which I can't remember, that his handlers gave him.*

*I stopped the interrogation after that, once I had established that he was an informer. Now the question was: what the hell was he doing in the prison? He then admitted he'd been sent into prison. He was told the day before his arrest that he and McGrogan would be sent into the jail. 'What for?' I asked. He replied that he didn't know; he would be told that in the prison by someone. This really was concerning. So I asked the I/O, Tommy, to put a bit more weight on McGrogan, to question more deeply, not to use violence. Heatherington then began to break down a bit more and told me about a group of people he had been working with, a network working for the Brits. I was passing on to Tommy information that Heatherington was giving to me, and obviously the way they were putting it to McGrogan, McGrogan knew that Heatherington was*

---

\* On the north-western edge of Belfast.

*talking to me. We broke for something to eat and McGrogan was seen walking past Heatherington's cell and he threw something into Heatherington's cell, into a small rubbish bin. The note was found; Tommy Dougan went to the cell, searched through the rubbish and found this note which said, 'Talk and you die.' That's all it said: 'Talk and you die.' That was given to me. I then realised that this is getting a lot more serious. So I put more mental pressure on Heatherington. He then broke down and told me about some of the operations he was involved in. I brought Junior Fitszimmons in on the interrogation. He told us more about the group – they were based in Holywood Barracks, they were supplied with money, with women, along with their handlers. They were allowed to come and go as they pleased. The Special Branch initially employed them but . . . they were then handed over to the military – but the backbone of the operation was British Intelligence. He had been taken away for training in Essex; they lived in a large country house. They were given weapons training, explosives training and anti-interrogation training and sent back. He told me about a flat that they had in Dublin, beside Connolly station, about the women who were involved with them. I can't remember their names but one of the women was a Protestant from the Shankill. They were given explo-sives and weapons to be brought to Belfast. They also had a house near a police station on the Lisburn Road. Heatherington really began to open up now. I asked him what operations was he involved in. And he told me about this particular operation in Corporation Street, near the docks, when he and McGrogan drove a car bomb into the street with a five-minute timer on it. According to Heather-ington, he had seen two kids swinging on a lamp-post and he tried to talk McGrogan into defusing the bomb but McGrogan said no. So they left, and the bomb went off and the two kids were killed. McGrogan was the dominant figure; Heatherington was the weak-ling. This was around Hallowe'en 1972. It was made to look as if it was the IRA had done it. What they also did was when the IRA put bombs into the town they would slip one in as well. And I know this happened, because there were times when bombs exploded that we could not account for. He told me about raping a young girl on Kennedy Way, about robbing a garage. When Heatherington admitted to the shooting at the Gaelic football match, Junior, who was a big fella, immediately went for Heatherington's throat. I had great difficult pulling Junior off. He had been at the match that day along with his wife and kids.*

*I then asked him for the names of the other people in this group with him. And he began to give me them. He named one of the guys that came in with him who was an IRA Volunteer, ———. So more trustworthy Intelligence Officers had to be pulled in, to interrogate [him]. Heatherington then gave me a list of other names, of people in the jail. Names such as ———; ——— from the Strand; he gave ———'s name as well. So all these people had to be interrogated and some of them were up in Long Kesh. I asked him, 'Well, what was the purpose of this group?' And he told me this. I mean, this is a kid telling me this. In the event of major confrontations in Belfast that they would be the sabotage unit. In the event of barricades going up, they would be sent in to plant bombs at barricades and they would be sent in to disrupt as much as they could, to break down defences. Fifth columnists, that's what they were. Now I believed him when he said McGrogan was involved but of the rest of them I wasn't sure. We still couldn't understand or work out their mission. He then told me that he had been sent in to poison the wing, when he got the OK. I said, 'How were you going to get the poison?' He says, 'A prison officer . . .' They didn't know the name of the prison officer. They were told the prison officer would approach him with instructions and the poison. They were to put the poison in the water we used to make tea. But before that they had major targets. Me, I was to be targeted first. Tommy Roberts. Junior Fitzsimmons. Curly Coyle from Derry.*

*Now, by this stage, there were people being interrogated all over the wing and in Long Kesh. So we started to take precautions. We put guards on the water tanks, guards on our food. Once Heather-ington told me about the poison plot, I got word up to Davy Morley who was O/C at Long Kesh, to warn him that some of the names*

that I was getting were on his staff. The next day, I got word back
from Morley giving me a whole rundown on British Army intelligence activities in Aden. Then poison was found in the Loyalist
wing, behind a cistern. It turned out to be Lenny Murphy* who
poisoned a Loyalist prisoner in the hospital wing, if I remember.
So the plot thickened and there was mad hysteria in the wing and
suspicions everywhere. Heatherington then retracted all the names
he had given me, withdrew them, saying they weren't involved, and
. . . started to give me other names. So I asked him, 'Why did you
give me the wrong names?' He says, 'That's what we were told to
do.' I asked, 'Why?' 'To cause as much confusion as possible,' he
answered. I hadn't actually broken him during interrogation as I
thought I had done; he was playing with me. It was basic counter-
intelligence disinformation that they were spreading. I asked
Brigade what to do and they sent an order in to go and inform the
Prison Governor. It was a very weak response [and] I felt they
weren't taking it as seriously as they should. I just felt totally
isolated. The interrogations began to get out of hand. I did not order
anybody to be physically beaten or tortured although I certainly
ordered people to take a heavier hand in getting this information
together because we were in a panic situation here; we were in a bad
situation. Everybody in the wing knew it. And I remember going
round all the people getting interrogated and I went into a cell on
the top wing, and there was a young lad sitting there with his feet
in a bucket of water, cigarette burns all over his arms, and totally
shattered. They were doing Japanese torture on them . . . They were
breaking people in Long Kesh who were naming people on A Wing.
So we were in a total disarray here. You trusted nobody; we didn't
know where we were going. You didn't know who was a tout, or who
was going to poison you or . . . stick a knife in your ribs. Total and
utter confusion. I went to Hilditch, the Governor of the jail. Hilditch
told me that the poison plot was nonsense, that it was to do with the
Loyalists. And I gave the order in the wing, you know, and I told

---

* Leader of the UVF murder gang, 'the Shankill Butchers'.

*Hilditch, 'I'm not eating any food.' So I gave the order in the wing: 'No one touches the prison food.' We were allowed parcels in at that time, so I said, 'Live off your parcels; we're not touching the food.' I said to Hilditch, 'You come in every day and taste the food.' So he agreed and I would pick out something for him to taste. It must have been really demeaning for him, you know, to do this. But he did it.*

Heatherington and McGrogan were spirited out of A Wing one night and held in the security annexe in D Wing, used in the early 1980s to house paramilitary 'supergrasses'. They were not heard of again until the IRA caught up with them just a few years later. Vincent Heatherington's body was found in West Belfast, in July 1976, dumped beside a wire fence on the Glen Road. He was blindfolded and his hands had been tied behind his back. A single shot to the head had killed him. He was twenty-one at the time of his death, nineteen when he messed with the minds of the IRA in Crumlin Road jail. On 9 April 1977, Myles McGrogan was found dead on the far outskirts of West Belfast. Like Heatherington, he had been shot once in the head, the classic hallmark of an IRA execution. He was twenty-two years old. A third alleged member of the group, James Green, also twenty-two, a taxi driver from the Divis Flats area and a former soldier in the Royal Irish Rangers, a British regiment, was shot dead in his cab on 5 May 1977.[59]

*Heatherington was shot dead in Belfast. McGrogan was shot dead in Belfast. Green was shot dead. There were other people involved in this. It finished up, I think, that there were eight people in the group, all shot dead in Belfast. I believe that all we got were the small fry. I believe the large fry got away.* *

As the IRA moved, furtively but steadily, towards a ceasefire in the autumn of 1974, the British were starting a fundamental

---

* Former British Intelligence operative Fred Holroyd has spoken of the loss of eight or so agents around this time, but otherwise this claim is unsubstantiated.

reassessment of the way they dealt with paramilitary violence in Northern Ireland. In January 1975, a committee headed by British judge Lord Gardiner recommended the phasing out of special-category status for paramilitary prisoners and the ending of internment as soon as conditions allowed. A week later, Northern Ireland Secretary Merlyn Rees announced that a new, supposedly temporary, prison would be built at Long Kesh, next door to the special-category prisoner and internee compounds. On 4 November, he announced that internment would be ended by Christmas and on 1 March 1976 special-category status, or political status as the IRA had called it, formally ended. Also that month, Rees announced that the RUC would resume prime responsibility for security in Northern Ireland with the British Army in a supportive but secondary role. The changes signalled an intention to deal with the IRA in the same way criminals were treated: the police would arrest and question them; they would be convicted in a court and they would be held in a jail firmly under the control of the authorities. Except that in Northern Ireland, *circa* 1975 to 1978, the courts had no juries, hearings were tried in front of a single judge and convictions were invariably secured via confessions made in police interrogation centres and often surrounded by allegations of brutality.

The policy adjustments made by the British very nearly did the trick and the years immediately following the second ceasefire saw the near defeat of the IRA. But it survived thanks to two factors. The first was the combined effort of Gerry Adams, Ivor Bell and Brendan Hughes to put in place organisational and political changes to rescue and rejuvenate the IRA, specifically to make the organisation more difficult for the British to penetrate. The IRA was reorganised into cells and the Company system scrapped, replaced by small Active Service Units (ASUs). The creation of Northern Command was another major change, intended to make the IRA more efficient and place it more firmly under the control of the Northerners, the people who were fighting the war. The group around Gerry Adams also set out to capture the national IRA leadership away from those who had given the British, in their eyes, the time and opportunity to make such a damaging assault on the IRA. Three men were singled out: Ruairi O Bradaigh, Daithi O Connail and Billy McKee, who became the symbols of a failed IRA leadership. The second factor that helped rescue the IRA derived, ironically, from the very regime changes that the British had made to the prison system. The ending of special-category status sparked a five-year-long protest by IRA prisoners to restore their lost standing and that had two consequences. The protest gave the IRA's political leadership a cause to mobilise and build around outside the jail, while inside the prison it produced two hunger strikes, the last of which would usher in changes that would eventually transform and end the conflict. Brendan Hughes, as he always seemed to be, was in the thick of it.

Although these prison-regime adjustments were not detailed by government ministers until 1975, there were, in hindsight, unmistakable signals of a new toughness and willingness to confront IRA prisoners on the part of the British some time before. Coincidentally or not, they became apparent not long after Heatherington and McGrogan appeared in Crumlin Road jail in late 1974 and it is possible to see what happened as an attempt to soften up the prisoners for what was to come. The authorities in Crumlin Road began to chip away at privileges while in Long Kesh they took an increasingly unyielding approach to demands from Republican and Loyalist prisoners for better conditions in the jail. If anything, there was more overcrowding, dampness and vermin in the camp than ever. On 15 October 1974 the tension in the jail exploded. There was a confrontation with warders and soon the British Army was deployed to end it. First the huts in one cage and then in another were set on fire by the prisoners. Troops charged them with batons swinging while CR gas, a rarely used and controversial anti-riot weapon, was fired into their ranks along with rubber bullets. Scores of prisoners were badly beaten. With much of the camp a smouldering ruin, the prisoners erected improvised shelters which became their homes for two-and-a-half months. Similar scenes were enacted in Crumlin Road jail.

*... at that time in Crumlin Road jail, I was dealing with a guy called Gibson who was second in command to Hilditch, the Governor. He was the man really making the decisions. They began to cut away at certain privileges we had. For instance, they limited the amount of food we were allowed in. They limited the amount of tobacco we were allowed in. They tried to introduce plastic forks and spoons into the jail; they limited the amount of time we were allowed out of our cells every day. There was something every day. It was constant. The same thing was happening in Long Kesh where they were cutting back on the privileges there ... The order was given in Long Kesh to burn the camp. I was really reluctant to do anything in Crumlin Road jail because I knew there was little we could do. But, because Long Kesh had gone, I sent word out that [if the IRA leadership wanted] we would riot that day. I remember getting the order back, now, to riot, to wreck the jail. And the jail was duly wrecked; cell doors were taken off ... it was quite easy to take a cell door off, you just put a heavy book between the two hinges – we used Bibles – and you pushed the door the opposite way and it just fell off. We made petrol bombs. We threw all the furniture down onto the main wing; ripped the whole place apart. And that was it. There wasn't a great deal more we could do except wait to see what they were going to do. We didn't have long to wait. They gassed us and sent the riot squad in. There were hundreds of screws ... with batons. They savagely beat every fucking body they could find. A group of us were able to fight our way back up to the top landing and barricaded ourselves in the canteen. They didn't even try to get into the canteen; they just fired tear gas in. There was total pandemonium. We finished up pulling the barricades away because we were smothered and we couldn't get air [and] ... we bolted out. The first thing we saw was a line of screws with batons ... and we had to run the gauntlet, along the top floor, down the second floor onto the bottom floor. They lined us up against the wall and there was one screw there called McConnell who was in total hysterics and he was running about with a gun in his hand. He'd a weapon in his hand and he was, he was crazed, totally crazed. Bill McConnell,*

*Assistant Governor. He was shot dead by the IRA in 1984 . . . the beating continued, they beat the crap out of us. Then they lined us up, threw us in cells and put the hoses in as well. We had busted eyes, busted heads, busted ribs . . . five or six of us were piled into a cell and they left us there for, I think, a couple of days. All visits were stopped, so there was no communication with the outside . . . after that they began to change the whole system in the jail. We had actually played into their hands, I believe. We had brought forward the inevitable – they were attempting to take away political status, they were attempting to control us. We'd lost it . . .*

When Brendan Hughes eventually made it to Long Kesh the evidence of the recent fire was everywhere and prisoners were still living in makeshift shelters. Gerry Adams was still in jail, now as a sentenced prisoner thanks to his unsuccessful escape bids, and so was Ivor Bell. Adams was in Cage 11 and Bell in Cage 9. The Long Kesh prisoners were organised in the same fashion as the IRA outside. The prison was regarded as a separate Battalion and each cage as a Company. The cages had their own staffs, from O/C downwards, and there was a Battalion staff above them, whose O/C was the equivalent of the Battalion Commander. And the IRA ran itself in the jail according to the rules of military discipline, the paramount aspect of which was the requirement to obey orders from a superior officer. The most senior officer in Long Kesh when Brendan Hughes returned there was a former British soldier from Newry, David Morley, a martinet who modelled his management style on the military code most familiar to him; the IRA cages in Long Kesh during Morley's command, Hughes complained, were run like a British military barracks.

Morley was also a leadership man, loyal to Billy McKee whom he had succeeded as Camp Commander. McKee had been released from internment in September 1974, and rejoined the Army Council to become its Chairman, its senior diplomat in effect who represented the Army Council in discussions with outside parties, such as the British. It was from this position that McKee helped steer the IRA to the 1975 ceasefire. When Hughes told Adams and Bell about his experiences with Seamus Loughran and Jimmy Drumm, the Feakle meeting was about to take place and they did not have to wait long for confirmation that what Hughes had seen and heard during his stint of freedom were signs of the impending cessation. Led primarily by Gerry Adams, as Hughes told Boston College, they spearheaded the opposition to the leadership and fashioned policies and strategies to correct the IRA's decline. In the jail, taking on the IRA leadership meant taking on David Morley.

*When I was brought to Long Kesh I had just ended a hunger strike [in protest over conditions in Crumlin Road] and the camp had just been burned . . . there were makeshift huts . . . and people were cooking on small gas stoves and fires. A guy called Bobby Campbell . . . looked after me and . . . made me beans on toast and said that was the best thing I could eat after coming off the hunger strike, which I believe is true . . . I settled into Cage 10, in one of the big huts. Davy Morley was in the small hut [of Cage 10] which was called the 'Generals' hut'. I asked to meet Morley to try and compare notes over what had happened in Long Kesh and in Crumlin Road jail . . . but my request was denied. The following day I made another request to see him and eventually he agreed. I was brought into the small hut, what's called the 'half-hut' and Davy Morley was sitting on the bed in a posing position and one of the prisoners was painting his portrait. I asked could we have some sort of sit-down to discuss what exactly happened and what the consequences of it were and about the interrogations that were taking place because I had heard in Crumlin Road jail about the torture happening in Long Kesh. Republican prisoners were being tortured by other Republican prisoners to try and force confessions that they were involved in MRF/UFF [Military Reaction Force/Ulster Freedom Fighters] activities. He had sent stuff to me about this being British counter-insurgency; he was the expert in counter-insurgency and . . . that he had it all in hand; I was a Volunteer and I should fall into line which of course I was quite happy to do.*

*... over the next few weeks there were attempts by Morley to undermine me. Not that he had any need to because I didn't want any position on the camp staff. My experience in Crumlin Road jail had given me enough of leadership ... I remember one particular instance in Cage 10: drilling was taking place, which was normal, and we marched around the yard ... I was put in the front row of two ranks of men, and we marched round and round the cage to orders ... All of a sudden I found myself marching on my own and everybody else was ... laughing. [This was done] to undermine me ... and to try and make a laughing stock out of me; this was part of Morley's tactics. I had never heard of David Morley before but ... my first impression was that [Long Kesh] was being run like a British Army camp ... where recruits were treated with disdain and degraded and put down, especially anyone with any sort of potential. It was the most uncomfortable few months that I've ever spent in prison. Morley ran the jail with an iron fist, which I resented right from the word go. I resented the fact that Morley had refused to meet me and then, when he did, he was sitting having a portrait done of himself. After the fire people lost everything and so clothes were sent in. There were these monkey hats amongst it all and there was only one white one – and Morley was wearing it ... He made himself just like Gusty Spence\* who had done the same, wearing water boots and distinctive caps or hats. I could see this quite clearly. We were using British Army manuals for training. It reminded me of my time in sea school in Sharpness in England, training for the Merchant Navy; it was the same type of regime as that, where you fell into line, you took orders, you didn't question it, you did what you were told. If you didn't do what you were told you finished up in the glasshouse. What I walked into at Long Kesh was very similar to that regime. The only thing that was missing were uniforms. Here we all had different berets on except the Commander-in-Chief who wore a white one; everybody else wore blue ones or brown ones or purple ones or whatever but there was*

---

\* Leader of Ulster Volunteer Force (UVF).

*only one white one and that was for Morley. It was a frightening, degrading and demoralising experience for me during that period in Cage 10 of Long Kesh.*

*. . . Two people from Cage 11 were opposing Davy Morley. One of them was the person who helped me when I first got there, Bobby Campbell, and the other was a guy called Jimmy Dempsey. Morley gave an order that Campbell and Dempsey be beaten and thrown out of Cage 10. And this is exactly what happened: Jimmy Dempsey and Bobby Campbell were severely beaten and left at the gate of Cage 10. And the prison regime was informed that they were no longer acceptable as Republican prisoners of war. They were taken in a prison van, brought to what was called 'the cells' or 'the boards', put into a cell and kept there; they were totally isolated from the rest of the Republican prisoners in Long Kesh.*

*When I was arrested along with Gerry and Tom Cahill, I was caught with some money stolen in a robbery from Hughes tool factory and all the notes had been marked. I didn't expect to be charged but all of a sudden, in 1974, I was brought down from Cage 10 to court, given two-and-a-half years for handling stolen money. That was me now a sentenced prisoner. Cage 10 was used to house remand prisoners who they wanted out of Crumlin Road so they put me back in Cage 11 instead . . . I wanted to get into Cage 11 [anyway] because I knew a lot of the boys [there] like Big Juice McMullan, Wee Danny Lennon, Tom Boy Louden, Bobby Sands, people I had been interned with. There was a much more down-to-earth sort of atmosphere in Cage 11, something similar to what internment was like. It was a relief when I was arrested the first time and interned. It was the same sort of relief getting from Cage 10 to Cage 11 where I felt much more comfortable among people I'd spent time with before. By this time it was late 1974, early 1975 . . . Gerry Adams was taken out and sentenced to eighteen months for an attempted escape and returned to Cage 11 along with Tom Cahill.*

Hughes and Adams had been reunited and although Bell was in Cage 9, from time to time the three could talk 'at the wire', as it was called: holding conversations through the wire fences during recreation. It was from this point on that the three began analysing events, devising ways of spreading their subversive gospel and plotting their opposition to the Davy Morley prison leadership, and through that opposing those they regarded as being ultimately responsible for the ceasefire. Hughes was eager to tell Adams and Bell all about the bizarre affair in Crumlin Road involving Heatherington and McGrogan, but the conversations quickly turned to the ceasefire and what to do about it. Their critique was grounded in the view that the British wanted to entice the IRA into a long debilitating ceasefire. That, they believed, is what the British had tried to do in 1972 and now they had a second chance. The evidence was there, in their eyes, firstly in the manipulation of internee releases to facilitate the ceasefire and secondly, in the false if ambiguous assurances the British had given the Army Council about their intention to withdraw. If the British wanted to leave, they asked, why were they building a new prison beside the Long Kesh camp? Then there was the willingness of the IRA to join a tit-for-tat sectarian war with Loyalists, singling out Protestants for assassination in retaliation for a wave of Loyalist killing. The South Armagh IRA's killing of ten Protestant workers dragged off a bus and machine-gunned to death in January 1976 and claimed in the name of a non-existent organisation, the 'Catholic Reaction Force', was particularly chilling example. The same was happening in Belfast and, in that instance, they blamed Billy McKee; he had become the new Belfast Commander and this was happening on his watch. That was a second strike against him. Not only did this suit Britain's efforts to portray the Troubles abroad as an unreasonable sectarian quarrel that they were trying bravely to referee, they argued, but it also diverted IRA resources away from fighting the British, the real enemy in the trio's eyes. They began recruiting converts to their cause but, remarkably, one figure they didn't even try to win over, because of his intense loyalty to Morley and Billy McKee, was a prisoner who would later become an icon of the Adams era: Bobby Sands.

*We discussed [Heatherington–McGrogan] pretty regularly. Certainly myself and Gerry discussed it because we were in the same cage [although] Ivor was in Cage 9. We used to meet at the wire, myself, Gerry and Ivor. There were two football pitches, one facing onto Cage 9 and one facing onto Cage 11. So Ivor was able to come up if there was a football match on and we would have debates about what we should do. But to be honest the biggest debate going on at the time was what was happening on the outside. What was happening to the leadership; where were they going? By and large the discussion took a turn towards what were we going to do about it. The leadership were starting to tell us that internment was going to end, there was talk about 50 per cent remission coming in. At the same time, right beside us, there was this major prison being built. We had seen the walls going up; they were working twenty-four hours a day, seven days a week, and yet we were still being told by the leadership within the prison that the war was over. People like myself, Ivor, Gerry and other people began discussing these issues. I wouldn't include Bobby Sands in this, because Bobby would have been seen then as a Davy Morley man. So Bobby wasn't involved. Bobby was in Cage 11 along with us but he was more into the cultural end of things and he was running classes in Cage 11 in the end hut. So Ivor, Gerry, myself and others, we decided that Morley had to be opposed because he had control of all communications going out of the prison [to the leadership]. Morley saw people like us as a threat to himself. What he was being told by the leadership on the outside I do not know. But he saw us as a threat to his leadership in the prison and he took measures to try and counter us. The way he did this was to get people who wouldn't have been known openly as Davy Morley men to listen in to our conversations and report back to him. People in Cage 11 were reporting anything they came across . . . and the jail became a cauldron of conspiracy, people listening and reporting back . . . A whole gang of informers had been set up and they were usually the worst type of character . . . set up by the camp staff to spy on myself, Adams and Bell . . . When Gerry arrived in Cage 11, he gave some direction to our opposition . . . and actually it was Gerry who planned and co-ordinated the opposition to Morley. I would have been probably much more anxious, to just dump Morley over the wire. One of the first things we did was to campaign to get Bobby Campbell and Jimmy Dempsey out of the blocks, where Davy Morley had sent them. As time went on, opposition grew to the Morley regime. It was a very oppressive regime and, as I say, based on British military practices.*

*. . . we believed that when myself, Gerry, and Ivor were [put] in prison, the British government was releasing people from internment who they believed they could deal with, people like Billy McKee, Jimmy Drumm, [and] that sort of . . . conservative type . . . People like Davy Morley were being released every other weekend to go for private talks with the leadership. Jimmy Drumm was allowed into the prison. A softening up . . . was taking place and people like myself and Gerry, specifically Gerry, realised that it had to be stopped one way or the other. And that's when we started to conspire to get rid of the leadership. This leadership was leading us up the garden path. We saw the hand of the British in this . . . I believe they controlled the release scheme so as to allow selected people out . . . to get into positions . . . in the six counties. And right up to the end, the last people they let out were those . . . they believed or perceived as the biggest danger. Those they didn't want out were people like Adams, Tom Cahill, people like that. So Gerry was seen as the person who could best oppose this regime. Morley obviously was being told this as well. As I say, I had never met Morley before in my life . . . He was obviously being briefed by the [leadership] outside to keep us under control . . . Davy Morley was not important; Davy Morley was only . . . an idiot with a hat and big boots . . . he was following orders. Davy Morley was a safe pair of hands . . . But things escalated to such a degree on the outside with a sectarian war going on, with the ceasefire being called, the incident centres being opened. There were communications from the outside leadership to the prisoners . . . every other day, directives telling us that: 'We have fought the British to a standstill, the British want out, we are negotiating with the British now and it's only a matter of time before the*

*boats sail out of Belfast Lough.' They were advising people not to [make] escape [attempts] because it was only a matter of time before they'd be released. At the same time there were bombs going off in the Shankill Road; there were bombs going off in the Falls Road; there were Protestants getting shot, Catholics getting shot. But there were no British getting shot. I was, myself, getting more and more frustrated at the lack of progress we were making [in opposing Morley] . . . at one stage I began to voice my objections and my perception that it was a sell-out, [and] I was arrested by Dickie O'Neill, Gerry Rooney and Bobby Sands, taken out and threatened with court-martial for my open dissent towards the leadership, and given a caution. I was sharing a cubicle with Gerry Adams at the time and I packed my gear. By this time the INLA had been formed and had prisoners in Cage 13, and I was heading there; I was going to leave the Republican movement and join the INLA. They had just been formed after a split within the Workers' Party. I was talked out of it by Gerry and remained. He convinced me that the only way to defeat these people was to oppose them from within. That was always the argument, oppose them from within . . . they would be quite happy for me to walk away. That was basically the line he gave me, that they'd be quite happy for me to walk away. But here we were in this situation; it was very, very demoralising. We then got the word that we must prepare for civil war and, Jesus Christ . . . we had to start training for that possibility . . . The British were pulling out and the Loyalists were going to rebel and we had to be prepared for that – we had to figure out ways of getting out of Long Kesh and joining the war against the Loyalists because the British weren't going to be there. So we were given all these instructions to start training and soon we were climbing over huts and marching and drilling as if we were at war. We also had to make survival kits which consisted of . . . a pair of laces, hard sweets, polish for your face for creeping out of the place. Oh, it was so, it was absolutely fucking crazy, but we had to go along with it . . .*

*[After ten Protestants were killed in South Armagh] I had arguments with the camp leadership . . . I put my name to a couple of*

*letters going out to the army leadership, complaining about the sectarian turn that the war had taken . . . and asking for it to be stopped . . . I don't know whether the petitions actually reached the leadership. Certainly I don't believe that they reached GHQ or Army Council level. I think they were probably stopped in Belfast. But these were communications sent out officially through the proper lines because if you didn't go through the lines they were not even read. If they went through the lines they were supposed to be officially responded to. We never got any responses . . .*

*At one time, I actually advocated shooting the Belfast leadership, which Gerry and Ivor were opposed to . . . at this time we were getting so frustrated with the direction that the leadership had taken. I believed it was being manipulated by British Intelligence because it suited the British at that time. And we could see . . . quite clearly from within the prison that the British were allowing this to take place and encouraging it actually. Even though some people were getting arrested, the main operators were not getting arrested. We knew because when people arrived in the Cage they were debriefed and most of us . . . knew the names of the individuals on the outside who were planting the bombs. Most of the people in Ardoyne knew who they were because [afterwards] they went straight into drinking clubs and it was quite obvious who they were . . . This sectarian war that the British were able to manipulate the IRA into was part of the Ulsterisation of security. The RUC were moved to the front line, slowly. The H-blocks were being built for the criminalisation part of it. And then, when the British were ready to move, they knew all the operators, they knew who were planting the bombs, and they moved against them. There were major round-ups with people [being] brought in and charged. I remember Brendan McFarlane\* coming in . . . Bik would not have been a sectarian bigot and he was arrested for a bomb that was planted, I think, on the Shankill, the Bayardo Bar that killed . . . a lot of people . . . I*

---

\* IRA Prison Commander during the 1981 hunger strikes, convicted of bombing the Bayardo Bar on the Shankill Road, Belfast, in August 1975, killing five people.

*remember him being confused, disorientated and deeply depressed about what he had done because by the time he got to Cage 11, he'd had time to reflect on that period . . . he realised by the time he got to Cage 11 that the British had allowed this sort of thing to take place. The policy on the outside was that only defensive action should be taken and British soldiers were no longer targets. Volunteers on the outside were not allowed to shoot British soldiers but they were allowed to take action against Loyalists and defensive action against the RUC. And the incident centres were there meaning that there was a hotline between the IRA and the British during all the time of the sectarian bombing campaign and . . . when Catholics and Protestants were shooting each other. When the time came, the British moved against the IRA, closed down the incident centres, arrested all these involved, moved the RUC up and pulled the British Army back . . . We started to hear words like 'Godfathers', 'Chicago-type killings'. The British sent a guy, Peter Jay, as Ambassador to America, and he went there to convince the Americans that this was a sectarian war here and the British were caught in the middle. The IRA had facilitated this image . . . by the time Bik and others like him arrived in the jail, they realised this. That was the weakness of the leadership at that time, that they were fooled into that. At the same time we were getting communications from the outside telling us that the British were withdrawing, that we're going through a phase that would probably finish up in a civil-war situation. Thus all the preparations in the jail, a ridiculous situation where men were crawling over huts and along the ground at nights to practise for night-time combat . . . it was like something out of a Mel Brooks film, putting survival kits together for the civil war in which the IRA was going to come up and break into the jail and get us all out . . .*

Brendan Hughes's story of his experiences with Seamus Loughran and Jimmy Drumm during his brief bout of freedom had clinched the matter as far as Gerry Adams and Ivor Bell were concerned. This was damning evidence that the leadership had conspired behind their backs to produce the ceasefire and that steeled the three in their determination to oppose David Morley. But there were other factors at work. The trio regarded themselves as much more politically radical than the older generation which currently led the IRA. But in one respect Hughes and Bell differed from Adams and that was in their attitude towards Catholicism; in that respect Adams had more in common with the leadership.

*. . . these people [the McKee–O Bradaigh–O Connail leadership] were still living in the 1940s. They still had the mentality of the 1940s generation. People like Billy were about protecting the Catholic people whereas we were developing into . . . a revolutionary organisation that wanted much more than that. I mean, who gave a fuck if Loyalists blew up a Catholic church . . . we weren't there to protect the Catholic church, we were there to bring about a united Ireland. The old Brigade attitude was: 'We must protect the Catholic religion; we must protect our faith.' We were developing into an organisation that really didn't care about such things. Certainly I was, and so was Ivor. Ivor was anti-religion. Gerry was still very much in the religious mould, but a modernised religious mould. And to this day I'm not sure exactly where his thoughts were. I mean, I shared a cubicle with him, and when I was reading Che Guevara and Fidel Castro speeches, he was saying his rosary. There was always that sort of contradiction: here he was a revolutionary socialist, yet he was very much involved in his religion and his Catholicism which conflicted [with] what we were trying to achieve. But I think because of the friendship and the comradeship that had built up [between us] during the early 1970s most of these apparent contradictions were put aside because we were fighting a war. And the main thing was to fight the war.*

Brendan Hughes, Gerry Adams and Tom Cahill were by mid-1975 living in the smaller hut, the so-called half-hut, in Cage 11. Many internees and sentenced men such as Bobby Sands had been released but had gone back into the IRA, been arrested – in Sands's case during an attempted bombing – and were now back in Long Kesh, some in Cage 11, as sentenced prisoners. Opposition to David Morley's leadership of the camp, and to the Army Council outside, was expressed in three ways. Adams gave lectures and held debates about the ceasefire strategy and other political topics; Ivor Bell stood against Morley in the election for Camp Commander and Adams wrote heavily coded critiques of the leadership strategy for *Republican News* under the 'Brownie' byline. The 'Brownie' articles allowed Adams to make veiled criticism of the ceasefire via comparisons to other, similar phases in the history of Irish Republicanism when a cessation was a prelude to defeat or decline. He also introduced concepts that would later define the era of his leadership, among them the idea of a long war, the espousal of left-wing ideas, and the need for a fusion of the IRA's military and political strategies which implied a much higher profile for Sinn Fein. He also introduced the idea of 'active abstentionism', which was a clever way of both defending and subverting abstentionism by advocating IRA involvement in creating alternative governing structures at community level. In this and the emphasis Adams gave the need to relate to the political and economic needs of the community from which the IRA sprang can be seen traces of the subsequent political and electoral strategy of Sinn Fein. In later years, during the peace process, Adams would deny, through spokesmen, that he was the sole author of the 'Brownie' articles, claiming that others in Long Kesh had shared the byline. The reason was that in one article 'Brownie' had spoken of his membership of the IRA, something that in the era of the peace process Adams was eager to deny. But Brendan Hughes told Boston College that there was only one author of the 'Brownie' articles during this time: they 'were totally his baby, totally Gerry's baby':

*What was important about [standing in] the election [for Camp Commander] was that if you did not get into some sort of position in the prison then you didn't have a voice on the outside – you had to go through army communication lines. There was no such thing as allowing an ordinary Volunteer . . . to write to the leadership straight from prison. You had to go through the lines. So if you had something to say, it had to be sent first to the leadership within the prison and they . . . would send it out. You could not do it yourself. There was one way around that and Gerry was able to find it . . . by writing the Brownie articles. His name was never on the articles but the Brownie articles being published in* Republican News *at the time provided a way around that. And there were people on the outside who . . . still had enough influence to get these articles printed in* Republican News, *people like Ted Howell\* . . .*

*We began to have debates. At this time the biggest issue was the Middle East conflict . . . the Israeli and the Palestinian situation and you actually had people like Cleaky Clarke† advocating the Israeli position, a Zionist position at this period. That was the level of debate that was going on, the level of intellectual awareness . . . there wasn't a great deal of it. Certainly in Cage 10 there was absolutely none. Actually in one period, in 1974, all the Marxist books were burnt in Cage 10 and James Connolly was thrown at the top of the pile. All communist material was burnt, and it happened in Cage 10 . . . Morley had so much control over these people that I used to joke about the Morley pill. You had guys who you thought were politically astute and aware who all of a sudden would go along with the Morley line. Perhaps it was something to do with [being in] prison. Morley was telling people that if they behaved it wouldn't be long till they were out of prison. Now he was getting this, obviously, from the outside and . . . he was pushing the line that the war was over, that everybody would be released. We were pushing the line that the war was not over. The British were trying what they had done in 1972, to get us involved in a long-drawn-out ceasefire. A long-drawn-out ceasefire destroys an army, and we were pushing that line that the leadership was wrong.*

*Adams's point of view, all the time, was that we must turn out a politically active, politically educated rank and file. That was the*

---

\* Close ally of Gerry Adams and future chairman of his think tank.
† An Ardoyne Republican and future Adams bodyguard, now deceased.

*key phrase, a politically educated rank and file so that control is taken off the leadership [and put] into the hands of the fighting men . . . Gerry was constantly pushing [the need for] an educated rank and file, that the reason why we're in the position that we were in, being involved in sectarian killings, was because the IRA was leadership-led and the Volunteers were not politically educated. The whole emphasis from 1976 on . . . was to bring about a situation where you had such people being released from the prison to go back into the IRA. That was the aim and objective of all . . .*

*The election was held; Ivor was put up as a candidate for Camp O/C . . . Ivor had won the election for O/C of Cage 9. They'd done a pretty good job down there in Cage 9 and that made him eligible to stand for Camp O/C . . . And I can't remember the exact result but Ivor lost . . . everybody had a right to vote – all Volunteers had a right to vote [but] suspended Volunteers were not allowed to vote. So up until the election, people were getting suspended for silly things . . . anything they could do to sabotage our campaign they did. People were suspended; they pulled me in and threatened me with court martial; people like Gerry Kelly and Hugh Feeney were suspended for canvassing on behalf of Ivor. Gerry and Hugh were in the same cage as Ivor. Threats of court martial were made; anybody caught undermining the leadership would be immediately court-martialled and would lose their status as Volunteers. Every other day men were ordered [to] parade: 'Parad anois'; 'Everybody out.' All but the suspended men lined up in the big hut and we had to suffer the humiliation of these statements being read out to us. And one that I can remember most clearly was a communication from the Commander of Republican Prisoners, Long Kesh, which said: 'This group of conspirators, the niggers in the woodpile, the anti-IRA people in this camp will not be tolerated. This conspiracy will be crushed.' Statements like that and we would be standing there biting our lips. But while the election [result] did have a slight demoralising effect . . . what gave me great inspiration was . . . that people were beginning to listen, people like Bik McFarlane. Gerry was absolutely good in organising Cage 11. Not so much openly, but*

*going round talking to . . . people like Bobby [Sands], Jim Gibney,*
*not Jim Gibney that's the Sinn Fein face now, but the other wee Jim*
*Gibney from Short Strand. But the more this went on, the more*
*debate took place and we would organise major debates in Cage 11 . . .*

*. . . by that time I was I/O of Cage 11. We had lectures; we were . . .*
*debating the whole situation and people were beginning to listen.*
*And I used to dander in to what we called the 'intellectual hut', the*
*end hut. You had . . . people like Bobby, like Rooney, a bunch of*
*other guys who were studying, learning Irish, reading books. And*
*then you had the other crowd like the Big Juice McMullans and the*
*Big Cleakys . . . who just wanted to do their time and do it as well*
*as they could. There was a gap between those two types that began*
*to break down. As discussions took place . . . the barriers began to*
*fall, certainly in Cage 11. It had already happened in Cage 9 under*
*Ivor and Martin McAllister.\* And we began to have debates about*
*what was happening on the outside, about the sectarianism, about*
*the 1972 truce, and international politics. Gerry used to do a lot of*
*these debates, and he was impressive . . . the type of person he is, he*
*could walk into the so-called intellectual hut and sit down with the*
*people there and debate with them. People like Gerry Rooney and*
*Bobby Sands would have opposed myself and Gerry; we were saying*
*that what was going on was a ploy by the British to get us involved*
*in a long-drawn-out ceasefire. But he began to impress them.*

*I was also into giving lectures and . . . talks and having debate*
*about the political situation, how it had gone wrong on the outside;*
*how we [had] allowed people to get into positions of power and*
*allowed the leadership to dictate where we were going and what*
*tactics were allowed, with men not being allowed to think for them-*
*selves. What we were trying to do was to bring about a situation in*
*which Volunteers could think for themselves and could work them-*
*selves into leadership level.*

*Well, by late 1976/1977 the situation had developed and there was*
*growing opposition to the Morley regime, to the ceasefire. It had*

\* A South Armagh Republican.

*largely built up in Cage 9 and Cage 11. And people began trans-*
*ferring out of Cage 12 and Cage 10 into Cage 9 and Cage 11 . . . So*
*Cage 9 and Cage 11 became the focus of opposition to the Morley*
*regime . . . and to the leadership outside. We intensified the lectures*
*and training in those two cages to the extent that special internal*
*camps were set up. For a whole weekend, eight or nine men would*
*go into the half-hut – usually in Cage 9 – and stay there for the*
*whole weekend, studying, training, debating, weapons training,*
*explosives training, all taking place over the weekend. They would*
*move out on the Monday and another six or seven men would*
*move into the half-hut again. There was a lot of concentration on*
*explaining the cell system that would come in . . . that the old*
*Brigade, Battalion, Company structure was not going to survive*
*[and] a different structure would take their place.*

Weapons training was sometimes very realistic and the authorities
were not beyond exaggerating this to strengthen the case that special-
category status served only to validate the IRA's authority over the
inmates. This was when Long Kesh began to be described in briefings
to the media as the 'University of Terror', the implication being that
a normal, criminal-type regime would change this for the better. At
one point, following the discovery of a realistic mortar in 1976, Cage
11 was briefly closed down and the inmates moved elsewhere.

*. . . it actually wasn't a mortar. There was an Armalite and an*
*imitation mortar that we were using in lectures. Actually there's*
*a photograph of me giving one of the lectures, and I think there's*
*a photograph of the mortar [as well]. The mortar was so realistic-*
*looking that the camp authorities believed it to be real and there*
*was a panic and everybody was moved out and the cage was pulled*
*apart. But it was excellent workmanship . . . but it was not a real*
*mortar, it could never have fired.*

The divisions in the IRA's ranks in Long Kesh deepened with
time with Gerry Adams leading the assault, courtesy of the

pseudonymous 'Brownie' articles in the Belfast Brigade's weekly newspaper, *Republican News*.

*. . . as I say, the only avenue we had . . . was through the 'Brownie' articles. And if you read the 'Brownie' articles they had hidden messages in them which tried to explain exactly what was going on, that the British had tried this in 1972 and the ceasefire lasted only two weeks but this time the British were getting away with it. And I believe that the 'Brownie' articles were first to highlight the Ulsterisation, criminalisation, normalisation policies.*

*The camp had practically split in two: you had the Morley camp and you had the Adams camp. Gerry and myself were, most of the time, in the same cubicle; at the start the huts used to be just open but they were then converted into cubicles, two main cubicles. They weren't cells; there were no doors, just curtains . . . And myself and Gerry would have had debates about what was going on outside the jail; about the cell system, about the leadership, about our opposition to the leadership. Gerry would, most nights, be writing the 'Brownie' articles for the paper . . . The 'Brownie' articles . . . weren't allowed to go out unless they were passed over to Morley for censoring. And there were great arguments over that. Many a night or day Gerry would be called to the wire by Davy Morley and there would be arguments and disputes . . . between the two . . . There was no physical contact, but a lot of shouting at each other . . . There was a great deal of tension, a great deal of hostility. At that time Gerry was O/C of Cage 11. Morley was under instructions from the outside to censor anything . . . coming out of Cage 9 or Cage 11, especially Gerry's articles. And Gerry was the most prolific writer at the time. And . . . by and large, he was seen as the person leading the criticism. And by and large he was.*

*Up until that point of his release he was responsible for all the 'Brownie' articles . . . all the 'Brownie' articles were his. Then when he got released Hugh Feeney wrote under the 'Salon' byline.*

Q. *Were the 'Brownie' articles a collective effort or were they simply the product of Gerry alone which he would then give out to others to assess, evaluate, etc.?*

A. *No. They were totally his baby, totally Gerry's baby. Every time he wrote one he would show it to me to read and to go over. Often we would have arguments . . . because most . . . times . . . I would just glance through it and he would say that he wanted [proper] feedback from me and . . . I really didn't. Often I would have to read [the article] two or three times. But the 'Brownie' articles were aimed at the rank and file on the outside and to a large extent they were coded in such a way that they would get out [past Morley]. Some of them were just . . . very funny articles based [about] life within the camp . . . But the main aim of the Brownie articles was . . . to get the message out that . . . the war was going wrong and calling on people to re-involve themselves . . .*

Q. *The point that I would raise is that in the book which you, yourself, are reading at the moment, on Gerry Adams:* Man of War, Man of Peace?, *by Mark Devenport and David Sharrock, Adams is quoted as denying that he was 'Brownie' and he has said that 'Brownie' was actually a number of authors. Although Devenport and Sharrock convincingly, compellingly refute that argument with decent evidence. I'm just wondering what you feel about that denial by Gerry.*

A. *That's a lie, I mean, I know what 'Brownie' means. And not many people know what 'Brownie' means. Do you know what it means? [It was a code] for making love [to his wife]; that's right, that's what it was. And it was purely his baby. Certainly, after Gerry got released, the 'Brownie' articles went out under different bylines – Joe Barnes was one who wrote some 'Brownie' articles . . . but during that whole period Gerry was exclusively Brownie.*

With the IRA Commanders in Long Kesh accusing the Cage 11 and Cage 9 rebels of fomenting a rebellion against the national leadership, Gerry Adams was careful not to give the Morley camp any more ammunition, displaying the great caution that has characterised his career in, and later leadership of, the IRA. Hughes and Ivor Bell wanted openly to involve other key players such as Martin McGuinness and Brian Keenan in their developing conspiracy, but Adams wouldn't hear of it, insisting that they communicate only through the 'army lines', the authorised lines of authority which meant communications to other IRA figures had to go through Morley, who would read everything.

*. . . you couldn't have a line to anybody outside the [recognised] structures. And that was a rule that we had to stick by, myself, Ivor and Gerry. And we did stick by it because if . . . someone had sent an unofficial comm. [communication] out and it was reported, then the person would be suspended. And I believe that happened to . . . Martin McAllister. Gerry was emphatic about this, that we had to stay within the Army [IRA] line, the same cliché. And they would have loved it if anybody had been caught. We were constantly warned about it. There was no direct line to Twomey, no direct line to anybody. There were communications coming in to us complaining about what was happening on the outside, mostly [sent] to Gerry, but he would not respond. If my memory serves me well, I think there was contact with Brian [Keenan] and I think that was because myself and Ivor were putting on the pressure. Gerry was adamant that we should not go outside the army line, always. Was he right to be cautious? Yes, because he realised that until we had some sort of hold on the reins of power in the camp, it would have sunk us all. We would have lost our ability to oppose them because they would have been in a position to court-martial us and then we would have no voice. Once you're court-martialled and suspended – you didn't even have to be court-martialled – once you were suspended you lost all your rights. So there was great caution over that.*

*I do believe there was unofficial contact with Keenan; we didn't collectively decide to do it but I believe it was Ivor. I remember Terry Crossan being pulled in and interrogated [about communicating to*

*McGuinness]. Terry Crossan would have been trusted at that time. I don't believe there was any written communication. That's what saved the day, I believe, because . . . they had no proof, they [just] had Terry Crossan's word against Gerry's. And I don't think it was enough to suspend or court-martial . . . it was a conversation and it was argued that there was no conspiracy taking place. There was, I think, an attempt to make contact on a friendly basis [with McGuinness] not on an official basis. McGuinness was seen as probably the one person on the outside who could make any . . . difference. He was held in high esteem by our group. Certainly he was one of the people who was always taken into consideration regarding the replacement of the leadership on the outside. McGuinness would have been seen as a potential ally, even a certain ally in this whole thing. I knew McGuinness reasonably well; Gerry knew him very well. But I don't think there was a great relationship between McGuinness and Ivor.*

By the end of 1976 and the beginning of 1977, the Morley era in Long Kesh was drawing to a close. Morley himself was due for release at the start of 1977 and he stood down to become Adjutant to his replacement, Jim Scullion, a close ally. Gerry Adams was due for release in February 1977, and as his release date approached, he and Brendan Hughes plotted and planned the IRA's future, both inside the jail and outside.

*. . . the last thing that Gerry and I did was to walk the yard [on] the day he was getting out . . . discussing what needed to happen inside the prison and outside the prison; the whole organisation, the whole movement on the outside needed to be reorganised. And the last words that Gerry said to me as he walked out the gate with his bag was that I was the lucky one staying behind; that he had a much, much harder job than me on the outside. So at that stage, obviously, Gerry was very confident that he was going to reorganise on the outside and my job would be to reorganise on the inside and that was a clear indication of intent. Gerry wasn't going out to go to*

*cross the border; he was going to go straight back into the movement
and start reorganising. And that's what . . . we'd been talking about
from 1975 until 1977 when Gerry was released.*

*. . . by that stage the movement on the outside was in disarray.
Most of the operators were in jail. The British government had
moved so heavily and closed down all the incident centres which
had become the Army's [the IRA's] wee base of power. And it was
quite obvious that [there was a chance] the whole struggle was going
to be called off; I think the British actually expected this . . . I believe
many of the leadership were quite happy to walk away because the
whole thing had been brought to such disarray and such a mess . . .
I believe there were people there in that leadership who would have
been quite happy to hand over the reins because none of them were
capable of taking the Army anywhere . . . so it was quite obvious
that a new leadership would emerge.*

*. . . by 1977 before Gerry got out, we knew that Sinn Fein and the
Army [the IRA] needed to run in tandem. That was the intention,
that was the strategy, that was the policy, [creating] a politically
educated rank and file, that politicisation had to take place on the
outside and politicisation had to take place on the inside and there
was going to be a massive reorganisation on the outside . . . there
were people on the outside doing nothing except waiting on people
like Gerry and Ivor getting out and perhaps myself as well. Except
I would have had to escape. I wasn't getting out for a long time. But
when Gerry got released I saw myself fitting into that role, because it
was quite obvious that once Gerry got out then the leadership in the
prison was going to be changed.*

*Within a week he contacted me and we had a direct line of
communication. He hadn't moved into any sort of leadership
position but certainly it was only a matter of time. I can't remember
exactly how long it was but elections were due within the cage and
I believe that Keenan was a main mover here, Twomey and Gerry
and Keenan. Within a short period of time we got a request to send
out nominations for the Camp O/C.*

It was actually seven or eight months before Adams moved to change the IRA regime in the prison, which Republicans still stubbornly called Long Kesh rather than the British name, the Maze. In a sign that the poacher was about to become gamekeeper, the method of choosing the Camp Commander was changed in a significant way. In the past an election would have to be held if there was more than one nomination for the job, meaning that candidates could also propagandise and make trouble among fellow prisoners; the Cage 11 rebels had used this procedure to advance and articulate their opposition to Billy McKee and his allies. But the change introduced after Adams rejoined the national leadership closed off this route to future rebels. Any prisoner could be nominated as Commander, to be sure, but from thereon the IRA leadership outside the prison would choose which of the nominees would get the job. Cage 11 and Cage 9 had been preached to about the need to democratise, to educate politically and empower the rank and file to curb an errant, arrogant leadership. But in this move could be seen a hand that relished the dictatorial powers that military leadership always brings. It was the IRA's version of democratic centralism, the Army Council being the equivalent of the Soviet Politburo. By the end of 1977, courtesy of his friend and long-time comrade, Gerry Adams, Brendan Hughes was appointed Commander of the special-category prisoners in Long Kesh, those who had not yet been moved over to the new H-blocks and still represented the bulk of all IRA prisoners. This, as much as anything else, marked the beginning of the Adams era in the IRA.

# 7

The first signs that Gerry Adams had made good his promise to Brendan Hughes and Ivor Bell to oust the IRA leadership of 1975 came several months before Hughes was made Commander of IRA prisoners in the Maze prison. They came on one of the most revered days in the Republican calendar. On the Sunday nearest 20 June each year, Republicans gather at Bodenstown cemetery in County Kildare to celebrate the birth in 1763 of the founder of modern Irish separatism, Wolfe Tone. It is an occasion to meet old friends, to reaffirm core beliefs and to hear the IRA leadership's take on the struggle to eject Britain from Ireland, and their analysis of how this will be achieved. The June 1977 Bodenstown ceremony was all of this and much, much more. The main speaker that day, the man chosen to pronounce the most radical shift in IRA policy since the Provisionals came into being, was none other than Jimmy Drumm, the same Jimmy Drumm whom Brendan Hughes had discovered was having secret meetings behind his back with either the British or their proxies in the spring of 1974. Drumm's surreptitious rendezvous were part of the complex dance that led to the 1974/75 ceasefire, an event that Adams, Hughes and Ivor Bell had long regarded as a disaster for the IRA. They had determined in jail to remove those responsible and now Jimmy Drumm, once that leadership's loyal water boy, climbed the platform beside Wolfe Tone's grave to announce that the new regime had taken over.* It was an exercise designed to demonstrate that Gerry Adams and his allies now held sway at the highest levels of the IRA; but it was also staged to humiliate the deposed leaders.

* See p. 168.

Drumm's speech said two significant things: first, the IRA no longer believed, as had the 1975 leadership, that the British had any plans to withdraw from the North; in fact the view now was that Britain was in for the long haul, determined to stabilise Northern Ireland and to defeat the IRA. Second, the IRA could come back from this setback only if the isolation of Republicans around the strategy of armed struggle was ended. Any struggle to achieve Irish independence that was confined to the North and based solely on 'hatred and resentment of the [British] army',[60] as the speech composed for Drumm put it, could not succeed. The old leadership had gone or was going and so too had their ideas. The new leaders – Adams, Bell, who was released later in 1977, Martin McGuinness, Brian Keenan and others – were signalling ever so subtly that the IRA had shifted leftwards and was committed to a broader level of political activity in both parts of Ireland. At the time, the leftward lurch got the attention and before long the tag 'Marxist' would be attached to the Provos; but it was, arguably, the latter development that in the long term made the greater difference. The expansion of Sinn Fein and the demand that it make itself relevant to people's normal needs, all implied in Drumm's speech and soon official policy, led directly to eventual Republican involvement in electoral politics, out of which came the peace process. But, long before that, the IRA's struggle against the British would once more be fought out in the prisons where Hughes would play a central role. The outcome of that battle would make the goals outlined in Jimmy Drumm's speech so much more achievable.

A few months before Jimmy Drumm made his reluctant way to the podium at Bodenstown, Brendan Hughes had passed his twenty-ninth birthday. He had courted death – and inflicted it on others – in the tangled streets of the Lower Falls since he was nineteen, had spent nearly four years in Long Kesh and now faced the best part of another decade behind bars. He and his wife Lilly had agreed to separate when he was sentenced, their marriage of just six years a casualty of the Troubles like so many others and their two children, a boy called Brendan and a daughter, Josephine, would grow up seeing their father only on jail visits. To add to all this he had become O/C of Long Kesh at a time when the camp's IRA prisoners were still deeply, even bitterly, divided. And he discovered alarming evidence of the cordial chumminess that had characterised the relationship between the prison authorities and the IRA camp staff during the Morley years.

*Things were very much the same [after Morley stood down], you could cut the tension with a knife. It was almost two enemy camps. And there were people in Cage 11, people like Big Juice McMullan, Wee Ginty Lennon and lots of others who had suffered under the Morley regime. When my appointment came in . . . the tension got even greater because there were people here who were really scared. And there were others who were busting to get at their throats, those who ran [Morley's] ruthless spying regime. The tension was even worse than before because . . . I heard the comments: 'Hang them from the fucking barbed wire.' A lot of these people had been inter-rogated, you know and beaten . . . by camp staff. The image I had once [my] appointment was made known was of these people scurrying into corners, waiting on the heavy hand coming down on them. There were two cases in particular; two of these people were actually caught in one of the tin wardrobes – listening to other people's conversation. There were numerous occasions when people were suspended by informers in our cages. So there was a great deal of hatred there. The first thing I had to do was inform the prison authorities that I was the new O/C . . . It was quite friendly actually, on the face of things. [But] I believe, underneath it all, there was a great deal of resentment and fear on the part of the authorities . . . because I had a reputation of being totally disruptive in the Crum-lin Road jail, when I was O/C there . . . I believe they were quite aware that the new leadership in the jail was subject to the advice and influence of a then-emerging, new Army [IRA] leadership on the outside. When I told the Governor and the Chief Prison Officer, Geordie Dixon, what the situation was, I sat down with them . . . I was called 'Mr Hughes' or 'O/C' by Geordie Dixon. Some of them*

*called me 'Dark' or 'Darkie'. It was always very pleasant and I was*
*. . . offered a cup of coffee, which I refused. I was then shown the*
*books of the camp staff and there was . . . I believe it was twenty-two*
*thousand pounds in the 'Jim Scullion Fund' which had been trans-*
*ferred from the 'Davy Morley Fund'. And I asked, 'What is this for,*
*what's this about?' He says, 'Well, it's, it's the prisoners' money.' I*
*says, 'Well, where did it come from?' He says, 'It was part of the*
*agreement that Morley and Jimmy Drumm came to with the camp*
*committee.' Apparently the UVF got money, the UDA got money*
*and the IRA prisoners got money. When I asked him what was the*
*money used for, he says, 'Ah, well . . . it's your discretion, it's up to*
*you now, it's in the Brendan Hughes Fund, it's for when prisoners*
*are getting out on parole or if you have any needs . . .' It was a fuck-*
*ing bribe. I immediately went to Scullion and had a head-to-head*
*with him: 'Where the hell was this money from?' And he couldn't*
*explain to me. I says, 'Why weren't the Volunteers informed of this*
*if . . . it's supposed to be there for their use? If prisoners' wives had*
*financial problems, should they not have been allowed to come and*
*get this money, if it was their money?' And I asked him, did he ever*
*hand over any money to prisoners who were having difficulties, and*
*he says, 'No.' There were never any suggestions that he was using it*
*for his own ends, but certainly there was suggestions that Morley*
*did. It was a large amount of money and I . . . told them to stick it,*
*I wasn't touching it, it was nothing to do with me, I didn't want the*
*money, which I think took them back a bit.*

Realising that the festering divisions within the IRA prison
community could be hugely self-destructive, Hughes set about
defusing the quarrel.

*I then concentrated on calming the situation because it was an*
*explosive situation . . . I requested a tour of all the cages, which I*
*proceeded to do. And the first cage I went to was Cage 12. And I*
*called them all to attention, or someone called them all to attention*
*and I gave them the talk I had planned. I tried to assure them as*

*much as possible that my intention was to unify the camp and to stop this antagonism . . . and I asked every Volunteer in the place to try . . . to co-operate with me to try and bring about unity within the camp: 'Forget about what happened in the past, we need unity here, there's a new situation developing, the Army [IRA] needs people on the outside, the movement needs people on the outside . . .' And to a large extent I was successful. I then went to the people who were the most angry and attempted to do that with them. And again I think I was largely successful. We made an attempt to make sure that this antagonism didn't finish up in a split . . . I had to forget a lot of things as well – [like] people who had been out to get me. I had to put that to the back of my mind as well, which I was quite able to do. And then the camp went pretty well. Changes were made. For instance, staff were no longer immune from prison duties, from now on all staff had to do exactly what every other Volunteer in the place was doing. And so I think that went a long way as well to break down . . . animosities and tensions. I was always a great believer in bringing about discipline through comradeship and through showing a lead, whereas before the discipline was brought about through fear, intimidation and threats.*

*A lot of the people who were with the previous leadership moved into Cage 10 . . . As I say, there was a great deal of fear in their ranks, but after some months or weeks that was quietened. And we went about organising and radicalising and preparing people to go outside. On the outside Gerry was reorganising the movement, [rescuing it] from the disarray that it was in. I carried on. We organised debates about things like 'What happened with the previous leadership?' . . . A lot of people within the jail – including people like Bobby Sands – did not really accept what we had been preaching. A lot of people were very, very loyal to the [old] leadership. Whatever the leadership said, the leadership must be right, and of course that's not always the case. The key words at that time were 'a politically educated rank and file' – a leadership that is controlled by the rank and file, an educated rank and file who were able to make their own decisions about what was right and what was wrong . . . The previous leadership was leadership led with little or no control or input from the rank and file. That was why we were in this mess. There weren't enough people in the rank and file who would speak up with their opinions.*

Days before the IRA leadership appointed him Camp Commander, Brendan Hughes's life was changed in another way and the consequences for him and the course of Irish politics would be profound. It started when an IRA prisoner called Joe Barnes had what the prisoners usually called 'a bad visit', one that turned into a quarrel with a wife or girlfriend, and he took his irritation out on a warder, hitting him as he returned to the cage. He was detained at the front gate and as Hughes attempted to negotiate his release, other prisoners climbed the wire and began beating the warders holding Barnes with bed irons and fire extinguishers. Hughes ordered them to stop and went to the help of one warder who had been felled and was choking on his own blood. Hughes turned him round to the recovery position just as more warders arrived. Although he had helped to stop the attack and had assisted an injured warder, Hughes was charged with rioting and assault and given an extra five-year sentence. That meant he was transferred out of the cages and special-category status section of Long Kesh into the new H-blocks whose construction had begun during the 1975 ceasefire. It was well into 1978 when Hughes entered the H-blocks and by then a group of IRA prisoners had been refusing for some time to wear the prison uniform in protest at the loss of their status.

The 'blanket protest', as the prisoners' campaign was called, was by no means a thought-out, well-planned action by the IRA but its consequences made it look as if it had been. British Secretary of State Merlyn Rees had scrapped special-category status on 1 March 1976 for any prisoner charged thereafter. Existing prisoners kept their political status but that too was removed in early 1980. The first prisoner convicted after Rees's edict was a former D Company member by the name of Kieran Nugent, an eighteen-year-old who had been in the IRA for two years. Nugent was convicted of hijacking a car and sentenced to three years. When he was taken to the H-blocks, he refused to put on the prison-issue uniform, famously telling the warders they would have to 'nail it to my back'. Nugent was placed naked in a cell and the next day was given a blanket which he used to cover himself, and so the protest was born. Sinn Fein figures discovered this only when, four weeks later, Nugent's family contacted them because their son had gone missing.[61] Through a lawyer, Sinn Fein and Nugent's family learned that the blanket protest had begun. Slowly Nugent was joined by others; and by 1980 around 300 prisoners, perhaps a half of all Republican prisoners in the new Maze prison, were 'on the blanket', a figure that would eventually rise to 450. Those on the protest were punished. They were held in their cells twenty-four hours a day, lost the 50 per cent remission of sentence available to conforming prisoners, and were denied access to television, radio, newspapers, books – except the Bible – and to writing materials, letters and family parcels. They lost their once-a-month statutory visit unless they wore a uniform at the time and totally forfeited three other privileged visits available to other inmates.[62]

What happened in the Maze prison between 1976 and the winter of 1981 was much more than a battle of wills between the IRA inmates and the prison authorities. It was a struggle about the meaning of Irish history and an attempt to redefine the narrative of the Troubles. By saying that the Provos were mere criminals, devoid of any political motive, the British were implicitly placing previous Republican struggles in the same category. If Brendan Hughes and his comrades were common criminals, then what did that make Terence MacSwiney, or the 1916 rebels, Robert Emmet, Wolfe Tone and the United Irishmen? That question resonated throughout Nationalist Ireland, way beyond the narrow confines of Long Kesh and in a way the British had failed to anticipate. It struck a sympathetic chord even among Nationalists who otherwise abhorred IRA violence. And for the Provos, it helped make the struggle in the H-blocks what Gerry Adams's skilled propagandist, Danny Morrison, would call 'Our 1916'.[63]

The battle in the H-blocks grew more violent and dirtier with the passage of time. When prisoners refused to take orders from the warders, they were beaten and such clashes often ended with serious injuries, mostly on the prisoners' side. When they smashed their cell furniture in response, their cells were stripped of all but a mattress and a blanket. Since virtually all the IRA inmates were Catholic and Nationalist and most of the warders were Protestant and Unionist, that gave the confrontations a sharper, sectarian edge. There were, however, some Catholic prison officers in the Maze and they invariably fell into two categories: those who were as violent and hostile as their most Loyalist colleagues, and were thus hated by the prisoners with a special intensity, or those who treated them decently, and these the prisoners would leave alone. As the violence intensified, the IRA outside intervened and began shooting prison staff dead. Those warders regarded as the most violent and bigoted were targeted and Brendan Hughes helped choose them. As the prisoners became better organised, the confrontations with prison staff intensified. The prisoners began a 'no-wash protest' when bathroom visits became an occasion for violence and humiliation. The prisoners' refusal to shower or determination to wash only infrequently meant that they soon stank; their hair became manky, long and tangled and they grew wild straggly beards. Because they refused to leave their cells they had to use the chamber pots in their cells as toilets and confrontations over that led to a new and unprecedented escalation of the protest, one that would define events in the H-blocks during these years almost as much as the later deaths on hunger strike. The decision to begin smearing their cell walls and ceilings with their own excreta was something that had never happened before in the long history of Irish Republican prison protests and it was a disturbing, if stomach-turning harbinger of what was to come.

Nationalist Ireland knew instinctively where this was heading if a resolution was not found. It would conclude in a hunger strike and if any IRA hunger-striker died, the consequences would be evident, very quickly and bloodily, on the streets of Belfast and

Derry and the country roads of Armagh and Tyrone. Hunger striking against a wrongdoer has cultural roots in Irish society that go back to the pre-Christian era but during the Anglo-Irish War of 1919–21 it was made into a political weapon. In 1917, Thomas Ashe, a 1916 veteran, refused to wear a prison uniform or do prison work and died while being force-fed. The Lord Mayor of Cork, Terence MacSwiney, died on hunger strike in Brixton jail in 1920 and, like Ashe's, his death became a rallying call for Republican Ireland. There were more IRA deaths by hunger strike for political status during and after the civil war and again during the Second World War, all of them south of the border where now the jailers wore Irish not British uniforms. In 1972, Billy McKee had fasted for political status and helped win it. If the H-block protesters went on hunger strike they would be following in a long and respected tradition whose impact on Nationalist sentiment throughout the island was bound to be significant.

As the prison protest entered its fourth year, Brendan Hughes and his colleagues began threatening to use this ultimate weapon. Alarmed at what could come next, the Catholic Primate of Ireland, Cardinal Tomas O Fiaich, and the Bishop of Derry, Dr Edward Daly, intervened in the hope of settling the dispute. O Fiaich was from Crossmaglen in South Armagh and like so many in that area he was a Republican – although he opposed the IRA's violence. He had already interceded once before, in July 1978, when he had visited and talked to prisoners in the worst-affected H-blocks. Afterwards he angrily compared what he had seen in the Maze to 'the spectacle of hundreds of homeless people living in the sewer pipes in the slums of Calcutta' and he voiced another heresy which particularly irritated the British and the Unionists: those on the protest were not ordinary prisoners, were not criminals, he declared. O Fiaich's intervention made him an acceptable mediator in Republican eyes and so he and Daly began a dialogue with British prime minister, Margaret Thatcher, and her Northern Ireland Secretary, Humphrey Atkins. Mrs Thatcher had swept to power in 1979 two months after her Shadow Northern Ireland

Secretary Airey Neave had been blown to pieces by an INLA bomb inside the Palace of Westminster and his death seemed to harden her already uncompromising hostility to all things Irish Republican. Not surprisingly, the dialogue with O Fiaich was the start of a stormy and troubled relationship.

When Hughes was taken from court after receiving a five-year sentence for rioting, the hunger strike was two years and more away and there were more immediate matters on his mind, notably the shock of finding himself in the H-blocks. He could have pursued an appeal against his conviction but dropped it when he realised the protest was the sort of issue Gerry Adams could use to build support for the Republican cause outside the jail. There were two blocks on the protest at that point, H3 and H5 and their leaders asked Hughes to become their overall Commander. He agreed but, surprisingly, he argued at first that the prisoners should end their protest, become conforming prisoners, at least in name, but then subvert the prison regime from within. His view was that no prison can run without the collaboration of its inmates, so withholding that co-operation gave the prisoners great power to effect change. When that was rejected, he urged the prisoners to show tactical flexibility, to make compromises that could enhance their leverage and help publicise the situation in the H-blocks, which they did. If the British had intended to punish Hughes by transferring him to the H-blocks they had certainly succeeded; but they also provided the protesting prisoners with a new, energetic leader.

*. . . that afternoon after coming out of the courthouse we were put into a van and brought to the H-blocks. I was first stripped naked and then thrown into a cell . . . I had been in communication with the people in the H-blocks, but I had no idea really what it was like and what they were going through until I got there. My first impression was that it was so clean, so organised and the screws were so much in control, so arrogant and cocky . . . [you could tell] by their appearance and by their strutting that they were in charge now. This was a different situation; we were no longer POWs, we were*

*naked criminals who were going to be treated as such. It actually did come as a shock to me [that I had been sent to the H-blocks]. We did not consider it and hadn't talked about it until that morning when Oliver Kelly\* arrived at the courthouse and warned us that . . . they could throw us into the H-blocks. It was only then that it struck me that this was a possibility. The screws didn't say a word [about] where we were going. It was only when we were driven into the H-blocks [section] that we realised we had lost our status. So . . . obviously it was a shock to the system . . . Here I was that morning being called 'Mr Hughes' or 'O/C', now being called '704 Hughes' and dumped into a cell. The cell was Tom McFeely's.† He was O/C of that particular block. I believe they put me in that cell because Tom McFeely was a very, very strong character and . . . I think they expected conflict between myself and Tom. He actually wasn't there at the time . . . he was on the boards for hitting one of the screws. But after a few days Tom arrived back into his cell . . . and we talked. I had put an appeal against the five-year sentence but after a week [in the H-blocks], I dropped it. And I think the reason was because so many people believed that I had all the answers. Obviously I didn't. I was as frightened and confused as anybody else. But I knew what was taking place on the outside [Adams leading a takeover of the IRA] . . . so I dropped the appeal and decided that the protest had to be escalated . . . something had to be done. My first suggestion to Tom and the others was that we put on the prison gear [clothes] and go into the system to destroy it from within. That was rejected almost out of hand by the prisoners. They had been there for over two years and they just couldn't face that – it was OK me coming in, clean-shaven and not having been there as long. These people had become . . . entrenched in the protest, but as far as I could see the protest wasn't going anywhere. The screws were quite*

---

\* A criminal solicitor and former internee; Oliver Kelly's family included founders of the Provisional IRA. He died in 2009.
† From Dungiven in County Derry, Tom McFeely was one of the seven prisoners who went on the first hunger strike, in October 1980. He is now the owner of a successful construction business.

*capable of containing and handling it as it was. People on the out-
side really had no idea. I mean, I was a couple of hundred yards
away from the H-blocks and I had no idea of the conditions that the
men were in. At that time we were not taking visits, so there was
little or no communication with the outside. To take a visit you had
to leave your cell, go up to a small cell at the top of the wing, put on
the prison uniform and go through the taunts and abuse handed
out by the screws. But I believe that it had to be done. We had a
general agreement on the escalation of the protest, but we had no
idea where it was going to finish . . .*

*When I became O/C I suggested that . . . the two blocks had to be
co-ordinated in some way, that there was no sense in H5 and H3
going separate ways. So the agreement was . . . an O/C of H5 and
an O/C of H3 and I would be the overall O/C, similar to the way
the structures were in the cages – a Camp O/C and then you had
the Cage O/Cs. We began . . . organising and collaborating with
each other to get some sort of coherent strategy going. That was
quite easy . . . Tom McFeely was O/C of H5 and was quite agree-
able to this; in fact he was one of those who asked me to become
O/C and Joe Barnes was O/C of H3 . . . The idea was to co-ordinate
and to escalate the protest – to get word out to the outside, to get
a propaganda machine going within the prison and find ways of
smuggling stuff out, smuggling stuff in. When I say 'stuff', I'm
talking about pens, cigarette papers and things to write on. I asked
people to start taking visits. Bobby Sands was in the next cell to
myself and Tom McFeely. Bobby was a prolific writer . . . and was
made PRO [Public Relations Officer] of H5 and some time later of
the two blocks . . . He was Camp PRO in a sense. And we began to
write notes. Bobby did most of it; I would give him ideas and tell
him, 'Put some meat on that.' He would have been the most prolific
writer in the blocks even at that time. So we began to co-ordinate
between H5 and H3 and we did that by taking visits. People . . .
weren't ordered to take visits, they were asked. Some . . . just refused
to come out of the cells, people like Big 'Bloot' McDonnell. I had
heard his voice, oh, for months and months and never saw his face,*

*didn't know what he looked like. He was one of those who refused to take any sort of visit or even to come out of his cell to go to Mass . . . We were allowed to go to Mass every Sunday but you had to put the prison trousers on and that was a way of communicating. Another way was through the priests who came into the jail. Some of them would carry communications from one block to another. Another way was to meet on the visits. For instance if we wanted to communicate with H3, the message would be passed on to someone taking a visit . . . Marie Moore\* was one of the principal couriers between ourselves and the Army [IRA] leadership on the outside; at that period she was one of the best couriers. Now going out on the visits, obviously you were searched. At this time we had very little in the cells. You'd a Bible, but no radios, no newspapers; so we had to find ways of getting information in. This was done, again, by taking visits. Now obviously . . . the prison authorities realised what was happening, that we were beginning to organise ourselves, and that two blocks had become co-ordinated. They attempted as much as pos-sible to stop it all, they stepped up the harassment, they stepped up brutality. When you were called for a visit, you left your cell, you went up, you put on the prison uniform and people were told that when they put on the uniform to rip the trousers around the crotch area to allow access to your rear end. Communications were written mostly on cigarette papers and the writing was very, very small. It could be carried in your mouth or up your rectum. This was prior to the dirt strike; this was [at] the stage of getting organised and getting communications going. But the prison administration knew what we were doing and searches were stepped up. I can't actually remember when they brought the mirror search in; I think that was after we had wrecked the cells. This would have been at the end of 1978, early 1979. As time went on we became more organised and more proficient at getting communications in and out. On Sundays, at Mass, we were able to communicate even more. But there was no mixing. People went to Mass in H5 and to a separate Mass in H3,*

\* Former Sinn Fein councillor and Deputy Lord Mayor of Belfast who died in 2009.

*so there could only be communication between ourselves . . . within the one block. And you could see each other and talk on visits as well. Sometimes communications had to be sent out from H5 and then brought back in again to H3 through another visit. As I say the communication system became pretty good.*

While the conflict in the H-blocks was fundamentally about who controlled and defined the prison regime, Hughes was conscious of the big picture. The prison protest could help Gerry Adams rebuild the movement and give it an issue around which Sinn Fein could agitate; this was one reason why he had accepted leadership of the protesting prisoners. But this raised a question about who ran the protest. Traditionally, the prisoners themselves made all the key decisions but during the blanket protest, the needs and agenda of the outside leadership would intrude in important ways.

*I saw the situation in the blocks as a tool to help the leadership on the outside – specifically Gerry – to build up a propaganda machine. The Army [IRA] leadership needed an issue that would help them organise street protests . . . to rebuild the Republican movement on the outside. I was very conscious of that. Myself, Tom [McFeely], Bobby [Sands], who became more and more a central figure, would discuss this aspect with as many people as we could at weekly Mass. The outside did not try to push us at any time to escalate, there was no attempt to do that. If anything we were left to our own devices. They would give advice but they would not encourage anything at all. It was up to us how we would escalate the protest. I was quite conscious of the need to escalate things [and] I was quite conscious that outside could really do with an issue. [But] it was basically left to ourselves in the blocks . . . That was always the case or it was sup-posed to be the case, right through the whole Republican struggle, not just the 1970s, right back till the 1920s. The decisions on the inside were exclusively taken by the prisoners [but] at times it was hypocritical and not true. Even before I left the cages, people knew I was going to be appointed O/C of the blocks. But by and large the* *decisions of the prisoners were theirs to make. But obviously there are contradictions in that because, for instance, during the hunger strikes there was a large input by the leadership on the outside. Another example were the five demands.\* I had nothing to do with them. They came from the outside . . . I was a bit concerned about this because . . . we had been demanding political status or special-category status. The outside came up with the so-called five demands, without any great input from the prisoners themselves. Danny Morrison was sent into the prison on a visit to explain the five demands to me . . . [They were formulated as] humanitarian demands that no one could really object to, whereas they could object to political status. The British government would find it easier to implement the five demands rather than give in to political status. It was an attempt to lessen problems for the British government . . . But as I say, we did not devise them. I think probably Gerry [played a big part], him and probably Danny Morrison. I don't even know, that's how much input I had into it; I can't say with any great certainty who came up with the so-called five demands, but certainly it didn't come from within the prison.*

The opportunity that Brendan Hughes had been seeking to intensify the protest came in March 1978, with increasingly violent confrontations between prison officers and IRA protesters in the bathrooms and showers of the blocks. It was a short journey from there to the dirty protest.

*. . . you were allowed one shower a week. And it was at the discretion of whichever screw was on [duty] at the time whether you got a shower or whether you didn't get a shower. And going to the showers was an ordeal in itself because you had to go through the humiliation and the snide remarks. And often with a lot of the younger ones there was brutality and beatings and slappings. And we made a*

* Announced the 1980, the five demands were: the right to wear their own clothes; the right to abstain from penal labour; the right to free association; the right to educational and recreational facilities; restoration of lost remission as a result of the protest.

*decision to stop taking showers. So the order was given . . . From my point of view, it was a tactical move. This was the first attempt to escalate the protest. So that was the beginning of the no-wash protest. The reaction from the prison authorities was to bring in basins of water every morning and [this was done by] orderlies, or 'ordinary decent criminals' who . . . got bonuses for this work: extra cigarettes and tobacco and . . . more food. And these people would come round every morning. The door would open and a small basin of water would be thrown in. Often cells were missed. And sometimes empty basins were thrown in so there was no water to wash with. So the order was given to smash the basins and stop washing altogether. By not going out to take showers that meant you did not get out to go to the toilet. So the wastage, the excreta and the urine built up in the small chamber pots that everyone had. So the prison authorities organised for this to be collected . . . The orderlies would come round with a large bin, they came to the door and you emptied your wastage into it . . . quite often it was thrown back into a cell – they would pick a cell, and the wastage would be dumped into it. So the order was given to stop co-operating with this waste collection.*

By mid-1978 there were over three hundred prisoners on the protest and, to accommodate the growing numbers, a third H-block, H4, was turned over to the protesters. Because of the refusal to slop out, the prisoners threw their waste under the doors and soon the cells became filthy and stinking. When prison staff removed furniture from one wing, prisoners elsewhere smashed their furniture and beds. The furniture was removed from all the protesting cells after that. The warders began dousing cells with heavy disinfectant which caused some prisoners to pass out and so the cell windows were broken to create some ventilation. After the prisoners had started to smear their cells with excreta the authorities sealed the windows, a move ostensibly prompted when the protesters threw other waste outside but whose effect was to intensify the stench inside each cell. The dirty protest that Cardinal O Fiaich would soon compare to the Calcutta slums had begun.

*A lot of this was caused . . . by the reaction of the prison authorities to us becoming organised. But certainly underneath it all was this intent on our part to escalate the whole thing. I had no intention at that time of ending up in the dirty protest. I had no idea where this was going to finish. In fact, before it ended, I got really frightened at the momentum that this had taken on. I mean it was like getting on a bike at the top of a hill. Your intention is to get to the bottom of the hill. But you've no idea what obstacles you're going to meet on the way down. It gained its own momentum to the point . . . that if the screws did something, we reacted to it. We wrecked all the furniture, the beds, the chairs, the tables . . . and we smashed the windows. So we were left with wreckage and this was co-ordinated between the two blocks. The brutality just seemed to be stepped up and stepped up and I was quite often fearful that someone was going to be killed. Once the excreta went up on the walls, I don't think they knew how to handle it. But they found a way of doing it. What they did was to empty one wing and shift us – 'wing shifts' they were called. This took place in the early hours of the morning and they just came in . . . and systematically, cell by cell, a man was trailed out, spread-eagled across a mirror, which lay on the floor, to check the rectum, which was a totally ineffective way of finding contraband that was there, it was . . . degrading; the whole point of it was to degrade. I don't believe they ever found anything by mirror searches. Maybe once or twice, when some, some fool had it hanging out. But largely, when you put something up your rectum it goes up and a mirror isn't going to find it. So it was an attempt to degrade and brutalise. And it was a frightening experience, the mornings of wings searches. And the most frightening bit was to be the very last man. They would take all day sometimes or a good part of the day to shift a wing of men – I think there was maybe fifty men in a wing, forty to fifty men in a wing. You can imagine what it was like – I remember really well the cries and the thumps and you knew exactly what was happening. But for the last two men to be moved across from the dirty wing to the clean wing it was an everlasting day. The last two men had to listen to all this. I had to go through it* *as well. But by and large I escaped most of the brutality because I think . . . they were more careful with me. And so . . . I can't remember ever being beaten. [The prison authorities] accepted that I was who I was . . . but they never ever made any sort of approach to me. I remember —— coming into my cell. I had already gone through the wrecking of Crumlin Road jail with this man. And I knew how devious he was. He was . . . a . . . one of the most brutal people. I don't know how he survived . . . he was a . . . But I remember him coming into the cell and just standing looking at me – the cell was just filthy. I had a blanket round me, with a long, long beard and long hair. And I remember the sarcastic look on his face. Another memory I have, and I'll never forget the man till the day I die, a Labour Party MP called Don Concannon . . . strutting down the wing and cells being opened for him to have a look. And I remember him laughing at the men lying in these cells with blankets round them and filthy. It was another telling memory of that man. I don't know where he is now, I hope he's dead.\**

*Towards the end of 1978 the screws were brutalising prisoners, and they decided to introduce compulsory haircuts and forced washing for all the blanket prisoners . . . I sent an order round at the time telling the prisoners to fight physically and to resist this. Well, the first person who was force-washed and shaved was a guy called Muffles Trainor who was in the cell with me. He went on a visit one day with the long beard, dirty and filthy. And I remember him being a bit late coming back from the visit. And he came back from the visit and he was thrown into the cell, spotlessly clean . . . I remember one particular screw, Girvan, a big fat screw who loved his job, who loved doing this, standing laughing. Muffles was a wee bit slow, and when I say 'slow', he wasn't backward, but he never spoke to me the whole time in the cell. He just lay on his back and shook his head from side to side, and he would laugh to himself. I never knew what he was laughing at. He was that type of a character. He was the*

---

\* Former Prisons Minister Don Concannon died in December 2003, three years before Brendan Hughes.

*least violent type of person, so he was an easy target. And it was a message to me . . . that this was going to happen [everywhere]. But when they started to move in to H3 to do the forced washing and the shavings, myself and Bobby – by this time Tom McFeely had been moved somewhere else, and it was just myself and Bobby. Bobby was always in the next cell, for some reason . . . If he wasn't in the next cell to me, he was very, very close by . . . Whether it was pure luck or . . . intentional, I don't know, but he was always there. So when they started this forced washing we had a long discussion [that lasted] most of the night. They had already force-washed some of the boys in H3. Bobby and I believed that if we didn't find some way of stopping this, then the whole protest would be . . . in major trouble. I knew there were going to be casualties; I knew people were going to get hurt and possibly killed. But I knew if that happened that the prison administration would be in trouble. I knew we were taking a great risk. And it was the second . . . hardest decision that I took during the whole prison situation, to send an order over telling naked men to fight these screws who were coming in with batons, helmets, all the protective gear. It was a really agonising decision to make. But the order was given and I remember the silence. It was shouted over that night to Joe Barnes to fight back. Bobby shouted over the order in Gaelic and there was total disbelief. I don't know if there was any great understanding of the real danger, [that] this whole protest could fall apart. Men were going to be hurt anyway by getting trailed out and thrown into a bath and scrubbed with hard brushes and shaved in a most violent way. So we discussed all this, as I say, for most of the night before the order was sent over . . . it took five or six times for Bobby to shout that over before it sank in. I know how hard it was for people to accept this. And I don't think people really know how hard it was for me to give the order. Me and Bobby . . . certainly discussed the possibility that men could squeaky-boot\**

---

\* 'Squeaky-boot' was prison slang for coming off the protest. Prisoners who agreed to conform were first given a new prison uniform, including boots. The distinctive sound made by new rubber heels making contact with shiny tile floors as the prisoners walked out of the wing told those still on the protest that their number had just been reduced by one.

*the next morning, that they could not face having to fight these people. We discussed all that, and decided that we had to take the chance. I don't believe anyone squeaky-booted the next morning. There were casualties ... two men taken to hospital ... Tom Boy Louden and Martin Hurson.\* I remember it well, the squeals and the shouting the next morning. About 8 a.m., they came in, implemented it and the men resisted. I think it did work ... the screws got so frightened that somebody was going to get killed that they stopped the forced washing. I remember talking to Kevin Lappin afterwards – and Kevin Lappin was the Principal Officer – that was his reasoning ... they, or Stormont was afraid ... that somebody was going to get killed and they stopped the forced washing. So as far as I'm concerned the tactic worked.*

The increasingly violent battles between the prisoners and the warders drew the IRA outside the jail into the conflict, especially as the dirty protest spread and intensified during 1979. Brendan Hughes put pressure on the IRA to target the warders and names were sent out, with prison officers regarded as the most brutal or bigoted at the top of the lists. Warders who were, in the prisoners' words, 'decent' were spared. One prison officer, a Principal Officer called Paddy Joe Kerr, a Catholic warder who was in charge of one of the first H-blocks to go on the protest, was so hated by the prisoners that even four years after the protest ended the IRA singled him out for assassination. Between early 1978, when Brendan Hughes began organising and co-ordinating the blanket protest and December 1980, thirteen prison warders were killed by the IRA, nearly half of all prison officers killed in the Troubles. The most senior was Albert Miles, a Governor at the Maze who was shot dead in his home in North Belfast.

*A Principal Officer called Kevin Lappin was in charge of H5. Paddy Joe Kerr – actually they were two Catholics – was in charge of H3.*

---

\* A member of IRA's East Tyrone Brigade from Cappagh. He died on hunger strike, 13 July 1981.

*Paddy Joe Kerr was a bully, but Lappin was . . . not as aggressive or as brutal. After saying that, Kevin Lappin was not always there. People like Paddy Joe Kerr took great enjoyment in beating prisoners and [he] was quite proud of the fact – he was a major target. The IRA eventually caught up with him coming out of Mass on a Sunday morning and he was shot dead.\* We took great satisfaction out of that . . . there was one less brutal screw who was going to brutalise anybody . . . the type of prison officer that went into the H-blocks at that time were mostly . . . bigots and hated everything that Republicans stood for; not just Republicans, hated everything Catholics stood for. Once the protest was stepped up, I certainly put pressure on the outside to take some action . . . And that entailed the shooting of screws and specifically the shooting of administrators, governors, chief screws – screws who were particularly brutal towards the prisoners. Names were sent out . . . names of the prison governors were sent out . . . people like Kevin Lappin, who were not a bit brutal and found themselves in a situation that they had no control over, I would have tried to protect. I remember sending his name out [so that he wouldn't be harmed]. He came into my cell one time . . . and told me that he was warned by the prison administration to check his car when leaving work, not because of the IRA but because of his own colleagues. People like him were under threat, not from the IRA, but from his own. I don't know how effective it was, but certainly when we got news of [a shooting] we were quite pleased . . . that the people on the outside were taking action on our behalf. [After the shootings began] the half-decent prison officers [were] pulled out of the blocks and you . . . were left with the hard core of bigots and the Catholic and Republican haters . . .*

In early 1979, the prison authorities changed tack. They moved all the senior figures in each wing and block to a separate block, H6, separating them from the rank-and-file IRA prisoners. A tough

---

\* Principal Officer Patrick Kerr was shot dead by the IRA as he left St Patrick's Cathedral, Armagh.

prison officer was put in charge and it seemed the authorities hoped to break the protest by breaking the leaders. They would stay in H6 until September 1979 when they were moved back. During their time there, not long after the move, Hughes and Bobby Sands decided that it was time to use the ultimate weapon, the hunger strike. Hughes sent a 'comm.' out to Gerry Adams telling him of the decision and an alarmed Adams wrote back saying a hunger strike would be suicidal, that Margaret Thatcher would let the prisoners die.

*Well, the time they moved us to H6, the intention was to break up the leadership. They took most of the O/Cs of the wings and of the blocks themselves and transferred them all . . . I think there were twenty, twenty-three, twenty-four people in all. They put what they believed to be one of their strong-arm prison officers, a man called Davy Long, in charge of the block. It was an . . . attempt to break the leadership . . . That was the first time that myself and Bobby . . . spoke about the possibility of a hunger strike . . . The decision for the hunger strike was taken in H6 . . . A communication was sent to the leadership on the outside. A few days later I received a communication back advising us against [it] . . . from Gerry to me [saying] that Thatcher would allow us all to die. [His] recommendation was that we should not go on hunger strike; [it] was a personal letter from Gerry advising me that it would be 'suicidal' – that was the word. It was left to us – we were not ordered not to go on hunger strike, we were not ordered onto it – but strongly advised not to partake in hunger strike at that time. So we took the advice of the leadership . . . You see, no one was arguing for a hunger strike and no one was arguing against a hunger strike . . . There wasn't a great debate amongst us in H6; by and large it was left with myself and Bobby. I can't recall any great arguments against hunger strike apart from Gerry 'Bloot' McDonnell. Bloot was opposed to any form of hunger strike. Obviously there were other people there who would have been opposed . . . but I can't recall anyone voicing that to any great degree. There were obviously other people there with an input into*

*suggestions . . . but it was by and large down to myself and Bobby.*
*Brendan McFarlane, or Bik, at that time was going through a bad*
*time. He was . . . in and out of depressions. There were times when*
*he never spoke to anyone at all. So he didn't have a great input at*
*that stage. It wasn't until later on that Bik came into his own at any*
*sort of leadership level. It became clear that the [prison authorities']*
*tactic of moving the leadership away from the bulk of the prisoners*
*had not worked and we were reintegrated with the rest of the*
*prisoners . . . The talk of hunger strike intensified. We began to*
*discuss it again after we got back into the blocks, where the level of*
*brutality had been stepped up . . .*

When Hughes and Sands were moved back to the H3, a number
of issues were clearer to them: the regime in the blocks had not
softened, quite the reverse; the protesting IRA prisoners were
edging closer to a hunger strike and without a resolution, the
protest was certainly going to end in disaster. The Provisional IRA
and constitutional Nationalists were divided on many matters but
on this there was accord: no one wanted to see a hunger strike. The
Provos were terrified it might fail, while the fear that deaths would
inflame Republican sentiment to the IRA's benefit alarmed the Irish
government, the SDLP and the Catholic Church. The growing possibility of a hunger strike was enough to activate Ireland's senior
Catholic cleric, Cardinal O Fiaich, and with Bishop Eddie Daly
beside him, he was soon talking to Mrs Thatcher and Humphrey
Atkins, her Northern Ireland Secretary, about a settlement that
would bring peace to the jail.

The exercise on the Nationalist side was an early preview of a
central feature of the later peace process: pan-nationalism in action.
Bishop Daly represented the SDLP's view of the world, and therefore Dublin's [the SDLP leader John Hume was a good friend]
while Cardinal O Fiaich was the voice of mainstream Republicanism, albeit of the non-violent sort. To demonstrate its desire for a
negotiated settlement, the IRA agreed to suspend the campaign
against prison officers while the talking went on. Graham Cox, a

thirty-five-year-old prison officer stationed at Magilligan prison in County Derry, who was shot dead on 18 January 1980 as he drove home from work, was the last warder or prison official killed by the IRA during the blanket and dirty protests. O Fiaich and Hughes arranged to keep in touch and the channel they used was a Redempterist priest from Clonard monastery in the heart of West Belfast, Father Alex Reid, a friend and confidant of Gerry Adams and a long-time mediator in intra-Republican disputes.

*There was one person [who] was a line of communication from me and the leadership on the outside, actually me and Gerry, and that was Father Alex Reid. I had a line of communication through him, a straight communication to Gerry. Cardinal O Fiaich visited me in my cell . . . He was deeply affected by what he had seen in the H-blocks – I know that. He was very emotional about the whole thing and very angry . . . but that was the only time we met in the jail . . . my contact with him after that was through Father Reid. He [Reid] would visit me in the cell, I would speak to him after Mass every Sunday and he would visit me on normal clerical visits . . . for a long period the O Fiaich thing looked promising . . . a way for us to get the five demands. I was pretty hopeful through this contact and through Father Reid. Reid would build our hopes up, not for a devious reason, but he would keep trying to persuade me not to go on hunger strike. After the experience in H6 the hunger-strike option was discussed quite openly and I talked about it to Reid. He would tell me, 'There are things happening behind the scenes.' Thus his nickname, 'Behind The Scenes'.*

Hughes had used Father Reid as a courier before this, to carry messages to Gerry Adams and to bring his replies back into the jail. As a result he would sometimes be searched by prison staff. Not all priests were so obliging. Father Denis Faul would smuggle in tobacco and writing materials but drew the line at carrying messages. One of a small group of priests who were regarded by the authorities as pro-IRA, Father Faul would turn against the IRA leadership, and Adams in particular, before the prison protest was over. Father Reid went on to play a crucial enabling role in the later peace process, a role made possible by his relationship with Gerry Adams.

*With Father Faul, initially the relationship was pretty good and I had a fair bit of time for him. He was not involved in any way with O Fiaich except in an advisory way. Obviously he would have met O Fiaich but he was not involved in the contact between myself, Father Reid, the Cardinal and the [IRA] leadership. Faul was very supportive of the blanket protest, right up until the hunger strike and he would bring in pens, sometimes tobacco and news and everybody liked going to the Mass when Faul was there . . . But other than that most of the contact I had with O Fiaich, after the the initial visit, was through Father Reid. He was always trying to give some hope and encouragement. There was a naïveté about him though. I remember him coming into me with his story about the American Embassy [actually Consulate]. Father Reid came in and said to me that he was making progress, that he was at the American Embassy in Queen Street in Belfast and he had met these British and American politicians. He came out of that meeting with great hope; he was bubbling actually when he came to visit me in the cell . . . But when I asked Father Reid who were these people, he told me one of them was the American Consulate [Consul] but he didn't know who the other Americans were. And the British one, I asked him what was his name, and he replied, 'Maurice something' . . . I said, 'Maurice Oldfield?' He says, 'Yeah, that's him, that's him', Maurice Oldfield being the Head of British Intelligence.* Thatcher's man. That was him, the same man. It shows his naïveté . . . and I asked Reid, 'What, what did he ask you? Did he ask you any questions?' And he says, 'Yeah, he asked me about . . . you*

---

* Former head of MI6, the British foreign espionage service and reputedly the model for John Le Carré's Smiley. Margaret Thatcher made him Security Co-ordinator in 1979 with a brief to improve relations between the British Army and the RUC.

*[Hughes], Kevin Hannaway, Gerry Adams.' And what actually was happening was that Reid was getting debriefed by British Intelligence; he was giving background information on us to British Intelligence and he hadn't a clue what he was doing. I've also no doubt that Gerry was informed by Reid of exactly what took place in the American Consulate, because as far back as 1970, Father Reid has been a close associate of Gerry. Anything that was going on at that time [like that], I've no doubt that Gerry knew about it and was informed . . . by Father Reid, even though I was not informed by the leadership, by Gerry or anyone else . . .*

*. . . the Adamses were very involved in Clonard monastery. Gerry's uncle, Liam Hannaway\* and another Adams, Gerry's father's brother, were pillars of Clonard monastery. There was a group of priests in Clonard, headed by Father Reid, who were involved in settling disputes between the Official IRA and the Provisional IRA. If a feud broke out, Clonard monastery would mediate between the two groups. So there was always a connection there between Clonard monastery and the Republican movement . . . and contact between Reid and the leadership of the movement. When Gerry became the leader of Belfast [in 1972] that communication with Clonard monastery was stepped up obviously. Reid was there from a very early stage. He knew every member of the leadership in the movement. So it would have been quite intelligent and proper for British Intelligence to get hold of someone like Reid who knew so much. But I also believe that at any given time, if the leadership had wanted Reid out of the way, he would have been stopped. This could not have happened without the OK of the leadership of the movement, specifically Gerry at that time. He's been there right from the start; he has a great deal of information and knows most of the individuals in the leadership of the movement, and he would be under the sway, I believe, of Gerry.*

---

\* An uncle on Gerry Adams's mother's side, Liam Hannaway was a founding member of the Provisional IRA. His son, Kevin Hannaway, Gerry's cousin, was IRA Adjutant-General at one point.

Behind the scenes, the O Fiaich–Daly initiative was heading for the rocks. The clerics had suggested that a concession on prison clothes could settle the dispute but Thatcher and Atkins responded with smoke and mirrors, offering a promising proposal to allow prisoners to wear 'civilian-style clothes' that on closer inspection was merely the old prison uniform redesigned. It was seen by Nationalists as a piece of bad-faith negotiations by the British, an insult to the Church, and it settled many minds about what sort of prime minister Margaret Thatcher was going to be, certainly as regards Ireland. With the collapse of the talks, a hunger strike seemed unavoidable. But there was another factor at work: violence meted out to the prisoners by the warders had driven the dispute over the edge. At one point Hughes had to order the protesters to stop resisting mirror searches, because those who did were being beaten terribly. Hughes heard that the O Fiaich initiative had failed during a visit with Sinn Fein's publicist, Danny Morrison, and returned to his cell knowing that between events outside and inside the jail, the die had been cast.

*I would have weekly meetings with Reid either on the visits or after Mass and we took a great deal of encouragement from . . . the O Fiaich–Thatcher meetings, until the day Danny Morrison arrived on a visit and I was sent for. I went down and met Danny and he gave me a big King Edward cigar and then told me that Thatcher had slammed the door on O Fiaich; the talks were over and there was nothing. It was a great shock to me and I remember having to walk back from the prison visits, back to the cell. But before that Danny Morrison said, 'What are you going to do now?' and I said, 'We've no choice but to go on hunger strike.' And I asked him to start preparing outside . . .*

*. . . there was always a possibility of a hunger strike, because of the upsurge in brutality after we came back from H6. I knew we had to do something drastic because I didn't believe that the men could take much more of that without [having] some light at the end of the tunnel. People were so demoralised and getting much more so*

*because of the upsurge in brutality and because the actions that the IRA were taking on the outside, assassinating screws, was not having the effect which we believed it could have . . . The tactic of shooting screws did not work, and did not lessen the brutality. Because of this and the breakdown of the O Fiaich talks, that left us with no alternative. People's hopes had been built up because of the O Fiaich talks. The day Danny Morrison said that Thatcher had practically thrown O Fiaich out of the place, I knew then that the only option left was a hunger strike. People were waiting with great expectations of me coming back with good news. I mean, the common phrase at that time was: 'When are the brown bags with our clothes coming in?' It was the loneliest walk back from the visits that I ever had. I knew I was going to have to inform the men that the whole thing had collapsed. But at the same time the decision to have a hunger strike was at least giving some hope that the prison protest would end eventually, because this was the last step we could take. I remember that lonely walk up the prison yard with people looking out [of] windows and waiting for me to bring them the word that it was all over, that the brown bags were coming up behind me. And I didn't have that news to give them. I sat and talked. Bobby was obviously in the next cell to me as usual, and he was straight down at the pipe, talking through the small hole at the heating pipe. And I told him what had happened. He was the first one I told, that there was nothing – and he knew right away that we had no option but to call a hunger strike. And that night I got up to the door and informed the men that the O Fiaich talks had collapsed and we would be preparing for a hunger strike. I remember the total silence in the wing.*

The decision made, Hughes set about organising the hunger strike, informing the other protesting blocks, seeking volunteers, setting a date and negotiating with the other Republican paramilitary group on the protest, the Irish National Liberation Army (INLA), a violent offshoot from the Provos' nemesis, the Official IRA.

*. . . so the decision was taken that day for a hunger strike and communications were sent around the blocks informing the men that a date would be set . . . and names of volunteers were to be sent to myself. I can't actually remember how many names we got. I believe it was over ninety . . . out of three hundred. It was a high figure . . . It was now a matter of sorting out how many men [had volunteered] and who would be picked . . . We went through the list, myself and Bobby, and eliminated anyone with health problems, anyone we believed would be too weak. And then we had to decide how many of us would go. There was some argument between myself and John Nixon who was the O/C of the INLA in the prison. He wanted to have two INLA prisoners on the hunger strike and I was insisting on only one; the rest would be Provisional IRA Volunteers. This argument went on for some time, through comms and through the cell door, in Gaelic. Nixon was in the same wing as me and . . . I remember the argument out the door with him. It got pretty heated at times, but I insisted there would be no more than one. So John Nixon volunteered to be that one. Sean McKenna's name came in as well and I initially ruled out Sean because I believed him to be . . . physically weak. After I eliminated Sean, he tortured me, sending me comms, insisting that he should [be allowed to] go on the hunger strike. I eventually conceded . . . and put his name down . . . We decided we would take one from each county, if possible, to maximise the support in the six counties. People thought we chose seven because of the 1916 Proclamation but the reason for seven men . . . was the six counties plus one INLA Volunteer. The intention was to maximise support in all of the six counties.*

Brendan Hughes and Bobby Sands had, by the way they structured the protest, almost guaranteed that it would run into difficulties, although they didn't realise it at the time. Hunger strikers have to be very determined people but the two men chose candidates based on geo-political considerations rather than their character. On the morning of 27 October 1980 seven prisoners –

Brendan Hughes, Tommy McKearney, Leo Green, Tom McFeely, Sean McKenna and Raymond McCartney from the Provisional IRA and John Nixon, the former O/C of the INLA – refused breakfast. The hunger strike had started. It would last fifty-three days and, for Brendan Hughes, it would end in controversy, deceit, regret and guilt.

*I remember the first day of the hunger strike . . . I was in the cell with Muffles Trainor . . . They left the food at the door of the cell, and I told them, 'I am on hunger strike, as from now.' I remember . . . looking round the cell and saying to myself, ' . . . this is the first of the last days of my life' . . . and feeling pretty isolated and lonely. As time went on they moved us from the cells and put us into a wing that was clean and empty. It became the hospital wing. Every morning they would . . . take our blood pressure, weigh us. We would then pass that information over to Bobby. I had great faith in Bobby at that time. That information would be sent to the outside, you know: 'Tom McFeely lost three pounds today; Brendan Hughes lost six pounds', and so forth . . . I can't remember how many days we were in this hospital wing, when they moved us up to the proper prison hospital. We had separate cells, which they called rooms . . . Again we were taken out every morning, up to the medical room, weighed, blood pressure taken and so forth. And again these details had to be sent out. By and large it was the priests who did that, particularly Father Toner. I would be allowed to visit each of the hunger strikers . . . Later, I needed help and the person who did that was usually Toner or Father Murphy, the two prison chaplains. Sean [McKenna] was the biggest problem. He was the weakest mentally and physically and I paid great attention to him. One day he informed me that he didn't think he could die on hunger strike. It came as a shock to me . . . Obviously he was going through a bad period of doubt.*

*As time went on we had an approach from the British and we all met. By this stage Sean was in a wheelchair, and we met in the prison hospital canteen. I can't recall the civil servant's name but the Governor of the prison was there and the Chief Prison Officer was* *there. They informed us that they were prepared to concede, not political status, not the five demands, but something similar. And we asked for some time to discuss their proposals. I can't remember specifically what the proposals were. But Tom McFeely who was . . . probably one of the most strong-willed of the hunger strikers, informed me that it was something similar to the conditions in Portlaoise that they were offering us.\* So the deal they were offering us became known as the 'Portlaoise-type settlement'. But we decided to hold on for as long as we could, to try and extract more and we insisted that someone from the leadership of the movement on the outside be brought in as a guarantor and Father Faul and someone else as a guarantors. We wanted guarantors. And this was when the brinkmanship started – we were holding out; they were holding out. After this initial meeting, we went back to our cells, Sean was very ill. I told him I would not let him die. And he took me at my word . . .*

Q. *Firstly, is it true to say that this completely limited your nego-tiating room for manoeuvre? And secondly, it also put a man's life directly in your hands, and you couldn't really violate your word after you'd given it because he [McKenna] was in a coma knowing that his life depended on you honouring your word. And, I mean, in your own mind there was no way that you could break your word to him?*

A. *No, I don't believe so.*

Brendan Hughes's promise to Sean McKenna effectively meant the hunger strike was over since McKenna was likely to be the first to approach death. But there were signs that others on the protest were having second thoughts. When McKenna slipped into a coma Hughes kept his word, saved his life and ended the hunger strike. It is evident from his interview that Hughes suspects the British had learned of his exchange with McKenna, possibly via a bug planted

---

\* The regime in Portlaoise jail, the prison used to house Republicans in the South, allowed inmates to wear their own clothes, to associate at times, defined prison work in broad terms and gave implicit recognition to the command structure of Republican groups.

in his cell, and maybe tailored their approach accordingly. Only after the protest had been called off did Hughes learn about a document sent into the jail by British Intelligence which purported to offer a deal.

*But Sean was not the only one – Sean was the weakest . . . So all those weaknesses were there. After Sean asked me, I gave him a guarantee that I would not let him die. A few days later – now, I want to try and get the sequence correct here. Dr [David] Ross – he was the main doctor looking after the hunger strikers – came and informed me that Sean had only hours to live. It's possible they were playing brinkmanship with me at this stage. And it's possible that the cells were bugged and that they picked up what I had said to Sean. And they knew that if Sean went into a deep coma, that I would intervene. And that's exactly what happened. Dr Ross came to me and told me that Sean would die within hours and he wanted permission . . . to take Sean to hospital. And this took place. There was a sudden rush of activity; prison orderlies took Sean on a stretcher up the wing. I was standing in the wing with Father Toner, Father Reid and Dr Ross . . . and I shouted up after Dr Ross, 'Feed him.' I had no guarantee at that point that anything was going to come from the British, no guarantee whatsoever. We all knew that they had offered us this deal but we had no guarantee that the deal would go through. We only had their word for it. The hunger strike was called off before the British document arrived. It was only later that night, I think; it was very late at night that Father Meagher\* and Bobby [Sands] arrived at my cell with the document.*

Q. *So is it fair to say that the hunger strike then did not end as a result of the document but the hunger strike ended prior to the document and it was in many respects the humanitarian decision on your part – you were bound by your word?*

A. *Yeah.*

---

\* A Redemptorist colleague of Father Alex Reid.

Q. *In many senses, I mean, it ended not because you sensed political victory but as a need to save Sean McKenna's life?*

A. *Yeah, that would be true, even though we had a promise, which was eventually boiled down to nothing, of this Portlaoise-type agreement. That night, as I say, when Meagher and Bobby arrived with this document, obviously this was taking place when we were still on hunger strike. But I didn't know that a meeting had been arranged at the airport, that Father Meagher was to go to the airport and a man would approach him wearing a red carnation in his coat. That's the only information Meagher had. He duly did that, went to the airport, picked up the document, picked up Bobby and came to my cell with it. Obviously I could not read it at the time. Father Meagher was jubilant; Bobby was cautious. And I asked Meagher and Bobby what did they think: was there a settlement there? And they both agreed that there was, but it would need further clarification and more work done on it. We were obviously jubilant as well because we believed that we had secured a solution to the hunger strike. I then went round and informed all the boys.*

*I made the decision to take Sean off the hunger strike, thus taking everyone else off because I knew that the hunger strike was going to collapse anyway . . . There were people on the hunger strike, I believed this at the time, I don't know how much truth was in it, who were waiting for Sean to die, knowing that then the hunger strike would be called off . . . I had seen the weaknesses in certain people. And I'm sure Bobby had sensed it as well.*

*I remember meeting Sean [McKenna] some time later and Sean didn't come out of it unscarred . . . He was brain damaged, and his eyesight was badly damaged. I remember him saying to me a few years ago, when I met him in Dundalk, 'Fuck you, Dark, you should have let me die.' I remember being really taken aback by that. It was just an example of the type of stuff that the man is still going through today. And I've since heard – I don't know whether there's much truth in it – he is now suffering from throat cancer.\**

* Sean McKenna died in December 2008.

240

The IRA and Sinn Fein leadership outside the prison pretended that the hunger strike had ended in victory while *faux* negotiations took place between the prison authorities and Bobby Sands, Hughes's replacement as Prison Commander, aimed at implementing the British document brought to Brendan Hughes after he had ended the protest. The authorised version of the first hunger strike, the version put forward by Sinn Fein then and ever since, has the British reneging on the document during these talks. The hunger strikers won, in other words, but perfidious Albion lied and deceived, as she always did. In his interviews with Boston College, Hughes called the Sinn Fein version a 'lie'; the hunger strike, he declared, was a failure. Most Provo supporters at the time seemed to side with Hughes. When the Sinn Fein leadership in Belfast announced a victory parade through West Belfast to celebrate the hunger strikers' triumph, so few people turned out it was an embarrassment.

*I remember feeling embarrassed at the whole thing taking place outside . . . I had no control over anything any more. People on the outside and Bobby were . . . dictating the line. It was largely taken out of my hands . . . I mean, the first hunger strike was a failure. We did not win our demands and the lie was perpetrated. It's happened twice in my life. I remember when the [1994] ceasefire was called the procession of cars going round West Belfast, bumping horns, 'Victory, victory, victory', and I knew damn well there was no victory there . . . So, as I say, that was the end of my leadership in the prison. [Ending the hunger strike] was the last decision I had to make. At that stage I had come out of the prison hospital . . . back to the prison cell that I had left, and I was totally and utterly demoralised, full of feelings of guilt, and thinking, 'Should I have let Sean die? It was murderous. I remember one time tensing myself up, pushing to try and stop my heart; I was suicidal. I had a constant clear image of having a gun and just blowing my head off. That went on for a long, long time after the hunger strike, and especially during the second hunger strike when men began to die. I mean, it was the worst period of my life; it was even worse than the hunger strike itself. It took me years and years to get over it. I still have feelings about it and it's very difficult for me to talk about this. It brings it all back. I have a clear image now of the prison hospital. I've a clear image now of people dying . . . There is a smell when you die; there's a death smell, and it hung over the hospital the whole period during the hunger strike . . . I can smell it sometimes, that stale death smell. I couldn't have spoken like this a few years ago. I wasn't able to do it. I put it out of my head. Even when the book* Ten Men Dead *was written,*[64] *I couldn't read it. I started it, and read one chapter, I think, and put it down. I still haven't read it. And I'm told that it's probably the most authoritative book that's been written on the hunger strikes.*

Brendan Hughes had ended the hunger strike when he was told that Sean McKenna was about to fall into a coma from which he might never recover. The advice came from Dr Ross, a senior prison medical officer, who would himself play a tragic, and until now untold, part in the story of the H-blocks during the terrible summer that followed the first, failed hunger strike. Hughes regarded Ross as the eleventh person to die on the protest.

*. . . a footnote to all this is that myself and Bobby had disagreements about the doctor who was in charge at the time of the hunger strikes. Bobby believed Dr Ross to be a mind-manipulator. I didn't believe that. I believed him to be OK. But it's important to remember that after the second hunger strike, Dr Ross blew himself away with a double-barrelled shotgun. He shot himself in the stomach and then blew his head off. I don't know if it was to do with the hunger strikes [but] I believe it was. And I would sometimes refer to Dr Ross as the eleventh hunger striker, the eleventh victim of the hunger strike. I mean, anybody who could stand by and watch ten men die and not be affected . . . is a very, very ruthless man indeed . . . and I don't believe that Ross was as ruthless as that. Bobby had no time for him, did not trust him, believed him to be, as I say, a mind-wrestler,*

*trying to get inside people's minds. But he used to sit on my bed for so long sometimes I would wish he'd go, [but] he would talk to me about fishing, about the mountains, the rivers and the streams. And for a man to bring in spring water every morning for the hunger strikers because he believed it to be much richer and would help the prisoners was not a ruthless man. That's what he did, every morning he brought spring water in instead of the tap water that we had. And you know during a hunger strike it's awful to drink salt and water. And I remember throwing it up, many's a time throwing it up. But you had to try . . . the memory of that salt water and the sickness and . . . and the smell and watching your flesh. I mean, the body is a fantastic machine – it'll eat off all the fat tissue first and then it starts eating away at the muscle to keep your brain alive. When that goes, all that's left is your brain, and it starts to go as well. And that's when the brain damage sets in. Your body needs glucose, and the last supply of glucose is in your brain.*

The British document handed to Father Meagher at Belfast airport by a mysterious courier from the British government and then rushed to the hospital wing of the Maze prison may well have contained, within its carefully constructed ambiguity, the seeds of a Portlaoise-type settlement – but if it was there, it didn't exactly jump out of the page. The narrative of what happened next is disputed to this day: did the British renege on a good deal or did Bobby Sands realise that Brendan Hughes and his men had failed and that another hunger strike was inevitable? If it was the latter, as Hughes himself believed, then the days and weeks following 18 December 1980 were spent by Sands and his fellow inmates creating the conditions in which a second hunger strike would seem like a justifiable response to British double-dealing.

Whatever the truth, the second hunger strike commenced on 1 March 1981 with Bobby Sands leading it alone. The first hunger strike suffered from a structural weakness that proved disastrous and that mistake would not be repeated the second time round. The flaw in the first protest was that the seven prisoners had all started their fast on the same day but since they would not deteriorate at the same rate, one of their number would approach death before the others. The healthier hunger strikers would then have to decide whether their failing comrade should live or die, and the likelihood that they would intervene was always going to be high.

The second hunger strike, by contrast, was a staggered and weighted affair. First Bobby Sands began fasting, then some time later Francis Hughes, followed after another short interval by Raymond McCreesh and Patsy O'Hara, and so on. Not only was the sense of interdependence undermined by this arrangement but very soon the pressure would all be the other way, not to end the protest but to stay on it, even to death. The die had been cast with Sands's decision to lead the fast alone. No other prisoner would hold Sands's life in his hands as he approached the end, while the pressure on Sands to expiate the failure of the first hunger strike by sacrificing his own life was huge. Only a concession by Margaret Thatcher could stop that happening, and it didn't come. Those following Sands carried the weight of his dead body on their shoulders. To end their own protest would be a betrayal of his death and as the toll in the Maze increased, that burden grew exponentially heavier. Sands's death was virtually unavoidable once the hunger strike began, as he himself must have known. It is this very Republican and Catholic quality of self-sacrifice that made Bobby Sands's death so special and transformed him into such an iconic figure for the Provos.

Sands died on 5 May 1981 after sixty-six days without food. Between then and the last week of August 1981, nine more prisoners followed him to an early grave. Outside the jail, sixty-two people, civilians, policemen and British soldiers, died in the riots and violence that accompanied the procession of coffins from the Maze. All this would have been enough to mark out the hunger strikes as a seminal moment in the history of the Troubles. But the protest was significant for another reason. It represented the fork in the road for the Provisional movement, a moment when its leaders

were presented with a political alternative to the IRA's violence –
and it happened entirely fortuitously. The Independent Republican MP for Fermanagh–South Tyrone, ex-IRA man Frank Maguire,
died suddenly, leaving the seat open. After some tense toing and
froing, the way was cleared for Bobby Sands to stand as the sole
Nationalist candidate in the resulting by-election and he won quite
easily, against conventional expectation.

Sands's election to the British House of Commons transformed
the IRA hunger strikes into an international media event and
greatly intensified the pressure on Margaret Thatcher to end the
protest peacefully and without further loss of life. But his victory
in Fermanagh–South Tyrone had greater consequences for Sinn
Fein and its soon-to-be leader, Gerry Adams. The Provo leadership
had been mulling over the idea of standing for elections for some
time, weighing up the likely opposition there might be internally.
Sands's triumph in Fermanagh–South Tyrone provided a risk-free
opportunity to adopt the strategy. An article in *Republican News*
under the Adams byline, 'Brownie', in April 1980, long before even
the first hunger strike, gave a glimpse of the thinking at the time.
Under the cover of challenging conventional and simplistic IRA
notions about how British withdrawal would happen, the author –
whose famous Long Kesh nom de plume gave the article huge
authority – argued for 'a strong political movement' to supplement
the IRA's armed struggle and said that the aim of establishing a
socialist republic 'is only viable from a Republican position if
those representing such a radical Republican Movement . . . secure
majority support in government'.[65] If the desire to enter the electoral arena and to develop into a more conventional political party
was at this stage embryonic, then the hunger strikes functioned as
a fast-acting growth hormone. Sands's election had broken the
taboo against standing in elections, which had been a defining part
of who the Provos were since 1969. In June 1981, the Irish general
election was held and H-block candidates won two seats in the
Dublin parliament, causing a change in government. A month later,
in August, Sands's election agent, Owen Carron, won the second

Fermanagh–South Tyrone by-election and by that November, Sinn
Fein had formally embraced electoral politics as part of its overall
strategy. The era of the Armalite and ballot box had dawned but
rather than the two working in harmony, it was not long before the
IRA violence was getting in the way of electoral success. This
fundamental contradiction could be resolved only by either the
Armalite or the ballot box prevailing. The rest is history.

Brendan Hughes's memory of the weeks and months after the
first hunger strike ended, as he admitted to Boston College's inter-
viewer, are hazy and indistinct, a possible reflection of the emotional turmoil he went through at that time. Of one thing, however,
he was absolutely clear and that was his opposition to the second
hunger strike. As the protest continued and more bodies were
carried out of the jail, his opposition intensified in proportion to the
guilt he felt for not having died himself on the first fast. He argued
with the new Prison Commander, Brendan 'Bik' McFarlane, urging
him to end it, but to no avail. In the end Hughes concluded that
McFarlane kept the hunger strike going because the IRA leadership
wished it so.

*. . . the first hunger strike ended with the situation . . . unresolved.
Myself and Bobby had meetings afterwards and Bobby indicated to
me that he was going to go on another hunger strike. I opposed him,
I disagreed with him at the time, agreeing with him [only] that the
first hunger strike had not resolved the situation; that we were still
in a rather severe situation within the H-blocks. But Bobby was the
person in charge. I know for a fact that my memory was messed up
. . . I don't know why . . . but certainly my recollections of that
period are a bit fuzzy. I have a slight memory of John Hume [the
SDLP leader] visiting me in the prison hospital, and I don't know if
that actually happened . . . I went back to H6 and I had this vision
about [being] back to square one . . . I remember feeling a lot worse
then than I did even on the hunger strike because I was back into
the situation that I had left months before, hoping to come back to
a resolved situation and here we were going back onto the treadmill*

*again – only this time me being a passenger or an observer and Bobby taking the lead role.*

*I had advocated . . . from a very early stage . . . and I advocated it again to Bobby in the prison hospital, that if the situation was not resolved then . . . we could go into the system and bring about the destruction . . . of the structure that they were imposing on us by participating in the prison regime, which we had done before. We had done it in Crumlin Road jail . . . A hunger strike was always seen to be the very, very last resort. Now after the first hunger strike, that, that's what I was advocating, that we go into the prison, into the system, and sabotage as much as possible and bring about a situation where the screws could not control us, which eventually is what we did. We went into the prison system and just sabotaged all round us. This is after ten men had died, but . . . I was advocating at the end of the first hunger strike that we should go in even without our own clothes, that we should go in and wear the prison uniform . . . I was advocating that rather than embark upon another hunger strike . . . We had something like three hundred men . . . and no prison can operate without the co-operation of the prisoners. The prison regime has to find some ways of keeping the prisoners content. If three hundred men went into a system refusing to co-operate with that system, that system will inevitably fall apart. We had tried the hunger strike and it failed. Bobby was insistent . . . And after Bobby died, I openly opposed the continuation of the hunger strike. When Brendan McFarlane was in charge, I remember standing in the canteen beside the hotplate, advocating to Bik to call the thing off, that enough people had died. And I remember Bik being in turmoil. He was the person in charge, he was the person that had to make the decisions. I met him at Mass on Sundays . . . There was no shouting out the doors about ending the hunger strikes or anything like that, it was done privately, I did it privately . . . Richard O'Rawe, who now tells me that he is writing a book about the period,\* also*

---

\* Richard O'Rawe's controversial and revealing memoir of the hunger strike, *Blanketmen*, was published in 2005, some four years after this interview.

advocated ending it. At least he tells me that. But outside of that
I don't know of anyone else who was . . . as well. I was an observer.
I was just another number, whereas up until this period I was the
person who was . . . in some sort of position of influence. This time
I was totally out of my depth in that I had no . . . input into the
decisions that were being taken.

I disagreed with the continuation of the hunger strike. I did not
know what was going on in the minds of the people who were allowing this to go on. And yet I was still a passenger on this moving train
that was slowly killing people. I sensed that . . . one person in particular was pushing Bik (and that) was ———. I always thought that
this man was in the background, stirring the pot . . . but not prepared
to step into the pot . . . And remember this, that Bik was, during the
whole blanket period, going through periods of depression and here
we had Bik in the position where he could have ended . . . the hunger
strike there and then. I do believe that Bik felt really restrained by
the powers that be on the outside, by the IRA leadership . . . I
believed the IRA leadership . . . should have and could have done
a lot more to ensure that people did not die . . . And I think Bik felt
that outside did not want him to do that. I can't speak for Bik or
what was going through Bik's mind at the period, but I believe he
felt really restricted on what decisions he could make. And no one
on the outside was giving him any sort of advice to call the thing off,
even though most of the prisoners by this stage were getting disillusioned. Even though there were still plenty of volunteers prepared
to go on the hunger strike, I think most men were getting to the
position where they felt enough was enough.

The feeling of utter futility that I had came after Bobby died. I
mean, you had to remember that I disagreed with the second hunger
strike in the first place and I had been quietly advocating the calling
off of the hunger strike after Bobby died. By the time it got to Joe
McDonnell* dying, I was openly opposed to the continuation of the
hunger strike and I think it became clear to most prisoners in the

* The fifth hunger striker to die, on 8 July 1981 after sixty-one days without food.

248

*jail. I remember feeling really, really guilty . . . talking to Francis Hughes\* before he went on hunger strike. Francis came over and gave me a hug and told me that I shouldn't feel bad about it [the way the first hunger strike ended], and that he had no reservations, no objections to me . . . He was obviously quite prepared to do what he was doing. And I felt . . . 'What can I say here?' And I didn't say anything to him . . . You don't say to a person who is just about to embark on a hunger strike, 'I think you're wrong' . . . I sometimes regret . . . my not saying that even though I did say it to Bik. But you don't say it to a man who is walking to his death. And besides that . . . I was disillusioned and embarrassed . . . Here I was alive, and here was another man . . . walking onto the treadmill I had just left . . . The job was only half done and here were these people like Francis Hughes and Bobby going on to finish the job that I had failed to do. So there were these feelings of being like an outsider. Here were men I'd been with for years, you know, on the blanket and coming through things like that and I felt like an outsider among them . . . I never finished off the job that I set out to achieve and these people were going to finish it for me. So . . . it was as simple as that, I felt guilty. And I continued feeling that way for many, many years afterwards . . . I found it very, very hard to live with myself because I felt that possibly I should have been dead rather than the other ten men.*

In his interviews with Boston College, Brendan Hughes touched upon some of the most controversial, sensitive yet recurring questions that arise out of the 1981 hunger strikes. Why did they last so long? Were any of the deaths needless? Why didn't the IRA leadership step in and stop the conveyor belt when it became clear that the campaign for political status could not be advanced by further loss of life? Was there an ulterior motive for keeping the protest alive? At the start of it all, the IRA leadership, including Gerry Adams, had made their attitude crystal clear. Fearing a devastating

---

\* The second hunger striker to die, on 12 May 1981 after fifty-nine days.

defeat, they had declared against the tactic of hunger striking, while Adams had gone so far as to describe plans for the first fast as 'suicidal'. The second hunger strike risked being a bigger setback than the first, if only because failure would see the Republican struggle staggering from the second of two knockout blows delivered within months of each other. Victory or defeat hung in the balance. Shouldn't the leadership therefore have intervened to alleviate the damage? And if not, why not? Hughes's answer is a controversial one: the hunger strike was kept going for political advantage, he claimed, specifically to help build up Sinn Fein as a political and electoral force.

*I know for a fact that there were people on the outside, people like Ivor Bell\* who were totally opposed to the second hunger strike and I know people like Ivor . . . pushed from his own position to stop the hunger strike taking place. So if the leadership – and I believe they had a responsibility even though we have this old tradition of not interfering with . . . the prisoners' decisions . . . I believe in this particular position where men were dying off . . . I think, morally, that the leadership on the outside should have intervened . . . This is an army; we were all volunteers in this army; the leadership had direct responsibility over these men. And I think they betrayed to a large extent the comradeship that was there and they eventually allowed people like Father Faul and families to make their own decisions of ending or stopping their sons, husbands from dying. I remember talking to my sister afterwards and she informed me that if I had gone into a coma, she would not have let me die. So the pressure that was put on the relatives, like Bobby Sands's mother and all the rest of the sisters and wives, I believe was totally unfair and unjust and a total disregarding of the responsibility that the leadership had. [It was] cowardly in many ways as well to allow mothers and sisters and fathers to make these decisions . . . allowing*

---

\* Ivor Bell was on the Army Council at this time and succeeded Martin McGuinness as Chief of Staff the following year.

*that to happen was a total disregard of the responsibility that they had to these people.*

Q. *Would the prisoners have ended the hunger strike, in your view, had the leadership ordered them to?*

A. *Yes. Yes.*

Q. *You do not think that the prisoners would have rebelled?*

A. *I don't believe so, I don't believe so. Maybe at an early stage of the hunger strike the prisoners might have . . . rebelled. But I think the prisoners had enough responsibility and enough dedication . . . to the leadership and to the Army [IRA] that I believe the order would have been taken . . . just like there were people during the blanket [protest] who refused to leave their cells even to go to Mass, or for a visit, certainly there would have been people who would have [protested] . . . but I think as time went on and more men died, I think the order from outside would have been accepted, I do believe it. I mean I was certainly advocating that the hunger strike be called off and I . . . would have stood up and accepted that.*

Q. *In your conversations with Ivor Bell, who was a senior figure in the IRA leadership at the time on the outside, in your later conversations with him in relation to the hunger strike, did he give you any indication of the type of opposition that he met within the leadership to his suggestion that the leadership should in fact intervene and call it to an end, bring it to a halt?*

A. *As far as I can make out, Ivor was a lone voice in his opposition to it. I mean, Gerry Adams is a powerful figure within the Republican leadership and what Gerry says normally goes. And possibly at that time Ivor Bell would have been the only person that would have been strong enough to stand up against Gerry . . .*

Q. *Do you think Gerry himself had any particular reason for not wanting to intervene?*

A. *I've always suspected that . . . there were more reasons than would appear for allowing the hunger strike to go on for so long, political reasons, ambitious reasons . . . And I have heard some stories which I cannot confirm . . . where people were ignored, parents were ignored, mothers were ignored when they went to the leadership and asked the leadership to order an end to the hunger strike. I have heard stories that the leadership ignored these requests, which leads you to suspect that there were other reasons rather than the five demands . . . The five demands were no big deal. We could have survived without the five demands; we could have continued resisting the prison regime without the five demands. The five demands were something that were developed on the outside, they didn't come from the prisoners . . . So there was always that suspicion that there was a lot more to this than just prisoners' demands. I mean, not one death was worth those five demands, not one death, never mind ten deaths. The regime and the conditions that the prisoners had come through over the years did not deserve one death. So I believe that . . . from outside's point of view [there were] purely . . . political reasons to keep the thing going.*

Q. *Is there a possibility that the leadership wanted to keep it going for the purpose of building a political party?*

A. *I believe so . . . that's the point I'm trying to make. I believe that was the reason why the leadership on the outside did not intervene, because of the street protests that were taking place, because of the political party that Sinn Fein was building. I think that was [the] outside's foremost priority – it wasn't the five demands, I don't believe it was the five demands. As I say . . . the five demands wasn't worth one death.*

Q. *Have you ever discussed the issue with Gerry since release?*

A. *Not in any, any depth. I mean, I talked to him obviously because when I got released from prison I stayed with the man, I stayed in his house . . . but it's been something that I have constantly avoided confronting . . . It's only lately that, that you can get me to even talk about the hunger strikes, never mind analyse ... to try and come up with a reason why it went on for so long. And so if ever I talked to Gerry about it, it was sentimental, it was not investigative, it was not questioning. It happened; I mean, that was the attitude I took because I was a good Republican and ... as the old cliché goes, 'Stay within the army lines, stay within the army lines, don't dissent, don't dissent, stay within the army lines' – I was still of that calibre when I got released from prison. So I didn't question ...*

Q.  *Did Ivor ever give you any indication of any tension between him and Gerry on it or are you surmising from general conversations with Ivor that he was the sole voice of opposition?*

A.  *No, I'm not surmising, I know Ivor was opposed to it because I've spoken to him about it and I know he was opposed to it. He was opposed to the whole direction that this leadership was going, to the point where Ivor was actually sentenced to death by the same leadership for his dissent and for his so-called attempt to dislodge the leadership ... I'm not suggesting that Ivor's [subsequent] opposition to the leadership was over the hunger strike, no. [But] I know for a fact Ivor was opposed to the hunger strike and he was advocating that the leadership must intervene to end it ...*

## 8

The last hunger striker to die was Michael Devine, a twenty-seven-year old member of the Irish National Liberation Army from Derry whose death on 20 August 1981 after sixty days without food came on the same day that Owen Carron won the Fermanagh–South Tyrone by-election to replace Bobby Sands as the constituency's MP. While more prisoners joined the protest in subsequent days, others were taken off by their families as they neared death. One of the prison's Catholic chaplains, Father Denis Faul, had come to the same conclusion as Brendan Hughes, that the Provo leadership was keeping the hunger strike going for political gain, and he persuaded more and more families to intervene to save the lives of their loved ones. Finally, on 3 October 1981, nearly seven months to the day since Bobby Sands had started his fast, the hunger strike was called off and, three days later, the new Northern Ireland Secretary, James Prior, announced a number of changes in the prison regime. Prisoners would be allowed to wear their own clothes; there would be a measure of free association within the H-blocks; extra visits were granted, and half of the lost remission caused by the protest would be restored. The prisoners had secured the bulk of their demands* but the more lasting consequence came at the end of that month when Sinn Fein's annual ard-fheis at the Mansion House in Dublin backed the idea that all future elections, North and South, should be contested, albeit on an abstentionist basis.

It was a moment of huge change for the Provisionals whose real significance was not properly understood at the time, even intern-

---

* According to former IRA prisoner Richard O'Rawe the same offer from the British or better had been accepted by the prison leadership in July 1981, when just four hunger strikers had died. He claims that the Prison Commander, Brendan McFarlane, changed his mind and rejected the offer on the urging of Gerry Adams.

ally. While sold to the rank and file as a way of expressing and build-ing support for the armed struggle, the effect, and possibly the intention was actually the opposite. Adopting electoralism was the first tentative step in the move away from armed struggle towards politics. Danny Morrison, Brendan Hughes's contact with Gerry Adams and the Provo leadership during the first hunger strike, helped swing the vote by asking delegates at the October 1981 ard-fheis two questions that also gave the new strategy a name: 'Who here really believes we can win the war through the ballot box? But will anyone here object if, with a ballot paper in one hand and the Armalite in the other, we take power in Ireland?'[66] But within a few years pressure would grow to drop abstentionism, at first as it affected the Dublin parliament, the Dail, and then to restrain IRA violence for fear of the damage it was causing to Sinn Fein's electoral prospects. The Provos had emerged in 1969 partly in protest at the then IRA leadership's intention to 'go political' but the wheel had turned full circle. From now on, Sinn Fein would stand for election at every opportunity in their own right and not in the guise of hunger strikers or protesting prisoners. The ballot box and Armalite strategy had arrived.

Thanks to Britain's new direct ruler, Sinn Fein did not have long to wait. James Prior was a leading 'wet', or economic centrist, in the British Conservative cabinet, an opponent of the Prime Minister, Margaret Thatcher who, in 1981, was attempting to sell her govern-ment on the buccaneering free-market policies of Milton Fried-man and Friedrich Hayek. Prior's dissent brought him exile to Belfast but the demotion spurred his determination to make his mark there. So he launched his own political initiative, a modest attempt to create a power-sharing administration that might have a better chance of survival than Sunningdale. Under Prior's plan for so-called 'rolling devolution', power would be transferred to local politicians gradually, in a piecemeal fashion as they demon-strated their readiness and ability to share it with opponents. His plan also called for a new elected assembly based at Stormont and elections were duly held in November 1982. This was Sinn Fein's first electoral outing under the party's own flag and the result shocked the Irish and British political establishments. The party won five seats, 10 per cent of the overall poll and over 40 per cent of the Nationalist vote, a result that demolished the conventional view that the Provisionals' popular support was minimal. Gerry Adams, Martin McGuinness and Danny Morrison, all current or soon-to-be members of the Army Council, were transformed overnight into elected politicians. A year later Gerry Adams won the Westminster seat of West Belfast and the journey towards the peace process was under way. That year the last of the old guard was seen off when Adams succeeded Ruairi O Bradaigh as Sinn Fein President. Two years later, the growing rift over the Provos' political and military direction between Adams and his old friend Ivor Bell spilled into open conflict and Bell was court-martialled and dismissed from the IRA. In 1986, Sinn Fein and the IRA both supported an Adams-led proposal to end the party's refusal to take seats in Dail Eireann. That same year, Father Alex Reid began overtures to the Fianna Fail leader and soon-to-be Taoiseach, Charles Haughey, to discuss ideas he and Gerry Adams had developed to end the IRA's armed struggle. Three-way talks between them opened up the next year and soon after, with both the British government and the SDLP leader, John Hume. Gerry Adams had parted company with Brendan Hughes in Long Kesh in 1977, vowing that he was leaving to rebuild support for the Provisionals. That he had certainly done, but not quite in the way Hughes had anticipated.

While all this was happening, Brendan Hughes was still in prison, attempting to come to terms with the new circumstances created by the ending of the protest. Although Prior had given prisoners the right to wear their own clothes, the outside leadership ordered the blanket protest to continue. Faced with the prospect of staying on an increasingly futile protest, Hughes decided to leave the non-conforming H-blocks. He had long advocated joining the prison system in order to undermine it and this was his chance.

By early 1982, a new leadership had taken command of the IRA prisoners from Bik McFarlane. First Sid Walsh, better known as

Seanna Walsh, followed by the team of Bobby Storey and Martin Lynch. The three men represented a new generation of activists who would become known for their utter devotion to the Adams–McGuinness leadership outside the jail. Seanna Walsh would be chosen to read out the IRA's valedictory message in July 2005, announcing the end of armed struggle against Britain. Bobby Storey would become Adams's spymaster and fixer, trusted to carry out sensitive missions such as piecing together the story of the 'disappeared'. He has also been accused, in the British parliament and elsewhere, of having organised some of the IRA's more spectacular operations during the years of the peace process, notably the £26.5 million robbery of the Northern Bank in central Belfast in December 2004.* Lynch, known as 'Duckser', preceded Storey as the IRA's Intelligence Chief and helped Gerry Adams survive a concerted challenge to his leadership by anti-peace-process dissidents a year before the 1998 Good Friday Agreement was signed. Storey and Lynch came into the Maze a year or so after the prison protests had ended and had little in common with prisoners such as Hughes who had gone through years of the blanket and dirty protests. Their leadership style, Hughes complained in his interviews with Boston College, was dictatorial, in sharp contrast to his own: he led by example, he insisted, never asking those under his command to do things he wouldn't do himself.

Hughes and the new prison leadership clashed early on. While the Prior reforms had granted the bulk of the prisoners' demands, the authorities were still planning to integrate Republican and Loyalist prisoners in the H-blocks. Achieving segregation – separation from Loyalists – became the next battleground for IRA inmates. One proposal put forward by the new leadership was to single out elderly Protestant prisoners and give them a beating in an attempt to force the prison authorities to separate the two sets of inmates. When a Protestant inmate was singled out for a beating,

---

* In January 2005, a Unionist MP, David Burnside, named Storey in the House of Commons as the IRA's Director of Intelligence and accused him of organising the Northern Bank raid.

Hughes threatened to intervene physically to defend him; the targeted prisoner had served time in H6 at the same time Hughes was on the blanket protest.

*. . . there was one person in particular, Maxi Maxwell, who [had] actually helped us during the blanket protest. He was a Protestant but he wasn't a bigot, he wasn't a Loyalist, he was [just] a Protestant prisoner. I had concern about people like that being abused just . . . because they were Protestants. Not all Protestants are Loyalists and not all Protestants are involved in sectarian activity. Maxi was not involved in any sectarian activity. He was just a hood. There were people during the blanket protest, Catholics from Republican families, who abused us more than people like Maxi did. There was one guy in particular from the Falls Road, whose brother, an IRA Volunteer, was killed in a premature explosion, who actually went out of his way to abuse us. And, so there was no clear line . . . There was Protestants who helped, and people from Republican families who abused us.*

The very real threat of violence between Republican and Loyalists prisoners eventually persuaded the prison authorities to separate them but before that happened, Hughes struck up an extraordinary relationship with one Loyalist prisoner. Robert 'Basher' Bates was a leading member of one of the most bloodthirsty and violent gangs spawned by the Troubles. Known as 'the Shankill Butchers', the UVF gang terrorised Catholic Belfast in the mid-1970s. Their speciality was to snatch victims from the streets in Catholic districts, take them to garages and the back rooms of bars in Loyalist areas and then torture them for hours, cutting and mutilating them with knives. Others they beat to death in back alleys. Hughes found himself in the same H-block as Bates and discovered they had domestic problems in common. They became so close that Bates actually saved Hughes's life, stopping a UVF plot to kill him.

*Basher Bates . . . was not the leader of the Shankill Butchers, but he was certainly one of them. The Shankill Butchers cut people up, cut women's breasts off, cut men's testicles off and shoved them in their mouths. After I came off the blanket, they put us into a wing with people like that. I wanted to understand what made people [kill like] that because I have no recollection of any Republican ever engaging in that sort of bestiality or brutality . . . We were in a wing together and I was a well-known IRA man. Basher Bates was going through a bad period with his wife, as a lot of prisoners do, you know, jealousy or loneliness or whatever. I happened to bump into him in the wing one day and he mentioned something to me about his wife and at that period I had gone through the same; my wife left me when I was in prison so I had an idea what he was going through. And you have to remember this as well: I mean, I was never sectarian, I was never a bigot. All my life I was brought up and lived with Protestants and ran about with Protestants; I had very few Catholic friends. So I was never a bigot. He mentioned this to me and I said, 'Right, come on, talk about it.' And we had periods at that stage where you could associate freely. We had a conflict going on between Republicans and Loyalists – we wanted segregation but at one time I actually suggested that we shouldn't push for segregation, if we were the organisation that we claimed to be, nonsectarian and trying to bring about a united Ireland that involved everybody. I saw a certain contradiction there. If that's what we stand for, if we're fighting for a united Ireland, Gaelic and free and for Protestant and dissenter, why are we pushing for segregation? This was the frame of mind I was in when I talked to Basher Bates . . . [There was] total opposition [from fellow IRA prisoners] to it. I can't remember any person in favour. As I say I wasn't 100 per cent in favour of it myself. And it may well have been just a weakness in me. But I believed, and I believe to this day . . . that we could have made big differences within the prison; we could have made big differences within Ireland if that idea had been pushed and nurtured . . . And so that was my frame of mind . . . when I talked to Basher Bates . . . I asked him to come to my cell, and he sat and told me about his marriage problems, that he was losing touch with his young daughter. And I remember asking him during the many*

259

*conversations I had with him, trying to find out where the hatred was coming from and how they could cut people up, how they could butcher people. And he told me that he was not by nature a bigot, he was not by nature a butcher, he was not by nature someone who hated people. And I believed him, listening to the guy talking about his family, talking about his background, talking about growing up, and I asked specifically this question: 'How the hell can you cut people up and how the hell can you take some innocent Catholic off the street and kill him?' And he answered: 'Drink, drugs and company.' And he specifically mentioned Lenny Murphy,\* who was the leader of the Shankill Butchers . . . He actually said to me that he wished he had met me years ago. I was just talking about Republicanism and where we came from and how much we had in common and so forth. I wasn't preaching hatred, but hatred had been preached to him all his life. And it's an example to me of how you can turn a human being into a monster. Basher Bates turned into a monster because that was the environment he was brought up in. He wasn't a natural-born killer. I think there were people there who were natural-born killers; Lenny Murphy was one of them . . . at one period the Loyalist leadership in the jail were planning an attempt on my life. And I'm sitting in the cell talking to Basher Bates and his mates are sitting in a cell across from me planning my assassination. Basher Bates heard that they were going to put a home-made bomb under the bed in my cell. I remember the day that it happened, when Basher Bates walked into the middle of the wing in the H-block and shouted to every Loyalist in the wing that if anybody attempted to kill me, they would have to kill him first . . . that's the point I'm trying to make here; I was able to build a bond with one of the Shankill Butchers to the point where he was ready to put his life on the line for me . . .*[†]

\*   \*   \*

\* Shot dead by the IRA in November 1982.
[†] 'Basher' Bates was shot dead in June 1997, eight months after his release from jail, by a member of the rival UDA whose father was killed by Bates in the mid-1970s.

Brendan Hughes was released from the Maze in November 1986, thirteen years after he and Gerry Adams were arrested at a Belfast Brigade staff meeting. The world had changed enormously in that time for the Provisional movement. Adams was into his third year as an MP and Sinn Fein was well established as a political force, albeit mostly in the North. The South was still unfriendly territory while in the North Sinn Fein had hit an electoral ceiling. One way and another, Sinn Fein had mobilised virtually all of its base support by the mid-1980s and any further expansion could come only by persuading SDLP voters to switch over, an unlikely prospect as long as the IRA was killing people. By this stage it was becoming painfully clear to the Sinn Fein leadership that IRA violence was a check on Sinn Fein's growth on both sides of the border, and very soon pressure would grow to put the military wing on a tighter and tighter leash, to avoid operations that could lose Sinn Fein votes. At the same time IRA violence was at a fraction of the level it had been when Hughes was vaulting backyard walls in the Lower Falls. As things stood, the IRA certainly couldn't defeat the British but neither could the British defeat the IRA; a military stalemate had been reached. But while Sinn Fein activists debated the reasons for the party's stalled growth, IRA militarists dreamed of renewed military vigour and success. An embryonic split existed in the Provisional movement in which the Armalite and ballot-box factions found themselves more and more at odds and as these tensions were developing, Sinn Fein leaders worked secretly on a plan to end the war while the IRA plotted to intensify it.

Sinn Fein's political plans were ambitious. Gerry Adams had opened secret peace talks with Father Alex Reid, Cardinal O Fiaich and others in the Catholic Church not long after the 1982 Assembly elections and, when Hughes got out of the Maze, approaches aimed at advancing their ideas, including an IRA cessation, would soon be made to the Fianna Fail leader, Charles Haughey, the SDLP leader John Hume and the British government.[67] Sinn Fein's growing electoral success had given Adams and those around him a political alternative to violence and a route to power. The peace process was about to come into its own but not quite yet. Gerry Adams and the small group of advisers around him had, with one hand, approved an ambitious plan to end the IRA's war while, with the other, and in concert with hardliners on the Army Council, given the go-ahead to import hundreds of tonnes of modern weaponry from Libya which they planned to use to launch a Vietnam War, Tet-style offensive designed to sicken British public opinion and stimulate withdrawal sentiment. By the time of Hughes's release, the first shipments had arrived safely and their cargo been stored away. The last and largest shipment, on board the vessel *Eksund*, was due to sail to Ireland in 1987 and once it arrived the IRA's version of 'Tet' would begin. But the *Eksund* was betrayed, dashing the IRA's military ambitions and leaving the Provisionals little choice but to pursue the surviving option, the peace process. That would all come later. Unaware of any of this when he was released from prison, Brendan Hughes had only one thing on his mind: rejoining the IRA.

*I remember clearly the day I was released. My first thought was I just couldn't believe that I was getting out of that place . . . I had my mind up that I would go back into the IRA . . . I insisted on that, and I went straight to the IRA and reported back the day I got out. I still had faith in the leadership; I still believed that they were going for a thirty-two-county democratic socialist republic. I went straight back and immediately I was put on GHQ staff as Operations Officer.*

Brendan Hughes's domestic situation had changed for the worse during his imprisonment. Because his marriage had disintegrated Hughes had no home to return to when he was released, so Gerry Adams and his wife Colette took him in, giving him a bedroom in their spacious detached home off the Glen Road in West Belfast.

*. . . when I got out of prison I actually lived with [Gerry] in his house in the Glen Road. We had . . . many conversations and again I say that I trusted the man at that time; I trusted his political*

*manoeuvring and his political direction. I saw myself then as more
of a soldier and not a politician . . . [I was] not as naive as I was in
the early 1970s where I would say, 'I'm a soldier, not a politician.' By
and large I saw my strengths [as being] within the Army [the IRA]
and I was pretty well accepted throughout the whole of Ireland with
IRA Volunteers. There were places . . . I could go and sit down with
IRA Volunteers where . . . Gerry could not because some people
believed . . . that Gerry was not really an IRA soldier, that he was
more of a politician. I saw myself [being] in the position where I
could strengthen Gerry's position by being . . . his physical-force arm
within the movement. That's the position I saw myself in. And you
had to remember that we had been fighting the war together for a
good few years and we were very, very close . . .*

*Q. Did you still feel at that time he and the leadership were totally
committed to the prosecution of the armed campaign?*

*A. I did, I did.*

Hughes threw himself back into the IRA and was placed near the
very top of the organisation, a sure indication of Gerry Adams's
friendship and patronage, at least at that time. Given a double brief
in GHQ as Director of Operations and assistant to the Director of
Intelligence, he was to plan and organise IRA activity outside of
Northern Command – which meant, *inter alia,* taking an interest in
IRA activity in England – while helping the Intelligence Chief, Pat
Doherty,* §uncover the British spies who now riddled and weakened the IRA. Doherty's brother Hugh was arrested in London in
1975, a member of the so-called Balcombe Street gang, while he
himself was named in the House of Commons as a member of the
Army Council, along with Gerry Adams and Martin McGuinness.[68]
Hughes soon discovered that distrust of the Sinn Fein element in

---

* Known within the Provos as 'Smiler', Glasgow-born Pat Doherty, whose family hailed from
County Donegal, was elected West Tyrone MP in June 2001. In 2002, Unionist MP David
Burnside named him in the Westminster parliament as a member of the IRA's Army Council.

the IRA – and of the Belfast IRA – was widespread, fuelled by a suspicion, which he later came to share, that the politicians in the Provos were trying to run down the IRA and its war to facilitate the peace process. By the late 1980s there were two types of Provisional Republican leadership figures: military men who distrusted politics and never had any truck with Sinn Fein, and those who rode both horses, balancing their IRA and Sinn Fein careers. Brendan Hughes was instinctively in the first camp and his ear was on the same wavelength as the IRA's militarists. The Provos' soldiers had a sensitive nose for compromise, and were always on the lookout for potential sell-outs. It had been that way in the IRA for as long as the organisation had existed and it was in Hughes's political DNA. The 'disarray' that he found the IRA in after his release, the shabby treatment of Seamus Twomey, the angry words of military men and veterans whom he respected and the havoc caused inside the IRA by informers hardened his suspicions. Steadily, Hughes moved to question and then doubt his old friend Gerry Adams. Ivor Bell had broken with Adams in 1985, a year or more before Hughes's release from the Maze and, by the end of the decade, Brendan Hughes would do the same and for the same reasons. It was the oldest story in the IRA, friends and comrades parting ways over compromise. Michael Collins had Harry Boland. Gerry Adams has Ivor Bell and Brendan Hughes.

*I reported straight back to the IRA and I was sent to Intelligence on the GHQ staff [where] my job was to work with a man called Pat Doherty who was GHQ Director of Intelligence. I was his assistant. My job entailed travelling around the thirty-two counties and going into any particular area I needed or wanted to go into, [as well as] planning particular operations. At that time I didn't know what was going on but there was a rundown taking place within the IRA . . . in many places, especially Cork and Kerry, Pat Doherty was not trusted because he was seen as [one of those] intent on running the IRA down and . . . he was deeply mistrusted by people. I didn't understand where the mistrust was coming from because I had just*

*come out of prison; I didn't have an ear to the ground, and so on
many occasions I defended Pat Doherty – but on many occasions my
defence of him was not accepted. Operations were my thing and . . .
my priority, and I wasn't a great deal into the politics of it. I remember going into Parnell Square, which is Sinn Fein headquarters in
Dublin, and seeing all the activity taking place, but I wasn't actually
part of that . . . Not that I was opposed to political activity – I
believed it was necessary. But I also believed in the war, and I was
primarily an operative. The IRA was in a very bad state; it was in
disarray. I argued on many occasions that operations should not
take place, especially in places like South Armagh, Tyrone and
Donegal; they should be suspended until such time as the Army [the
IRA] was strengthened, reinforced and [made] more disciplined.
But I believe now – I didn't believe then and didn't realise then –
that it was probably being done purposely, that the Army was being
run down purposely.*

*Q. What did you think was the major cause of the Army's weakness
at the time?*

*A. Lack of leadership, lack of discipline, lack of foresight about
where we needed to go. I believed we needed to go to England and
that we would be more effective by attacking England.*

\*   \*   \*

On 8 May 1987, some six months after Brendan Hughes had
rejoined the IRA, the cream of its East Tyrone Brigade was wiped
out in an ambush mounted by the elite British special forces unit,
the SAS. The East Tyrone unit had just blown up the unmanned
police station at Loughgall in County Armagh when the SAS
opened fire on them from hidden positions, riddling the IRA men
with a withering fusilade. When the SAS ceased fire, eight of the
most experienced activists in Tyrone were dead. It was the single
most devastating blow suffered by the IRA in over three decades of
violence and, in the intervening years, recurring questions inside
the Republican community about how and why such a disaster

could have happened have made the Loughgall ambush a constant focus of speculation and suspicion. The bulk of the unit was on the verge of defecting and forming a rival unit when they were killed. Seven or so months earlier, in the autumn of 1986, the IRA and Sinn Fein had separately dropped the rule forbidding members to take seats in the Irish parliament, Dail Eireann. Although Stormont and Westminster remained off limits there was little doubt that the decision was a key moment in the Provisionals' political journey. The move forced out the older generation of IRA leaders, people such as Ruari O Bradaigh and Daithi O Connail who had been clashing with Gerry Adams and his supporters ever since the cease-fire in 1975. The East Tyrone unit was wiped out before they could follow suit. At first the Loughgall ambush was for Brendan Hughes an example of everything that was wrong with the IRA – infiltration by informers along with poor intelligence, planning and training – but, alongside that criticism, a mustardseed of doubt was planted in his mind that the neglect of the IRA had been done deliberately, encouraged by Gerry Adams and his new right-hand man, Martin McGuinness, so as to accelerate the move into politics. He saw evidence for this not just in Loughgall but in the neglect of the vitally important England Department, which organised bombing operations in London, and in the rush to launch the 'Tet' offensive in the face of evidence that the IRA was just not fit for that purpose.

*I don't believe [the Loughgall ambush] was bad luck. I believe there were informers involved there. I also believe that the operation went ahead without the proper intelligence, without proper organisation and without proper training. I remember arguing against operations [like this] going ahead. I sat in a house in Donegal along with Martin McGuinness and the rest of the GHQ staff where they were planning . . . this major upsurge in the campaign; we were going to go in and take over [British] army billets and so forth, major operations involving major weapons. Gaddafi had come on board. Shipments of weapons came in, money came in, all the weapons*

266

*were there, all the money was there. What was lacking was the training but there was this sort of bullish attitude from people like McGuinness to push ahead with these operations. I argued against them because we didn't have the proper training. I had done a tour of the whole six counties, I went round and spoke to most of the operational companies . . . and I believed that [the IRA] wasn't ready for a major push. This meeting took place . . . over a twenty-four-hour period; I mean, we sat well into the night and slept in this house in Donegal, and the next morning as well. We were not ready for those type of operations. We didn't have the intelligence, we didn't have the organisation, we didn't have the discipline. But people wanted to go ahead with it, and one person in particular . . . Martin McGuinness . . . I believed that what we needed to do was to pull as many operators out of the North into the South, retrain them and beef the whole Army [IRA] structure up. The structure was not secure enough for these type of operations to take place [but] it didn't happen; what I was suggesting did not happen.*

*I didn't meet outright opposition [but] a passive type of opposition where I didn't get any encouragement, I just got negative thoughts back . . . there were people like Kevin Mallon\* . . . who agreed with me. But this push seemed to be coming from the top; there were invisible people pushing [for] this, Army Council people like Joe Cahill.*

Q. *Do you ever get the sense that there may have been an attempt by some elements within the leadership to sabotage the whole war by pushing Volunteers into a conflict, a confrontation too early and for which they weren't ready?*

A. *I believed that then and I believe that now; that things were moving so fast, people were coming on board, weapons were coming in, and I think some people got frightened by it. I think people did not want this to happen . . . I think there were other people there*

---

\* Tyrone Republican and IRA member since the 1956–62 campaign when he was convicted of murdering an RUC sergeant.

*who were scared of this escalation . . . I think there were people there who didn't want it to happen. There was the English Brigade, people like —— and the handful of people who ran the English operations. They were burnt out; I met them in Dublin and . . . I argued for them to be pulled out of England . . . and for a new group to be formed. I really believed in the England Department because it could be the most effective . . . [but] there was opposition to that from people, I can't pinpoint . . . I wish I could point the finger at particular people, to say that they planned this or stopped this or discouraged it. I suspect, I know . . . who was behind this . . . I was working with Paddy Doc [Doherty] at the time and people . . . believed that he was the person who was holding back the war. I don't believe it was him in particular, because Paddy Doc wouldn't have had the strength for it.*

Q. *He was somebody else's front man?*

A. *Yes, I believe so. I believe it was probably Adams behind it.*

Q. *Although there's no proof of this?*

A. *No, I have no proof of it, no.*

Q. *Do you think his responsibility at any rate lies in the fact that he made a bad decision and ultimately that bad decision meant that people moved prematurely and in Tyrone, Loughgall, May 1987, eight lost their lives?*

A. *Aha. I believed at the time that it was a mistake. I suspect now because of the situation that we're involved in now, that there might have been intent as well, to bring about a disaster . . .*

Q. *Sabotage?*

A. *Yes. Yes. I believe that there's a possibility of that, [and] that . . . this premature move was intentional . . . you're talking about McGuinness and Adams, who . . . were involved in the decision to go ahead [with the 'Tet' offensive]. I remember [by contrast] the Four Square Laundry. I was one of the those who interrogated*

*Seamy Wright, and we got the rundown on the other people [involved] like Beaky McKee and the rest of the squad . . . involved in the MRF. I wanted to move quickly, to remove these people and to remove the Four Square Laundry and the offices in College Square and so forth. And Adams held me back: 'Sit back, sit back, do more intelligence, do more intelligence.' And we did hold back, and it was the right thing to do . . . I would have moved too quickly, prematurely, and we might have missed some of the people that we eventually did get. When . . . Loughgall and the other operations happened, when I was arguing to hold back, to get more intelligence, to get more training, I was vetoed, which was a contrast to the Four Square Laundry . . .*

Q. *But was Adams at any of these meetings, for example, where McGuinness was advocating a military push?*

A. *Yeah, always.*

Q. *And was he of the same frame of mind?*

A. *He was, yeah. And it was a complete reversal of positions that I found myself in, as I say, from the Four Square Laundry – where I wanted to push ahead right away. I was advocating caution and to take our time. These people wanted to go ahead right away, a total reversal of positions.*

Q. *Do you think there's any merit in the suggestion that the [IRA] leadership, as much as the British, needed certain areas removed, areas that would have been opposed to a ceasefire or a peace process, areas such as Tyrone and South Armagh?*

A. *I suspect that to be the case now; I didn't then. I thought then that it was a mistake, that we had thrown caution to the wind. Now looking at . . . the way things have developed, I suspect that there may well have been a great deal of collusion there, a great deal of conspiring.*

Q. *But it has to be said that it's speculation . . . ?*

A. *It's speculation . . . I don't know. It's because I'm so suspicious of the people in positions of power now that [it] leads me to think that there's a possibility that there was collusion there. I don't know – it may be fair, it may be unfair.*

Hughes's doubts, however, grew slowly and in the months that followed his release from jail his confidence in Gerry Adams remained undimmed and unaffected, as was Adams's support for Hughes. In 1987, he was brought into the inner circle and given a seat on the Army Council, the ultimate expression of the leadership's confidence in him. In retrospect it was the high-water mark in the renewed Adams–Hughes friendship, but from thereon it was mostly downhill.

*. . . I was on the Council, but I wasn't happy being there. I was asked to go to America by Adams because of my profile, because of who I was – 'Darkie' Hughes, ex-hunger striker and all the rest. And I was sent to America . . . and met the Noraid people, who supplied the money. There was one group of people I met in a hotel outside New York and they had a suitcase full of money . . . I had already met small groups of people in New York, in the Bronx area, who were unhappy with the type of people giving the money. They were basically socialists. There was one guy called Kilroy who was a lawyer, who fought cases for Mexican immigrants . . . he was arrested, badly beaten, tortured and dumped across the border. He was one of the people I tied in with in New York, and other younger radical-type people. Kilroy was seen as a socialist, so he was disliked by these people with the briefcase and [they were] suspicious of people like me. I argued Kilroy's case, that the guy was a Republican, he was an Irish Republican, [but] it finished up in an argument in the hotel room. And this particular person who . . . had the briefcase full of money, he said he was taking the money away, and I said, 'OK, go, I don't want your fucking money.' I was there as an Irish Republican. I was there to try and build support among ordinary working-class*

*people. This particular person was not prepared for that and he upped and left with his briefcase full of money . . . I'll give you an example of the type of person that he was. He reckoned that we were not fighting the war properly, that we should be shooting the Queen, anybody who wears a crown on his helmet or anybody that's associated at all with the British regime. And I said to him, 'Do you mean postmen; we shoot postmen?' He says, 'Yes.' I says, 'Right, I'm going back to Belfast in a couple of days, and we'll get another ticket and you come back with me and you shoot the fucking postmen.' That's when he walked out of the room . . . I don't even think he'd ever been in Ireland, never mind Belfast, but he had the money and he was trying to dictate to me how to fight the war. But he held a pretty high position in Noraid. So he came back into the room and I eventually got the money . . . I eventually raised something like a hundred thousand pounds; I'm not sure exactly what the amount was. But I was staying with a group of young people, practising lawyers, sympathetic to the Irish cause. And I used these people; one would have brought ten thousand pounds, another fifteen thousand pounds, whatever, back in, into Ireland . . .*

Q. *Well, what was the money for? Was it for Sinn Fein or was it for the Army [the IRA]?*

A. *Absolutely not for Sinn Fein. I raised this money; I went to meetings with people. I met one particular person in New York who was a millionaire, a Tyrone man [in the pub trade], and I met him in one of his pubs, or one of his restaurants, and I was asking for donations and . . . he asked me was the money going to politics or was it going to the Army. I says, 'Going to the Army; it's for weapons; it's for keeping IRA Volunteers on the streets or in the fields.' And that was the only condition. He gave me the ten thousand dollars.*

Q. *But did the leadership who sent you out agree with this, that it was going to the Army, and it wasn't going to the party?*

A. *Well I never thought for a minute that it was going to the political organisation. I went to America to raise money to buy weapons, to buy explosives, to continue the war.*

*Q. You weren't sent out on a Sinn Fein brief; you were sent out on an Army brief?*

*A. I was sent out on an Army brief. Obviously other people had different ideas, but the money that was sent back, I did not think for one minute that it wasn't going anywhere except towards the Army. I raised the money in America, to prosecute the war, not to prosecute political objectives.*

\*   \*   \*

Sinn Fein's entry into electoral politics after the 1981 hunger strikes was accompanied by persistent allegations from across the political spectrum that Sinn Fein's impressive performance was due in no small measure to an extensive vote-stealing effort. Personation, as the practice is called, has always been and still is a regular feature of elections in Ireland (and wherever the Irish have migrated) and nowhere was it practised with more skill and enthusiasm than in Northern Ireland. While personation was present long before the Troubles, there were unwritten rules that ensured that it never really got out of hand. That all changed, or so it was said, when Sinn Fein started fighting elections in the 1980s and brought a degree of military planning, magnitude and discipline to the effort, which badly tipped the scales.

At first, personation was clearly visible to the electoral authorities, as a Northern Ireland Affairs Committee report on electoral malpractice in 1998 noted: 'The Chief Electoral Officer was shocked by the organised personation which he saw during his visits to polling stations during the two 1981 by-elections in Fermanagh–South Tyrone. Afterwards, he reported his concern to the Secretary of State.'[69] The British then pushed through a legal requirement on the part of voters to provide some form of identification at the polling station. Medical cards turned out to be the most popular document used by voters and soon there were allegations that a small industry existed devoted to forging them. After that, though, the evidence of personation became much harder to find, as that same Westminster Committee admitted: '. . . the allegations have not always been precise. Much of the evidence of fraud is anecdotal and circumstantial. Gossip has not translated into hard evidence. In particular, there is a notable lack of concrete information on the prevalence of voting fraud. As a result, the extent of the problem is hard to define.'[70]

The Provos indignantly denied the charge and countered that the allegations came from rivals and elements opposed to everything Sinn Fein did. On one occasion Gerry Adams was confronted by reporters who had seen what looked like a batch of medical cards in a Sinn Fein caravan parked outside a polling station, but he denied that forged cards were being used to steal votes: 'The allegations are not true. The electoral office has asked the SDLP on numerous occasions to produce evidence and they have not been able to do so. It's the worst sort of negative campaigning.'[71] While one former Sinn Fein official, Willie Carlin, had publicly claimed that a huge voting fraud in Derry had got Martin McGuinness elected to the 1982 Assembly, the value of his claim was devalued by the fact that he had been working secretly for the British at the time.[72] There was a lot of smoke, to be sure, but not much sign of flames.

All of which makes Brendan Hughes's account of his role in Sinn Fein's personation efforts all the more significant. He ran, he told Boston College, the personation campaign for Gerry Adams's first re-election bid to the House of Commons in 1987 and did the same in the 1989 council poll, each time stealing 'massive' numbers of votes. Adams held on to his seat and his success might well have been due to Hughes's efforts since the gap between Adams and his SDLP rival, Joe Hendron, was around the two-thousand-vote mark, close enough to mean that personation could have influenced the outcome. As the years went by the conviction that something needed to be done to clean up elections in Northern Ireland grew and in 2002 legislation was passed obliging voters to produce

b
d

d
VOICES FROM THE GRAVE

photographic identification. But by that time, as Hughes noted wryly, the Sinn Fein boat was sailing the high seas, leaving him and others like him behind.

*. . . I worked on the elections out of Connolly House.\* I was the main person in charge of personation. I organised busloads, carloads; I'd a fleet of taxis at my disposal to bring people to the polling booths . . . I did this right after I got out of prison, during the council elections and the [Westminster] election . . . I hear Unionists complaining about it all the time, [and] they're right, it was massive . . . I was the impersonation master. I did it from my house, from Connolly House, I did it from the Sinn Fein centre on the Falls Road; I had loads of dead people, I had babies' names, I had babies who weren't born, babies who were in the graveyard; they all voted. And that's how we got to the position that we're in now. It was like getting a hundred people to push this boat out; a boat that is stuck in the sand . . . and then the boat sails off, leaving the hundred people behind. That's the way I feel; the boat is away, sailing on the high seas . . . and the poor people that launched the boat [are] left behind sitting in the muck and the dirt and the sand.*

\*    \*    \*

Hughes began to develop concerns, as he put it, about the direction the Provisionals were taking when he saw how Seamus Twomey had been thrown onto the scrap heap by his successors and had died lonely and mostly unvisited in a Dublin hospital despite his lengthy service with the IRA and the career boosts he had given years before to people like Gerry Adams.† The other influence on him was a legendary IRA figure from the 1940s, Harry White, who was a leading participant in the so-called 'Northern' campaign between 1942 and 1944 led by the semi-autonomous Northern Command. When Tom Williams was due to be hanged in September 1942 for killing an RUC officer, White took part in a raid on a British Army base near

\* Sinn Fein headquarters in Andersonstown, West Belfast.
† See p. 110.

Crossmaglen in South Armagh, hoping to capture a British officer
and hang him if Williams was executed. The plan failed when an
RUC patrol came upon the IRA unit and a gun battle ensued. White
and another IRA man, Maurice O'Neill, moved to Donacloney in
Dublin, where they were pursued by the Irish Special Branch. A
detective was shot dead during a raid on their hideout and O'Neill
was captured and later executed, while White escaped but was subsequently arrested and sentenced to death. Sean MacBride, the
lawyer son of the 1916 leader and a former IRA Chief of Staff, managed to get the death sentence commuted to a lengthy jail term.
When the Provisionals were formed, White was an early and
enthusiastic member and, as a devotee of physical-force politics, he
later became something of a sounding board for criticism of the
Adams strategy.

*I started to have concerns when Seamus Twomey was treated the
way he was. People like Harry White began to have doubts. Harry
actually threw Danny Morrison out of his house and Harry White
is his uncle. Harry was a 1940s man. People like Harry began to
become disillusioned. I was going in and out of Harry's house and
Harry was putting up objections to the direction that the war was
taking. Harry was one of the hard men in the IRA. There was one
time at the funeral of Jack McCabe,\* the Gardai tried to stop a
firing party and Harry pulled a weapon and put it to a policeman's
head. So that, that's the sort of person that Harry was. Now, I was
involved, as I say, largely naively involved in the Army structure and
I missed a lot of the things that were going on, politically . . . Harry
didn't. Harry realised what was going on.*

Brendan Hughes's concerns about the IRA's political direction
might have been growing but they were dwarfed by his realisation
that the organisation had been heavily infiltrated by British
Intelligence. He had been appointed to one of the IRA's most

\* IRA Director of Engineering, killed while mixing home-made explosives in his garage in
Swords, County Dublin, 30 December 1971.

important posts, heading up the Security Department, and was charged with running its counter-intelligence operations, designed to uncover and remove British double agents.

*There was a major problem with informants. And one of the jobs that I had taken on was to try and find informers. The Army, the IRA, always had a problem with informers; there were always informers around – low-level informants, high-level informants – but by that stage, by the late 1980s, there was an awful sense of mistrust. Certainly the South Armagh men believed the major problem was in Belfast. I was one of those trusted by the South Armagh people . . . and the South Armagh people did not trust Belfast. They believed there was a major problem in Belfast with informants and what I believe now, looking back, was [that this was about getting to] where we are today . . . people like Gerry Adams, who I had 100 per cent trust in, Martin McGuinness, people of that calibre, were actually directing the movement towards the position they're in now where they've become part of the Establishment. I believe people in places like South Armagh, Kerry, Cork, saw this long before I did; they mistrusted the people at leadership level; they were physical-force people, but they were not stupid people . . . I believe they had detected what was taking place within the movement and that was to establish . . . a constitutional political party.*

When Gerry Adams and Ivor Bell set about reorganising and reviving the IRA after their release from Long Kesh in the late 1970s, the guiding star in their journey was the concept of the 'long war', which brought along with it the necessity for a whole new and systematic way of dealing with British Intelligence's penetration of the IRA's ranks. The 'long war' idea was itself an admission that the violence of the early 1970s could never be repeated. It was also an acknowledgement that British Intelligence had put the IRA on the defensive, and between them the three groups ranged against it – MI5, Military Intelligence and the RUC Special Branch – had a better measure of the IRA than at any point before.

Although it was never explicitly stated, the 'long war' doctrine also seemed to be founded on the hope that if the IRA could survive long enough then something might come along to improve its fortunes in a dramatic way. As it turned out that was not a bad approach, the 1981 hunger strikes being evidence that this is exactly what did happen. But to do all this, the IRA had to pay closer attention to its internal security than ever before. It is an astonishing feature of the IRA's story that for the first decade or so of its existence it had no dedicated section entrusted to countering hostile penetration. Keeping an eye out for treachery was a job performed by Company Intelligence Officers (I/Os) but that was only part of a brief that otherwise devoted more resources to collecting information for targeting purposes. Occasionally, as in the case of the Four Square Laundry operation, an I/O such as Brendan Hughes would hit paydirt, but as Gerry Adams himself admitted, the IRA 'took their eye off the ball' after that success.[73]

By the late 1970s the integrity of the Company structure had been undermined by British penetration, forcing Adams and Bell to propose a cellular structure for the IRA so as to make infiltration more difficult. Inside Long Kesh, Adams and Bell made the debriefing of new internees and sentenced prisoners mandatory. Newcomers to their cages would be closely questioned about their experiences at the hands of RUC interrogators for any clue that they might have been turned. Reports would be smuggled out to the IRA leadership for any necessary follow-up. This was the start of a much more rigorous and organised approach to counter-intelligence. When Adams and Bell had secured control of the IRA, by 1979 or so, this debriefing requirement was extended to every IRA member arrested for questioning by the RUC. To handle this task, the Security Department was established and the hunting of agents became a priority for the IRA. Initially the Department's brief was confined to Belfast but gradually its reach was extended throughout the organisation, making the Security Department a larger and more powerful part of the IRA. As part of this process, the so-called 'Green Book' was drawn up to give IRA recruits lessons in how to resist police interrogation and what the consequences would be if they failed. The manual instructed IRA members to stay silent during questioning, but it became accepted in the IRA that any recruit who had not been 'green-booked', that is who had not been given the chance to read what it said about resisting interrogation, could not be executed for informing. At its peak the Department had a staff of around a dozen and it had sweeping authority to investigate virtually any aspect of the IRA. And like all secret police forces, the Security Department was feared and hated in equal measure by those it kept under watch, not least because its members policed the IRA for signs of dissent.

The Security Department worked a little bit like an electrical junction box in the IRA. So many wires passed through the box, so extensive was the Department's knowledge of activists and operations, that British Intelligence made penetration of this inner sanctum the highest priority, not just because of the information that would come its way but because this could help Intelligence Chiefs protect and advance agents in other parts of the IRA. Not surprisingly therefore, the story of the Security Department is replete with allegations of high-level treachery. At least two former Directors of the Security Department are suspected of having worked for the British over the years. The first to fall under suspicion was a former British special-services soldier, John Joe Magee, who headed the Department for around a decade. The extraordinary aspect of his tenure is that it should never have happened. Magee had been sentenced to death by the IRA in the mid-1970s after it was learned that he had been consorting with two members of the UVF and a number of prostitutes. He and the Loyalists were to be shot dead and the prostitutes given punishment shootings but the operation against them had to be postponed and then it was somehow forgotten. Magee rehabilitated himself and then made his way into IRA Security by joining a bombing team attached to the Second Battalion in Belfast that would later form the core of the new Security Department. During Magee's time with the team a number of city-centre bombs failed to explode, creating the suspicion that the devices had been tampered with. When he was put in charge of security in North Armagh, the IRA there 'collapsed'.[74] Those who oversaw John Joe Magee's appointment, in the mid-1980s, would later claim they had known nothing of the IRA death sentence against him. In such a way, the person given the job of protecting the IRA from British infiltration had a track record sure to make any agent handler salivate in anticipation of what was possible.

While the case against John Joe Magee, who is now dead, was never proved, there is less doubt about the other Internal Security Chief named as a spy, Freddie Scappaticci. A member of one of several Belfast-based, Italian-Irish families that have been involved in the Provisional IRA, 'Scap' as his IRA colleagues called him, was John Joe Magee's deputy and succeeded him as head of IRA Security. He joned the IRA in 1970 but was interned a year later. After his release in 1975 he got involved in IRA intelligence work and then moved into the Security Department when it was established. He spent the next fifteen years or so working for it. In 2003 he was outed in the Irish media as the infamous double agent known as 'Steak knife', about whose identity there had been feverish media and Republican speculation for some years. 'Steak knife' had been named as an agent working for a section of British Military Intelligence known as the Force Research Unit, which ran agents inside the IRA and Loyalist groups in conjunction with MI5 and the RUC Special Branch. 'Steak knife' or Scappaticci had been working for the British since the late 1970s and was a 'walk-in' agent who volunteered his services allegedly after being given a bad beating by an IRA colleague. Although Freddie Scappaticci denied claims that he was 'Steak knife', the assertion that he was had been made by a credible source: a former Force Research Unit NCO who had first revealed 'Steak knife's' existence in 1999. 'Martin Ingram', the soldier's pseudonym, claimed Scappaticci had been allowed by his handlers to get people killed in order to protect his cover. Some estimates put the number of his victims at fifty. Three years after he was exposed, the Belfast High Court heard that Scappaticci had gone into hiding because of a fear he could be killed. The court imposed a media ban on revealing his whereabouts and banned the publication of recent photographs.

By the time Brendan Hughes took over, the Security Department had been well infiltrated by the British and the suspicion that the IRA, especially in Belfast, was being subverted by double agents was widespread elsewhere in the organisation. But the immediate problem facing Hughes was a very different one: to root out torturers in the Security Department, in particular a much feared duo known within the IRA as 'Burke and Hare', after the notorious nineteenth-century Scottish bodysnatchers. The pair routinely used violence and sensory deprivation against suspects and employed the IRA equivalent of water-boarding against some. Hughes got them court-martialled and thrown out of the IRA but they were soon allowed back into the Security Department, albeit at a lower level.

*. . . these people tortured guys. There was a friend of mine who owns a bar, Paddy McDaid, an IRA Volunteer who was taken away by these people and tortured. I mean they burned him with cigarettes, they put his head in water, they kept him starved for four or five days in an old . . . barn somewhere across the border. Paddy McDaid came to me not long after I got out of prison and told me about what happened to him . . . he was accused of being a tout. Burke and Hare, that was their names, —— and Monaghan . . . Burke and Hare, the Body Snatchers. But Paddy wasn't the only one I spoke to. I spoke to other people [who had been tortured]; other people came to me. And this is sacrosanct; I'm not supposed to talk about this, but I will. When a court martial is called you're sworn to secrecy; you're not allowed to speak about it, no matter what the decision is. But myself and Billy McKee were on the court martial when this man [told us how he was tortured] and there were lots of others who didn't survive it; they're buried down the countryside somewhere by these people, these Internal Security people. I got into major controversy with these people and their court martial was*

*organised. I prosecuted the case. They were both dismissed from the IRA with ignominy. The charges were brutality, cruelty and disobeying Army orders that [said] people are not to be tortured. They were dismissed for that reason. After that I disappeared off the scene to Dublin. Within months the same two people were back [but] they never had the power and the control that they had. It's hard to believe how people within the IRA were so scared of these people. [But] I went to school with ——; he was a friend all my life [and] I was frightened of him. I went to work in England with him at one time and I was sleeping. When I woke up, he was trying to kill me. He's into devil worship – Dennis Wheatley, is it? He's into his books. I woke one night and he'd his hands round my throat trying to kill me, a dangerous, dangerous man. But, I mean, every army attracts psychopaths . . .*

When Brendan Hughes agreed to take on the Security Department brief as well as GHQ Operations, he had unwittingly begun a journey that was to end in disillusionment with the IRA and flight from Belfast. Thanks to an incident so infused with chicanery and double-dealing that it could easily have leapt from the pages of a John Le Carré novel, his conviction grew that the IRA was thoroughly infiltrated by the British. He also suspected that a blind eye was being turned to corruption on the part of well-connected activists and that the leadership, for whatever reason, was not willing to do much about it all.

The figure at the centre of the drama was a gregarious thirty-five-year-old estate agent and wheeler-dealer by the name of Joe Fenton from the Andersonstown area of West Belfast. Although not an IRA member himself, Fenton was a friend to many people who were and had so fully won the IRA's trust in the city that he had become a facilitator for the Belfast Brigade, providing cheap homes to well-placed figures, safe houses for IRA meetings or lovers' trysts and empty houses whose floors could be opened to make hiding places for IRA weapons. His connections in the property business meant that for Republicans he was the person to go to if they wanted a mortgage, especially when they were unemployed and not eligible for a home loan. Joe Fenton would happily forge evidence that the applicants held down good, well-paying jobs, even if this made the mortgage-holder guilty of fraud. He also provided the Belfast IRA with vehicles to transport explosives and weapons across the Irish border from mother dumps and fenced stolen goods for those IRA members who engaged in private-enterprise robberies on the side. All in all, Joe Fenton was a great friend and helper to the IRA in Belfast but he was also an agent working for the RUC Special Branch, possibly one of the most valuable ever. The homes and safe houses he provided were bugged; the weapons hidden in empty houses were 'jarked' so the security forces could keep track of them, and the vehicles used to ferry weapons put under close surveillance. As for those who had arranged fraudulent mortgages via Fenton, they were perfect candidates for blackmail by the police.

Joe Fenton survived as an informer because he had a powerful protector and sponsor in the IRA. Harry Burns was a scion of one of Belfast's oldest and most respected Republican families, and he was related by marriage to Gerry Adams. From the St James district of the Falls Road, Burns had been badly disabled when a bomb he was carrying exploded prematurely. Whether it was due to his disability or because he so trusted his friend Joe Fenton, Burns would break IRA rules and get Fenton to drive him to supposedly highly secret IRA meetings. How much information he helped the Special Branch obtain in this and other ways, how many weapons and explosives shipments he helped betray and how many IRA members were blackmailed into becoming informers themselves because of his treachery can only be guessed at. When the Belfast IRA finally moved against Joe Fenton they killed him before he could be thoroughly interrogated and so his hugely valuable secrets went to the grave with him. Joe Fenton was killed before Brendan Hughes could properly question him.

*. . . I got out of prison; I had nowhere to live so a friend of mine called Fra McCullough\* brought me to an estate agent called Joe Fenton. The two then brought me to a house in Rockville Street. I was immediately suspicious: here's me just out of prison, brought to a house and told that it was mine, it was my house . . . I didn't take it. I instinctively got suspicious. And then I started to look into the background of this man . . . He was an estate agent, right, so what other people did he get houses for? Then a house was raided by the IRA in that area, in the Rockville Street area, and a bug was found. It was a house that Fenton had handled [and] it was a key house owned by a man called Harry Burns who is dead now but he was a senior player with the IRA in Belfast. He was O/C of Belfast Brigade and he ran the whole explosives smuggling operation from across the border and loads of people were getting caught. Even when Harry wasn't running Belfast there was nothing moved in it without his say-so. Because of my job in Internal Security I was looking at the connection and I found the connection between Harry Burns and Fenton. Fenton was supplying the property and some-times also the cars that were sent across the border to bring stuff in. And I had a major run-in with Harry Burns in his own house. His wife was sitting in the back room and we had a row. Harry was an operator; he lost an arm, lost a leg, I think he lost an eye as well, Cushendall, 1976, when his own bomb exploded in a shop doorway . . . I argued that there was a security problem with Fenton. Harry swore by Fenton. But then what Harry did was to warn Fenton that I was checking into him. Fenton did a runner; he went to England on the pretext of going to a boxing match and was away for about ten or eleven days. I was running Internal Security on the GHQ staff. Fenton returned. He was told to return by his handlers, that everything was all right; Harry would fix it up. Fenton returned. I was in Dublin, I think, when Fenton returned, and I heard it on the news – Fenton was found dead. Fenton returned to Belfast and was immediately executed by the IRA before I could get to interrogate*

\* Former comrade of Hughes in the 'Dogs', D Company from the Lower Falls area.

*him. I believe he was executed to protect someone bigger than him. I believe he was executed by the person in the IRA who was handling him. And I believed that the Special Branch threw Fenton to the wolves to protect the major informer. I think Fenton was a runner more than an informer – it was a whole murky business I found myself in. I actually got very frightened that I had discovered something here at a high level. I was getting no help from anybody in Belfast. I mean, people like ——, ——; Fenton got them their houses. And there was half a dozen others. All the houses were bugged. And that was the precondition, they got the houses [but] the Brits went in first and bugged the house. So the whole thing in Belfast was rotten . . . rotten. And you were taking your life in your hands just by asking questions. I believe that if I had have got my hands on Joe Fenton the first thing I would have done was put him in a car, take him across the border, and hold him for as long as possible. Because there were other people involved, higher-ranking people . . . As I say, Joe Fenton was only a squirrel,\* right. And somebody had Fenton executed before I could get talking to him. And I have no doubt if I had have got my hands on Fenton I could have unravelled a whole lot of – [but] I might have got myself killed. I was largely based in Dublin by that time and I had a squad of people around me in Dublin and Kerry who I trusted. I didn't trust Belfast. Belfast was rotten. When I say 'rotten', it was fucking riddled with leaks, with informers, and nobody was making an attempt [to clean it up]. You had people like Paddy Monaghan, ——, lifting wee lads off the street and taking them away and torturing them, but not really looking at the overall picture of where the major informers were. People were getting arrested, people were not getting arrested, people who you'd have imagined should have been arrested were not getting arrested. It was only the main players getting arrested and getting taken out, when I say 'taken out' and getting shot.*

---

\* A term used in the IRA, mostly in jail, to describe a leadership snitch.

Q. *But the Army Council must also have approved Fenton or at least one of them must have approved him getting killed. And I suppose they went on the evidence that was presented to them by the people that wanted him killed?*

A. *By Belfast Brigade. I mean, there are other people who are still alive who probably know, who definitely do know more about the execution of Fenton than I do. I wasn't there when he was executed. If I had have been there he wouldn't have been executed as quick as he was. Somebody had him executed to cover up someone else. I've an idea who it was but I don't know exactly who it was.*

Q. *Do you want to say? It's a question I have to ask but you don't have to . . .*

A. *I think —— was involved in the execution of Fenton. —— certainly benefited from Fenton's involvement in the IRA . . . It has been said that Fenton's execution came as a result of people who had massive dealings with him and who needed him out of the way in case he exposed them. I have no doubt that is the truth.*

Q. *But were —— and Cleaky Clarke\* not involved in robberies at that time? Was there not something dodgy going on there?*

A. *There was . . . and, as I say, I wasn't there at the time, but there have been accusations that ——, Cleaky and other people were involved in dodgy jobs. Fenton was the key to it: he was the fencer, he was the money launderer, he was the setter-up of the jobs . . . Fenton could have exposed all this. And I think —— would have been one of the big [names] exposed. But again Fenton was the key, Fenton was taken out. Fenton was a British agent, given a free hand, he took on board other people . . . I hate to say this [but] —— was one of the people who was involved with Fenton and there are people still there who can answer these questions better than I can because I just touched on it . . . Fenton was the key to getting*

---

\* IRA activist from Ardoyne in North Belfast, from a family of active Republicans. He was one of Gerry Adams's bodyguards in the 1990s. Died of cancer in 2003.

*into the middle of this. And he was taken out when I was outside Belfast, when I was in Dublin.*

The Joe Fenton affair convinced Hughes that he woud be safer in Dublin than Belfast, that if he stayed within the Belfast IRA then his life could be in danger. There was, he believed, no IRA member in the city that he could trust any more, so widespread was corruption within the organisation, not least his old friend Gerry Adams. When he tackled Gerry Adams about it all, Adams told him he was paranoid. After that he left Belfast for Dublin and when eventually he returned to the city of his birth, he had cut all his ties to the Provisional IRA for good.

*I just didn't know who to trust any more. The people I had trusted with my life I couldn't trust any more. Gerry Adams I couldn't trust; —— I definitely never trusted, and the other people around me in Belfast I could not trust either. I knew there were robberies taking place; I knew people were getting immunity from arrest; I knew there were touts there; I knew there was corruption there. And that's what led me to go to Dublin. I was living in Iveagh [mid-Falls Road area] with a girl and I moved to Dublin to get away from all that because I knew my life was in danger, not from Loyalists, not from the British, but from IRA personnel.*

Q. *It was that bad?*

A. *It was that bad . . . Other people certainly didn't see it, but I had touched . . . the corruption in my own movement and I knew there were people there who would need to protect their interests. I couldn't find the main mover . . . and I knew that I wasn't getting any support from anyone and I had to get out.*

Q. *Did you, did you confide these problems in any senior leadership figures?*

A. *I confided them to Gerry Adams, yes.*

Q.  *What was Gerry's response?*

A.  *That I was exaggerating, that there might be a wee bit of fiddling going on but there's not the sort of scale that I was alleging. I confronted —— in Gerry Adams's house and there was a major blow-up, and —— walked out. I sat and talked to Gerry and Gerry says I was getting a wee bit paranoid. So after that I left, I went to Dublin and I lived in Dublin for a while. I didn't leave the IRA . . . I moved onto the GHQ staff. I was actually asked by Pat Doherty, who was Chief of Intelligence, to go back to Belfast to try and clean it up and I refused. I said, 'If I go back in there and start digging up shit, I'll not last a week.' He had asked me . . . because he realised how dirty it was, how corrupt it was. But he wasn't prepared to go to Belfast and do it himself . . .*

Q.  *So was that more or less the beginning of the end . . . ?*

A.  *It was for me. Well, when I came back to Belfast I got a job in a bar in Trinity Lodge. And I was approached on at least two occasions by Brian Keenan who asked me to come back into the IRA, that there was a problem within the IRA and there was things that I could help deal with. And I admit I thought about it, I considered it. And then I considered the . . . person who was asking me, and I refused. I wouldn't go back in because I wasn't going to go through all that again. I didn't trust anybody; I didn't trust the man who was asking me to come back in. I didn't trust the people I was going to be working with.*

*. . . last year [2001] I was sitting in a bar and I saw these people eyeing me. Keenan was one, Paddy Adams [Gerry Adams's brother] was another and a guy from St James's . . . Bernard Fox.\* And I walked up to them and I asked them did they have a fucking problem with me and not one of them said a word to me. But the*

---

\* Former hunger striker and long-time IRA member who subsequently was appointed to the Army Council when Gerry Adams and Martin McGuinness resigned. He resigned in protest at their continued efforts to control the organisation from behind the scenes. He is now a member of the independent Republican group Eirigi.

*following day Bernard Fox came here where we're sitting and told me he didn't have a problem with me. And I says, 'What about the rest?' And he says, 'I can't speak for the rest.' . . . there was total hostility there that night. Actually . . .*

*a couple of women I was sitting with walked out with me, because they believed I was in danger, as I certainly believed I was in danger . . . there's a Republican repression of anyone who dares to object or who dares to question the leadership line . . . we've been told all along that this is not a leadership-led movement, this is a movement led by the rank and file. That's a load of bollocks. This is a movement led by the nose by a leadership that refuses to let go and anyone who objects to it, anyone who has an alternative, is either ridiculed, degraded, shot or put out of the game altogether.*

## 9

In his much praised biography of Michael Collins, Tim Pat Coogan described Collins and Harry Boland, two of the most influential Irish revolutionaries of their time, as 'partners in crime'.[75] It might be difficult to find a more apt phrase to describe the alliance between Gerry Adams and Brendan Hughes during the years when their lives were most closely intertwined. A committed Republican long before they met, Boland introduced Collins to the secret Irish Republican Brotherhood, the IRB, from where the two friends and comrades together plotted and schemed their domination of the IRA in the coming decade. They fought together in the Easter Rising in 1916 and in the subsequent war with Britain but with the Treaty of 1921 came the parting of the ways. Boland took de Valera's side against Collins, denouncing the deal with Lloyd George as a betrayal of the Republic for which they had both fought and their long friendship ended. When Boland died, shot dead near Dublin in disputed circumstances by troops of the new Irish Army, just three weeks after the shelling of the Four Courts, he and Collins were confirmed adversaries. Within three weeks Collins was also dead, shot in unclear circumstances at Beal na mBlath in County Cork.

Gerry Adams and Brendan Hughes did not meet until after their war had started but when they came together their influence on the direction and growth of the Provisional IRA in the city was decisive. They were different in key ways but dovetailed perfectly, albeit that the product of their partnership was invariably more death and destruction. Adams was the strategist and thinker, Hughes the man of action and organiser. If Adams was the one who knew how to make the best snowballs, Hughes was far better at throwing them. Together, in the Belfast of 1970 to 1973, they made a formidable team. The partnership deepened when both were imprisoned in Long Kesh, strengthened by their joint detestation of an IRA leadership they viewed as naive and dishonestly defeatist. When Adams was freed and set about restoring the IRA to what it had once been, Hughes committed himself to advancing Adams's cause inside the jail. As he happily admits in his interviews with Boston College, many of the tragic events inside the Maze prison between 1977 and 1981 happened in consequence of that mission. As with Collins and Boland, their break came when the time arrived for compromise, although what is striking with Hughes is that he was affected as much, if not more, by how it was all done as what was done: the deliberate running down of the IRA that he saw, the tolerance of informers and corruption, the lies, stealth and deception that he detected and, most of all, Gerry Adams's own denial of IRA membership.

Nothing better captures the special closeness between Brendan Hughes and Gerry Adams in the early days than the photograph of them as prisoners in Long Kesh, Hughes wearing a 'Melbourne Irish Club' T-shirt, his arm wrapped around the neck of a taller, hairier Gerry Adams, a little like an older and a younger brother. These were two men who shared a tiny cubicle in a small hut, who conspired nightly on ways to confound their common enemies and intimate enough that Hughes was let in on the secret meaning of the 'Brownie' byline that Adams used to promote his subversive views to the wider Provo audience. Hughes would nail that photograph to the wall of the small flat in Divis Tower where he spent his last days, as a memoir of the special comradeship he had with Adams and to remind him that it had ended in disappointment, at least for him. Gerry Adams's refusal to acknowledge his own IRA history was, in Hughes's mind, the ultimate disavowal of their friendship and he spent a considerable portion of his interviews with Boston College putting the record straight in that regard. Hughes doesn't give that as the reason for breaking the IRA's rule of *omertà* and agreeing to tell the story of his life in the IRA to American academics but it is clear that it was never far from his mind, a metaphor that conjoined personal and political betrayal. When Gerry Adams first publicly denied his membership of the IRA, in June 1983, instructing his solicitor to protest in writing to the editor of the *Irish Times* when the paper described him as the Vice-President of the IRA rather than of Sinn Fein, Brendan Hughes believed Adams must be telling the truth in some way. Boston College's researcher, Anthony McIntyre, was in jail with Hughes at the time and later wrote about an exchange they had about the matter. Hughes, he wrote, 'expressed the view that Adams might have stepped down from the Army to take up a party role given his very public discourse on the issue. The Dark felt his old comrade was too straight a guy to mislead people.'⁷⁶ Did the time to tell his story arrive when finally he came to reject all that he once believed about his old friend, when his god grew feet of clay?

*I believed 100 per cent in Adams: I believed in his leadership, I believed in his direction, I believed almost everything that he would have said to me. I went along with it and believed in it. And you have to remember this as well, that I was one of these non-political Volunteers. I always saw myself, up until [I served a] few years in prison, as a soldier, not a politician, naively so but that's the way I saw it. I eventually learned. And I believed in the direction that Adams was taking. I remember when he left Cage 11, when he was released, him saying to me that I had the easy job, he was going out to the hard job. I believed that we needed to take control of the leadership of the IRA and of Sinn Fein [and] I believed that the two organisations needed to combine . . .*

*I don't think anyone can take away from Gerry that he is an intelligent man and a very shrewd operator. I don't know anyone else in the whole Republican movement, during the history of my involvement, who could have brought this movement to the position that it's in today . . . I was one of those, and I wouldn't class myself as being stupid, who went along with Gerry for so many years without realising what direction he was taking us . . . Thanks to the loyalty factor in the IRA, Gerry was able to control and manipulate people like myself and many others. Obviously there were other people who would give him encouragement and would welcome the direction that the movement moved to. But I don't believe it could have been done without him . . . There's no one else in the Republican movement with the intelligence, the shrewdness and the ruthlessness that was needed to bring the movement to the position that it's in today. Gerry was the only person, to my knowledge, who would have been capable of doing that.*

*I don't condemn him for it. I criticise him for the devious way that it was all brought about. There were people still dying when they were talking and these people who were dying – fair enough the war has to carry on – should have known the talks were going on.*

*I would have died for him; I would have jumped in front of him to save him from being shot and took the bullet myself. I would have done that because I believed, really believed what he was saying in his writings, in his talks . . . I believed him and I feel betrayed by him; I feel really betrayed. I feel it personally . . .*

*Where I differ now is that what the IRA and Sinn Fein have done is [that] they've just upstaged the SDLP. The revolutionary socialist direction that . . . I was fighting for has been dropped. And all Sinn Fein have done, all the IRA have done is just to become another SDLP . . . all the things that were important to me, that we fought and died for, mainly the . . . betterment of the working-class people in Ireland, have been dropped . . . There's a sectarian thing here as well and Sinn Fein have been very good at manipulating and bringing bigots along with them . . . The sort of people who have come into Sinn Fein are not the sort of people that I would have associated with during the IRA struggle. They're middle-class, career politicians. I came down the Falls Road yesterday to see Fra McCann\* because I lost my income-support book . . . and he was standing talking to Tom Hartley.† People like that who never fired a shot . . . but hung onto the aprons of dead Volunteers. Not that I wanted to talk to him but he made a point of ignoring me . . . he's [Hartley] the type of person that was always there waiting on the sidelines, the type of people like Caoimhghín O'Caoláin,‡ career politicians . . .*

*To me now, it's all about getting into positions of power. I go back to Liam Mellows again – people will go into positions of power and hold*

---

\* Sinn Fein Assembly member for West Belfast and former member of D Company.
† A key member of Gerry Adams's think tank, a former Sinn Fein General-Secretary and Belfast Lord Mayor in 2008.
‡ Sinn Fein TD (Teachta Dala, member of the Dail Eireann, the Irish parliament) for Cavan–Monaghan. A former banker, he joined Sinn Fein in a full-time capacity in 1982.

*onto them because of the privileges that power brings. I see so many of them people about now within Sinn Fein, within the movement. And you have the other poor fools that run about with the badge of IRA written across their chests and the British government sitting back and laughing. They eventually got the IRA into the position they've always wanted. They tried it in 1972, they tried it in 1975, and failed both times. They've now succeeded in turning a revolutionary movement into a conservative organisation, one that they can deal with and are quite happy to deal with . . . This is the crime that I see: they have left behind kids, young people, Republicans that are not going away, you know. All the contradictions, I think, will begin to emerge because they haven't brought about a solution here. All they've done is to guarantee that this is going to last for another generation and that basically is where my objections arise to this settlement. I agree eventually there has to be negotiations but I believe negotiations need to be fair and just, and a guarantee that they will not move onto another generation. Sinn Fein and the IRA have not done that. They sentenced young people, young Republicans and young working-class people to another generation of fighting.*

*. . . a few months ago I found a bug in this apartment that we're sitting in now. I don't believe it was . . . planted by British Intelligence [but] by someone else. I don't know who, because loads of people have come through this flat. It could have been a journalist; it could have been someone working for some other agency. But the fact remains is that it could have been a Sinn Fein person . . . the thought is always there. The reason why I'm doing these interviews is because of my trust in you, no one else. I don't believe there's anyone else in this country could talk to you [in] the way I'm talking to you. I've never done it before, not in this detail . . . It's not going to do me any good but I believe it's important for later generations when I'm dead and gone . . . I have absolutely no reason to tell any lies about my involvement . . . I have never admitted publicly to being a member of the IRA because to do so would land me straight back in prison. If I stood up on a platform or gave an interview with a journalist, I would always refer to myself as a member of the Republican movement. I think it's important*

*for future generations to know that I was a member of the IRA, a high-ranking member of the IRA and here I am, fifty-three years old, for the first time in my life, admitting it publicly . . . History is written by the victors. In this particular case, the defeated have a chance to put on record their role and their perspective of this so-called victory. And therefore I think it's of absolute importance. There is still doubt about who killed Michael Collins, who killed President Kennedy, and I see an opportunity here of having something for future generations so people can say who killed [our] President Kennedy, who killed [our] Michael Collins. I don't find [the interviews] easy; I find them quite difficult sometimes because it's always in the back of your head – who the hell else is listening to this? I'm at the point now where I really don't care who else is listening . . . the important thing about this is that my war is over. I've lived over thirty years sitting in dark rooms, sitting in houses, organising operations, organising the war . . . maybe it's because I'm getting old and I just don't care any more . . .*

\*    \*    \*

Not long after Brendan Hughes gave his last interview to Boston College, in August 2002, he began the long mental and physical decline that would end less than six years later in his death. After his return to Belfast from Dublin in 1991 or thereabouts, the drift away from the IRA was well under way. One of his last jousts with the IRA leadership came in 1994 when he opposed efforts to block released prisoners from rejoining the IRA because they included figures sceptical of the peace process. He worked where he could, mostly in low-paid building jobs; for a while he and some friends ran a small business but that failed, coinciding with the break-up of his relationship with his girlfriend, Marguerite. 'After that the downfall came,' his brother Terry explained. One of his last jobs was as a part-time barman in Andersonstown but for the last seven or so years of his life he was unemployed and, according to his sister Moya, increasingly gripped by a clinical depression caused in large measure, she believes, by the political situation. By 2002, the IRA had begun decommissioning its weapons and Sinn Fein was edging closer to accepting all that he and

Gerry Adams had fought against in their youth: the existence of Northern Ireland, the policing system, Stormont and so on. He lived alone in a flat in Divis Tower, visited by his sister and daughter, Josephine, and by journalists eager to hear a Republican take on the peace process at variance with the Sinn Fein orthodoxy. He was particularly exercised by the neglect shown towards ageing IRA veterans by the Provo leadership. There were hundreds of men, he told one reporter, 'carrying around problems from that time. If not physical problems, there are men with mental problems, alcohol problems, depression, trouble holding a job or relationship.'[77] He was especially angry about the death of Kieran Nugent, whose refusal to wear a prison uniform in the H-blocks in 1976 had begun the IRA prison protest. 'They called him a "river rat" because he spent his last days drinking by the river in Poleglass. Why didn't someone in the movement not see he'd problems and help him? He was the bravest of the brave.'[78] His other concern was Sinn Fein's close relationship with a certain building firm which employed a lot of IRA veterans at low wages, people who would have trouble getting work elsewhere and in defiance of labour laws, paid them in a bar they owned, retrieving a slice of their money when drink was bought. It reminded him of his trip to Cape Town as a young merchant seaman where the black dock workers drank their wages in the boss's drinking club. But as time went on, he ventured out less and less. 'He felt secure in his wee flat,' recalled Moya Hughes.[79] His brother Terry, a former internee, believes the IRA's political journey sapped his will to live: 'He hurt too much and he felt isolated. When he lost the [Republican] movement, he lost everything. I think he lived for that movement.'[80] Increasingly his health became a problem, a possible legacy of his fifty-three-day hunger strike in 1980. He had a heart attack and then bypass surgery but continued to deteriorate. 'He was in and out of hospital all the time,' remembered Moya. In early February 2008 he developed a chest infection and contracted influenza. Although his condition was worsening, he wouldn't go to hospital. Moya Hughes eventually sent for a doctor who ordered him admitted to the City hospital where he soon fell into unconsciousness. A week later, on Saturday, 16 February, he died.

Unsurprisingly, Brendan Hughes's funeral in Belfast was a major Republican event. Several thousand mourners from all over Ireland and beyond, many of them former IRA comrades or fellow prisoners, journeyed to the Lower Falls to pay their tributes. His coffin, draped with a Tricolour and with the black beret and gloves that constitute the trappings of IRA membership, was taken from his sister's home to St Peter's Cathedral for Requiem Mass. Afterwards it was carried through the Lower Falls, along some of the streets where he and D Company had fought gun battles with the British, to the memorial erected on the front of the Falls Road by D Company veterans to their fallen comrades. Then a hearse transported the remains to Roselawn cemetery in East Belfast for cremation. If the media coverage of the funeral zeroed in on the Sinn Fein presence, that was only to be expected since there was great curiosity about what stance the Provo leadership, Gerry Adams in particular, would take towards the obsequies for their foremost critic. The Sinn Fein leader was accompanied to the ceremonies by some heavyweight colleagues, all of whom had crossed Hughes's path, not always happily, in jail: Bobby Storey, Adams's right-hand man and a senior figure in the IRA prison command staff after the 1981 hunger strikes; Brendan 'Bik' McFarlane, the prison leader during that protest, and Danny Morrison who brought him the news in jail that launched the first hunger strike.

Gerry Adams had twice visited Brendan Hughes in hospital, the last time just before he died. Ivor Bell was there at the same time and so, briefly, the trio that had terrorised the British Army and much of Belfast in the early 1970s was reunited, physically if not in spirit, and with just two of them, Adams and Bell, conscious. When Hughes died, Adams released a statement full of praise for his critic, calling him 'my very good friend' and 'a sincere and committed Republican who was very proud of his working-class roots'.[81] His hospital visits had fuelled speculation of a deathbed reconciliation and when he and fellow Sinn Fein member Fra McCann helped shoulder Hughes's coffin into the church that, or something like it, seemed to be confirmed. Photographs of the moment accompanied reports in the next day's newspapers of the reconciliation between the Sinn Fein leader and former friend. The *Daily Mail* ran a story with a headline that captured the media consensus, 'Sinn Fein makes its peace with The Dark', quoting a Sinn Fein source as saying, 'There was still a lot of respect and fondness for Brendan, despite all the things he said in recent years. Mr Adams's decision to carry the coffin is seen as a sign that any rift had been healed.'[82]

If that was the impression, it was what Brendan Hughes had not only not intended, it was what he feared might happen. Some time before his death he had contacted Paddy Joe Rice, a leader of the D Company veterans' group with instructions for his funeral. 'We do that a lot, make arrangements for D Company funerals,' explained Rice. 'He came to me a few months before his death – he must have had a feeling something was going to happen – to say that if anything did happen that Adams, Sinn Fein members or Provisional IRA were not to have anything to do with the ceremonials, that they weren't allowed to speak at it. He was very adamant that none of them should have anything to do with it. He was afraid they would use his funeral to try to say that he ended up agreeing with Adams, that the breach had been healed when, if anything, it had grown wider.'[83] As the funeral approached, Adams contacted D Company with a request to give the oration but Paddy Joe Rice turned him down. Ivor Bell had agreed to speak and when Adams heard that he withdrew his request, although as it turned out Bell became ill and couldn't give the speech. An effort to have Francie Brolly sing the H-blocks anthem during Mass was also blocked since Brolly was a Sinn Fein Assembly member and a fan of Gerry Adams. But when the Sinn Fein leader asked to carry the coffin for a while, Rice relented and the photograph duly appeared, visible evidence, it seemed, of a frendship restored. While Sinn Fein was doubtless content to see the story covered in this way, there is no evidence that Gerry Adams and Brendan Hughes ever exchanged a word in the City hospital, much less settled their differences. 'He was unconscious [during Adams's visits] and not lucid at all,' recalled Terry Hughes. 'When he went into that coma he never came out of it.'[84]

In accordance with Brendan Hughes's wishes, his ashes were buried or scattered in three places in Ireland: at his parents' grave; at the ruins of his grandfather's home in the Cooley mountains in County Louth, and at the D Company memorial on the Falls Road in West Belfast – but not at the IRA plot in Milltown cemetery in West Belfast. Every June, the month of his birth, friends and former IRA colleagues gather in the Cooley mountains to remember him and to discuss the latest twists and turns in the journey taken by Sinn Fein and what remains of the IRA. People who go there report that this year the gathering was larger than it had been the year before.

When the funeral ceremonies in West Belfast had ended, a much smaller group, family and close friends, travelled out to the crematorium in the far-off Castlereagh hills, beyond East Belfast. Among them, with no camera crews around to capture the moment, went Gerry Adams. Terry Hughes remembers the scene vividly: 'He stood there looking so forlorn. He actually walked over to talk to me; no one was speaking to him. He didn't seem to know where he should be; he was sort of a lost soul.'

August 1969. Catholic families in Belfast flee their burning homes in the wake of Loyalist attacks. The IRA's failure to defend their communities split the republican movement and brought the Provisionals into being.

The Falls curfew in 1970 was a turning point for the Provisionals in Belfast. Afterwards support in Catholic parts of the city swung towards them and away from the Officials.

IRA Belfast commander Seamus Twomey confronts British troops at Lenadoon during the IRA ceasefire of 1972. At his signal, Brendan Hughes and other IRA members opened fire, ending the two-week-long cessation.

British troops patrol Divis Street, in the heart of D Company territory, after rioting. Brendan Hughes first met Gerry Adams during a riot in the same area: 'I can't remember if he threw anything but he certainly directed everybody else to do it,' he recalled.

Bloody Friday, July 1972. Brendan Hughes was operational commander that day, in charge of the IRA bombing teams. Twenty-two bombs exploded in the space of around an hour, killing nine people. Six of the deaths happened at Oxford Street bus station above. The violence persuaded David Ervine to join the UVF.

Jean McConville with three of her ten children. The widowed mother was killed and disappeared after the IRA discovered she was an informer for the British Army. Hughes interrogated her and said she admitted her role.

Gerry Adams, Ivor Bell and Brendan Hughes photographed by British military intelligence after their arrest in July 1973. When soldiers asked him what he was going to do next, Hughes replied, 'I'm going to escape.'

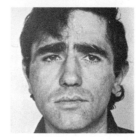

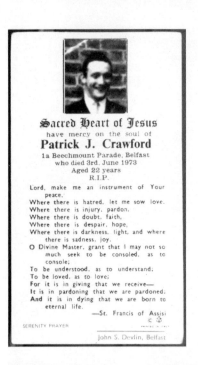

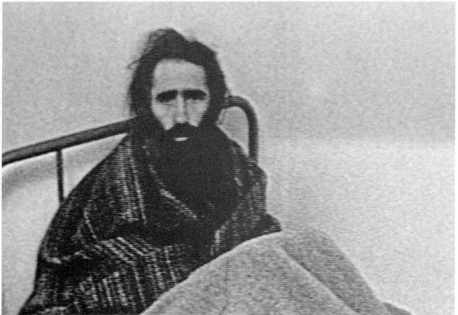

A Mass card for Paddy Joe Crawford. His death was judged a suicide but the IRA hanged him in jail.

Robert 'Basher' Bates, one of the Shankill Butchers, a UVF gang that murdered Catholics indiscriminately in the mid-1970s. Bates befriended Hughes in jail and halted a UVF plot to assassinate him in his prison cell.

Brendan Hughes in prison hospital during the failed 1980 hunger strike. Guilt over his decision to end the first hunger strike, which led to the second strike and ten deaths, haunted him for the rest of his life.

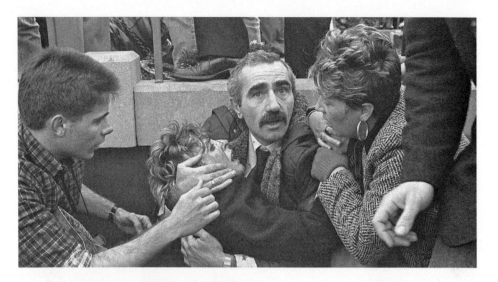

Brendan Hughes comforts a woman wounded by grenade splinters in the attack on an IRA funeral in 1988 mounted by Loyalist Michael Stone.

Hughes in his Divis Tower flat with Boston College researcher Anthony McIntyre.

Barred from giving the oration at Hughes's funeral, Gerry Adams briefly 'lifts' his coffin.

McGurk's Bar, December 1971. One of the first UVF bombings after the break with Tara. Fifteen Catholics were killed in the blast, which was never admitted by the UVF.

Thirty-three people died and over 250 were wounded when the UVF sent car bombs into the centres of Dublin and Monaghan during the 1974 Loyalist strike against Sunningdale. Twenty-six were killed in Dublin in three explosions, fourteen of them, including twelve women, at Talbot Street above.

David Ervine (standing, far left) poses with Gusty Spence and fellow UVF internees in Long Kesh.

Gusty Spence ran the UVF compounds in Long Kesh like a British Army barracks, a sense of discipline that David Ervine relished. Here he reviews UVF internees parading the colours.

Gusty Spence, regarded as the founder of the modern UVF, poses with 'Buck Alec' Robinson, a Loyalist gunman from the 1920s who is believed to have assassinated Brendan Hughes's great-uncle.

David Ervine and Billy Hutchinson after their election to the Northern Ireland Assembly following the Good Friday Agreement in 1998.

Gerry Adams, a welcome presence at David Ervine's funeral, commiserates with Ervine's widow, Jeanette.

# DAVID ERVINE

1

Of all the twenty or so bombs that shattered Belfast in just over an hour on the afternoon of Friday, 21 July 1972 – 'Bloody Friday' – none was more destructive or deadly than the one hidden in a Volkswagen estate car driven into the Ulsterbus station at Oxford Street. The bus station, situated where the city centre abuts the River Lagan, was well placed for those heading to or from the downtown shopping districts, and always a busy spot, especially so on a Friday afternoon when rural visitors and out-of-towners began to make their way home after a day working or shopping in the city. That Friday was no exception. The IRA had picked out five public transport termini as targets that day – two bus stations, two railway stations and the Belfast-to-Liverpool ferry terminal – and since these were all places that attracted large numbers of people, the chances of civilian casualties and deaths were always going to be high. As much as stretching the resources of the British Army and the RUC by exploding so many bombs in such a short space of time, this feature of the IRA plan guaranteed that 'Bloody Friday' was going to be a disaster.

The various accounts of 'Bloody Friday' differ in important detail. Some say nineteen bombs detonated that day; others twenty or twenty-one. One account has the Oxford Street bomb being the tenth to explode, at 3.10 p.m.[1] but the Northern Ireland Office, in a news sheet hurriedly published shortly after, said it was the fifth to explode and the device exploded at 2.48 p.m. The consequences were beyond doubt, however. Six men were killed in the explosion, two of them British soldiers and four employees of Ulsterbus, a public company responsible for all bus services outside Belfast. The *Irish Times* report described what happened:

301

The bomb was left in a car driven into the station which was at the time crowded with travellers. Two men left the car and ran away. The crowd in the bus station at the time took cover because of the suspicion of a bomb on the Queen Elizabeth Bridge near by. There was panic when the bomb went off. The two soldiers had driven in to give a warning but were killed almost immediately as they jumped out of their car. The civilians died instantly too. Women and children were among the frightened victims here and even as rescue work went on more bombs could be heard going off in the city. A large fire broke out after the explosion and again as at the Smithfield [bus station] blast, buses were severely damaged.[2]

As Belfast's major bus station dissolved into broken bodies, shattered buildings and burning buses, bombs were exploding all over the city. At the same moment that the Volkswagen estate crumpled into flames and deadly, flying shards of metal and glass, a van bomb detonated in the car park of the railway station in Great Victoria Street, destroying four buses and damaging forty others. Two minutes later, a car bomb exploded outside a bank on the Limestone Road in the north of the city while at the same time a bomb hidden in a bread van blew up the York Hotel in Botanic Avenue in the south of the city. The bombs kept exploding, one after the other, until 3.15 p.m. when the last device, a car bomb, blew up outside shops on the Cavehill Road, again in the north of the city, killing two women and a fourteen-year-old boy, Stephen Parker. By the end of the day IRA bombs had killed nine people and injured a hundred and thirty, seventy-seven of them women and girls.

Kevin Myers was a reporter for Radio Telefís Éireann (RTE) on 'Bloody Friday', based on the top floor of Fanum House, a modern and famously ugly office building on Great Victoria Street, but one of the tallest structures in the city. Myers raced up to the roof with a camera crew and, as plumes of smoke from successive explosions rose over his shoulders, gave one of the more dramatic and memorable broadcasts of the Troubles. Many years later, on the thirtieth anniversary, he described how he saw the day:

> It seemed as if a malevolent god was showering bombs on the hapless, cowering citizens beneath him. The statistics – twenty bombs, nine people dead, a hundred and thirty injured within an hour – do not even begin to tell the true horror of the day. As the bombings started, thousands of panic-stricken shoppers began to stumble backwards and forwards, seeking safety. The endless explosions, the columns of smoke rising everywhere, the crowds stampeding into one other, declared this simple, inescapable truth: there was no such thing as safety. Long after the last bomb had exploded, terrified people skulked in clusters, paralysed, not knowing where to go, with hundreds of children screaming amid the acres of broken glass.[3]

Oxford Street was the ground zero of 'Bloody Friday'. At first the authorities thought eight people had been killed in the explosion there, such was the extent of human debris at the scene. Only when the dismembered body parts were reassembled was it realised that the death toll was lower by two. When people who were alive at the time think of 'Bloody Friday', they remember the television pictures of a fireman shovelling into a plastic bag the blackened, butchered remains of a torso, virtually all that was left of one of the Oxford Street victims. 'Bloody Friday' was a catastrophe for Belfast but it was also one of those turning-point days of the Troubles, when the IRA balanced the books for Britain's 'Bloody Sunday', turned constitutional Irish Nationalists against them with a fury and put themselves for ever more on the military defensive. Ten days later the British Army, taking advantage of the IRA's new political weakness, launched Operation Motorman to retake the IRA enclaves in Derry and Belfast from which the organisation launched its violent attacks. History may judge it to be the day that the IRA began to lose the war. But that is not how it was seen then.

'Bloody Friday' was also the day when the lives of Brendan Hughes and David Ervine intersected. As Hughes crouched at a street corner on the Falls Road, an Armalite rifle in his hands to give cover to the returning bombing teams, nineteen-year-old David Ervine was making his mind up to join Northern Ireland's most violent Loyalist paramilitary group, the Ulster Volunteer Force. One of those killed at Oxford Street was an eighteen-year-old East Belfast Protestant called William Hull Irvine, who lived in a street near the Ervine household. For a while anxious relatives and friends believed that it had been their David Ervine who had been killed and it was this, as he told Boston College, that pushed him 'over the edge'. As it turned out, William Irvine was a member of another, newer Loyalist outfit, the Ulster Defence Association (UDA), and he was given a full paramilitary funeral, complete with a uniformed guard of honour, all wearing dark glasses, which accompanied the cortège from a funeral home on the Newtownards Road towards Roselawn cemetery.[4] All of which makes Ervine's decision to follow a similar path a choice that was full of tragic irony.

David Ervine had been weighing whether or not to join one of the Loyalist groups and if so, which one, for a while. In that respect he was little different from many working-class Protestants in places like East Belfast at that time. The three years since August 1969, when British troops were first deployed on the streets of Derry and Belfast, had changed Northern Ireland beyond the recognition of most Unionists and Loyalists and the unsettling effect was profound. A Catholic civil rights campaign had begun the turmoil and not only had the result been an upsurge in violence but the Unionists had been cast – by the entire world, it sometimes seemed – as the baddies, the Bull Connors of Ireland enforcing Jim Crow against their Catholic neighbours. Sympathy was on the side of the Nationalists and there were voices in Britain calling their homeland a political slum. As the IRA and the forces of Irish Nationalism made advances, it seemed that Unionists could only retreat, virtually powerless to control events. The civil rights agitation had become, in their eyes, a Republican insurgency, the B Specials had been disbanded, the RUC disarmed and all the while the IRA grew in strength and audacity, seemingly beyond the reach or the will of the authorities to curb them. Worst of all, the Stormont parliament had been suspended and Direct Rule imposed by a British government that at heart many Protestants did not trust. Betty Magee, the sister of one of Ulsterbus victims, Thomas Killops, wrote an angry letter to British Prime Minister Edward Heath that caught well the mood of Northern Protestants in the wake of 'Bloody Friday'. Northern Ireland was being torn apart, she wrote, by terrorists 'who can openly flaunt [*sic*] the law and the British Army and walk in the streets of Belfast scot-free, and who are allowed to appear on television and openly boast about what they are going to do'. She issued a challenge to Heath: 'If you were man enough to come to Belfast and visit all the hospitals yourself, maybe then you would be a bit more concerned for the people of Ulster . . . You can go to bed at night and be sure of a good night's sleep. But the people of Belfast and other Ulster towns do not know what it is like to get a good night's sleep because of the IRA campaign.'⁵

Their power taken away and fearful of worse to come, convinced the police and Army were unable or unwilling to take on the IRA and distrustful of their new masters in London, more and more Protestants such as David Ervine were doing what their forebears had done: banding together to defend and to strike back. Since the autumn of 1971, in the wake of the communal violence that greeted the introduction of internment, Protestant vigilante groups had mushroomed, especially in Belfast, and then amalgamated into one body, which they called the Ulster Defence Association. The UDA was a large organisation, boasting at its peak some forty thousand members who would don camouflage and dark glasses to march through Belfast and other towns in shows of Protestant strength. If, in 1972, the UDA specialised in mobilising bodies onto the streets, then the UVF offered angry Protestants a chance to meet violence with violence, often paying the Catholic community back with interest. It was this that drew David Ervine to its ranks.

*There had been a couple of attempts to recruit me by various organisations, and I didn't move towards any, [although] I was increasingly getting fed up with attacks on my community . . . That culminated on the day of my nineteenth birthday, witnessing 'Bloody Friday'. The following Sunday I joined the UVF. I made a judgement that the UVF were more likely to do the business. Around that time you had the growth of the UDA, and this is not to be pejorative about individuals in the UDA, but they did a lot of marching, they did a lot of drilling, they did all of that, and that looked great . . . but I wanted to sort of hit back, I wanted to hit back with an absolute ruthlessness and I perceived that the UVF was the vehicle that I was most likely to do that with . . . When I try to look back at what happened with me, all of that was clearly significant and painful . . . I think I was inching in the direction of having to do something about [the situation] but it was only the moment of 'Bloody Friday' when there was a lad killed with the same name as me. He lived close by and people thought it was me, and it could have been me. At that point I went over the edge, I suppose . . . Maybe we'd need to do statistics on that to find out how many people became embroiled because they had grand ideological spirit, how many because this is the duty of a community, and how many because . . . they've had an experience of some trauma.*

Not long before this, in one of those intriguing 'what if?' moments of the Troubles, Ervine had tried to join the RUC as a way of standing up for and defending his community, but a minor boyhood misdemeanour over a stolen bicycle barred him from membership. But for that, Northern Ireland's recent history might have been quite different.

*I did try to join the police, but they wouldn't allow me in . . . I remember when I was ten or eleven buying a bicycle off someone for ten bob, which is [now] fifty pence, and it turned out the bike was stolen. The next thing there was a rap at the door and I ended up in court; it was a misdemeanour, but later in life when [I was] about*

*nineteen or twenty, I actually explored the idea of . . . joining the
police and was told that this huge criminal conviction was a barrier
to me joining the police, so they said. Whether I would have ever
gone through with it or not I don't know, but that was an interesting
barrier. I was more or less told by the desk sergeant at Mount-
pottinger police station, 'We don't need the likes of you.'*

*By the time of 'Bloody Friday' my view was that my community
is in difficulty, we need to do something about it and that would
have culminated with my experience of 'Bloody Friday' and then
the determination that maybe the best means of defence is attack.
I could kid myself that I'm tracing a line from not wanting to be
involved, and I think that's genuine, to wanting to join the police to
help with defence, to wanting to join the UVF for attack, but I had
a sort of a growing intensity. I'd have had a basic understanding of
paramilitary values, or at least what I perceived to be values. You
knew who people were, but you maybe didn't know exactly what
happened when they were with each other apart from tittle-tattle,
bar talk, that type of stuff, but it always struck me that the UVF
were more concise and more effective than the UDA. They were the
blunt instrument, whereas the UVF seemed to me to be the cutting
edge, and that's where I wanted to be. My own view was that we
wouldn't [need to] exist if the security forces would deal with the
problem and there didn't seem to be a will by government either.*

*The day after 'Bloody Friday', on the Saturday, I made contact
with someone who had previously talked to me about . . . joining.
The understanding I had then, it may be a little covered by mystique,
but the theory was that the UVF could be joined if you were invited,
and that the UVF could be joined if you went and said, 'I want to
join', and I made it known to a UVF guy I knew that I wanted to
join, and I joined on the following day, on the Sunday, in a hall in
East Belfast along with a number of others . . . You get a quare shock
to your system when you join and you find that there were people
there you knew all along and you didn't know that they were in it.
That was great news for me, that was a boost of confidence, that the
sort of secrecy and cloak-and-dagger that the UVF seemed to offer*

*was something I admired . . . You stand up, you're sworn in and the trappings of swearing in are there, flags and weapons, but it was made very clear to me that . . . out of this you could lose your relationship with your family, you could lose your life, that this is deadly serious . . . nobody ever believes it's going to happen to them, so I suppose I heard it all but I didn't pay a whole lot of attention to it, but it was certainly told to me, it was not . . . like, 'Come on in and join the Boy Scouts'; that was not the case. It was pointed out to me very clearly the risks, the dangers and the sacrifice that were not only a potential but possibly expected.*

## 2

To read David Ervine's account of his family and upbringing in working-class East Belfast and of his journey into the UVF is to acknowledge the sheer force that communal pressure exerted in shaping people's views and actions during the Troubles in Northern Ireland. In his case this pressure prevailed over the strong influence of his father, Walter Ervine, who held, for that time, unusually progressive, even left-wing, views, not least about Irish nationalism and Northern Ireland's Catholics. Unlike most of his neighbours, Walter Ervine was sceptical about organised religion, scornful of sectarian politicians such as Ian Paisley, and was a man who had read hungrily all his life. Ervine's older brother Brian recalled a father who had been disappointed in life, an intelligent man who could have achieved much but never had the education, a man who continually provoked his sons to think outside the box. His mother Elizabeth was different; deferential to authority and politically 'to the right of Genghis Khan', as Ervine himself put it, but it was his father who had the greater impact of the two. Yet David Ervine went on to join a group, the UVF, that would become a byword for savage, even psychopathic violence against Catholics – everything that his father was not and was seemingly opposed to. That he did so was because more powerful and ancient forces swept him along, the same forces that pulled Brendan Hughes into the IRA: the call to defend one's own community against those who might overwhelm it. Still, his father planted seeds that many years later would sprout and grow.

*I was born [on 21 July 1953] and reared in East Belfast between the Albertbridge Road and Newtownards Road, in a very basic working-class community, close enough to be described as [being] in the shadow of the shipyard. I would imagine that a lot of the disposable income, not that there was much of it, was generated by people who worked in Queen's Island, which was the site of the shipyard, and ancillary industries. I was the youngest of five children; [we were] almost like two families, a brother and two sisters and then my brother and me. I think the youngest of those three was eighteen when I was born; my mum [was] forty-two when she had me, forty when she had my brother. Things were done differently in those days, and I suppose for many different reasons the sophistication of family planning hadn't yet arrived. But I was born into what, I suppose, was a happy enough home . . . I think my da was, in his own mind, an under-achiever, a very skilled tradesman but [he] missed the opportunity of an extended education and had to go out to work . . . with family requirements as a young lad.*

*I think that his travels around the world as a naval officer, an engineer, probably gave him . . . a very parochial attitude towards Northern Ireland; intolerant almost of our intolerance, he would have been. I would have described him as very liberal man, and my mother would have been the opposite, [one] to the left of Joe Stalin and the other to the right of Genghis Khan. I [had] a happy upbringing, I think, in that I don't ever remember being brutalised; I remember things in a very naive and genteel way, about playing in the street and my first experiences at school . . . I suppose up until about the age of about fourteen, [I had] a fairly basic little existence, you know, ran the streets, played football, get fed, get clothed and happy enough.*

Ervine went to Orangefield Secondary School off the Castlereagh Road, a state school that in the 1960s had a name for being progressive and liberal. It certainly produced an eclectic bunch of alumni. Van Morrison was a student there in the 1950s and, during the Ervine years, schoolmates included Brian Keenan, the teacher and writer who was kidnapped and held hostage in Beirut by Islamic Jihad; Gerald Dawe, the poet and writer, and Ronnie Bunting, the son of Ian Paisley's former right-hand man, Major

Bunting, who went on to become a leader of the violent Republican group the Irish National Liberation Army (INLA) and was the victim of a UDA assassination squad in 1980. David Ervine's brother Brian had passed the Eleven Plus and went to Grosvenor Grammar and then on to Queen's University, Belfast, where he graduated in theology. A career as schoolteacher, playwright and songwriter followed. David Ervine, by contrast, was no scholar and left Orangefield just before his fifteenth birthday to take up a series of unskilled jobs. When he joined the UVF he was working in a city-centre paint store.

*. . . I think I went through the nightmare of not knowing what school was about, just didn't understand it; it was, you know, 'somewhere where I have to go'. No, school was of no tremendous significance to me, [but] I got playing sport . . . the academic side was not a forte of mine anyway. My oldest brother, who was at least twenty years older than me, missed his opportunity for education much as my da missed his, but the brother nearest to my age went for it and I didn't and I can't understand why. In hindsight you could manufacture all kinds of reasons, but I'm not so sure that even now I understand why. It was a blur basically. It's almost like the story of the young kid that plays in the cup final at seventeen and by the time he's thirty or forty he can't remember the details, yet it was a great and very interesting moment of his life.*

*Our house was stuffed full of books, and my da was an absolutely avid reader, in fact, you know there used to be a bit of a giggle, my brother and I were chosen each week to go to the library and to get him three books. We would ask, 'Well, what do you want?' and he would answer, 'Well, anything', literally anything, and we brought those three books and my da read them and then the following week they were returned and another three books were got. I remember we had a couple of suitcases under the bed which were packed with encyclopedias. Now the very fact that they were under the bed [showed] there were no shelves; the house couldn't have held shelves, the walls were like paper. But, anyway, it's rather an indication of my interest in encyclopedias, that I don't ever remember taking them out of the suitcases.*

*. . . my father professed socialism, and I can remember we lived in a street where there was a church at one end, and people would have paraded along the street in their Sunday best to go to church and a woman would have come and collected my mum's church envelope and even though my mother and father didn't go to church, my mother insisted that you have to fill the envelope each week for the church. Interestingly enough every three months the church produced a little magazine in which they named everybody who gave money, and not only that, they named people who didn't, and I think that was probably a driving force for my ma. My da used to think that was disastrous . . . we would have certainly got a sense from our da that church was not necessarily all that it was built up to be. Which makes it quite interesting that my brother has gone on to be a Christian of long standing and is qualified as a minister but has never chosen to be ordained, and I could hardly say that I have gone in that direction.*

*. . . the news was avidly watched by my da, and that would have been news on anything. I can remember that we got* The Sunday Times *every week . . . I don't know whether we were the only people on the street to get* The Sunday Times; *it was a big long street, but there couldn't have been many. We got this huge paper that it took my da till about Wednesday to read, and I remember it used to have a magazine which pleased me no end. I could look at the pictures in the magazine, but that was the sort of attitude that my da had; he wanted to know the news, he listened to the news and he would have talked about it. There used to be a guy came round to our house to sell clothes to my sister; he was from India, and he and my da became great friends. My da would have invited him in and they would sit and talk politics all day and all night and about Hinduism and Islam and Christianity. So I can remember in that respect my da was always fuelling discussion of some kind or other. I think that we were . . . slightly more political animals in some respects than . . . other households . . . but he was in truth sickened by politics in*

*Northern Ireland. I remember [the Reverend Ian] Paisley cam-*
*paigning in our street, and I don't know who he was campaigning*
*for, but he came up as my mother was out scrubbing the front, and*
*you used to do a sort of semicircle of cleaning at the front step of the*
*house and he said something like, 'You keep these houses like little*
*palaces', and then my da, who was ill at the time, struggled up off*
*the chair and . . . in what would have been language that was shock-*
*ing to me, told Paisley to go away, I think the words he used were*
*'Fuck off', and it was harsh and agitated. I mean, we had electric*
*points that hung off the wall; you couldn't attach them to the wall,*
*the wallpaper sagged, the ceilings fell and cockroaches were an infes-*
*tation, and Paisley was patronising my ma and then my ma was of*
*course standing there saying, 'Ah yes, Mr Paisley, ah no, Mr Paisley.'*
*My da of course wasn't for any of that.*

*The street would probably have had about a hundred houses.*
*I think there were four Catholic families that I'm aware of. One*
*Catholic family had six children and the three boys were all Protes-*
*tant and the three girls were all Catholic; it was a mixed marriage*
*and . . . they were lovely people, great people, I've absolutely abiding*
*affection for those people, and my dad – and my mum, in fairness –*
*but more especially my da had a great relationship with that family.*

*I don't know that you were ever frightened of the Catholic you*
*knew; you were frightened of the Catholic you didn't know. My*
*da's argument was that 'We are just all people', you know, and as far*
*as religion was concerned, he used to go to the debates in Clonard*
*monastery, which was hardly the done thing.\* I don't think he was*
*anti-Christian, or anti-deity per se; I think it was anti the manipu-*
*lation and the sense of a false fellowship that he believed religion*
*brought. But I did sense, and at the same time didn't, that Catholics*
*were always different; you knew they were different but I didn't*
*know why they were different . . . but you knew enough to know*
*that they were different, and then I suppose there's the moment*

---

\* A series of ecumenical debates hosted by the Redemptorists of Clonard monastery in the 1950s and early 1960s.

*when you hear the word 'Catholic' and 'What does that mean?'*
*and you become au fait, if you like, and particularly in street lan-*
*guage. I certainly would not have been in any way encouraged to*
*believe in our superiority, even from my mother's point of view.*

David Ervine was just fifteen or sixteen when the civil rights
campaign began, triggering the events that would, a few years later,
spiral into the Troubles and then change his life utterly. His father
saw the campaign in a very different light from most Protestants
of the time, a view that Ervine could recognise as being present in
the peace process he helped to shape many years later.

*I think it only became evident to me [that Catholics could pose a*
*threat] around the time of the civil rights movement . . . [and] the*
*speculation that Republicanism or the IRA was infiltrating it. I*
*think that my da would have been a fool not to have considered*
*that, but I think in essence the basic argument he had was that . . .*
*rights are for everybody; they're human beings, you know. I remem-*
*ber one stunning comment which stuck with me for ever, when he*
*said, 'Now there's an interesting one', when a banner was being*
*carried by a civil rights march that said on it, 'British rights for*
*British citizens', and then we spoke about people wanting to keep*
*them separate as opposed to them being Catholic British citizens.*
*I'm not sure I fully understood it at the time, but for me that has*
*grown to have a greater resonance with some of the attitudes that*
*prevail even today.*

*Well, the broader community view [of the civil rights campaign]*
*seemed to be one of 'This is an enemy.' My da's words were harping*
*in the back of your head but I think that probably I was siding with*
*the community view . . . that civil rights was a sinister plot. My da*
*was saying, 'Well, hold on a minute', but certainly I probably would*
*have fallen to the community view. They [Catholics] were simply*
*bad people, and they were strategising around bad things; that was*
*the community view, and I probably went with that view. I was in*
*no position to theorise other than what would have been whispered*

*in my ear and was sitting on my shoulder, which was the comments of my da. In some respects he took the sting out of that, but I would not have seen it as alien that the civil rights movement met opposition from people who considered it to be the enemy. When the disturbances in Derry moved to Belfast, my reaction was very simple: 'You're either one of them or you're one of us', and I was one of us . . . It was our community being attacked . . . it became something other than civil rights, it became a conflagration between our two communities.*

In 1971, as his community pulled Ervine further away from his father and Northern Ireland moved closer to violence, he toyed with Orangeism but the flirtation was brief and unsatisfactory.

*I would certainly have been very aware of the Battle of the Boyne, King Billy and all the rest of it. I didn't understand it very well because it all came to us as cliché. But I was the only member of our family ever to join the Orange Order and I think I attended one meeting. My father wasn't a fan, my brothers never joined the Orange Order, I was the only one ever and I didn't last long, just a very short time. I was eighteen, and I think that from my point of view it was [because] something was happening in my community. I don't know that I fully understood, it was all a cliché, a simplistic thing that was there and I did not understand it, I really genuinely did not understand it. [But] it was there, it was of us, not of them, and us and them has greater significance today than it seemed to have then . . . It didn't for me mean anything other than: 'There they are and this is of us and we wave and cheer and they wave back', and, 'They make noise and there's music.' For me as a young person, no, it didn't mean anything other than that . . . I'd truly no concept of what it meant.*

But his father had introduced him to another aspect of his Irish Protestant heritage.

*I think I was probably fifteen when my da gave me a book called* Betsy Gray and the Hearts of Down. *It was actually the story of Henry Joy McCracken\* who was one of the leaders in the United Irishmen, and was hanged a mile and a half from my house and I didn't know that. I don't know why my da chose that moment or whether he'd just come into possession of the book. I doubt that. I think it was probably him . . . saying, 'Well, you'd better understand some of these things.' I didn't know that the 16th and 10th Divisions fought in the Battle of the Somme, or that one of them fought at Gallipoli.† I didn't know that Catholics were . . . fighting for Britain or [were] fighting in defence of small nations. I didn't know that because nobody told me, and I think it was only through my da that I was starting to get some kind of alternative view of what we'd been told. For me it was a confusing enlightenment, but it was coming from him, it wasn't coming in the classroom, it certainly wasn't coming in the history books, it wasn't coming from the street, it wasn't coming from anywhere else other than hearing it in the house, and it confused me, I have to say, it very much confused me.*

*Only later, when I was in jail, I think that some of the things that had been said to me inspired me to dig deeper and inspired me to look a little bit deeper. But you could argue that because I had the time and the reflective opportunity, that maybe if I hadn't gone to jail I never would have dug any deeper and never would have exposed myself to any of that. But, you know, in jail I learned more. I learned*

---

\* McCracken, a radical Presbyterian and industrialist, was a founder member of the Society of United Irishmen along with fellow Protestant radicals, Wolfe Tone, James Napper Tandy, James Hope, Thomas Russell and Robert Emmet. McCracken took part in the United Irishmen rebellion of 1798 and led an unsuccessful rebel attack on Antrim town. Afterwards he was arrested, court-martialled and hanged at Corn Market in central Belfast in July 1798. The United Irishmen rebellion, which was inspired in part by the French and American revolutions, marked the birth of modern Irish Republicanism although the dominating role played in it by Protestants is rarely acknowledged by their modern co-religionists.

† The Sixteenth and Tenth Divisions of Kitchener's Army were Irish units formed around the Irish National Volunteers who remained loyal to John Redmond, head of the Irish Parliamentary Party in 1914. Redmond helped raise the regiments in the hope this would ensure Home Rule for Ireland when the war ended. The 16th Division lost more men killed in the Battle of the Somme in 1916, some five thousand killed, than the 36th Ulster Division, formed out of Edward Carson's UVF, which lost some two thousand.

*about the Pope's sponsorship of King Billy\* and I learned that the
United Irishmen rebellion was put down in the main by Catholic
militia. I know lots of things now that I didn't know [then] . . .*

David Ervine had just celebrated his sixteenth birthday when, in
August 1969, British troops marched up the Falls Road, bayonets
fixed, to take positions on an imaginary line that divided Nationalist, Catholic West Belfast from the Unionist, Protestant Shankill
Road. Days of fierce rioting in Derry between the Bogsiders and
the RUC had left the police exhausted, demoralised and, as far as
the bulk of Catholics were concerned, discredited. The civil rights
campaign had set out to reform and democratise the Northern Ireland state but instead had exposed tensions and fissures within
Unionism and intensified sectarian friction between Nationalists
and Unionists. Unionism was separating between those, like supporters of Prime Minister Captain Terence O'Neill, who recognised
a need to accommodate Nationalist complaints and others, not a
few in O'Neill's own cabinet, for whom the idea was complete
anathema. For them the clamour for Catholic civil rights was just
a devious IRA plot to undo the union with Britain which must be
put down with as much determination as if it was a dangerous
military threat. Outside the confines of the ruling Unionist Party,
a young firebrand preacher by the name of Ian Paisley was setting
himself up as the bane of O'Neillism, and the man with the courage
and foresight to expose the civil rights conspiracy on the streets of
Ulster by blocking, hindering and hampering their marches and

---

\* The Dutch prince, William of Orange, known in Ireland as 'King Billy', became a hero for
Irish Protestants when he acceded to the British throne in 1689 and defeated the rival Catholic
monarch, James II, in 1690 at the Battle of the Boyne, a victory celebrated to this day each
12 July by Northern Ireland Loyalists. His invasion of England and then Ireland is widely
represented as consolidating the Protestant reformation and ensuring a Protestant ascendancy
and monarchy in both countries. The Orange Order, which David Ervine briefly joined, was
named after him but less well known is the fact that William's overthrow of James II was
supported financially by Pope Innocent XI who saw his success as a way to undermine King
Louis XIV of France whose defiance of Innocent had angered the Vatican. The Orange roots
of Northern Loyalism therefore lie as much in the tangled European politics of the day as in
hostility towards Catholicism.

protests. From January 1969 onwards, sectarian friction ramped up and confrontations between Nationalists and the RUC grew more frequent and violent. The Apprentice Boys' parade in Derry that August was the spark for a wider conflagration, which spread further afield to other Nationalist towns and to Belfast where Protestant attempts to burn down chunks of Catholic West and North Belfast forced the government in London to intervene militarily. The troops dispatched to Belfast were seen instinctively in places such as David Ervine's neighbourhood as the friends and protectors of Catholics, their presence evidence that the British had sided with Unionism's enemies.

*I can remember the Army coming in and the clear implication was that the Unionist community were the aggressors because they pointed their weapons at us and I think that this psychology was deeply damaging. It was perceived in the Unionist community, and I absolutely shared this . . . that those who advocated for civil rights were a mask for the behaviour of bad people . . . The perception that I had at that time was that . . . bad people were hell bent on causing mayhem. Shortly thereafter it was bodies up entries and alleyways and people being tortured and drive-by shootings and bombings of public houses . . . and I'm not sure it was a time of clear thinking.*

David Ervine's route into the UVF was a classic example of how personal experience joined together with communal pressure to nudge and cajole people to join paramilitary groups in Northern Ireland. Much more than mother's milk, an ideological fixation or words spoken on television, the anger-making experience of aggressive violence was by far the most compelling recruiting tool during the Troubles. The urge to hit back, to balance the scales, was a powerful, almost irresistible force, even though it might have been justified as an act of communal defence. It worked that way on the Falls Road, on the Shankill and in East Belfast. Except, in those early days, the Unionists were the bad guys in the eyes of most of the world, including Britain, while Nationalists were seen as the victims, and a source of guilt for many in Britain and the Irish Republic. The Nationalist narrative was accepted almost without question while the Unionist version was, except in their own community, largely ignored or repudiated.

One iconic event during the early stages of the Troubles captured all of this perfectly. It was the so-called 'Siege of St Matthew's', an event that entered Republican folklore, and most histories of the Troubles, as a watershed moment in the life of the infant Provisional IRA. It happened on one of the most tumultuous days yet in the Troubles, 27 June 1970, the last Saturday in June and traditionally the occasion for a mini-Twelfth of July parade in Belfast along a route that, at least back in 1970, took Orange lodges and their bands through many flashpoint areas of North and West Belfast up to the Whiterock Orange Lodge near Ballymurphy, in those days a mixed but increasingly Catholic housing estate. The parade that year was engulfed in major violence; clashes along the route spread to the interface in North Belfast between the Shankill and Catholic Ardoyne areas and soon the evening air was alive with the crackle of gunfire. The firing seemed to have come mostly from the Republican side, as evidenced by the fact that the three people killed that day were Protestants, all killed, it seemed, by the IRA snipers. From the ferocity of the violence it is hard to avoid the conclusion that, contrived or not, the events had presented the IRA with an ideal opportunity to give the Shankill Loyalists a bloody nose that day, and a warning that any attempt to repeat the burnings and mini-pogroms of August 1969 would provoke a ferocious response. The trouble moved to the East of the city that evening when local bands and lodges dispersed and the IRA had another chance to drive the point home.

The small Catholic area known as Short Strand is at the inner perimeter of East Belfast, situated near the River Lagan at the apex of two roads, the Newtownards and Albertbridge Roads, which lead to the main two bridges into the city centre from that part of town. David Ervine lived further up that apex, only a few streets away from the Short Strand. The area is surrounded by Loyalist streets on all sides and has its back to the river. Historically, the Short Strand had been the scene of some of the most vicious sectarian violence in Belfast's turbulent history, especially in the 1920s, and was regarded as the most vulnerable Catholic district in Belfast, a hostage to the good behaviour of Nationalists elsewhere in the city. That Saturday, a gun battle and rioting that lasted almost the entire night would dramatically change that calculation.

The Republican version of what happened is simple: when the Orangemen returned from the Whiterock parade they stormed the local Catholic church, St Matthew's, throwing petrol bombs and firing shots, while the British Army and the RUC stayed outside the area, seemingly on purpose. Had the Loyalists succeeded in destroying the church, Republicans said later, the heart would have been ripped from the community, which might then have been destroyed. But the IRA, under the command of Billy McKee, the Brigade Commander, came to the rescue and fought off the Loyalists, killing two of them. McKee was badly wounded and an IRA Volunteer, Henry McIlhone, shot dead. The narrative was crucial to the infant Provisional IRA because it made good the promise implicit in its raison d'être, to defend Catholic Belfast from Unionist extremism. There was another bonus. Having protected the Short Strand in such a violent way, the IRA was then at liberty to start bombing Belfast city centre and to attack British soldiers without fear of the consequences being visited on the Short Strand. Mostly though, the story fitted neatly into the larger narrative: Catholics were trapped in a hostile state, and were under siege from bigots. As a local Sinn Fein activist, Deborah Devenney, recently put it: '. . . we were under attack by Loyalist mobs assisted by the British government and the RUC. After Bombay Street there was writing on a wall in the Falls – IRA: I Ran Away. After the battle of St Matthew's, no one could say that any more.'[6]

The Protestant version of the 'Siege of St Matthew's' is very different and, interestingly, the most recent account[7] from within that community draws its evidence in large measure from Nationalist accounts of the battle published over a quarter of a century later when the passage of time had permitted greater candour. This rendering of events claims that East Belfast Protestants had fallen into a trap carefully laid by the IRA, one that had been set in order to create the circumstances that would allow the IRA to present itself to Catholics as their defenders. Their evidence comes in a description of preparations for the battle inside Short Strand compiled in 1997 by a Nationalist community body, the Ballymacarrett Research Group. The preparations suggest not a hurried defence of the area but something more organised and planned: 'When the IRA formed up that night in Lowry Street just off Seaforde Street', the Group's account read, 'it was the first time since the 1920s that the IRA had paraded before going into action. There were around thirty men that night which comprised of Brigade Staff Officers, local volunteers and volunteers from the Falls. Supporting them were Fianna who acted as runners ferrying ammunition and messages between the various positions taken up around Seaforde Street and the Church.'[8] In other words IRA leaders and members from elsewhere in the city had been drafted in before the trouble started and the fact that they had time to form up for a parade suggests the gunfire had yet to begin. The violence erupted, both sides agree, when Nationalist youths began waving Irish Tricolours at the Orange marchers. Nationalists say shots were fired from within the crowd, which the IRA answered, while the Unionists say the only firing came from the grounds of St Matthew's Church. According to the Unionist version of that night's violence it was not until much later, long after the initial bursts of IRA gunfire, that the local Protestants were able to arm themselves – with two pistols, a .303 breech-loading rifle and a Mauser rifle that had been smuggled from Germany to Carson's UVF in 1914 – and return fire. All the while the British Army and the RUC stood aside, unwilling or unable to come to their defence, while the IRA poured fire into the Loyalist streets.

So the version to which David Ervine would have been exposed was the mirror image of that believed by Nationalists. In his community, the IRA was the aggressor; in one local Protestant account

the violence is called 'our Pearl Harbor';[9] whose immediate consequence was 'the formation of both the UDA and the UVF in East
Belfast'.[10] That account was published only in 2003, thirty years after
the event, and evidence of how emotive the violence still is for
Loyalists in the area. In a sense the truth of what happened on the
night is secondary, since the competing mythologies are too firmly
embedded in the group psyche to be dislodged. What is beyond
doubt is that the violence in Short Strand set the tone for the
Troubles that followed. It is worth noting, however, that one
important part of the IRA's version has now been exposed as a false-
hood. The sole Catholic killed that night, Henry McIlhone, was not,
in fact, a member of the IRA, even though Billy McKee and Gerry
Adams among others have claimed he was, and nor was he shot
dead by a Loyalist gunman. He was killed, it now seems, by his own
side, very possibly by Britain's IRA spy, Denis Donaldson, in a
friendly-fire accident.[11] So the question becomes: if the IRA lied
about that part of the incident, did it lie about others?

David Ervine was present on the Newtownards Road that night
when the gunfire erupted and it is clear that it was an important
way point on his journey into the UVF.

*I didn't go rioting . . . but, you know, young people are inclined to
follow excitement. There was a lot of rioting at the bottom of the
Woodstock and Lower Newtownards Road [and] I can remember
going and having a juke. I was there the night in 1970, when two
people were shot dead, three actually, two outside the chapel
grounds and one inside, and [Robert] Neill, [James] McCurrie and
[Henry] McIlhone, and I can remember a guy getting shot and it
wasn't like the movies. The guy got shot in the hip and, and the
blood spurted about three feet, and I just thought 'Jesus' you know,
you saw John Wayne and there was a stain. That just wasn't the way
the world worked; it was horrendous, the noise, the fear, the atmosphere, it was incredible stuff . . . My community was savagely beaten
that night, it was savagely wounded, and I remember walking up
the next day. It was the road that I was born and reared on . . . and*

*it was just like a war zone, you know, it was like something you'd seen in the Second World War, gutted properties and rubble and all of that. It was a rather horrendous time I have to say, and I have no doubt in my mind whose side I was on then, although I hadn't yet made a move towards being active in any of that. In some ways I think I probably saw [the growth of the UDA and UVF] as a community rallying to its needs, I think that's what it was . . . It has become many other things since then but for many I think that's what it was. It came from the process of vigilantism and vigilantism was protecting your own little street, your own little house, and then [it] generated into something much larger. Now the UVF already existed, but in general terms the growth in paramilitarism came from vigilantism which was a determination that you were under attack and you were going to do something about it . . . and then it was one step away from defence to attack . . .*

## 3

The Ulster Unionist leader Jim Molyneaux once said that, for Northern Ireland Protestants, loyalty to Britain was a two-way street. It is rare indeed for a politician, especially one as ill at ease with words as Molyneaux was, to capture in such a pithy way the dominating, even defining, characteristic of his community's political culture. But the 'wee man', as his colleagues fondly called him, put it well. He was setting forth in simpler terms what political scientists call 'conditional loyalty', which is the idea that citizens and the state are bound together by a contract in which the citizens agree to support and defend the state only as long as the state supports and defends them. It is almost impossible to understand the world of Ulster Loyalism, to grasp why Protestants take up arms and threaten to defy the government they claim as their own, or why someone like David Ervine would join the UVF, without recognising how fundamental the doctrine is to the culture of Northern Unionism.

The centrality of this contractual relationship to government in Northern Irish politics has its origins in the Plantation of Ulster in the early seventeenth century. The Plantation was an extraordinarily ambitious effort by the late Tudor and early Stuart monarchies to secure England's western flank and subdue the most lawless and rebellious part of Ireland. The English fear of an enemy invasion through the back door of Catholic Ireland – by the Spanish, the French or the Germans – shaped the relationship between the two countries from the Reformation through to the Second World War, providing the strategic interest that invested Britain's claim over the country. The idea of transplanting loyal, dependable Protestants from England and Scotland to Ulster took root in the final years of the reign of Elizabeth I, when fear of another Spanish armada was still very real, and it was put into place by her Stuart successor, James VI of Scotland, when he ascended to the English throne in 1603. Not only did the presence of a trustworthy population in the part of Ireland that is nearest to England and Scotland offer a buffer to an invading foreign army, but granting the new inhabitants land once owned by the rebellious O'Neill and O'Donnell clans also helped deny the successors of these troublesome tribes the resources for new uprisings and mischief-making.

The Planters were supposed to be half English and half Scots but in practice the numbers who migrated from the Scottish lowlands exceeded by nearly sixfold those from England. Over the next century or so they brought with them the distinctive values of the Kirk, Scotland's Calvinistic Presbyterianism, prime among which was the dogma of conditional loyalty. James VI, who was crowned James I in England, had conceded the principle in 1581 to the Scottish Kirk in the face of fear that Catholic plots originating in France and Spain could undo the Reformation and restore the Papacy to Scotland. In return for James's promise to 'maintain true religion', his Scottish subjects pledged themselves to defend his person and his authority. In other words as long as he kept his word to keep Scotand Protestant the Kirk would be loyal to James but if he didn't then the deal was off. This covenant was renewed in 1590 and again in 1638, during the rule of Charles I, when the monarch's threats to impose his Catholic-sounding prayer book on the Scots put Scottish Presbyterianism again under threat.[12] Prior to all this, it had been the practice of the Scots gentry and nobility to 'band' together for self-defence when their interests were under threat, a product of decades of weak central government, and that practice was absorbed and imitated by the Kirk and the Covenanters. It meant that if the monarch threatened to renege on his or her part of the deal then it was permissible to use force against the Crown for self-protection, as the Covenanters demonstrated to Charles I on the eve of the English Civil War. The doctrine of conditional loyalty failed to be assimilated into English political culture but it survived and thrived, along with banding, in the political climate of

Ulster and it provides a way to understand the Unionist paradox: Loyalists being disloyal. Both the UVF and the UDA owe their origin to the idea.

The turmoil caused by the impending English Civil War contributed to another abiding characteristic of Unionism, a deep, chronic sense of insecurity. The Irish Rebellion of 1641, which took place just months before hostilities began between Charles and Parliament, was sparked by fears among the Catholic gentry of an invasion by English Parliamentarians and Scottish Covenanters who suspected that, in Ireland, Charles I would raise an army that would first put down the rebellious Scots and then help him impose his will in England. What started as a rising turned into a Catholic onslaught against the Protestant Planters, motivated in no small measure by a desire to regain confiscated lands. Contemporary pamphleteers in England greatly exaggerated the subsequent killings, claiming that over two hundred thousand settlers had lost their lives; it is likely that the true figure was nearer to twelve thousand, who were either killed or died from starvation, disease or cold when they were expelled from their homes that winter. The most notorious incident took place in Portadown, County Armagh, in November 1641 when between a hundred and three hundred English Protestants were marched by Irish soldiers to the bridge over the River Bann, stripped and herded into the icy river, where they either drowned or died of exposure. The stories of Irish butchery, both the exaggerated versions and those closer to the truth, during the 'massacre of 1641' entered Ulster Protestant mythology and culture as evidence of the enduring threat they faced from those native Gaels whose ancient lands they now occupied.

Those three elements which made up the Ulster Protestant political persona – conditional loyalty, banding and insecurity – all found expression in the Home Rule crisis of 1912, out of which emerged the military force whose name and methods would be co-opted sixty years later by David Ervine and his colleagues. Throughout the latter part of the nineteenth century, the British Liberal Party had become the champions of limited self-government for Ireland. The party's leader and four-time prime minister, William Gladstone, had first tried, and failed, to steer a measure granting Irish Home Rule through parliament in 1886 and then again with the same result in 1893, when the House of Lords vetoed his Bill. A third effort was made by Gladstone's successor, Lord Asquith, in 1912, a course he was persuaded to follow after John Redmond's Irish Parliamentary Party had secured the balance of power in the House of Commons. This time the auguries seemed good for Irish Nationalism. The House of Lords had by this point lost its veto power and the Liberal–Irish Parliamentary majority in the House of Commons was sufficiently large to ensure the measure's safe passage through Westminster. As the Edwardian age faded into the past, Ireland confidently looked forward to managing its own affairs.

At this point Dublin barrister Edward Carson and the Ulster Unionists entered the story, leading the opposition of Northern Ireland Protestants to Home Rule and bringing them to the edge of insurrection. Carson won the support of the British Conservative Party and set out on a whirlwind campaign throughout Ulster mobilising grassroots Loyalists to the cause. His efforts culminated in the signing of the Ulster Covenant at Belfast City Hall in September 1912 by over half a million men and women, some using their own blood for ink. Declaring that Irish Home Rule would be 'subversive of our civil and religious freedom', signatories of the Covenant pledged themselves to use 'all means which may be found necessary to defeat the present conspiracy'.

The phrase 'all means' captured the essence of conditional loyalty, signalling that if the British parliament reneged on its bargain with them, then Ulster Protestants were entitled to take their defiance to the point of using violence. What those 'all means' meant in practice was apparent long before the Covenant was signed. By the spring of 1912, Carson was reviewing columns of marching men, members of an armed force of some hundred thousand men he had helped raise, led by a former Indian Army general, equipped with 35,000 rifles and 3 million rounds of ammunition smuggled from Germany to the port of Larne on the Antrim coast. Their intent was clear. If Home Rule went ahead and efforts were made to impose it on Ulster, then there would be resistance, led by Carson's Army, by now called the Ulster Volunteer Force (UVF), and with all this came the distinct possibility that Ulster would secede from the Union and organise her own government. It was a classic example of banding together for self-protection, as the Scottish Covenanters of old had done, and its success encouraged Irish Nationalists to do something very similar.

Some, but not all, of the volunteers raised by Irish Nationalists did go to war against Britain – in Easter 1916 and again in 1919 – but not the UVF. The outbreak of hostilities with Germany in 1914 put Home Rule on ice and the UVF volunteered virtually en masse to fight for Kitchener's Army in the trenches of France and Belgium. The slaughter of the 36th (Ulster) Division on the Somme in July 1916 was an act of sacrifice by the UVF which, in Ulster Protestant eyes, both deepened Britain's contractual obligation to their cause and would serve to legitimise the grievance that any future betrayal coming from London would represent. Irish self-rule was not revisited until 1920 when the Government of Ireland Act, some-times called the Fourth Home Rule Act, was passed, creating two states in Ireland and granting both a measure of self-rule. The Southern part was de facto amended by the terms of the 1921 Treaty, but the Northern part remained untouched, thus creating the Northern Ireland that exploded in violence in August 1969.

The creation of the new Northern Ireland state, the preservation of the link to Britain and escaping absorption into an Irish and pre-dominantly Catholic state did little to reduce the Unionists' real or imagined sense of insecurity. A large section of the population, at least around a third, was Catholic, and Nationalists in outlying parts of Armagh, Fermanagh and Tyrone especially resented their separation from the rest of the island. The rest accepted their fate sullenly, a stance reflected in the posture of Nationalist MPs at Stormont, who boycotted the parliament during its early years. With a large slice of the population antipathetic to the new state's existence, a panoply of coercive laws was drawn up, designed to curb Nationalist or Republican threats. In addition to the new Royal Ulster Constabulary, the Unionist government led by James Craig raised a large part-time police reserve, the Ulster Special Constabulary, to enforce them. The 'Specials' or 'B' men, were substantially composed of elements of the UVF who had survived the trenches at the Somme. This was such a defining part of their identity that Scottish historian Michael Hopkinson said that the force, which was widely involved in reprisal attacks on Catholics in the North during the 1919–21 period, 'amounted to an officially approved UVF'.[13] It was one of these Specials who shot Brendan Hughes's great-uncle dead in a tram in York Street in 1922. When the modern UVF appeared in the mid-1960s and began targeting Catholics, Unionist politicians, not least of them Prime Minister Captain Terence O'Neill, were at pains to contrast the imitation with the original, as if the old UVF had never been involved in such killing. Far from having 'misappropriated' the UVF name, as O'Neill asserted, it is arguable that the new UVF had much in common with its predecessor.

The new UVF of the 1960s appeared on the scene, not by coincidence, with the first signs that the inflexible politics of Unionism might be softening and in this regard it is impossible to separate the arrival of Ian Paisley and the resurrection of Carson's Army from one another. By the 1960s, Northern Ireland's traditional industries – shipbuilding and linen in particular – were in serious decline or at risk of extinction. It was evident that to survive and replace the lost jobs, Northern Ireland had to tempt new foreign investment to set up shop and a fresh, friendlier image was required, one that suggested stability and peace rather than division and conflict. The Northern Ireland prime minister since 1963, an affable but shy former Irish Guards officer called Captain Terence O'Neill, who could trace his lineage back to the Chichester family, the pioneers of the Plantation, began reaching out slowly and cautiously to the Catholic community, visiting schools and shaking hands with nuns, sending condolences to the Catholic primate on the death of Pope John XXIII, and the like. O'Neill's ecumenism was hardly earth-shattering but in contrast to his entrenched predecessors, Lords Brookeborough and Craig, it was dramatic, seismic stuff. Economic pragmatism dictated the next tectonic shift, when O'Neill invited Sean Lemass, an IRA veteran and successor to Eamon de Valera as the Fianna Fail Taoiseach of the Irish Republic, to Belfast for talks, mostly about economic co-operation. That O'Neill failed to inform his cabinet beforehand, and in the eyes of many Unionist MPs at Stormont had broken his word to them never to talk to Dublin, only fanned the flames of discontent.

Opposition to O'Neill built up within the Unionist Party and outside, where the raucous Ian Paisley, the latest in a long line of fire-breathing, political preachers in Northern Ireland, mobilised discontent to first build his church, the Free Presbyterians, and then his political machine, the Protestant Unionists. The rise of O'Neillism coincided with a worldwide surge in ecumenical friend-ship between the Catholic Church and mainstream Protestant denominations, a rapprochement that was as alarming to many Northern Ireland Protestants as O'Neill's inclusive politics. It all helped to fuel Paisley's rise.

Easter 1966 marked the fiftieth anniversary of the Rising in Dublin and many Unionists expected that the IRA would use the occasion to launch a new campaign in the North. The IRA's last military crusade against the Northern Ireland state had been launched in 1956 but had petered out within a year. It had failed to attract significant Catholic support and was formally ended in 1962. What followed was a peace that was often uneasy, thanks not least to Ian Paisley. In 1964, threats by him to invade the Falls Road to remove a Tricolour displayed in the window of a Republican election office sparked several days of rioting between Nationalists and the RUC, who pre-empted Paisley but outraged Nationalists by breaking into the office to carry away the offending flag. The incident reinforced the view that the police were the servants of Unionist extremists. Despite its military collapse and failure to win

Catholic backing, Unionists found it difficult not to regard the IRA as anything but a permanent and tireless threat and so, by the spring and summer of 1966, tension and apprehension had grown noticeably.

Just how apprehensive some Protestants were in 1966 is evident from an account of the time given many years later by Billy Mitchell, a UVF leader at an early stage of the Troubles and at one time a devoted member of Paisley's Free Presbyterian Church:

> I remember being told that the police had evidence that the IRA intended to take over the town of Newry during the 1966 Easter Rising commemorations and emulate the stand taken by Connolly and Pearse at the GPO in 1916. The IRA's intention, we were told, was to make an armed stand and call for United Nations intervention. Gusty Spence recalls that some Unionists also believed that the IRA in Belfast intended to take over the City Hall and that this resulted in an RUC guard being posted. There was also a widespread belief, whipped up by hard-line Unionists, that the IRA intended to use the 1966 Easter Rising Commemorations to orchestrate civil disturbances in Belfast and Londonderry. Preparations for the Easter Rising Commemorations appeared to confirm that something was happening within Nationalist areas. Both the political climate and the stories about the alleged intentions of the IRA in 1966 ensured that the time was ripe for the reconstitution of the UVF.[14]

March 1966 brought the first indication that matters could get serious. The RUC began investigating a series of petrol-bomb attacks on Catholic homes in Belfast while local newspapers reported that O'Neill's government was examining suggestions that the UVF was being re-formed to oppose Republican Easter parades the following month.[15] On 21 May 1966, the new UVF announced itself in a letter to the local press that declared war 'on the IRA and its splinter groups', adding, 'Known IRA men will be executed mercilessly and without hesitation.' It concluded, 'We are heavily armed Protestants dedicated to this cause.' Six days later a twenty-eight-year-old Catholic store man, John Scullion, was making his way home drunkenly from a bar on the Falls Road when he was shot, apparently from a passing car, and on 11 June he died in hospital. At first the RUC believed he had been stabbed but after claims of responsibility were phoned into the *Belfast Telegraph*, his body was exhumed and the shooting confirmed. It turned out that the Scullion killing was a botched operation. The gang had set out to kill an IRA man called Leo Martin but, when they couldn't find him, picked on Scullion when they heard him shout, 'Up the rebels.' The casual, random killing of Catholics such as Scullion would become one of the UVF's later hallmarks.

The next victim was an eighteen-year-old single Catholic barman called Peter Ward who had wandered into a Shankill Road bar called the Malvern Arms on the night of 26 June along with three Catholic friends. In search of a late-night drink after working their shifts in a hotel in downtown Belfast, the four men sat drinking for an hour or so. At around 2 a.m. they left the bar, and were met with a fusillade of gunshots. Three of the men were hit and a single bullet struck Ward, piercing his heart and killing him instantly. It later emerged that the UVF gunmen had been drinking in the Malvern Arms at the same time, had spotted the off-duty hotel workers and had concluded, without much evidence, that they were IRA members. Again they had been hunting for IRA victims that night without success and seemingly chose Peter Ward and his friends because they were readily available Catholic targets. In the wake of the murder, Prime Minister O'Neill rushed home from Somme celebrations in France where, ironically, he was commemorating the UVF of 1916, and banned its modern-day manifestation, calling it 'this evil thing in our midst'. A day later the new UVF claimed its third victim, a seventy-seven-year-old Protestant widow, Matilda Gould, who died in a house blaze caused by a petrol bomb meant for a Catholic-owned bar beside her home.

The RUC moved quickly against the UVF and soon arrested the major activists. Three men were subsequently convicted of the Peter Ward murder, all of them from the Shankill area. Their leader was a thirty-three-year-old shipyard stager and former soldier called Gusty Spence who had worked for the Unionist Party and whose brother was a Unionist election agent. Charges of murdering John Scullion were dropped but Spence was convicted of killing Peter Ward and given a recommended twenty-year prison sentence. Many years later Spence would claim that he had been inducted into the UVF at a meeting attended by some forty men in Pomeroy, County Tyrone, earlier that year. He had been invited to join, he would claim, by two Unionist politicians, both anti-O'Neill members of the party's ruling Ulster Council, but since he has consistently refused to name them, his claim has so far defied confirmation.

If the origins of the new UVF are shrouded in confusion and uncertainty it is because it was so tangled up with other paramilitary-style groups that found shelter under Ian Paisley's wide umbrella, Ulster Protestant Action (UPA) and the Ulster Protestant Volunteers (UPV). One of Spence's co-accused, Hugh McClean, later told RUC detectives how it was that he came to join the UVF: 'I was asked did I agree with Paisley and was I prepared to follow him? I said that I was.' While Paisley was quick to distance himself from the UVF after O'Neill proscribed it, and heartily condemned 'the hell-soaked liquor traffic' that constituted the background to the Ward murder, the truth was that he and the new UVF were part of the same overlapping and interlocking network of anti-O'Neill fundamentalism.

Gusty Spence would be transformed into a Loyalist folk hero, his bungled efforts to take on the IRA in Belfast soon regarded in places such as his native Shankill as evidence of remarkable foresight. When the Provisional IRA launched its campaign five years later in 1971, the painted slogan 'Gusty was right' peppered walls on the Shankill. For a while his prophet-like status was rivalled only by Paisley's. When the Troubles gathered steam and UVF prisoners began arriving in Crumlin Road jail and then in Long Kesh, Spence was the automatic choice for their O/C or Officer Commanding. Spence had served in the Royal Ulster Rifles in West Germany and in Cyprus where he had fought the EOKA uprising and he ran the UVF compounds of Long Kesh like a British Army barracks with tight discipline. The next Chief of Staff was Samuel 'Bo' McClelland, another Shankill man who like Spence had served in the Royal Ulster Rifles. He had lied about his age so he could join up to fight in Korea. His successor, Tommy West, was also a former British soldier, a special forces veteran. Between the three, the group's early leaders put a British Army stamp on the UVF, both inside and outside the prisons.

In the mid- to late 1970s Spence underwent a remarkable transformation, seemingly shedding his hardline Loyalism and addiction to violence. On 12 July 1977, the most hallowed day in the Loyalist calendar, he addressed his fellow UVF prisoners and made a call for 'a universal ceasefire' by Republicans and Loyalists, an appeal that failed to inspire his audience. Spence argued that Loyalist violence was redundant because Northern Ireland's place in the United Kingdom had been accepted by both the British and Irish governments and could not be altered without the say-so of its people. It also emerged that Spence had been learning the Irish language and studying Irish history and that he had sent condolences to the widow of Joe McCann, a prominent Official IRA activist who had been controversially shot dead by British troops. From David Ervine's interviews with Boston College it is clear that, inside the UVF compounds, Spence had also been preaching the merits of sharing power with Nationalists, much to the dismay of some of his fellow prisoners.

It was during this period of Spence's political regeneration that David Ervine was exposed to some of the ideas that later became central to the political approach of the Progressive Unionist Party (PUP), the UVF's subsequent political wing: not just acceptance of power-sharing with Nationalists but populist, leftish views on economic and social issues of a sort that could be found in the manifestos of most European Social Democrats. After his release from jail in 1984, Gusty Spence would describe himself as 'a moderate socialist',[16] while Ervine, when his spell in jail ended in 1980, would get into violent arguments in bars when he espoused his progressive agenda, on one occasion earning a punch in the mouth and the charge, 'You're a fucking communist!' On one level this highlighted the paradox that lies at the heart of the UVF: the co-existence of left-wing political sympathies with an often violent, racist-like hatred for Catholics, more redolent of the extreme Right.

The roots of the UVF and the PUP help to explain the anomaly. Gusty Spence and later David Ervine were essentially part of the same iconoclastic tradition as Tommy Henderson, the Independent Unionist MP for the Shankill at Stormont between 1925 and 1953. A housepainter and decorator by trade, Henderson was a founder member of the Ulster Unionist Labour Association, which had been set up in 1918 by Edward Carson to purge 'Bolshevism', with its sympathy for the Irish Republican cause, from the local trade-union movement. Carson's efforts to link Labour with Sinn Fein led on one occasion to the mass expulsion of left-wingers, trade-union activists and Catholics from the shipyards.

Henderson had political ambitions but when he ran as a candidate for the Unionist nomination for the Shankill seat in the 1920 Stormont election, he was rebuffed. Convinced that class bias had shaped the decision, Henderson stood as an Independent in 1925 for the North Belfast seat at Stormont and won, beating the mainstream Unionists. From 1929 onwards Henderson held the adjacent Shankill seat against repeated challenges from Glengall Street, as the headquarters of the Unionist establishment was known, and used his seat at Stormont to speak up for working-class constituents and to criticise the government's patronage of wealthy interests. At the same time he took an uncompromising line on the border and relations with the Southern state and Northern Catholics. Henderson held the seat until 1953 when, tellingly, a Northern Ireland Labour Party candidate captured nearly half his vote, allowing the Unionist nominee to slip in between them. That year Henderson was part of a slate of seven Independent Unionists who stood against the mainstream Unionists in protest at what they claimed was the government's appeasement of the Catholic Church over education reforms while demanding more jobs and housing for Protestants. It was the beginning of a revolt, in which Paisley and the UVF were key actors, against the Unionist 'fur-coat brigade' that ran Protestant politics in those days, a protest against appeasement of Nationalism and an expression of class antagonism.

The Independent Unionist tradition of hardline, populist Loyalism was again taken up in the Shankill area when the Derry-born barrister Desmond Boal won the seat in the 1960 Stormont election. Although standing for the mainstream Unionist Party, Boal was an adviser to Ulster Protestant Action (UPA), a ginger group cum embryonic paramilitary organisation, set up in 1956 in anticipation of the IRA's coming Border Campaign. Its other leading lights included a young Ian Paisley and a clerk who worked for Belfast Corporation by the name of Billy Spence, whose brother Gusty would soon become a household name. The UPA had encouraged Boal to run and backed him during the campaign. When Boal won, local UPA activists, including Billy Spence, joined the local Unionist branch en masse in an example of infiltration tactics the later UVF would imitate. After the IRA threat receded, UPA moved into the workplace, to the shipyard, to Shorts' engineering plant, Mackie's engineering works and elsewhere. Branches were set up and much of their energy was devoted to ensuring that jobs stayed in Protestant hands. Boal, meanwhile, led the parliamentary opposition to Terence O'Neill at Stormont and, according to one former colleague, his motivation had a lot do with class: 'I think he regarded O'Neill as the Big House still in charge and he resented that and O'Neill's arrogance bitterly.'[17] In 1971, Boal helped Paisley found the Democratic Unionist Party (DUP), persuading the Free Presbyterian leader to show a more secular face to Unionists. He also tried to steer the new DUP leftwards, as an early activist recalled: 'He explained that [the DUP] would continue to be right-wing on law and order but that there was a need in Northern

Ireland for a party with radical social and economic policies which could embrace all people . . .'[18] Boal remained Unionist MP for Shankill until Stormont was prorogued in 1972. The only time his seat was threatened was in 1969 when a Labour candidate called David Overend split the Unionist vote. By the 1990s Overend had become a leading member of the UVF's political wing, the PUP.

After Spence's imprisonment, the UVF, or what remained of it, dropped off the radar screen. The civil rights campaign launched by Catholics in 1968 intensified the pressure on Terence O'Neill and gave Ian Paisley and his growing band of followers repeated opportunities to further weaken the Unionist prime minister. The killer blow came in March and April of 1969 when three sets of explosions crippled electricity production in East Belfast and halted the supply of water to the city. The bombs were widely blamed on the IRA and this forced an exhausted O'Neill to resign at the end of April. But the bombs had been the work of people close to Ian Paisley, including figures who had overlapped with the Shankill UVF back in 1966, and the aim had been to discredit and topple O'Neill. In October 1969 a Kilkeel, County Down, Free Presbyterian and quarry worker called Thomas McDowell was badly burned by a bomb that exploded prematurely as he was planting it at a power station in County Donegal in the Irish Republic and died later in hospital. McDowell was a member of both Paisley's Ulster Protestant Volunteers and the UVF, further evidence of the close ties between the groups.

The year 1966 was a bumper one for Loyalist paramilitaries. In April that year Ian Paisley set up a body called the Ulster Constitution Defence Committee with the principal task of co-ordinating the activities of the UPV, a new, Free Presbyterian-linked paramilitary outfit. By the end of the summer of 1966, Gusty Spence was in jail and the UVF was, like the IRA, a banned organisation. The remnants of the Shankill UVF found themselves leaderless and without direction. Then, in November 1966, another group appeared that offered the UVF refuge until such time as their fortunes could recover.

Of all the Loyalist groups spawned by the Troubles there was surely none as bizarre or outlandish as Tara. Founded by an evangelical lay preacher called William McGrath, it took its name from the Hill of Tara in County Meath, the seat of the ancient High Kings of Ireland who McGrath believed were descendants of the kings of biblical Israel. McGrath also believed that the British people were the survivors of the ten lost tribes of Israel, that Ireland was populated by Celts whose origins were the same and that Tara would play a key role in a looming conflict in Ireland spawned by communism and Romanism. The re-emergence of the IRA in 1969 seemed to justify McGrath's warnings, bestowing on him the same oracular powers that had made Loyalist heroes out of Ian Paisley and Gusty Spence. Tara was a doomsday paramilitary group, however, and believed that violence was permissible only when the crisis arrived. Until then Tara's job was to recruit and warn of the impending Armageddon. Once Romanism and communism had been defeated, Tara's job was to reconquer Ireland for Protestantism after which the Catholic Church would be proscribed and the education of Irish children placed in the hands of evangelicals. Despite its place at the very edge of Unionism, not to say sanity, Tara attracted into its ranks people who would be prominent later in both the mainstream Unionist Party and Paisley's DUP. And it also brought into its ranks the residue of Spence's Shankill UVF.

The UVF stayed within Tara's fold for the best part of five years but left as a group in December 1971, four months after IRA internment had been introduced and at a point when Northern Ireland was spiralling into the bloodiest phase of the Troubles. Afterwards Tara, or those close to them, complained that the UVF had infiltrated the group to exploit it and left when that task had been accomplished. As one newspaper report put it: 'The tactic is to seek membership, then leave with any equipment and good men who can be seduced to the UVF.' By 1971 not only had Tara seemingly served the UVF's purposes but the underworld of Loyalist politics was alive with stories about McGrath's sexual excesses, that he was a paedophile who was using his Loyalist activities to facilitate his predatory sex life. His supposed speciality was the pursuit of rising young male Unionist stars and as it turned out the rumours were well founded. A decade later McGrath was convicted of sexually abusing boys at a children's home in East Belfast. The rumours also seem to have played a part in the break but, whatever the truth, the UVF re-emerged into a Northern Ireland where more and more Protestants were ready to pick up the gun and use it.

Almost immediately after breaking with Tara the UVF took human life on a scale inconceivable at the time, although a few years later the slaughter it was responsible for would become almost commonplace. On the evening of 4 December 1971 a bomb exploded in the doorway of McGurk's Bar in North Queen Street, adjacent to the Catholic New Lodge Road area of North Belfast. The bar and the accommodation above it collapsed like a house of cards, crushing and killing the bar owner's wife, daughter and brother-in-law and twelve other people, all Catholics, who had been drinking in the bar. The death toll of fifteen shocked and horrified Ireland and afterwards British Army officers, eager to blacken Republicans, briefed journalists that the IRA was responsible. An IRA bomb in transit, they said, had exploded prematurely. The myth of IRA responsibility persisted for years but in 1978 the truth of the bombing of McGurk's Bar was finally revealed when a UVF member, Robert Campbell, admitted driving the bombers' getaway car and was given fifteen life sentences. Planting no-warning bombs in Catholic bars would become a UVF speciality in the ensuing years, as David Ervine would testify in his interviews with Boston College, and so would the random assassination of Catholics, shot from passing cars, on their doorsteps or snatched from the streets to meet unimaginable deaths.

It took longer, nearly twenty years, for the UVF to admit another notorious bombing, on one of the bloodiest days of the Troubles, the 1974 car bombings of Dublin and Monaghan town in the Irish Republic in an effort to destroy the first major peace settlement since the start of the Troubles. In January that year a power-sharing executive comprising Unionists, SDLP and Alliance ministers took office at Stormont, the first step in implementing a political settlement that its architects, led by the British and Irish governments, hoped would create a measure of political stability in Northern Ireland and help to isolate and defeat Republican and Loyalist paramilitaries. Known as the Sunningdale Agreement, after the location in England where the negotiations had taken place, the settlement also envisaged the creation of ambitious cross-border institutions including a Council of Ireland which theoretically opened the way for Northern Ireland's long-term absorption into an all-Ireland state. Largely because of this, Loyalist opposition to the deal was fierce and on 14 May 1974 Protestant industrial workers, organised in a group called the Ulster Workers' Council, declared a general strike that began the next day. Anti-Sunningdale Unionist politicians and both major Loyalist groups, the UVF and the UDA, signalled their support for the strike and three days after it began, UVF car bombs devastated the centres of Dublin and Monaghan, killing a total of thirty-three people and injuring 258. Strangely, the UVF stayed silent about its part in the slaughter even though the devastation was welcomed by hardline Loyalists and the admission of responsibility would have scored points over the rival UDA. The more significant consequence of the two bombings was not immediately apparent but they probably marked the moment when enthusiasm for involvement in the North's affairs on the part of the South began to diminish and in that regard the carnage marked a high-water mark for Loyalist violence. Even so, it was not until July 1993, in response to a British television documentary that claimed British security forces had helped the UVF construct and plant the bombs, that the UVF announced that it had indeed been responsible, although without the aid of 'outside bodies'.

Whatever the reasons, the UVF had a history, dating back to the bombs that removed Terence O'Neill in 1969, of not always admitting responsibility for acts of violence, sometimes in the hope that Republicans would get the blame. Occasionally the ploy worked spectacularly well. On 1 December 1972 two UVF bombs exploded in the centre of Dublin, killing two bus drivers. In the immediate aftermath, and for some time, the IRA was blamed for the deaths and that suspicion helped ease controversial anti-terrorist legislation through the Irish parliament, or Dail. The Offences Against the State Act would allow the Southern courts to convict suspects on charges of IRA membership solely on the word of a senior police officer, an erosion of normal due process that prompted a large number of TDs to threaten to vote against. On the night of the bombs, the measure was heading for defeat and the Fianna Fail government was threatening a general election on the issue, when the city was rocked by the explosions. After an adjournment, the Dail resumed debating the measure and it was passed overwhelmingly.

Another violent effort to blacken Republicans turned out to be a military failure but it managed none the less to pitch the Irish and British governments into a bad-tempered spat, bringing the UVF an unexpected political bonus. On the night of 31 July 1975, one of Ireland's most popular musical groups, the Dublin-based Miami Showband, was travelling home to Dublin after playing a gig at a dance hall in Banbridge, County Down, when its Volkswagen van was stopped at a military checkpoint outside Newry, a few miles from the border. The checkpoint, however, was fake. It had been staged by members of the Mid-Ulster UVF, some of whom doubled as soldiers in the Ulster Defence Regiment, a largely Protestant militia established by the British in 1971 to replace the discredited B Specials. Their plan was to hide a bomb on the van which was timed to explode when the band had crossed the border and was in the Irish Republic. Had the plan succeeded, the band members would all have been killed; no one would have known about the fake roadblock and it would have looked as if the band had been transporting explosives for the IRA, a claim that would have embarrassed Republicans and increased the pressure on the Irish government to act against the IRA. But it all went wrong. The band members were ordered out and lined up beside the van as two of the UVF gang placed the bomb in the back. But the bomb detonated prematurely, killing the two UVF men, both of them also soldiers in the UDR. The rest of the gang opened fire on the band, killing three of them. The lead singer, Fran O'Toole, was shot twenty-two times in the face.

Afterwards, the Irish government summoned the British Ambassador, Sir Arthur Galsworthy, to complain 'that not enough has been done to stop sectarian assassinations . . .', this friction between the two capitals some consolation for what otherwise had been a disastrous operation for the UVF.[19] The Miami Showband massacre, as the event was called, was a staging post in a significant escalation of UVF violence, in part spurred by a new tougher leadership, which later in 1975 would see the group once again proscribed by the British government and the beginning of the Shankill Butchers era, one of the darkest episodes of the entire Troubles. The upsurge was fuelled by an IRA ceasefire and secret talks between Republicans and the British, events that sharpened Unionist suspicions of an incipient sell-out. This was the same ceasefire that Brendan Hughes, Gerry Adams and Ivor Bell saw as ruinous for the IRA but the UVF knew nothing of that. Like most Unionists, they suspected the worst and acted accordingly. Nervous about their political future, the UVF struck out, with more violence and bloodshed than any other Loyalist group. The record shows that in 1975 the UVF killed exactly one hundred people, the highest yearly death toll attributable to Loyalists in the entire Troubles and four times greater than the number killed by the UDA.

Like the UDA and the other much smaller groups in the world of extreme Loyalism, the UVF subscribed to the view that the best way to deter the IRA in the North was to terrorise the Catholic community from where it sprang and that fed, sheltered and protected its members. Billy Mitchell also dealt with this in the paper he prepared for the Progressive Unionist Party in 2002 and he explained or justified the sectarian nature of UVF violence in these simple, if chillingly honest, terms:

> The UVF regarded the conflict as a conflict between the
> Nationalist and the Unionist communities. The IRA was simply

a physical-force component of a wider opposing force. The IRA was conducting its campaign of terror for, and on behalf of, the Nationalist community. The Nationalist community provided the foot soldiers, the financial support, the safe operating environment and the moral support for the IRA. It also willingly accepted any political gains that were obtained as a result of Republican violence. In Nationalist areas west of the River Bann it is generally the so-called moderate Nationalists who benefit most when Protestants are expelled from their homes and farms by the IRA. The Nationalist community was, in the eyes of the UVF, culpable. It was the enemy that stood behind the IRA's campaign of terror and it was the only visible enemy that could be targeted. Many UVF volunteers did not believe that there was any real difference between physical-force Republicanism and constitutional Nationalism. The UVF has never sought to hide the fact that its campaign was aimed at subjecting the Nationalist community to a level of violence that would instil fear and terror in members of that community. The objective was simple – subject the Nationalist community to an oppressive force of violence as retribution for Republican violence.[20]

Although more secretive and much smaller in size than its often bitter rivals the UDA, the UVF was undoubtedly the most deadly Loyalist outfit in Northern Ireland. Between 1972 and 1977, the worst years for Loyalist bloodshed, the UVF outkilled the UDA by 3 to 2. Of the 1,050 deaths caused by Loyalist violence between 1966 and 1999, the UVF was responsible for 547, over half, while the UDA killed 408, or just under 40 per cent.[21] It was this sort of track record that lured David Ervine into its ranks after 'Bloody Friday'.

The UVF that David Ervine joined was, by his own description, somewhat more casual and laid back, even haphazard, than the IRA that Brendan Hughes became part of. While Hughes was sent to training camps across the border, the UVF gave Ervine 'a bit' of weapons training and 'basic' explosives training and was only beginning to put together a systematic training regime for new members when Ervine was arrested, over two years after he had joined the organisation. Hughes and his colleagues in D Company spent their days in call houses in the Lower Falls ready to launch attacks on the British Army or police at any moment. But in the UVF there was no daily routine; you turned up for active service when you were summoned by the local leadership, otherwise you could be idle 'for long enough'. All this was 'confusing', Ervine admitted, especially when the UVF remained inactive during the greatest crisis for Unionism since 1912, when Protestants went on strike to bring down the Sunningdale power-sharing Agreement. Despite all this Ervine was an enthusiastic UVF man, eager to impress his superiors and most reluctant to jump off the 'hamster wheel to hell' that constituted life as a Loyalist paramilitary. But in one respect he and the IRA were inseparable and that was in their opposition to the Sunningdale Agreement of 1974. To the IRA it was an internal settlement that would copper-fasten partition; to Ervine and his colleagues the Council of Ireland created by Sunningdale had the potential to end the Union.

*[The UVF] was broken up into what they described as units or teams and you would have only ever realistically known your own unit's members, [but] of course, tittle-tattle again, a nod and a wink, you knew who others were in different teams. But in the main you kept to your own group, [and] they functioned and operated internal to themselves. Each unit had a Commander and they . . . liaised with a Battalion Commander who had . . . overall authority, but you wouldn't have spent too much time in their company. I remember meeting in the back room of various bars, and there probably were no more, at any given time, than twenty of us. I was given a bit of weapons training and very basic explosives training, well, a fair bit of weapons training, mostly on pistols, so it was quite interesting. I actually think that just before I got arrested they were setting in train a whole programme of training, but I missed that.*

*I remember saying to the guy who was in charge of our wee*

group, 'I won't do armed robberies', and he says, 'You'll do what you're told', but he never ever asked me to do an armed robbery; whether he ever asked others to do armed robberies I don't know, because you wouldn't have been told; it was a need-to-know basis. I think that some groups ran better than others, and some groups had a greater discipline than others, but essentially you were expected to do exactly what you were told, but in the main there would have been enough cognisance by those in authority that . . . said, 'Well, horses for courses', you know. On a day-to-day basis it was all a bit confusing in some respects. I remember going through the Ulster Workers' Council strike, and never being asked to do anything, and I wondered, 'What's happening here?' You could have been called upon to move weapons, and I was a few times. You could have been called to a meeting . . . at that time, it seemed to me there were eighty UVF people to about eight thousand UDA in East Belfast; there was always tension between them, and you could have been called together to be given information about UDA threats. I remember one time being called to a meeting where everybody was told to be very cautious, because they believed that we were about to be attacked. There were quite a number of UVF homes attacked that night in the Woodstock Road area, so the UVF must have had intelligence on the UDA. I lived in the Woodstock area and my house was one of the very few UVF houses that wasn't actually attacked, which probably meant they didn't know I lived there. But day-to-day stuff depended on what was going on, but in the main, you'd have been called on expressly for specific reasons, and you could have been doing nothing for long enough. That didn't mean to say nobody else was doing anything. And then all of a sudden somebody could get in touch with you and say, 'Be here at such and such a time', or whatever, and that's the way it worked. It wasn't a case that you had a day-to-day routine or a day-to-day job. You were called on when required. Although, mind you, I think the issue of intelligence was something that you were always expected to be dealing with always . . . anything that was strange or anything that you stumbled across, you would have been expected to let somebody

345

*know right away. That would have been, I think, the only day-to-day thing that you would have been expected to be involved in.*

*. . . once I crossed the Rubicon my job was to do something about it; whether I was effective or not, that is for others to judge, but I certainly wanted to be, and I was committed to it, there was no going back. There was never a moment when I said, 'Have I done the right thing here?' That never happened . . . My sense would have been that I had no regrets other than probably not being as effective as they needed me to be, or felt they needed me to be . . . It was a hamster wheel to hell, and, you could argue, well out of control. Once you're on that hamster wheel, not only does there seem even with hindsight no way off, [but] I didn't want to get off. I wanted to get on with it, and we were embroiled in a battle and the battle was getting ever bigger and ever more brutal, ever more deadly. I didn't imagine that it could run for thirty years but, having said that, I don't know that anybody ever knew how it was going to all end. We were just locked into it and that was why I call it the hamster wheel to hell; it just goes on and on and on. I don't know that anybody in 1972 was thinking that this was sustainable for a very long time. But if you think back there was eventually an IRA ceasefire in 1974; there were negotiations between [the] government and the IRA around that time, and the UVF knew it and . . . went on a substantial bombing campaign to do one of two things, either stop the discussions between the government and the IRA or be part of them, so that rather indicates that there were people thinking, 'When is this going to end?' But it took a long, long time.*

*My view at the time [of the Sunningdale Agreement and the UWC strike] was that the Unionist community were being asked to sign up to something that was unfinished business, that had no bottom line. I don't think the theory of power-sharing was totally alien to all Unionists, but the . . . Council of Ireland was, especially when it was ill defined, in fact not defined at all and not a settled issue. The Unionist community had the right to feel that the world and its dog had gone over their head, and even though in the pressure cooker of Sunningdale, the Unionist political leadership seemed to sign up to it; they were always on a hiding to nothing on the basis that there was unfinished business. The ill-defined nature of the Council of Ireland was the death knell for the Agreement. The Unionist community are an extremely literal people, how do you get a literal people to sign up to things that have no basic parameters, or when the parameters weren't there?*

*I absolutely supported the anti-Sunningdale campaign and so did most Unionists . . . I lived in very Protestant working-class East Belfast, and I didn't see the intimidation that is supposed to have taken place; it didn't happen where I lived. People didn't go to work because they didn't think that they should go to work because . . . the withdrawal of their labour was as good an argument as any to say to the government, 'Catch yourselves on.' But the weird bit of this is that the UVF never used me during that period. I can remember that quite a number of fellas who were UVF with me weren't used either, so if there had been a great campaign of para-military muscle-flexing [during the UWC strike], I think I would have been involved in it, but that wasn't the case. I don't think that the UVF became expressly active, [although] in some areas there may have been more activity than others, but where I was – and I don't know what was in their mind – it was a period of immense inactivity. I wasn't asked to man barricades; I wasn't asked to do anything. There were UDA people on the barricades, and I don't remember seeing UVF people there. I never ever asked the leader-ship whether this was a deliberate decision, because I was arrested relatively soon afterwards and I never got the chance . . . but talking to other UVF people I discovered that I wasn't the only one, quite a number weren't used at all.*

*The Dublin and Monaghan bombs were harrowing, shocking, but [I had] no understanding that it was the work of the UVF, I didn't know it was the UVF. No one was hinting to me, even within UVF circles, that it was the UVF. The UDA always seemed to silently take credit or should I say responsibility, depending on what side of the argument you're looking at. It was only later in life that I became aware that it was expressly the UVF, although, mind you, if you* were talking about explosives, the UVF were always more proficient and more likely to use explosives than the UDA, massively more so. So all the logic would have said most likely it was the UVF, but the UVF didn't claim it, and there wasn't a whole bucketload of UVF activity suggesting that it was them.

I think I probably would have been supportive of those bombings, not so much because of the massive loss of innocent life – that's certainly not what I mean – but in terms of returning the serve, in terms of saying, 'Here, do you know what it's like?' and in the inimitable words of one great Nationalist leader, 'One bomb in London is worth a hundred in Belfast' – well, maybe that applies to Dublin as well. I don't doubt there was massive support for it in the Unionist community, massive support. Again not because of the individual loss of life and the horror and tragedy that goes along with all of that, no matter who you are. But there was a sense that yes, somebody was hitting back: 'Now you know how we feel.' [It was] really simplistic and really brutal, but I have to answer the question honestly; you're asking me it, and I'm answering it: yes, I would have thought that massive numbers in my community felt that it was dead on. I've seen myself in circumstances where the police messages were on [the radio] in a pub and a bomb goes off, and I knew where the target was, and once the police message declared that the target was clearly a Nationalist target, the bar cheered; people who were never going to go out and do anything themselves, maybe voted DUP, UUP, maybe went to church on a Sunday, I don't know, but they cheered, and little did they know that some of the people who'd been responsible for the [radio reports] were standing in the boozers along with them. You've got to remember, there'll be arguments that communities refuse to have with themselves, that what you do may well be perceived to be wrong, but your simplistic response to that is: 'Aye, but look at what they're doing to us', and that was very much the case, and that the Dublin–Monaghan bombs were very much about saying, 'Well, now they know how we feel; this isn't a one-way street, you know.' What is it they say in a divided society: 'Each action has an equal and opposite reaction'?

*On the allegation of collusion [with the British in the Dublin and Monaghan bombs], there comes a point when the concept insults me, insomuch as that a Provo could lie in bed and with a crystal ball . . . could pick their targets but a Prod could only do the same if there was an SAS man driving the car. It is sheer unadulterated nonsense. I don't dispute that there were probably kindred spirits in the security services, being from the same community, and there being individualistic degrees of collusion, but I am not aware, and I genuinely am shocked at the notion that at that time there was a clear and structured process of collusion. It wasn't the fucking case. I do get insulted by it. One of the reasons why the Loyalists have probably not been perceived as [being as] effective as the Republicans was dead simple: they were too tolerant of the forces of law and order. If the Loyalists wanted to be equal to the Republicans they should have shot peelers dead; they should have put police families out of their communities and shut down the avenue of intelligence that saw hundreds of Loyalists go to jail. The Royal Ulster Constabulary arrested me on possession of explosives; now why did they do that if we lived in a process of collusion? When I went into jail there were 240 UVF men in three compounds, packed in like sardines, and the UVF were a relatively small organisation in comparison to some of the others, but they made up a hell of a percentage of that jail. Where's collusion there? Is this a joke or what? And if there was all this massive collusion, why weren't IRA men in greater numbers taken out by the roots? Like there's a whole bucketload of questions that Republicans can't answer . . . I don't think there's any doubt that Loyalists were capable; all the evidence was that they'd already detonated substantial numbers of bombs in Northern Ireland, so all they had to do was work out how you put one into a car and how you take it a hundred miles. If you can take it ten miles you can take it a hundred miles. To those who understand, no explanation is necessary; to those who cannot understand, no explanation is possible. If people choose to believe that then they're living in cloud cuckoo land, and they also underestimate . . . their enemy, massively underestimate their enemy.*

Although David Ervine was unwilling in his interviews with Boston College to speak in detail about his role and activity in the UVF, he dropped enough broad hints about his life in the organisation to suggest that his paramilitary speciality was the use of explosives. In particular, his arrest in November 1974 while driving a car with a bomb in the boot and the fact that he was able, when ordered by a British bomb-disposal officer, to make it safe enough to be defused, strongly suggests a close acquaintanceship with the manufacture and delivery of such devices. At the same time it is worth noting that there would have been very few in the UVF in the days when Ervine was active who were not involved in some way with that side of the organisation, as an analysis of UVF violence at that time demonstrates. Between September 1972, two months after Ervine joined up, and July 1974, three months before his arrest, the UVF killed fifty-four people, thirty-six of them in the Republic and eighteen in the North, the bulk of them in Belfast, and in only one killing was a bomb of some sort not used, either hidden in the boot of a car or tossed into a building.[22] Planting bombs was undoubtedly the UVF's forte, especially when the target was a bar or club where Nationalists drank or socialised. Fifteen of the eighteen Northern Ireland victims of the UVF during this period were killed in bar explosions, eleven bombings in all, and all but two of the victims were Catholics. The first to be killed during the Ervine years was Daniel McErlean, a forty-eight-year-old waiter at the Carrick Hill Social Club, patronised by Catholics from nearby Unity Flats, who died when a hundred-pound no-warning bomb exploded. The worst of the bombings came in May 1974 when the UVF threw a canister bomb into the Rose and Crown pub on the Ormeau Road in South Belfast, killing five men instantly and a sixth who died some days later. A seventy-five-year-old man lost a leg and another man an arm in the explosion.[23] Whether any of these provoked cheers in bars from customers unaware that some of those drinking alongside them, such as David Ervine, were responsible, is a secret he took to the grave with him.

*I was arrested on – I think it was a Saturday night – November 2nd
and I was transporting a vehicle and a bomb to Holywood, or
towards Holywood, County Down, when I was stopped ... There
had been quite a lot of UVF activity and, I believe, and you don't
know for sure, that a target had been picked [but] abandoned on
two occasions because of very serious police surveillance and activity
... it was a fortnight later that the attempt to move that device was
stymied, so there was quite a bit going on at that time. There was
something of a campaign being launched by the UVF in which the
group we were involved [in] were unable to take part because of
police activity. Now whether that meant that there was some kind
of information leaking to the police or whether it was just random
... it's hard to tell; there are those with views on both of those possibilities. I've always tried to avoid speculation because ... if you were
to go down the line of looking for some intelligence reason, you could
torture yourself. I was lying in jail shortly thereafter, and from my
point of view I wasn't going to be very helpful in assessing any of that.*

*I'd left the Newtownards Road with a vehicle, a bomb in it, up
the Holywood Road heading for Holywood with no reason to believe
that I wouldn't make it. I was in a vehicle on my own; there was a
car travelling behind me with five others, and when I was stopped
they just ... drove past me, and I'm sure they wondered, 'What will
he say, what will happen now?' I was held at the scene because it
was deemed that the bomb needed to be defused; I was held at the
scene whilst the bomb-disposal officers had a look at the device and
then they asked me would I assist them in making it easier for them.
I didn't have a problem with that; I mean at the end of the day I
wasn't going anywhere ... What I did was I went forward with a
rope tied round me and then tied round the ankle of the captain,
an ATO, Army Technical Officer, and he trained a pistol on me.
Frankly it would have been like Bonnie and Clyde had I have
thought of making any kind of dash, and I can remember just a few
hundred yards up the street there was a squad of young people and
they were all chanting, 'Die, die, die, you Provo bastard', and all
kinds of very disparaging comments on the assumption that of*

*course I was a Republican . . . To cut a long story short, the ATO
asked me to open the vehicle, the doors, bonnet, boot, in, in a very
specific sequence, the theory was if that you got the sequence wrong,
'I'll shoot you', so my capacity to retain the sequence was OK. We
got the thing done. I lifted the device out and set it on the footpath
and they took it away eventually and disposed of it.*

*Strangely enough the ATO, a Captain Walker, visited me after
they moved me. They arrested me and first took me to Mount-
pottinger police station in East Belfast, where I was questioned and
they put me in a cell that was literally like a wet dank dungeon and
I presume that they thought, 'Well, these aren't very good conditions.' It was a Saturday night, the earliest court hearing was
Monday morning, so they moved me to Holywood, County Down,
where they put me into a cell that was not a whole lot better but at
least it was dry. While I was in that cell Captain Walker arrived
and thanked me for my assistance, which is all a bit interesting. The
focus of attention was: where did I get the explosives; where did the
explosives come from? Now I didn't know where the explosives came
from, but the police were quite fixated with that. I was encouraged
to talk to a couple of long-haired gentlemen who turned out to be
police officers, but not your typical police officer, Special Branch or
something like that, and they were absolutely obsessed with where I
had got the explosives. I think the theory must have been that they
were trying to trace the source, but since I had no receipt, I didn't
receive the explosives until the vehicle was about to drive off, I
wasn't able to help them at all.*

*But I wasn't in a frame of mind to help them anyway, no. I had a
very simple view of it. I pleaded not guilty all along. I was arrested
in a vehicle, a stolen vehicle with a bomb in the car. Now there
wasn't much hope of beating that charge but I fought it because my
view was that the state's got me and if it wants to keep me, it'll have
to do the work, I'm not going to do the work for them, very simple,
total denial. I was charged with possession of explosives with intent
to endanger life. I'll never forget one night there was a police officer
. . . a guy called Frank Savage, a Shankill Road man, who said to*

*me, 'What are you going to do when the wife's got a lodger?' and I replied, 'If you say that to me again I'll pull your fucking head off', and he never said it to me again . . . That type of sleazy sick politics in the police room is frankly foolish and detrimental to the concept of justice and law. Anyway, I was then taken to the magistrates' court in Townhall Street and remanded in custody for a week, and I had always been told not to take long remand periods, that you want to appear every week, and I did appear every week for seven months in that courtroom. I would be brought out in a little blacked-out transit van which, when we were going through Carlisle Circus on the roundabout, we would try to overturn it. You'd maybe a dozen prisoners in the back and the theory was that in the mayhem maybe you'd just get away. It was highly unlikely; we'd probably all end up butchered in the back of the bloody thing, but that was the type of thing that we got up to. I was held in Crumlin Road jail for about seven months which seemed long enough but then I know others who were there two years on remand.*

*When I arrived at the jail, first of all I was taken into what's called the annexe base which is like a reception area. [They] have a look at you and process you, and then you're put into what's called the annexe base, B Wing, into a pretty sparse basic cell, on the ground floor, with a courtyard behind it between B Wing and C Wing. You'd have been lying in your bed and then the next thing you'd hear people out in the courtyard, prisoners from C Wing exercising, which was the Loyalist wing. They'd ask, 'Who are you, what are you in for?' I knew some of them and they shouted over, 'It'll not be long till you're over here', and literally a day later I was moved from the isolation of the annexe base into a collective jail regime . You were unlocked in the mornings; you got out for breakfast, if you wanted breakfast; I don't think I got up once for breakfast in the whole seven months, for a bowl of cornflakes, and a bit of sausage or potato bread floating about in gallons of grease. It was not what you wanted. Then you would have been locked up again after breakfast, for a relatively short time. We'd have got quite a bit of association when the wing was open, when the cells were open,* then you'd maybe four or five hours of discussion and conversation, you'd maybe play a game of table tennis and you just got your day in. I did a lot of reading, and eventually after a while you would have got a radio in. A radio in many ways was your only company, until the jail started to fill up, and it filled up massively at that time, particularly with UVF people. I can remember being three to a cell, although I had started off on my own but then ended up three to a cell. It was a large influx of UVF people. It seemed to me that the UVF at that time outnumbered the UDA and the UDA were considered to be a much larger organisation on the outside . . . and when I was remanded instead to Long Kesh, the UVF outnumbered the UDA in there as well. Then I was brought back to the Crumlin Road for two weeks to await trial which might have been May in 1975. I was sentenced to eleven years for possession of explosives with intent to endanger life. I had some very strange experiences in jail, [for instance] I found out that my security clearance or my security level was the highest that you could get. We used to call such people 'red-book men'. 'Red-book men' meant that you were considered very dangerous. I don't know why they considered me desperately dangerous, but I was a 'red-book man', and I thought, 'Why?' Usually that was reserved for murderers, maybe multiple murderers . . . and that carried with me the whole way through jail including Long Kesh. If I needed to go to the doctor, I had to have a prison officer all on my own, whereas prison officers could escort other prisoners who weren't 'red-book men' in twos . . . If I wanted to go to the study hut, for instance, it became a bit of a nuisance as I had to wait for a screw to be available. If there were, say, five of us going to the study hut, well that meant three screws, one each for a pair of prisoners and one for me. I wasn't the only one, there were a number of people, but I just never came to terms why.

In Crumlin Road the UVF command structure was very clear and very defined, but probably not as confident as the command structures in Long Kesh because they were long-term structures, whereas remand is a constant flow of people, it was a transitory jail process. In Crumlin Road you just had to take it on face value

354

*because the outside organisation said, 'Here is the way the world works', and that's the way the world worked. We had people in charge of floors, we had people in charge of landings, and then we had [someone in] overall control. The first time I was in [the O/C] was Tommy McAllister from Donegall Pass and when I was back for my trial it was Billy Hutchinson. The whole time I was awaiting trial we were locked up twenty-three hours a day, and it was three to a cell, and when you needed a crap in the middle of the night, and there's two other fellas in the cell, you may not feel too good about it. But it's easier to stand the smell of your own crap than it is for somebody else to stand the smell of yours. They were not good conditions, cockroach infested, parts of the jail were mouse infested, it wasn't good, but it was home, and actually quite interesting. I saw and learned a lot about people in that period of time. Young working-class Protestant people – and this is of course a generalisation – seemed to me to need alcohol to laugh, but in the jail we learned to laugh without it . . . for some it was character-building, for others it was destruction; there were those who just couldn't cope, there was those who grew in stature in jail, it's amazing. And of course that was carried on then in Long Kesh where the atmosphere was fundamentally different, where UVF had express and unshared control and processes of discipline that were substantially superior to those in Crumlin Road jail. It was interesting.*

When Gusty Spence was convicted and sentenced for the Malvern Street murder, legend has it that he complained bitterly, 'So this is what you get for being a Protestant!' It was a refrain that would be repeated by hundreds of Loyalists after him and it reflected an anger that far from Loyalists being jailed for taking up arms to defend a common cause, the Unionist establishment – RUC, polit-icians and judicial system – should instead praise them. David Ervine was no different.

*. . . here were the police officers who were defending the status quo just like me, the screws who were standing beside me in the dock*

*defending the status quo just like me, and the fucking judge defending the status quo just like me. Now there was plenty of talk in our community about 'Ulster will fight and Ulster will be right', and 'shoot to kill', and plenty of political mouthing, but when you actually went and did it, somehow or other you were the scum of the earth, and that was certainly on my mind . . . I'll never forget when Lord Justice Jones [sentenced me], I waited on him getting the black hankie and putting it on his head. He was renowned for harshness, and I remember him saying to me, 'The defendant has very unfavourably impressed me', and he chastised the policeman, Frank Savage, for being less articulate than the prisoner, which I thought was a rather strange comment. It came from the judge's interruption during the policeman's evidence when he asked him, 'Do you believe that the defendant is contrite?' and Savage didn't know what contrite meant. At that point the judge lost the rapper and said, 'I have absolutely no doubt that the defendant knows what contrite means', and here was this peeler getting sandbagged for not being a polished connoisseur of the dictionary. It was crazy, but behind it was a sense that: 'Hold on a wee minute here, you're a scumbag, you shouldn't be articulate.'*

*I think that the Loyalists found themselves very much misunderstood, that the community mood music was to fight back, even if they themselves would not necessarily do the fighting. There was a clear belief that the forces of law and order would not protect the people, would not protect the integrity of Northern Ireland's position within the United Kingdom . . . But there were other things, I mean, these judges were case-hardened. You weren't talking here about going into a court filled with your peers who would make a judgment on whether you were guilty or innocent. It wasn't about getting the truth, it was just about clearing the decks, the conveyor belt to Long Kesh. There weren't too many people who were walking out of the courts, and under the Diplock\* regime it was democracy defending*

---

\* The no-jury system of trials was introduced in 1972 ostensibly to avoid the intimidation of juries in terrorism cases on foot of a recommendation made by Lord Kenneth Diplock, a senior Law Lord, who had been asked by the British government to consider alternatives to internment without trial. In the Diplock courts, as the new system was christened, a single judge acted as jury and anyone found guilty had an automatic right to appeal before three judges.

*itself by undemocratic means. I think when democracy defends itself by undemocratic means then it is behaving wrongly, and in my case it's punishing me because I believed that I was doing the right thing for my society, on the basis of the refusal of the state to actually deal with the problem of IRA insurgency.*

*There's no such thing as justice. I think that there's loads of law, but I don't believe I ever saw justice, I don't believe that justice is done in courtrooms. I think that the independence of the judges is very questionable; not only was very questionable but still is very questionable. They get infuriated when they hear that said, but I cannot believe that they were an independent group of people. They were part of the state machine, and it was a state machine going through the illusion of normal democratic behaviour. I remember my mother coming to see me and I was telling her just some of the things that happened to some people in police stations, and she didn't want to believe it. I had never seen the institutions from the inside, I never really had any effective functioning with the police, I had no effective functioning in the courts, I had no effective functioning in the prison regime. But my experience of the institutions was that they were as corrupt as fuck, and if I thought they were corrupt as fuck, and I was a defender of the status quo, how much more when the young Nationalist got his first glimpse. I wonder was he surprised at the degree of shit that exuded from those institutions, or did they just reinforce the rightness of his cause?*

## 4

The British government did not start treating Northern Ireland's Loyalist paramilitaries in the same way as the Provisional IRA, as terrorist threats whose members needed to be removed from the streets, until February 1973, when the first two Loyalists, both leaders in their way, were interned and sent to Long Kesh. Loyalist violence had really escalated in the wake of the internment swoop aimed at the IRA in August 1971, not only because, far from dealing the IRA a fatal blow, it had boosted Republican violence and greatly increased Nationalist alienation. The moderate SDLP had walked out of the Stormont parliament a month before over some controversial killings carried out by the British Army and after internment it spearheaded an angry campaign to boycott Northern Ireland's institutions and to withhold public rent and rate payments to the state. The one-sided nature of the operation, which ignored Loyalists, fuelled Nationalist anger. The UVF was already there, albeit hidden inside the folds of Tara, and in September that year the various Protestant vigilante groups set up in Loyalist districts in and around Belfast during the year came together to form the Ulster Defence Association (UDA), which acted partly as a mass protest movement and partly as a deadly paramilitary force. By February 1973, well over a hundred and twenty people had been killed by either the UVF or the UDA. By 1973, Edward Heath's government in London was beginning to seek a political exit from the morass of Irish politics and had turned its mind to constructing a widely based deal around the concept of power-sharing between Unionists and Nationalists, and some form of relationship with Dublin, the so-called 'Irish dimension'. Exploratory meetings had been held in late 1972 but the SDLP, the major Nationalist party, was playing hard to get, raising demands that internment be ended.

The decision to intern Loyalists was thus seen as a sop to Nationalists and a one-day protest strike, a precursor of the UWC strike a year later, was called by hardline Unionists and led to confrontations between Loyalists and the British Army, during which one UVF member and one UDA member were shot dead.[24]

The first two Loyalists interned also came, one each, from the UVF and the UDA. The UDA internee was Edward 'Ned' McCreery who led a gang in East Belfast notorious for the viciousness of its killings. One of its victims was kidnapped, stripped, hung by his heels and repeatedly stabbed and beaten before being shot dead. Another had the shape of a cross and the letters 'IRA' branded on his back.[25] A grenade attack on 1 February 1973 by members of McCreery's gang on a bus carrying Catholic workers to a building site in East Belfast was the trigger for his internment. The UVF leader chosen for detention was not really a UVF member at all, but the founder of a small paramilitary group that aligned itself, to the point of virtual absorption, with the UVF. John McKeague founded the Red Hand Commando in 1972, and had a storied track record in the world of Protestant politics. Once a close associate of the Reverend Ian Paisley, he had been charged but acquitted of involvement in the 1969 bombings that ended Terence O'Neill's political career. He went on to found the Shankill Defence Association, which played a major role in the violence of August 1969 in West and North Belfast, then broke with Paisley, ostensibly over money but also because rumours about McKeague's sexuality – he was reputedly a paedophile – had become rampant amongst Loyalists.*

The decision to intern Loyalist paramilitaries, along with the burgeoning moves by the Heath government towards what became the Sunningdale Agreement, acted as a stimulus both to paramilitary recruitment and their violence. By the middle of 1974 the UVF and the UDA, in their different and often conflicting ways, had become major actors in the story, serious obstacles in the way of British policy. They had, for instance, played an important role

---

* John McKeague was shot dead by the INLA in January 1982.

in the UWC strike that brought Heath's efforts to nought in 1974, although by David Ervine's account it seemed the UDA, rather than the UVF, was more active, more ready to expose its members at street barricades and the like. By the time David Ervine was caught with a bomb in the boot of his car, the memory of that victory was beginning to fade and with it the central place the Loyalist para-militaries had created for themselves in the Unionist political firmament. And by then the British, led now by Labour's Harold Wilson, were frying different fish. A month after Ervine's arrest the first moves were made towards a truce between the British and the IRA and while Loyalists assumed the worst, that the British would sell them down the river, they were mistaken. None the less, the consequences of the IRA's lengthy ceasefire would be serious for the UVF. The change in British security strategy, fashioned during the ceasefire and introduced towards the end of 1975, criminalised Loyalists as much as it did Republicans and soon RUC holding centres such as Castlereagh in East Belfast were churning out UVF men whose admissions during interrogations would earn them convictions and often lengthy jail terms in the juryless Diplock courts.

The policy of 'criminalisation' officially came into effect on 1 March 1976 when special-category status for all paramilitary pris-oners was scrapped. The accompanying emphasis on confession-based convictions was soon felt by the UVF. Less than a year after Ervine had been removed from the scene, in October 1975, the bulk of the UVF in South-East Antrim – based principally around the towns of Carrickfergus and Larne – was arrested and charged with a series of murders, attempted murders, bombings and robberies. In February 1977, after a trial that lasted seventy-six days and at the time was the most expensive in Northern Ireland's legal history, twenty-seven South-East Antrim UVF men were convicted, twenty-one on the basis of verbal or written statements they had made to detectives in Castlereagh. Among the murders they were convicted of were those of two UDA members, shot and buried in a secret grave in the spring of 1975 during vicious feuding between the two groups. When the new policy picked up momentum, Long Kesh began filling up with UVF prisoners.

One of those imprisoned was thirty-five-year-old Billy Mitchell, the former Paisleyite turned UVF leader. Many early UVF figures had imagined the Troubles would be sharp but short; by mid-1973 it was clear that they could last a lot longer. Against a background of growing paramilitary impatience with Unionism's political leaders, Mitchell persuaded the UVF to call a ceasefire, which began in mid-November 1973, in an effort to prompt a Republican response. The ceasefire was enforced with impressive discipline and the UVF did not kill anyone for over five months, until the end of February 1974. During the cessation, Mitchell also met members of the Official IRA, who had been on a ceasefire against the British since 1972, and more controversially with leading Provisional IRA members, Daithi O Connail and IRA Quarter Master General Brian Keenan, for exploratory peace talks. The dialogue stumbled on the predictable issue of Northern Ireland's constitutional status and the violence resumed. Even so, the British took heart from these developments and in April 1974, just as the UWC strike was building, the Labour Northern Ireland Secretary Merlyn Rees announced that the ban on the UVF would be lifted, a move that reflected British hope that this might encourage the recent signs of moderation.[26] A similar ban on Sinn Fein was also ended for the same reasons.

Mitchell's move was supported by Gusty Spence from his compound* in Long Kesh. By that stage Spence had almost completed his remarkable journey away from violence and hardline, inflexible Loyalism but the first sight of Spence in Belfast since his arrest in 1966 was of the old, diehard Spence. In July 1972, he was granted forty-eight hours' compassionate parole to attend his daughter's wedding but as he was being driven back to the jail his car was blocked and Spence was 'kidnapped' by fellow UVF members. He spent the next four months or so of this contrived freedom

---

* While the IRA used the term 'cages', the UVF and other Loyalists preferred the word 'compound'.

helping to reorganise and restructure the UVF; he also designed a uniform for the organisation, the main feature of which was the black leather jacket that became the UVF's daunting hallmark. A British television interview with Spence made during his spell of liberty featured a taciturn, uncompromising figure whose answers came in unsmiling monosyllables. He was re-arrested in November 1972 but by the spring of 1974, some eighteen months later, he had performed a political U-turn, now advocating a peaceful, nego-tiated settlement to the Troubles. Before long he would also be quietly preaching the merits of power-sharing with Nationalists, a far cry from his adamant opposition to Terence O'Neill's mild reformism.[27] Spence also encouraged the UVF to create a political party, the Volunteer Political Party (VPP) which had a brief if unsuccessful existence contesting for the votes of Shankill Road Loyalists. Like Billy Mitchell, Gusty Spence opened dialogue with Republicans, reaching out to IRA prisoners of both Official and Provisional stripes, helping to set up a Camp Council to negotiate issues of common concern with the prison governor, on which sat the Commanders of UDA, UVF, Official IRA and Provisional IRA inmates. In these developments, along with an influx of hardline prisoners to the jail, can be found both the source of Gusty Spence's eventual estrangement from the mainstream UVF outside the jail as well as the influences that shaped David Ervine's later political odyssey in the Progressive Unionist Party, the VPP's successor.

The internment of Loyalists and a swelling conviction rate meant that by late 1973 the UVF's prisoners had to be moved from Crum-lin Road jail in Belfast to Long Kesh. Spence was one of the first to be transferred. He was the natural choice for Commander of UVF prisoners and introduced a regime strongly influenced by his years in the Royal Ulster Rifles, as he told BBC journalist Peter Taylor many years later: 'The compounds were run on British Army lines with made-up beds, highly polished boots, pressed uniforms, etc. There was a daily regime. Reveille was at eight o'clock in the morn-ing, followed by showers, breakfast, and then a parade. Then the day was laid out.'[28] By November 1974, when David Ervine was driven through the gates of Long Kesh, Gerry Adams, Ivor Bell and Brendan Hughes were beginning their battle with the IRA's Camp Commander, David Morley, another British Army veteran whose idea of prison discipline, while more eccentric than Spence's, was similarly derived from his days as a squaddie. This was the Long Kesh that would be Ervine's home for the next six years, first as a remand prisoner then as a sentenced man.

*For the short time I was on remand in Long Kesh, I was held in Compound 20. Compound 18 and 19 at that time were UVF compounds, 16 and 17 were UDA compounds and 21 was Official IRA. We were held in the remand compound, 20, which was mixed UDA, UVF . . . I remember the day that I arrived, I was met by Gusty Spence who actually lived in Compound 18, but he was in Compound 20 to meet the influx of new prisoners in his capacity as the O/C of the UVF in Long Kesh. So it was very clear that the [prison] structure was not only solid, but was established in the relationship between the UVF and the jail [authorities] . . . It seemed to me that here was clear recognition of the importance of the control factor in men. [The authorities] knew that they couldn't control UVF people; the only people who could control UVF people was the UVF leadership, and that was very clear. You were coming from a jail where you were locked up, allowed out, locked up, allowed out all day, every day, that's the way it worked. In Long Kesh, the huts had doors that opened out onto a fairly large hundred-metre-square compound and pretty much from seven o'clock in the morning till nine o'clock at night you could do what you wished. Or at least that's the way you might have thought, but then enter UVF rules and regulations where one had to be out of bed in the morning at a specific time . . . washed and preened by a certain time, that one's living space had to be spotlessly cleaned. Being tidy was not good enough. This wasn't what I was expecting . . . My remand period in Long Kesh was almost a grounding for what I would be coming back to, because in the sentenced compounds, 18 and 19, the implications of that discipline were actually much more acute than in Compound*

20. *They weren't invasive but they were about making the place function, and you learned very quickly a set of rules . . .*

*. . . there was a 'no conflict' policy [which meant] you weren't allowed to hit anyone. If you had a dispute [then] lifting your hands was actually a very risky business because you were then directly challenging the authority of the UVF in Long Kesh and that did not go down well at all. You would have been expected to deal with things in a manly manner. In other words if there was a real dispute then [it was into] the boxing ring and [on with] the boxing gloves. The venting of anger and frustration was done in a controlled manner rather than simply in a brawl. There were very, very few incidents of physical violence, but of course the other compounds around us did not necessarily function in that way. Other groups controlled their membership by violence. I remember the story about a guy in, I think it was Compound 16, the UDA compound, who apparently had infracted their rules and his head was put in a workbench vice and tightened. The UVF leadership did not advocate the use of violence for control purposes . . . and it worked. On one occasion I saw a guy use a knife and he was immediately stripped of special-category status, political status, if you like, and thrown out. I actually think that in terms of control mechanisms the UVF were away ahead of the game inside that jail . . . The cleanliness wasn't about telling anybody they were dirty; it was about absolute discipline, having pride in yourself. It was a lot of very subtle psychological things that I think Spence, perhaps in his army years and in Crumlin Road jail, had thought of, along the lines of: 'We know that people can get depressed; we know that there's a danger of disenchantment, they're fed up and depressed' . . . Spence had a lot of things in place that were about keeping you occupied and giving you a concept of pride . . . I have to say to you, I raised the odd eyebrow, but I got on with it, and over later years I would be in admiration for the style, attitude and nature of the way he controlled those men.*

*. . . there were many reasons why the discipline of the UVF was absolutely vital, but the point I make was that Spence was virtually*

*unassailable regarding fairness, [and the way he] used his authority.*
*He had been the O/C of the UVF before he came into Long Kesh,*
*and . . . a weaker leader would have been crushed from the outset.*
*There were a few wobbles but in the main the internal discipline of*
*the UVF held. The compound system was one of humane confine-*
*ment, particularly if it was augmented with psychologically sensible*
*attitudes on the leadership's part and not only that, a 'no conflict'*
*attitude by the leadership. You weren't, if you were five foot three,*
*going to be pushed around by somebody six foot four when the*
*dinner queue came; you just weren't going to get bullied, it wasn't*
*going to happen . . .*

The Wilson government's new criminalisation policy saw the eventual destruction of the compounds and huts of Long Kesh and their replacement by the H-blocks along with a more conventional and restricted prison regime. Ervine believed that the old Long Kesh regime encouraged cross-community contact and he blamed the Labour government and especially the new policy's overseer, Northern Ireland Secretary Roy Mason, for making changes that might have jeopardised the potential for some sort of peace process. As it was, the new prison system led directly to the IRA protests and hunger strikes of 1980 and 1981, which deepened the conflict. Ervine also condemned the changes because life in cells and wings discouraged prisoners from seeking further education.

*. . . I think that . . . it's a tragedy that the continuum of the com-*
*pound process until the end of the conflict wasn't allowed because I*
*think that the Ph.D.s would be coming out of our ears. Interestingly*
*enough, in the UVF compounds people were inclined to take classes*
*that were related to mathematics and very practical things, com-*
*puters and so on, whereas the Provos were inclined to take classes*
*related to social issues. I was doing a foundation course, an Arts*
*and Humanities foundation course, and part of it was the study of*
*poetry and I remember a big guy called John Wallace, who now is*
*living in Scotland, whose view of poetry was that poetry was for*

*pansies, poetry was for big girls' blouses. He would say things to me like, 'What are you doing that for, you big idiot you?' Totally disparaging. John Wallace eventually had to take the compulsory classes and out of that [he] did an Open University degree. He then left Long Kesh to take up Ph.D. work at St Andrews University in Scotland and stayed in university for I don't know how many years after that. So it was quite interesting to see the mindset changes in people with exposure to education . . . it was tremendous stuff.*

If the Provisional IRA in Long Kesh at this time had Cage 11, where Gerry Adams and Brendan Hughes discussed revolution, plotted the overthrow of the IRA leadership and recruited a following, then the UVF had its equivalent, Compound 21, where Gusty Spence was eventually housed. There, the UVF leader gathered around him his own band of followers who discussed ideas such as power-sharing – as unwelcome to the UVF outside the jail as Adams's left-wing inclinations were to his leadership – and nurtured the core of what would become the UVF/PUP leadership that twenty years later would embrace a peace process initiated by the same Gerry Adams.

*We were provoked, tortured almost, by Spence. I can remember sitting in the sunshine in 1975 minding my own business on the steps of the study hut and Gusty Spence came over. 'How are you doing, son?' 'I'm doing all right, sir, thank you very much.' He was always given the title 'sir'. I think anybody who begrudged that soon accepted it and 'sir' just rolled out. It would even today roll off my tongue without thinking when I meet him, but anyway we started talking about politics. I was just an average basic chap, and he started asking, 'Had anybody thought of the politics of the goldfish bowl?' 'What is this stupid auld bastard talking about?' you're saying to yourself . . . and he went on to talk about the politics of the goldfish bowl in a society where not only would one be fair but one would have to be seen to be fair, how this was the only way that you could ever have . . . power-sharing. 'Power-sharing! Power-sharing!*

*You mean let the fifth column inside the house? Sure you wouldn't want the fifth column inside the house!' And I think that Spence's theory was probably well enough summed up when he would say, 'Well, I'd rather have them pishing out from inside as pishing in from the outside.' And that was 1975, and Northern Ireland Unionists had not in any way come to terms with the concept of power-sharing. The power-sharing Executive had just fallen, à la the Sunningdale Agreement. Now whether or not people would have acquiesced in power-sharing and were more agitated by . . . the suggestion of a Council of Ireland is a debatable issue. I think for many . . . the Council of Ireland was used to justify the strike . . . In other words, my argument would be that I am not convinced, far from being convinced that the people of Northern Ireland or the Protestant or the Unionist community were wedded to any notion of power-sharing. Spence was away ahead of the game, and he was almost a devil's advocate. He was constantly facing us with theories that were weird. I mean, you had just come into Long Kesh and the basis of your life was hatred for the Republicans [and] the next thing you know there's a Camp Council in which every faction, an unheard-of thing, [were] all pulled together by Spence to [engage in] dialogue about the conditions in the jail, to challenge the jail regime about our conditions and circumstances. But that's not what his real reason was; it was to talk politics among all of the factions, and he nearly pulled it off. The Provos ran away from it eventually because the idea was that you would then extrapolate from these contacts to the outside, and the Provos ran away from it. It's quite interesting [that] it was the Provos who ran away, not the Loyalists, not even the UDA. That was Spence's baby, and here he had, by that time, two hundred and forty men who were all full of gung-ho hatred for the Republicans and yet Spence was able to pull it off; he was able to sleep in his bed among these murderers who were dubious about talking to the enemy, bringing in a fifth column. They would be saying, 'What is this man doing?' We got that all the time [from Spence]; it was constant, absolutely constant, and if you look at Billy Hutchinson, Billy Mitchell, David Ervine, Marty Snodden, 'Skittle'* *or Alistair Little, 'Winkie', Tom Winston, and others, you're looking at a class of '75 and the teacher was Spence. I think you were expected to do a lot of your own learning, but the provocateur was Spence . . . It was structured and unstructured, structured by Spence in ways that he would have tried to provoke debate and in an unstructured manner where he would have tried to collar you and make you think. You were in a cubicle or what some people would call a cell, and you were just sitting around having a yarn, up came politics, paramilitarism, all of that . . . and it was all the time. The violence outside and the fact that nobody outside was doing any-thing about it [was] probably . . . part of the reason why we our-selves took steps that took us into arenas that people had never been before, testing ideas on each other. I remember writing a letter to Combat\* about the possibility of power-sharing, and being attacked in the compound, well almost attacked. [The attacker] was stopped before he got to me . . . There was an intensity in our community about such issues and anything that looked like it was reasonable to the other side was seen as a weakness. You would have got that internally as well within the compound system, but in fairness, and it's been something that the UVF has been very good at since, and the peace process tells the tale. You could fall out with the UVF leadership on a Monday morning and Monday afternoon go back and do busi-ness. The UVF in that respect has always facilitated discussion and debate, in my experience, both inside and outside [jail]. I'm sure sometimes they sit with their fingers in their ears not wishing to hear what they're hearing, but this current leadership has followed on in that tradition. I think that is one of the reasons why the UVF as an organisation as a whole is more sophisticated and settled . . .*

*I remember a number of questions that were nightmare questions, and very simplistic I would have to say, but nevertheless I think of significance. Why do people hate people they don't know? Imagine [Spence] asking that of the murderers: why do people hate people they don't know? . . . Without personal basis or personal foundation,*

---

\* The UVF magazine, now called the *Purple Standard*.

*there's a capacity to hate, and out of the dialogues around that issue it was very clear that the process of manipulation in Northern Ireland is not a thought process, it's a taught process. So what is that manipulation about, what does it really mean, who does well out of that manipulation, who does badly? Big-house Unionism in bed with little-house Unionism, little-house Unionism goes home to its difficulties and big-house Unionism manipulates the difficulties and remains in the big house, you know. That's simplistic but nevertheless that was the style and nature of the debate and the discussions.*

Gusty Spence also initiated dialogue with the Provisional IRA leadership and that of the Official IRA, but not the group that split off from the Officials, the Irish National Liberation Army (INLA) which, inside the jail, took sides with the UDA during a violent feud with the UVF in 1975.

*Gusty Spence carried the mantle for most of that, but I can remember being sent to, I think it was Compound 9, [where] the Provo compounds bordered the soccer pitches and they were out playing soccer. I loved to play a game of soccer, and Gusty asked me expressly not to do that, but to go to the football game and I asked him, 'Aye, OK, well, what do you want me to do?' 'Well,' he said, 'I want you to get a Provo out to the wire and talk to him' . . . It was Hugh Feeney, one of the London car bombers, and I remember talking to Hugh Feeney expressly about a message that I was asked to pass on and then the conversation went on further. I said to him, 'Well, where's your victory?' And his reply was shocking in its simplicity: 'Our victory is every day we can hold down the might of the British Army.' And I said, 'Well, Hugh, I feel sorry for you.' And that's exactly the language that I used, because it really was not about the outcome, but that the war was the cause. I felt that was rather a tragedy, but it was interesting, in terms of the answer, a tragic answer and was one that was unsustainable.*
*We had lots of conversations with the Official IRA. They were in the same part of the jail as us, quite close . . . it was relatively easy to*

*have dialogue across the wire. Even though we were separated by about ten yards, you could have reasonable discussion, but then we both also had a penchant for education and the judgement call was made whether you let them share your education facilities or not, and we agreed to let them do that. So the UVF and the Stickies used the same education facilities but the UDA did not. Now whether [that was] because they hadn't got the interest in education, I don't know. I'm not aware of anybody who was doing any great degree of education in their compounds. But then again didn't John White\* get a degree, and he was in Compound 17, but he didn't avail of the study-hut opportunities, maybe because he didn't want to share space with either the UVF or more likely the Stickies. In those discussions with the Stickies, I mean, it just came quite naturally. You did your study and you had your work to do, but you also had quite interesting discussions about the history of the Republican movement. I have to say I was quite fascinated by a lot of their views and where they were coming from. I always had a grand desire to know my enemy and whilst they were somewhat less the enemy after 1972 when they called a ceasefire and expressed the desire to pursue any arguments it had politically, they also said that 'If you can't unite Northern Ireland then you can't unite the island of Ireland', which is quite interesting and quite practical in its outlook. So they in some ways ceased to be the enemy. You could learn a lot from them in terms of Republican ideology and the engine driving the agenda that lay behind it. It was also quite interesting to hear them talking about other Republicans or others who have adopted the name of Republican. I think we learned a bit all right . . . and the exposure itself was probably good because there was a difference between us. One had been brought up a Catholic and the other had been brought up a Protestant, so you were getting exposed to something . . . that you and many in your own community had never been exposed to before.*

* John White was a Shankill Road UDA man notorious for the frenzied stabbing murders in 1973 of SDLP Senator Paddy Wilson and his Protestant female companion Irene Andrews. In 1978 he was sent to jail for twenty years after pleading guilty to the murders. He completed a degree in Social Sciences while in jail.

Q. *And did you ever bounce your own conclusions and ideas off . . . ?*

A. *Oh yes, oh aye.*

Q. *And how were they received?*

A. *Usually with patience and fortitude, but you've got to remember that the core belief of the Stickies at that time was the socialist republic and the ruling elites and all of that stuff. Whilst we understood the process of manipulation, we would not have been gung-ho ideological communists, where they were, I think. There was always a form of socialism within us, a caring politics within us, but not in an ideological sense. Spence always tried to avoid ideology because he believed that ideology was the root cause of the destruction of the Stickies and that the purist emerges when the ideologue emerges and so far, in fairness, the UVF and the PUP have managed to steer a fairly steady course . . . in terms of the development or entrenchment of dogma.*

In March 1975, Gusty Spence was profiled by the *Irish Times*, which noted that he was 'a different man than the one who was given a sentence on October 14th, 1966, of life imprisonment' for the Malvern Street murder. He had become, the article went on, very critical of Loyalist politicians: 'He now says that the Unionists, and others, have conned the Loyalist population over the years, have kept them in deplorable housing and appalling slums, have played the Orange card once too often.'[29] Between Spence expounding views like this and consorting with the Official IRA in Long Kesh, the UVF had earned a name, at least in Unionist circles, for radical leftist beliefs and this surfaced in an intriguing way during 1975, in the midst of a feud with the UDA that had absolutely nothing to do with ideology. As rivals for the allegiance of working-class Protestants, the UVF and the UDA were constantly rubbing against each other in the early to mid-1970s, the years of Loyalist paramilitary growth, and from time to time violence would break out between them. Invariably alcohol, as much as politics, provided the trigger and such was the case in 1975.

The roots of the trouble lay in the UWC strike of May 1974 when the paramilitaries ordered bars and drinking clubs to shut down in Protestant Belfast. One UVF bar in North Belfast stayed open and when UDA men tried to close it, a fight broke out, guns appeared and a twenty-two-year-old UVF man was shot dead. Eight months later, on 15 March 1975, a quarrel broke out in another North Belfast bar between UVF and UDA drinkers which was settled when UVF gunmen arrived and shot two of their rivals dead. The UVF claimed that the two dead UDA men had killed their man back in May 1974 and they had been targeted because the UDA reneged on a pledge given to the UVF to deal with them. There then followed a series of tit-for-tat shootings and bombings, often in bars and mostly in David Ervine's home patch of East Belfast, which culminated in the kidnapping of two UDA men, one a local Commander, who were shot dead and buried in a secret grave in County Antrim. The UVF was tiny compared to the UDA but what it lacked in size it often made up for in the intensity of its violence.

As this was happening the world of left-wing Republicanism was being torn apart in an equally vicious feud between the Official IRA and a break-off group opposed to the Officials' ceasefire, the Irish Republican Socialist Party (IRSP) which soon had an armed wing called the Irish National Liberation Army (INLA). That feud prompted the UDA to allege that the Officials and the UVF had teamed up to assist each other in their respective feuds, a charge that fitted neatly into the left-wing narrative about the UVF then current within Unionism. There were even rumours circulating in both communities, unfounded it seemed, that a close relative of Gusty Spence had joined and become a rising figure in the Official IRA. The UDA claimed there was an 'agreement between members of the brigade staff of the UVF and the Officials to act against the INLA and other Loyalist paramilitary organisations'. It added: '. . . when met with opposition to their extreme left-wing politics, the political leaders of the UVF used the media to deny their Communist ideology. We regret that an organisation with the proud and historic name of the UVF should permit some of its brigade staff to bring the organisation into disrepute and work with the Official Republican movement to bring about the destruction of Northern Ireland.'[30] In an effort to deflect the left-wing charge, the next day the UVF claimed responsibility for the bombing, a month earlier, of the Bush Bar in Leeson Street, off the Falls Road, a well-known haunt of the Official IRA and an explosion the Officials had blamed on the INLA at the time. The Officials' Chief of Staff, Cathal Goulding, was in the bar when the car bomb exploded. The UVF 'had no Communist or Official IRA ties', two hooded spokesmen told the media.[31]

On the basis that 'my enemy's enemy is my friend', the feud eventually spilled over into Long Kesh, where the alleged UVF–Official IRA liaison was mirrored by the UDA and former Officials who had joined the INLA. In October 1975, the bodies of the two kidnapped UDA men, Hugh McVeigh and David Douglas, were found in Islandmagee and the RUC, assisted by an informer, swooped on the South-East Antrim UVF men responsible and arrested them. When they were convicted and sent to Long Kesh, the UDA with the help, Ervine asserted, of the INLA sought revenge on those responsible. He told Boston College what happened:

*. . . the UVF leadership in Long Kesh, I believe, operated very often with great wisdom by maintaining calm and by building processes of defence. We had a number of situations in Long Kesh where things exploded and when the UVF won hands down every time. It was simply about discipline and organisation and pre-empting [what] the UDA were likely to do . . . around that time there was a liaison between the UDA and the INLA and the INLA was semaphoring to the UDA the movements of UVF prisoners coming back from visits, that is South-East Antrim UVF prisoners coming back from visits. The UDA broke out of their compounds and attempted to attack a minibus carrying UVF prisoners.*

Q. *This would have been related to McVeigh and Douglas . . .?*

A. *Yes, the UVF then broke out of its compound and sorted that problem out.*

Authoritative estimates of the UVF's strength towards the end of 1975 put the organisation's membership at around fifteen hundred, with 'a hardcore' of some four to five hundred.[32] That compared to the some twenty thousand members that the UDA claimed, although when it came down to dedicated gunmen and bombers, the groups might not have had such a disparity. The UVF's internal structures were, like Provisional IRA's at that time, roughly modelled on the British Army and were testament to the influence of the three earliest leaders, all ex-British soldiers: Gusty Spence, 'Bo' McClelland and Tommy West. The UVF's military leadership was invested in a Brigade Staff, similar to the IRA's GHQ, and it would be led by a Chief of Staff, just like the IRA, except the UVF leader carried the rank of 'Brigadier'. His second in command was a 'Colonel' and the Brigade Staff officers were responsible for a range of activities, from prisoner welfare to intelligence gathering and so on. Above the Brigade Staff was the Command Staff which consisted of the Brigade Staff plus seven Battalion Commanders and sometimes, as during the peace process, the leadership of the Red Hand Commando. Modelling the UVF's organisational structure on the British Army made it, much like the pre-Adams IRA, vulnerable to security-force penetration. The IRA's solution was to attempt to reorganise into cells but the UVF dealt with the problem by varying the responsibilities of Commanders to make British Intelligence's efforts at identifying key members a little more uncertain. But the heart of the UVF, those on the ground, were not reorganised, making it somewhat easy to work out general responsibility for acts of violence. Northern Ireland was split geographically into seven Battalion areas: North, South, East and West Belfast, East Antrim, Mid-Ulster and North Ulster. There were also Battalions in Scotland and England, small in size, which were used in support of the UVF in

Northern Ireland. Battalion Commanders were called 'Lieutenant-Colonel' and the companies in each Battalion would also be determined geographically. Company Commanders held the rank of 'Major' and each company had platoons within which were located active service units. For special operations individuals could be drawn from different units.

Like their political antecedents in the Independent Unionist movement, disgruntlement with the Unionist political establishment along with economic and social populism characterised the UVF's politics outside of the constitutional question. Of the two Loyalist paramilitary groups, the UVF was the first to dabble in electoral politics, encouraged by the success of the UWC strike to believe there was sufficient Protestant disenchantment with the mainstream political leadership to sustain a market for their brand of Loyalism. In June 1974, the UVF created the Volunteer Political Party whose founding manifesto described itself as 'a progressive and forward-thinking Unionist party'.

The VPP contested the October 1974 British general election in West Belfast and one of its leaflets attacked the 'disgraceful' social conditions on the Shankill Road. One of the issues highlighted was a piece of public housing notorious for its shoddy construction known as the 'Weetabix' flats after a certain physical resemblance between the blocks of flats and the breakfast cereal. The candidate, Ken Gibson, a former UVF detainee from East Belfast, polled a mere 2,600 votes and the UVF leadership got the message. 'The general public', it conceded, 'does not support the political involvement of the UVF', and the VPP was wound up. Although one of the VPP leaders, Hugh Smyth, won a seat to a Constitutional Convention established by the British the following year, he stood as an Independent Unionist while the UVF went back to what it knew best. The UVF eschewed organised politics until 1978 when the Progressive Unionist Party was created and even then it was, for many years, regarded more as camouflage for meetings between the UVF leadership and the Northern Ireland Office, rather than a serious political venture.

The VPP experiment raises an intriguing question. If its first outing had been more successful, would this have planted the seeds of a political/military split in the UVF, of the sort that later transformed the Provisionals? The question is academic because until David Ervine's election to the 1998 Assembly, Loyalist paramilitary parties would invariably do badly in Northern Ireland's elections, although some individuals associated with them were more successful, as long as they stood in their own names, not that of their paramilitary group. Protestants might have been ambivalent about the UVF's and UDA's violence, as Catholics were about the IRA's, but they would never vote for them in significant numbers while the violence continued. For the same reason respectable, lower-middle-class and upwards Protestants would prefer the Queen's uniform to the balaclava if they felt the urge to get back at the IRA. Nor was there much of an appetite for politics in the ranks or at leadership level of the UVF, as one source put it: '... the leadership's view of politics ... was simply: "Go ahead, theorise, debate, discuss and write papers but we have a job to do and until there is a cease-fire from Republicans nothing is going to change."'

As the VPP experiment flopped, the scene was set for a dramatic change in the UVF leadership, one effected at the point of a gun but prompted not by politics but by military matters, in particular a series of what the British Army called 'own goals', UVF men killed by their own bombs and a number of 'reckless' operations such as the Miami Showband attack, which had harmed the UVF's image. The leadership was removed in a coup when gunmen walked into a meeting and told them they had been deposed and should leave the scene. The then Chief of Staff actually left the country for his own safety. The Shankill UVF had strongly supported the coup and so it is likely that so did Lenny Murphy, an activist who had built a fearsome name for violence by 1975 and would soon provide material for a notorious chapter in the history of the Troubles as leader of the Shankill Butchers. Put another way, if Murphy had opposed the coup it would have caused the rebels problems. The incident was testimony to the power residing with the UVF's gunmen.

Into this new mix was added a truce between the IRA and the British that lasted for much of the year and like all ceasefires it made many Protestants more edgy and suspicious. The ceasefire became tangible when 'incident centres' were set up to allow the British and the IRA jointly to monitor infringements and when legal weapons were issued to the Republicans manning the centres, all of which set Loyalist nerves on edge with predictably violent results. The following year saw UVF violence reach new heights. In July 1975, the Miami Showband massacre happened and then on 2 October twelve people died in an unprecedented wave of UVF bombings and shootings in Belfast, Antrim, Coleraine, Armagh and County Down. Six of the victims were Protestants, four of them UVF members killed in a premature explosion. The single worst incident was in Belfast at a bottling plant near the city centre. In a UVF gun attack cum armed robbery four workers, all Catholics and two of them sisters, were shot dead. Three of the victims, including the two sisters, were killed by the gang leader Lenny Murphy, who shot each in the head.

Murphy, who was from the Shankill Road, had joined the UVF at the age of sixteen and killed for the first time four years later in September 1972 when he shot dead a Protestant gun-dealer accused of having dealings with the IRA. Charged along with an associate with the murder, Murphy was remanded first to Crumlin Road jail and then to the remand compound in Long Kesh. In April 1973 he poisoned his co-defendant with cyanide in Crumlin Road prison after suggestions surfaced that he might co-operate with the police against Murphy. He was acquitted of murder but convicted of trying to escape from jail and was imprisoned until May 1975. After the explosion of violence in October 1975, the UVF was again placed on the list of banned organisations and within weeks the coup restored the leadership that had been in charge prior to the beginning of Loyalist internment. Among the new leaders was John 'Bunter' Graham who was Chief of Staff by 1976 and, aside from a time spent in jail on a 'supergrass' charge, has been Chief of Staff ever since. During the peace-process years his support of the positive approach advocated by Ervine and Gusty Spence was probably crucial. David Ervine's recollection suggests that the leadership changes in October 1975, which he called a 'coup', had a mixed reception from some, if not for ideological reasons then for personal ones. The overthrown leadership had treated Gusty Spence's politicking with something close to contempt. One position paper produced inside the jail for the leadership was returned to Long Kesh with a dismissive 'Fuck Off!' and that sort of behaviour would now end. Spence's emphasis on discipline also alienated some in the jail including the newly convicted Lenny Murphy. With some allies, Murphy got himself transferred out of the UVF compound.

*. . . there were, I think, little ramifications . . . some people ended up going to Magilligan from Long Kesh not long after that, and they were people who were less inclined to accept [the changes]; they didn't really want to accept the very sensible, relatively strict discipline in the jail. Joe Bennett\* was one of them . . . he went to Magilligan and came back eventually when they closed Magilligan, but there were a few Shankill Road men left and went to Magilligan around that time . . .*

Q. *[Anthony] 'Chuck' Berry,† Lenny Murphy, people like that?*

A. *Yeah, and I think that the [prison] leadership's view at that time was that the UVF had lost its way, it didn't have the degree of discipline that it needed to have, that there were excesses, and there were larger-than-life cardboard cut-out characters within the UVF whose outlandish behaviour was detrimental to the UVF as a whole, and I think that was one of the reasons why the leadership changed, that the coup took place.*

*[As far as the prison leadership was concerned] it was a fucking ignorance and an arrogance [on the part of the deposed leaders]*

---

\* An East Belfast UVF member and former Long Kesh Compound Commander, he was the first UVF 'supergrass' whose evidence resulted in the conviction in 1983 of fourteen associates on charges relating to murders, bombings, shootings and robberies.
† A Shankill Road UVF Platoon Commander.

*that saw people who hot-housed the issues, thought about them,*
*deliberated about them and then sent opinions and found those*
*opinions within seconds torn up and thrown in the bin . . . There*
*was no opportunity for a dialogue or a conflict, and in that respect*
*they had no interest in listening to analysis . . . it's always a treach-*
*erous and difficult time when something like a coup happens, but*
*set against the backdrop of a set of prisoners who were analysing*
*and doing anything that they could for their country in the confines*
*of Long Kesh and finding that they were being treated like fools . . .*
*I think sets in context my argument that over a period of time no*
*one was crying into their tea about the change of leadership.*

After being released from jail in May 1975, Lenny Murphy gathered around him a team of like-minded followers, which, at its height, according to one account, 'contained dozens of members'.[33] One was William Moore,* who worked in a meat-processing plant where his job entailed butchering cattle, and another was Robert 'Basher' Bates, who would befriend Brendan Hughes some years later in the H-blocks. On the night of 24–25 November, the gang carried out the first of the killings that would earn it infamy and a name for extreme brutality. Their victim was picked up late at night in the city centre as he walked from Crumlin Road to the Falls Road to pick up a taxi ride to his home in Andersonstown. The route he took was a sure sign that he was a Catholic and choosing their victims in this way became the modus operandi of the Shankill Butchers. Francis Crossan, a thirty-two-year-old married man with two children, was knocked unconscious with a wheel brace wielded by Murphy and bundled into a London-style black taxi where he was savagely beaten and driven to an entry off the Shankill Road. There he was beaten again before Murphy used a butcher's knife provided by William Moore to cut his throat almost through to the spine. Over the next two years the Shankill Butchers would embark on a savage carnival of death, taking an estimated thirty lives with

* Died of a heart attack, May 2009.

furious, bloodthirsty violence; their leader and murderous muse, Lenny Murphy, was directly involved in at least eighteen of the killings until his own death, at the hands of IRA assassins, in 1982. The bulk of their victims were Catholics although Protestants were killed in mistake for Catholics and some were killed in Loyalist feuding. However, it was the random selection and brutal murder of Catholics in North Belfast for which the gang became notorious, a reign of terror graphically captured in one account:

> They were killed using implements such as cleavers, axes and the butcher's knives, which earned the gang its nickname. Some of their victims were killed with axes while others had their throats cut. The victims were picked out solely for their religion. Some were tortured. In a statement to police about one murder, a member of the gang said, 'When he was lying on the ground I cut his throat. It was a butcher's knife I had, sharp as a lance. I just slit his throat right open.' In at least one case, an attempt appears to have been made to decapitate a victim ... In another Butchers killing, a man had all but three teeth ripped out with pliers.[34]

Five days after the killing of Francis Crossan, Murphy crossed swords with the new UVF leadership with such chilling violence that from thereon few in the UVF would wish to confront him. The clash began with the robbery by members of a separate UVF unit of a seventy-three-year-old Shankill woman who was tied to her bed as the gang ransacked her house. The UVF leadership ordered the punishment shooting of those responsible and this was carried out by some of Murphy's men. But during the operation one of the burglars, Stewart Robinson, was shot dead as he tried to run off. He was killed by Archibald Waller who had helped Murphy kill Francis Crossan. Robinson's unit demanded revenge and so they shot Waller dead. Murphy's response was to have the gunman responsible, Noel Shaw, brought to a drinking club. Murphy lined up his entire squad to watch Shaw's bloody death. After a pistol-whipping, Murphy shot him five or six times and the rest of his unit were forced to clean up the mess afterwards. It is easy to see why David Ervine concluded in his interviews with Boston College that the UVF leadership was too scared of Murphy to intervene in the Butchers' killing.

Murphy was arrested in March the following year and charged with attempted murder. In a deal with the prosecution, he pleaded guilty to firearms charges and was sentenced to twelve years. The Butchers' killings continued in his absence, with Moore and Bates leading the gang, but with Murphy, who had been present at only the first three knife murders, directing the killers from his cell. The authorities got their big break when the Butchers made their first mistake. In May 1977, a young Catholic man, Gerard McLaverty, was abducted by the Butchers, beaten and tortured, but somehow the gang failed to finish him off. He was dumped in an alleyway and, while badly injured, he survived. McLaverty's miraculous escape came just as Loyalists, led by Ian Paisley, were planning a general strike in protest at British security policy towards the IRA and when it began the Shankill Road was thronged with excited Loyalist paramilitaries. RUC detectives took McLaverty on a tour of the area in the hope that he would be able to identify his assailants from the crowds. He picked out two of them and they were arrested, questioned and eventually admitted their role in the Butchers gang, identifying in the process other members of the gang who also confessed. Eleven members of the Butchers, only a fraction of the gang, were convicted of a total of nineteen murders in February 1979. Forty-two life sentences were handed out, eleven to Moore and ten to Bates. Lenny Murphy was never convicted of any Butcher killing and was released in July 1982, killing four more times before the IRA, allegedly assisted by a Loyalist informer, tracked him down and riddled him with bullets. Although it was said that many of his former colleagues were privately relieved at his death, there was no question that the UVF might disown him. Far from that, he was given a full paramilitary send-off: a four-man guard of honour on the coffin all wearing the UVF's uniform of black leather jacket, balaclava and a commando hat, a similarly attired firing party that discharged three volleys from handguns in a nearby entry as his coffin was taken from his house, and a piper who played 'Abide with Me' as the casket was placed inside a hearse. It should not have surprised anyone that he was given such a send-off. After all, according to Billy Mitchell's definition, the UVF's job was to 'instil fear and terror' in the Catholic community and, by that light, Lenny Murphy was an exemplary UVF member. While someone such as David Ervine was very conscious of the bad image that Murphy and the Shankill Butchers had created for the PUP and the more politically minded UVF leaders, his carefully chosen words about the Butchers are probably as close to a reproof as he could safely go.

*. . . my personal view? One of abhorrence, absolute abhorrence. The difficulty you had was that there were divided loyalties in Long Kesh. Some of the people who would have been responsible . . . would have had friends in jail, and one had to be cautious. You weren't going out of your way to fight World War III in Long Kesh where you had little influence or control on the affairs on the outside.*

*There were those who believed that the UVF leadership were afraid of some of the personalities. It's as simple as that. Some of the personalities who were driving the excess were so powerful that they were bigger than the whole organisation; that was the view of many of the prisoners.*

*I have no doubt that the [prison] leadership would have lobbied and reflected not just their own views [about the Butchers] but the views within the compounds. There were a lot of UVF prisoners and UVF prisoners had the highest incidence of life-sentence prisoners in any of the compounds, so they weren't angels or pussycats. So I think when multiple murderers are saying, 'Hey, for frig sake', I think it's worth listening to them . . . but there was no opportunity for the volunteer or even the relatively low-level officer to hear the dialogue between the leadership on the outside and the leadership on the inside. That was all done very privately.*

*In many ways [we] had little control or influence over what was going on, but it was tragedy and it was sad. The Butcher stuff was . . . I'm not sure how to describe it other than to say that it was obscene, and nobody could defend it. I remember one suggestion that, 'Well, you know, there's not a lot of weapons and you use whatever weaponry you have', and that just never washed with me, ever, although I have to say maybe we were callous enough not to be dismayed but I always sensed a pride in the UVF. You only had to see us; you only had to watch the way we lived our lives, the discipline in the cages, the cleanliness, the sense of self-esteem that the UVF had. It stood out against all other sections of prisoners in Long Kesh, but certainly I have to say that there was abhorrence . . . now it wasn't just the Butchers. But I have to say we can set this in some interesting context. I was in Long Kesh the night that La Mon House hotel was torched and lots of people were burnt to death, incinerated.\* I wonder were the Provos dismayed? I imagine not, I suppose we lived in a callous world . . .*

*I think that the bombardment of information certainly makes a difference to how you view things, and that, yes, one could say that if there had not have been the hype around [the Butchers] that maybe they wouldn't have had the same degree of intensity . . . but when it's wrong, it's wrong, it's abhorrent, and we knew it. But there were many other things . . . remember the Maguire children; the Provo car mowed three young Maguire children down. We were watching this society of ours going to hell, there were bars with large numbers of people wiped out, whether it was McGurk's or La Mon or the Droppin' Well or the Mountainview, a whole host of these things. This was cruel and brutal and evil. We lost our way, our society lost our way, not just the UVF, our society was losing its way. Even as far away as Long Kesh you could hear the ambivalence within our own community about what was happening to the other side, and you could make the assumption that [there was]*

---

\* Eleven people were killed in a botched IRA firebombing of the La Mon House hotel and restaurant in February 1978.

*ambivalence in the Nationalist community about what was being inflicted upon our side . . .*

*But it was being said [inside jail], 'What a fucking mess that is', 'Jesus Christ, it was awful', and that was the attitude. One of the quite brilliant ways in which prisoners attacked that era was: 'Sure, they kill as many Prods.' Now from my own personal point of view, it didn't matter whether they were Catholic or Protestant. I believe if someone was an enemy, and was a legitimate enemy, that you didn't let it be perceived that there was enjoyment in taking their lives . . . but it was a bad time, it was a very emotional time for a lot of prisoners because there was no standing over that, you know, there was no standing over that at all and from my own personal point of view absolute abhorrence. I make no apologies for feeling that way.*

A year or so before the Shankill Butchers were jailed, in the spring of 1978, Gusty Spence resigned as Camp Commander. His health had been failing for some time and in March 1978 he suffered a heart attack which for ten minutes left him clinically dead. Recurring coronary problems meant he eventually had to have triple bypass heart surgery and it was clear that twelve years of prison leadership had taken its toll. He had also by this stage undergone his conversion to non-violence and when he quit there was predictable speculation that unease within the ranks at Spence's moderation had forced his departure. Mainstream UVF claims that this was untrue, while also to be expected, found support in the shape of his successor, his brother Bobby Spence, a former British naval gunner and an unlikely choice if grassroots sentiment had indeed moved so strongly against him. At the same time, commanding a group of people who believed that taking life randomly was a legitimate political tactic while personally espousing non-violence was a balancing act beyond his or anyone's ability. A campaign seeking Gusty Spence's early release from jail had begun and since one argument in his favour was his new political disposition, it made sense for Spence to stand down from the leadership job. In line with the campaign, the UVF leadership, 'Bunter' Graham and others, encouraged Spence to distance himself from the organisation for which he had become the byword. David Ervine would soon join Spence, still a major influence, in Compound 21. Ervine resigned as a Hut Commander in Compound 19 after friction with the new Compound Commander and joined a group of people who would form much of the PUP leadership during the peace-process years. It was here that the PUP's willingness to accept power-sharing was forged, foreshadowing similar moves on the part of UDA in the 1980s. One of the ironies of the Troubles was that those who were to the forefront in the killing of Catholics were the first to accept bringing Catholics into government, while those Unionists quickest to condemn their violence were so much slower. In the UVF's case, Long Kesh became home to people who had been involved in some of the worst anti-Catholic violence of the Troubles while elsewhere in the same part of the jail other UVF inmates were working out ways and means of sharing power with Catholics.

*I moved compounds and I went to live in Compound 21 where Gusty was and where there was still a rational . . . leadership. It was in the other two compounds that one worried, and the South-East Antrim mafia, as we used to call it, was on the rise, led by [Geordie] Anthony. I viewed him as an abomination frankly, and the style of his leadership encouraged sycophants [who were] not people that I really wanted to be around, so I moved . . .*

*Spence operated a system in which there were no bullies in our compounds, you didn't raise your hands, you were equal. Geordie Anthony's leadership was not like that; there was one rule for one and another rule for another. I remember him walking into my hut on one of his inspections, a real soldier, he couldn't get the sleeves of his short-sleeved shirt tight enough to bulge his muscles, you know, and a sort of hard-man swagger in a UVF uniform. There was a guy with long hair, who always had long hair and was spotless, 'Tombo' Clarke from Portadown, doing life. Gusty never had any problems with his hair, and as the person in charge of the compound I never felt that there was a need to tell him that he needed his hair cut . . . and here was Geordie Anthony walking in. 'Get two inches off that hair.' It was all about Geordie Anthony, it wasn't about making this lad's time easier. I told him that day that if he wanted to get Tombo's hair cut that he could come and do it himself, but that he had to get past me first, and that was the type of atmosphere that existed between us. But I should have stayed. I should not have resigned my commission.*

*Well, I moved to Compound 21 where Spence was, and there were an awful lot of the class of '74 who were there: Eddie Kinner, Marty Snodden, Billy Hutchinson. I just fitted in and kept my head down and, as a Volunteer, did my job. I think that Spence lit the touch paper and the flame raged on in terms of discussion. I would imagine that if you sat that class of '75 down and said to them, 'Give me an A4 sheet of paper, tell me what the plans for Northern Ireland's future will be', I think it'd be very, very hard to separate us. All right, some of us would use different language than others but I think in essence you'd find it very similar, and is that by accident?*

*I think the core politics, the power-sharing politics of the PUP, has its antecedence in Long Kesh, no question in my mind about that, in that those who were considered as thinkers within the Progressive Unionist Party in 1994, 1995, 1996, 1997, or before, were in many ways Long Kesh people . . . I was not in a position to know but I'm not aware of any great political prowess coming out of any other compound. I think Billy Mitchell and all ended up in Compound 21. Spence's regime was seen as harsh by some, and yet Compound 21 ended up being the most liberal compound of the three . . . Now work that one out.*

Nearly eight years after he had been arrested ferrying a bomb for the UVF in East Belfast, David Ervine was freed from prison.

*I first came out on [pre-release] parole in Christmas 1979. I was on crutches because I'd had a cartilage operation and I remember preferring to walk into the town with my wife rather than get the bus. I was afraid of the bus, I couldn't handle money, it was frightening to me . . . She eventually tortured me onto the bus and I was in one of the big stores, Anderson and McAuley, and there was a café there. We were sitting there getting something to eat and the noise was deafening. It was actually quite strange, it was exciting, but in its own way maybe a wee bit frightening . . .*

*I was released in May 1980 and came home very conscious of the fact that probably the greatest suffering out of my incarceration was by my wife and son as opposed to me and that it was really about time I got myself sorted out and got work and started to honour my responsibilities. So I did that. I became a milkman, would you believe, and in no way in my mind was there any idea of getting [back] into paramilitarism because I thought, you know, 'I've really got to focus here and do logical things for a family that's suffered.'*

*I didn't knock around with the people I used to before I went into prison, but with a totally different set of people. I'd drink in the Cosy Bar, and I would have been standing having a yarn and the next thing you're talking about politics and I can remember one time talking about equality and the responsibility of Unionism to sell the concept of the United Kingdom to Nationalists and what have you, and this guy, he hadn't a shoe on his foot nor an arse in his trousers, hit me a dig in the gob, and shouted, 'You're a fucking communist.' I was so taken aback I didn't hit back. It wasn't a question of whether I was or wasn't a communist; it was that he couldn't cope with the logic of the argument and that at some point he did what many working-class people do, they strike out as a conversation-stopper or potentially an argument-winner.*

*. . . when I came home it was with no great intentions of becoming involved in paramilitarism. It was later, must have been about 1983, 1984, when I got a rap at the door, and it was two people from the Progressive Unionist Party, saying that they had been alerted to my bar-room oratory and came to see whether or not I would be interested in joining, which I subsequently did. What I was saying about power-sharing was not particularly endearing in a working-class Unionist community, but I think that what the UVF had probably heard was my articulation, in terms of: 'Your man can put up an argument.'*

By the time David Ervine was released from jail, the UVF had
become a shadow of the group that had struck terror into Catholic
Belfast in the mid-1970s. But they weren't alone. All the paramilitary
groups, Republican as well as Loyalist, had quickly felt the impact
of the British government's new 'criminalisation' strategy and, by
the end of 1977, the general level of violence was on a downward
curve. Some 116 souls lost their lives in the first full year of the new
security policy, 1977, the lowest count since 1970. By the time David
Ervine walked out of Long Kesh, the death toll had settled at
around the hundred-a-year mark, nearly a third of the average of
the most violent years of the Troubles. All the paramilitary groups
killed fewer people in 1977 but the UVF's rate of decline was the
sharpest. The Provisional IRA killed 68 people, around half of the
year before; the UDA killed 12, a third of its 1976 toll, while the
number whose lives were ended by the UVF was 14, only 20 per
cent of the previous year's total.[35] The success of RUC detectives in
extracting confessions from suspects held in the new holding centres, in Belfast and later in Armagh and Derry, was evident by
the summer of 1977. The number of terrorist-type charges levelled
was up by 20 per cent on the previous twelve months while murder charges rose over 40 per cent.[36]

In the UVF's case, the RUC was rounding up its most active
units. The South-East Antrim UVF had been decimated in 1976
when one of its members turned informer; the Shankill Butchers
had been put out of action thanks to some inspired police work
and there were other successes, less high profile but nonetheless
significant. In November 1977, for instance, Belfast City Commission was told that in Ballymena, County Antrim, a Loyalist hotbed
and political base of the Reverend Ian Paisley, the UVF cell had

been rounded up more than a year earlier and since then there had been no UVF violence at all in the town. Sentencing the UVF's Ballymena unit of twelve men for a range of offences, Justice Basil Kelly praised the RUC's 'good police work'.[37]

There can be little doubt either that the fall-off in Provisional IRA violence had a knock-on effect. Since the Loyalist paramilitaries would often step up their killings in tandem with Republican violence, there was now less reason to strike back. The years after Roy Mason came to Belfast to implement the policy were also politically fallow ones. After the setback of 1974 and the failure of an experimental constitutional convention set up shortly afterwards whose principal achievement was to reaffirm the existence of an unbridgeable gap between Unionism and Nationalism, the British effectively abandoned the business of deal-making, and that settled Unionist nerves, including those of the paramilitaries. But there was another reason why the UVF, along with the UDA, was on the back foot in these years and they had Ian Paisley to thank for that. In 1977, Paisley and a number of political allies from other fringe parties managed to persuade the UDA and the UVF to launch another Northern Ireland-wide strike, like that in 1974, this time as a protest against one unexpected but potent side-effect of Roy Mason's tough security policy.

The sweeping away of political status, the decision to criminalise paramilitaries and the centrality of police-acquired confession evidence in the judicial system were known collectively by the British as the 'Normalisation' policy but others called it 'Ulsterisation' because of another feature of the strategy, the greater street role played by local forces, the RUC, the police reserve and the Ulster Defence Regiment (UDR), compared to the British Army. Just like the similarly named US strategy of 'Vietnamisation', the British aim was to reduce the exposure of their troops to violence and as in Vietnam the consequence was that local forces began to bear the brunt of casualties. The figures bear this out. In 1975, 14 British soldiers were killed and 18 locals, that is members of the RUC, the RUC reserve and the UDR. The following year it was 15 British to 40 locals. UDR

fatalities alone more than doubled, from 7 to 16. The impact in
Protestant Ulster was significant; it is at this time, for instance, that
Unionists began alleging that the IRA was ethnically cleansing
along the border, shooting UDR members to force their families to
flee their farms and homes so that Catholics could acquire them.
Unionists demanded action from the British and when it did not
come they went back to what they did best. In May 1977 the Pais-
ley-insired, UVF/UDA-supported Loyalist strike started with the
public goal of forcing a crackdown on the IRA and a more secret
agenda, which some believed amounted to an attempted *coup d'é-
tat*. But there was a key difference between the 1977 action and the
1974 UWC strike and that was that Unionism was divided about
the wisdom of such an extreme step. Significant sections of mainstream Unionism, the Official Unionist Party and the Orange Order
in particular, refused to have anything to do with Paisley's strike
and it collapsed after ten days, fatally weakened by Unionist divisions.

While David Ervine might be right, that there was no intimidation of factory and office workers in 1974, the same could not be
said about the 1977 strike. Showing a distinct lack of enthusiasm
for the action, most workers paid no heed to Paisley's call and so the
paramilitaries deployed fear and intimidation to force them to stay
home. At one stage a joint statement said that neither the UVF nor
the UDA could be held responsible for the safety of workers on the
streets. The power workers came under huge pressure, but they
forced Paisley into a corner. They would support the strike, they
said, but would close the power plant down in one fell swoop,
rather than the gradual slow-down the strike organisers wanted.
Knowing that doing this could permanently cripple the plant and
cause lasting damage to the economy, Paisley retreated and the
strike was over. The UVF and the UDA had a disastrous strike. Not
only had they alienated their own people by threatening and
intimidating in Loyalist neighbourhoods, but they had both killed
Protestants during the strike as they sought to enforce it. One was
a bus driver shot dead by the UDA and the other a part-time soldier

in the UDR, the son of one of the strike leaders as it turned out, killed by a UVF bomb set in a petrol station that stayed open during the strike. Afterwards both groups were in bad odour with their own communities and all the more vulnerable to police action.

Although the UVF and the UDA came out of the strike weakened, not so Ian Paisley – and that it ended this way was as perfect a metaphor for the relationship between paramilitary and political Unionism as could be found. While both Loyalist groups hunkered down for the security assault, Paisley found his political fortunes immensely transformed for the better, even though he had been humiliated during the strike. In council-wide elections held ten days afterwards, Paisley's DUP doubled the number of its councillors and won control of its first council, Ballymena. Paisley hailed it as evidence that Protestants had backed him but the truth was that the DUP, sensing the strike's defeat, had switched its resources to the election campaign in the last week, abandoning its political and paramilitary allies. The election ended with all the smaller Loyalist political parties swallowed up by the DUP, leaving only Paisley's party and the Official Unionists vying for the top-dog position in Unionism. For many in the UVF and UDA, this outcome encapsulated their unequal relationship with the mainstream. In a crisis they would be asked, and would happily carry out, the dirty work while respectable Unionists condemned them and afterwards they would be abandoned and denied a share of the political rewards while the politicians prospered.

The paramilitaries had urged Paisley to call the power workers' bluff over their threat to close their plant down but that Paisley wouldn't take up the challenge provided another lesson: the DUP leader made a great noise during crises but invariably fell short on delivery. It was after this that both the UVF and the UDA took to calling Paisley 'The Grand Old Duke of York', willing to march up the hill but never able to summon the courage or commitment to go over it. The 1977 strike was the last occasion that the UVF or the UDA would dance to Paisley's tune, although they would continue to work alongside some of his better regarded and more trustworthy colleagues. Four years later, in November 1981, when Paisley tried to revive street politics in the wake of the IRA's murder of South Belfast Unionist MP Robert Bradford, both the UVF and the UDA shunned him. A few weeks later, a Shankill Road UDA prisoner jailed in Dublin for a firebomb attack on the city, Freddie Parkinson, echoed a general Loyalist view in a statement issued to the press: 'I remember vividly the Parliamentarian megalomaniacs of the late 1960s and early 1970s who beckoned us to follow them but later left us abandoned to be scorned as common criminals. To my countrymen . . . I offer this sincere appeal: Do not allow yourselves to be used by the politicians who have created the conflict in which we live.' On Paisley in particular, he added, 'He uses words to create violent situations, but never follows the violence through himself.'[38] Many years later, the UVF's former South-East Antrim Commander, Billy Mitchell, identified another defect in modern political Unionism: 'Unlike the Ulster Unionist leaders of 1912 and 1920, and even 1965, who were prepared to go outside the law and give leadership to the UVF, the leaders of Unionism during the past thirty years have only been prepared to incite men and women to organise; they have never put themselves forward as either Officers or Volunteers.'[39]

As David Ervine noted, sympathy for Paisley's approach to politics was thin on the ground in the UVF compounds of Long Kesh/The Maze.

*I remember [the Reverend Ian] Paisley coming into Long Kesh and his view seemed to be that he knew that all of us Loyalists would stay in here for ever to keep the IRA in, and that went down like a lead balloon. He also talked about hanging the murderers, and we wanted to know did that mean us as well, and of course logically from his point of view it had to, even though he may not have meant it. There was always a sense of hurt and anger and hatred for Paisley's politics inside the Long Kesh camps, and not just that; I think within the ranks of the UVF, there's been consistently a hatred for Paisley's politics, which is quite interesting in that the funda-*

*mentalist found himself not very well appreciated within the ranks of those who were seen as the absolute extreme. Strange stuff, strange psychology.*

In retrospect, the abortive 1977 strike was something of a watershed in the relationship between the Loyalist paramilitaries and, if not with all Unionist politicians, then at least with the most boisterous and provocative of their number. The Loyalists were more inclined thereafter to plough their own furrows, more careful about associating with mainstream political leaders and more willing to embrace previously heretical ideas, such as power-sharing, which the mainstream Unionists were still too timid to touch. In 1979, for instance, the UDA's embryonic political wing advocated sharing power with Nationalists in the context of an Independent Ulster – the idea being to remove the vexed constitutional issue from any settlement – and later embraced it without that precondition. Signs that some in the UVF were ready to stray down a similar path came much earlier, within a few weeks of the strike ending, when Gusty Spence issued the first of several statements outlining his own change of heart. Spence's words were not liked by many in the UVF, or elsewhere in the Loyalist world, but his public utterances were, in hindsight, the beginning of a process that ensured that when the peace process arrived, the hardest of the hard men – or at least their leaders – were ready to deal. Without that, the process might well have failed.

Spence, in his eleventh year of imprisonment and now forty-four years old, chose the holiest day in the Orange calendar, 12 July, for his first statement, made to UVF prisoners in Long Kesh in what was described as 'a personal capacity'. Launching a verbal assault on Paisley, without actually naming him, Spence called for talks between the Provisional IRA and the Loyalist paramilitaries. Attacking the politicians, he said, 'We can do without the politically immature, emotionally unstable and bigoted element within Loyalist circles. As a political leadership they are a sick joke; a mixture of inane hacks and power-hungry clerics who could not recognise the truth if it kicked them in the face. These are the men who have cunningly and purposefully fused religion with politics and fostered fear among the Loyalist community for their own designs and to retain power. They have adroitly manipulated the Orange Institution and other working-class organisations to serve such ends, hinting that when the time came for action they would not be found wanting.' Spence's speech conflicted radically with official UVF policy, outlined in a 1974 mission statement, which set out an uncompromising stance towards the Provos: 'The UVF recognises the Provisional IRA and Provisional Sinn Fein as the No. 1 short-term enemy of Ulster. The Provisionals can only be defeated by military means and any form of "détente" with them is out of the question.'[40] Four months later Spence made another appeal for peace, saying that further violence would be useless and counter-productive because the aim of Loyalists – self-determina- tion – had been achieved with the 1974 strike: 'There is a need for reconciliation with our neighbours whose aspirations differ from ours,' he said. 'Negotiation and dialogue can fill the vacuum of violence.'[41]

Then the Peace People entered the story with unfortunate results for Gusty Spence. The Peace People had come into being as a result of one of the most pitiful incidents of the Troubles, the death of the three Maguire youngsters in August 1976. The children, aged six weeks, two-and-a-half years and eight-and-a-half years, had been killed in Andersonstown, West Belfast, when a car driven by a fleeing IRA man ploughed into them, as their mother, Anne Maguire, walked them home. The driver had been shot dead from a pursuing British Army Land-Rover and lost control of the vehicle. Anne Maguire's sister Mairead and a neighbour, Betty Williams, became the figureheads for a spontaneous anti-violence street movement that developed in the following days and they were joined by Ciaran McKeown, a journalist with the Dublin-based *Irish Press* newspaper, who would become something of a guru to the movement. By November 1977, much of the steam had gone out of the Peace People but they were still newsworthy. When

McKeown went into the jail to speak to Gusty Spence, the event was widely covered in the local media. He came out of Long Kesh/The Maze bubbling with enthusiasm for the UVF founder and full of stories about him, not all of which would do him much good in the UVF compounds but which did little harm among those who decide prison-release dates. Spence had become a fluent Irish speaker and had taught the language to some hundred fellow inmates, McKeown claimed. His interest in the language had been stimulated by a Catholic missionary nun, Sister Joseph, who had exchanged letters with him from Africa and he had developed a keen interest in Irish history. McKeown said that Spence's conversion to peace was genuine, and not done simply to gain remission. 'The judgement I came away with and retain', he said, 'is that Gusty Spence is an extraordinary man. I would love to see that amazing potential tested in the positive environment outside the prison compound.' Within three weeks Spence confirmed what many had suspected, that his Damascene trek hadn't gone down well in his own backyard. Rumours that a number of UVF prisoners had been transferred at their request to the UDA compounds were true, he admitted, but he denied suggestions that some prisoners were refusing to obey his orders. He also corrected some of McKeown's more embarrassing revelations. Only five UVF prisoners had learned Irish, not a hundred, he said, and even then just so they could better understand what Provisional IRA prisoners were saying to each other. The nun was actually an old neighbour of Spence's from the Grosvenor Road area whose pre-convent name was Molly Meenan. She had made contact again when Spence was sent to Long Kesh. And his interest in Irish history was of long standing, pre-dating his reunion with the nun. In March 1978, Spence announced his resignation as Camp Commander, although the given reasons were less than convincing: '. . . my health is not what it once was and I have a deep obligation to my courageous wife and children to devote more time to them.' How he was to do this from inside jail was not explained. The UVF still say to this day that he was not pushed but jumped in an effort to win early release, his abandonment of UVF leadership in the prison something that would be received positively by the authorities. If true then the encounter with Ciaran McKeown might also have been staged deliberately for the same purpose.

At around this time the Progressive Unionist Party (PUP) was formed, initially as a cover for the UVF, which was still illegal, to meet the British government, or at least to communicate with it. The two founders, Hugh Smyth, who had won election to two local assemblies and Belfast City Council, and David Overend, a former Northern Ireland Labour Party activist, also began to develop a political programme for that brand of working-class Loyalism. The PUP's predecessor, the Volunteer Political Party, had foundered in 1974, not just on account of its dismal electoral performance but because most activists believed the UVF's only role was to kill Catholics. In the words of one VPP leader, 'Politics was best left to the politicians.'[42] Four or five years later, however, the mood in the UVF's leadership had changed and Unionism's politicians were seen in a more unfavourable light: craven, unreliable and unimaginative. One way in which this antagonism cum disillusionment expressed itself was in a growing paramilitary appetite for drawing up their own political programmes and schemes for settling the conflict. In these years some of them veered down the road of Ulster independence, briefly bringing a few in the Republican camp with them, but the PUP's scheme was set firmly inside a British Northern Ireland. Called *Sharing Responsibility*, it was published in 1979 and advocated a devolved power-sharing government in Belfast made up of Unionists and Nationalists, the latter assumed to be of the SDLP variety. It was founded in the view that while most Protestants abhorred deals such as Sunningdale, which had a strong cross-border, Irish dimension, they could be persuaded to share power with non-violent Nationalists.

*In the period of time before I joined the PUP the party presented* Sharing Responsibility *to the Secretary of State at the time, Jim Prior, and he told them that he was very interested in it but they were twenty years ahead of their time, and I think they were, absolutely. Every Unionist political party nowadays effectively advocates exactly the line that the Progressive Unionist Party, the UVF, if you like, was advocating in the mid-1970s, and I find it absolutely fascinating that those who had the time and space to evaluate and offer leadership chose not to do so, [while] those who very often are spurned . . . because of the paramilitary origins of their leadership, but maybe more because they were working class, were beavering away through a thought process by themselves but also in conjunction with prisoners in the jail. I think it was of some significance, in fairness, that the UDA, through the Ulster Political Research Group, had created their* Common Sense* document, supposedly the brainchild of JohnMcMichael. I don't know whether it was fully his brainchild but it certainly indicates a process of thinking in the paramilitary ranks of Loyalism far beyond that of the serried ranks of besuited politicians on the Unionist side. There's no doubt in my mind about that, absolutely no doubt that had we waited for rational politics from Unionist constitutional politicians we'd have waited for ever.*

For all that this was the product of Loyalist paramilitary disenchantment with their community's elected politicians, the all-class alliance that had characterised the Unionism of 1912 and 1974 would be briefly revived again, in 1985, after the Anglo-Irish Agreement, and for some, including David Ervine, the experience served to deepen their disdain for the Unionist establishment and to confirm a determination to forge a separate route in the future.

The story began in the summer of 1981 with the deaths of ten Republican hunger strikers whose protest at being treated as common criminals and being denied their political status had escalated from 1976 onwards, first in their refusal to wear prison uniforms, then to smearing their cell walls with excreta and, finally, to the ultimate protest, the hunger strike. The first fast in 1980 had failed and

---

* A pro-power-sharing policy document published by the UDA in 1987.

a second was called three months later, structured in a way that ensured one of only two outcomes: death or victory. Like many Loyalists, Ervine's sympathy was with the IRA prisoners.

*Well, you've got to remember that, as a former prisoner, I was an advocate of special-category status. I believed it was a mammoth political mistake to replace the humane confinement [of the Long Kesh compounds] with the inhumane confinement [of the H-blocks] and the Provos rebelled about it and I admired them for it and was deeply sorry, as I know other prisoners were, that we couldn't in our own way fight the battle that we should really have been fighting . . . Loyalists per se should have been battling for the fundamental rights that we as special-category prisoners had but were about to be removed for other prisoners. We took out advertisements in the newspapers, we did letter-writing, we did a lot of stuff to try and lobby for an understanding of our position, but our community didn't want to know, our community had a very simplistic concept that: 'We don't challenge the British state because the British state is being challenged by our enemy and that you really can't do what your enemy is doing because then that somehow or other bolsters the arguments of your enemy.' Right is right and wrong is wrong and my argument would be that the introduction of criminalisation, whilst [people such as former Northern Ireland Secretary] Roy Mason may claim that it kept the lid on things in Northern Ireland, [actually] set the cause of peace back many, many years. Whilst one was conscious that your enemy was starving themselves to death, the cause upon which that enemy travelled, if you like, was a just one in terms of prison conditions, and the recognition that the problems in Northern Ireland are political . . . and that only by political means would they be resolved. [But our problem was] lack of support from the community, and I think that we had to measure our attitudes to what one could or would do on that basis.*

The IRA hunger strikes transformed politics in Northern Ireland. The election as MP for Fermanagh–South Tyrone of Bobby

Sands, the hunger strikers' leader and the first to die, followed by two more wins for hunger-strike candidates in the Republic's general election and Sands's replacement by his election agent, Owen Carron, in a second Fermanagh–South Tyrone contest strengthened the forces in Sinn Fein seeking to launch the party into electoral politics. The party's first outing as Sinn Fein was in 1982 when elections were held for an experimental assembly in Belfast and the result shocked Ireland's political establishment, North and South. Sinn Fein won 10 per cent of the vote, the support of four out of every ten Catholics and five seats. A year later, Gerry Adams was elected MP for West Belfast and this result set alarm bells ringing in Dublin. Unless Sinn Fein was stopped there was a real chance that the SDLP's domination of Northern Nationalism could be seriously challenged and the potential for instability arising from that deeply worried the Irish government. After some two years of frantic, and occasionally rollercoaster, diplomacy, the Irish Taoiseach, Garret Fitzgerald, persuaded Margaret Thatcher to sign up to the Anglo-Irish Agreement, known to Unionists as 'the Hillsborough Deal', which gave the Dublin government a physical presence in Belfast and direct access to the policy-makers in the Northern Ireland Office. A small group of Irish civil servants was stationed at Maryfield, an office complex in East Belfast and subsequently the focus for Loyalist marches and demonstrations. Although the deal came with solemn assurances from Dublin of respect for the consent principle, which said Irish reunification could happen only with the say-so of the Northern Ireland people, the deal looked like a Trojan horse to most Unionists and, as their forefathers had done before them, they banded together for greater protection and strength in the face of the threat.

In the angry days that followed the deal at least a hundred thousand Unionists gathered for a protest rally at Belfast City Hall, where Carson's Covenant had been signed, and a further three hundred thousand signed a petition protesting the deal. All fifteen Unionist MPs at Westminster resigned so that the resulting by-elections could, referendum-like, measure the scale and solidity of

Unionist opposition to Hillsborough, and government ministers were boycotted. The most contentious part of this 'Ulster Says No!' campaign, as it was called, was a plan for a one-day, UWC-style protest strike in March 1986 which, unlike the effort in 1977, gained support from across virtually the entire Unionist spectrum. Paisley's deputy, Peter Robinson, had formed a strike committee called the '1986 Workers' Committee' and it looked as if he was moving towards a repeat of what happened in 1974. The Loyalist paramilitaries looked at Robinson and liked what they saw. They participated in his Workers' Committee because Robinson seemed to be 'made of different stuff' from Paisley, as one Loyalist put it, prepared to go over the top, unlike his chief.[43] When the UVF and the UDA began intimidating RUC families out of Loyalist areas because of the force's firm stand against Unionist protests, all of mainstream Unionism condemned them except Paisley's deputy. Robinson's potential seemed confirmed when the DUP formed its own paramilitary force, called 'Ulster Resistance', and along with the UVF and UDA put together an ambitious arms-smuggling plot involving South Africans and Israelis, which brought tonnes of modern weaponry into Northern Ireland. Thanks to well-placed Loyalist informers, most of the arsenal was captured by the RUC and then, in April 1989, the plot was publicly exposed. French police arrested several 'Resistance' members in a Paris hotel as they were meeting a South African diplomat and an American arms-dealer. Two of the 'Resistance' men were traced back to Paisley's Free Presbyterian Church and Paisley promptly disowned them, to the disgust of David Ervine and other Loyalists.

*[Paisley's] denial was, I think, something that ordinary Loyalists expected and accepted; you know, here's the grand doyens of moral guardianship who would . . . with the side of their hand have indicated, 'Well, like, I have to say that, you know, I have to say that.' Well, what followed next was not good news, and effectively the people in Paris were abandoned, and [there were] whispering campaigns against them in DUP ranks, so there was something not very*

*nice going on. How widespread that would have been known is questionable, but certainly I was aware of it, and all it did was forever confirm in my mind that which I already knew: these people are not to be trusted, that their interest does not lie in Northern Ireland, their interest is self-interest.*

Robinson's promise evaporated when he spurned the thorny crown of martyrdom, paying a fine to a Dublin court rather than enduring a prison term in a Southern jail, and losing his seat at Westminster, for his part in a rowdy 'Resistance' invasion of the small County Monaghan town of Clontibret in August 1986. He and Ian Paisley had been cut from similar cloth after all.

The very fact of the Anglo-Irish Agreement was seen by Loyalists such as David Ervine as compelling evidence of the Unionist leadership's incompetence. Jim Molyneaux, the leader of the largest grouping, the Official Unionists, seemed to have won a great victory when, in May 1984, Margaret Thatcher rejected the Irish Forum Report, the product of a pan-Nationalist (except the Provos) conference in Dublin which outlined three constitutional possibilities to settle the Troubles, ranging from a Unitary all-Ireland state through to joint authority. Thatcher's 'Out! Out! Out!' response to each plan at a press conference was regarded as Molyneaux's finest hour and a tribute to the special relationship he seemed to have with the Iron Lady. But then Molyneaux took his eye off the ball and was as surprised and outraged as most Unionists when the deal was announced in November 1985. In the immediate aftermath, Molyneaux spoke of 'the stench of hypocrisy, deceit and treachery' surrounding the negotiations, and said he felt 'universal cold fury' at the Agreement such as he had not experienced in forty years in politics. But Ervine was scornful.

*I remember the day that the Anglo-Irish Agreement came out and I thought to myself, 'Fuck me, these geezers are running about Westminster every day, there are 635 MPs and there's not one of them would tell [Molyneaux or Paisley] what's happening! There was just one person in the PUP believed the Brits wouldn't do that to us, and I actually believed that there were a lot of the bedrock members of the two main parties who believed that as well, but I think their leaderships knew better. I think their leaderships were fucking cowards, I think that they knew, [and] particularly the Ulster Unionists knew. There's [James] Molyneaux, who wins prizes for taciturnity, was the man who kept telling us he had a great relationship with the British government and the Queen and all the rest of it, and meanwhile back at the ranch, no indications from Molyneaux of the manifestation that turned out to be the Anglo-Irish Agreement.*

*. . . the UVF's response at first to the Anglo-Irish Agreement was clear unadulterated anger and . . . street responses, but it didn't last and they didn't try to sustain it. They could have sustained it, it would have been relatively easy . . . [but] they didn't try to sustain it, and I think that the UVF were listening, if not accepting 100 per cent, our [the PUP's] analysis that the Unionist leaders 'got us into this pile of shite and effectively they've a responsibility to get us out of it'.*

The 'Ulster Says No!' campaign was just three or so months old when the Loyalist paramilitaries received an object lesson from mainstream Unionism about their perceived role in life and place at the bottom of the food chain. The Unionist political leaders, Jim Molyneaux and Ian Paisley, had put away their differences and joined forces to oppose the Hillsborough Deal. On the eve of the one-day strike they journeyed to Downing Street, having agreed with their parties to put a take-it-or-leave-it offer to Margaret Thatcher: agree to suspend the Agreement and hold talks on its replacement or face mounting Unionist protest action and even a general strike. But, with Molyneaux nervous about the impact the strike would have, the pair reneged on their pledge. Instead they proposed an all-party conference that would take place 'unconditionally'; that is the Anglo-Irish Agreement would be functioning as it met, a de facto acquiescence in Britain's 'deceit and treachery'.

Thatcher eagerly accepted the offer but the two men arrived back in Belfast to face a rebellion from their second-tier leaderships and rank and file who were privately accusing them of selling out. Later that night Molyneaux and Paisley performed U-turns, rejected the deal worked out earlier with Thatcher and backed the impending one-day strike. The hard men of Loyalism were drafted in to give them the necessary cover.

*The 1986 experience was fundamental. Paisley and Molyneaux were at Downing Street, and I heard in the lunchtime broadcasts that there was a potential deal between Paisley, Molyneaux and Thatcher. Paisley and Molyneaux spoke on the radio live, I heard it, and there was an indication of a deal all right. So we were all summoned as part of the 1986 Committee to a meeting in the DUP's headquarters in the Albertbridge Road. How did we get the invitation, did they not know who Billy Elliot [UDA's East Belfast Brigadier] was representing that night, not know who I was representing that night? Of course they did. Strangely enough Sammy Wilson and Peter Robinson came into the room, no Paisley or Molyneaux – they'd been delayed – but what we got from them was 'We put backbone into them', and I'm listening to Robinson and Wilson talk about how 'they put backbone' into that great charismatic figure, Ian Paisley, who in the view of the Unionist community is all backbone. Then the next thing, they announced that the meeting would have to be in Glengall Street [the Official Unionist headquarters] that there had been a change of plan, so we were all dispatched to the Europa [hotel] to be summoned over to Glengall Street. We eventually got into Glengall Street and —— was coming down the stairs, and he says, 'Put a bit of backbone into them', and we were shown into a room where we sat for a while and —— left and then down came Paisley and Molyneaux and they said they would support the strike, and the people from the '86 Committee asked, 'Well, let's make it very clear. Is this a joint call for a strike, Mr Molyneaux?' Because it was clear that Paisley was never getting a strike on his own, and Molyneaux said, 'Yes.' The interesting thing is that it was supposed to be a private meeting, some would say a secret meeting, and when the door of Glengall Street opened and we were leaving, we were met by banks of cameras, and the headlines in the* News Letter *the next morning was 'Hard men change minds', and it was a total fucking fabrication to . . . give the impression that our politicians were trying to do a deal with Mrs Thatcher but look, these hard men wouldn't let them. It was absolutely shameful, totally designed and orchestrated by the Democratic Unionist Party and the Ulster Unionist Party.*

*I wish I had a pound for the number of times Ulster Unionists would say, 'Oh, watch for the Protestant backlash. Oh, I don't know how we're going to sell this to the hard men.' Meanwhile, back at the ranch . . . us hard men were the people who had the policies that were twenty years ahead of their own. I mean, it was incredible, it was cynical, manipulative and dishonest . . .*

*I can only speak in relation to my understanding of the UVF's attitude and really for the first time it started to listen very carefully to the idea that we needed to learn how to speak for ourselves, we really did need to force our way into the political arena, and that began for sure in 1986 . . . I can never forgive the Unionist leaders because the way they behaved was not for the good of this community, it was not for the good of our people, it was for themselves, it was about their own fortunes, it wasn't about anybody else, it was about frightening the British government or the Catholic community, and they haven't tried it since, haven't quite tried it since, maybe they've realised the game was up.*

*I think that the Anglo-Irish Agreement threw Loyalism and Unionism into a state of flux but the debates within paramilitarism were quite interesting, certainly those within the UVF . . . quite a number believed that the responsibility for the political conditions that led to the creation of the Anglo-Irish Agreement lay with the Westminster MPs. They had singularly failed, and that whilst there were many UVF people who felt, 'We'll react because it's the . . . thing to do', there were others who were saying, 'Hold on a wee minute, really this is a political problem and these people have not done their job. Why didn't they warn society, why didn't they agitate, why didn't they create conditions which allowed the population to really know what was coming?' So there was some confusion, and maybe lack of clarity about where we were going because Loyalists didn't have any of the cards. The one card . . . they knew they had was the capacity to inflict violence and . . . rather than a reactive response in the Loyalist leadership, they seemed [instead] to be much more politically attuned in the use of violence.*

The graph of Loyalist violence, as measured by their killings, takes the shape of an inverted U between the years 1971 and 1976, the years of greatest political instability and therefore of Unionist insecurity. After that the line becomes a straight line, more or less, bumping along at the bottom of the horizontal axis, each year's toll of death a mere fraction of what it had been in the mid-1970s. Of the two, the UVF's killing rate declined at a slower pace than the UDA's but even so the change was dramatic: there were, for instance, more people killed by the UVF in 1976, a total of 71,[44] than in the entire next ten years, between 1978 and 1987. Even the two years of the Anglo-Irish Agreement, 1985 and 1986, saw no great variance from the new lower norm. By and large the two groups continued to do what Loyalist paramilitaries had done ever since Gusty Spence's killing spree in 1966. When they wanted to kill they targeted uninvolved Catholics, often at random, and, like Gusty Spence's victims in 1966, many met an unintended death due to sheer incompetence. It was not that the Loyalist paramilitaries did not have intelligence on the IRA or that they did not know where IRA activists lived or what they looked like. Lack of such information was never a Loyalist problem. It was an open secret, in the early years of the Troubles especially, that departing British troops would stuff UVF and UDA letterboxes with photomontages of IRA 'players' culled from intelligence files. If the UVF or the UDA had wanted to, they could have gone for real IRA targets but they mostly didn't. It seemed that killing Catholics randomly with the gun or bomb was a lot easier to do.

That started to change in 1980 when Loyalists began choosing their targets more carefully and strategically. The first such victim was a Protestant Republican politician and landowner called John Turnly who lived on the North Antrim coast. At one time in his life an officer in the British Army, Turnly had joined the moderate SDLP, but left to join a radical splinter group, the Irish Independence Party, from where he later supported the IRA hunger strikers. In June 1980 he was shot dead as he sat in his car with his Japanese wife and their two children. The assassins were members of the UDA and the Turnly killing marked the start of the most directed and coherent campaign to date organised by any Loyalist group. Their next victim was Miriam Daly, a former Sinn Fein activist, who along with her husband James had become a leader in the Irish Republican Socialist Party, the political wing of the INLA. She was shot dead in her Andersonstown home. In October the UDA killed Ronnie Bunting, the radical son of Paisley's former aide who had become a leader first in the Official IRA and then the INLA. He was shot dead by gunmen who used a sledgehammer to break down the door of his Andersonstown home, and alongside him was killed Noel Lyttle, a member of the Red Republican Party. The following year, in January 1981, UDA gunmen shot and seriously wounded the former civil rights leader Bernadette McAliskey and her husband Michael in their isolated home in County Tyrone. Other activists from the civil rights days were targeted, some fleeing Belfast for the safety of Dublin. The UDA said that their campaign was directed at what they called the IRA's 'cheerleaders' and it was notable that three of the victims had been active in the H-block campaign, supporting the IRA claim of political status for prisoners. The UDA killings were an effort to strike fear in that section of radical Nationalist politics which gave valuable support and guidance to some of the IRA's causes.

It wasn't for another seven years or so that the UVF went down a similar path. That it did so was in no small way the result of a new relationship between the UVF leadership and the PUP, one that gave the PUP influence over the gunmen's strategy. It was during these years that Ervine also became active again in the UVF as its 'Provost-Marshal', responsible for internal discipline, a move that seemed calculated to reassure the rank and file that he was one of them.[45] The change came about in the confused aftermath of the first moves in what would soon become known as the peace process. The story began, in public at least, on 11 January 1988 when a political earthquake shook Northern Nationalism. Delegations from the SDLP and Sinn Fein, led by their respective leaders, John Hume and Gerry Adams, met for the first of six meetings, the last one taking place in September that year. The contacts were extraordinary simply because the Establishment orthodoxy for many years had been that the Provos, elected or not, were pariahs, fit only to be shunned by respectable society. Such an approach was a matter of faith for some politicians in the South, especially Garret Fitzgerald, the Fine Gael leader and twice Taoiseach. If anything the sentiment was stronger south of the border, particularly in sections of the media, than it was in London and so Hume was seen as bucking his allies in Dublin by meeting Adams & Co. – or at least that is how it looked. More than that the SDLP and Sinn Fein had fought one election a year against each other since 1982 and by now they were bitter and sometimes physical rivals. The fact that they were now prepared to meet and discuss their different analyses of the problem suggested something unusual was afoot.

No matter what they really thought in private, the bulk of mainstream Unionist leaders responded to the SDLP–SF talks with suspicion, scorn and hostility, assuming that they were just part of another cunning Nationalist plot to undo the Union. With the exception of the UVF and the PUP that is. Seemingly alone of all the pro-Union groupings, the UVF/PUP realised that neither the SDLP nor the Irish government, which had to have approved the meetings, would entertain the Sinn Fein leadership in talks unless the IRA's use of violence was somehow on the negotiating table. This piece of astute reasoning shaped a sophisticated response, which had two major features. One was an open-minded approach that did not dismiss the possibility that the talks were aimed at ending the violence. The second was to assume the best, that the Provos were looking for a way out of the conflict and, to encourage them to move faster down that road, the UVF set about trying to kill as many known Republicans as it could. Like the UDA seven years before, the UVF set out to kill a specific set of targets, only their targets would be in the IRA, Sinn Fein and those around them. So intense was the campaign unleashed by the UVF and other Loyalists that, according to Ervine's interview with Boston College, an alarmed IRA sued for peace via intermediaries. The offer was rejected.

*. . . the PUP was a tiny and a very core group. It would have met on a fairly irregular basis at first with the leadership of UVF and hot-housed the political vista with them, if you like, but that changed over a period of time. I think the biggest change came in, it had to be about 1989, with the creation, at the behest of the UVF, of a kitchen cabinet. Out of that hot-house process came our understanding of the much talked about Republican strategy of pan-Nationalism. When the concept became public, Unionism was apoplectic, but the leadership of the UVF were not, and neither were the small nucleus of PUP people. The view that they had was no matter how much we disliked the SDLP or the Irish government, they were not going to get into bed with Sinn Fein as long as the IRA was using violence. So that was an indicator to the UVF that something was going on. The questions were: 'What is it that they're talking about?' 'What's [Gerry] Adams offering here to his own community?' And I and at least one other were then sent out to try and find out.*

*. . . part of that kitchen-cabinet discussion was about how you escalate the war to end the war, which again was an indication . . . that there were people in the leadership of the UVF who believed this war could end, unlike many of their foot soldiers for whom the war was just a way of life. There was a change, a mindset change . . . and the focus switched to a more acute political analysis of every word, of everything that was being said, everything was being done . . . and more fundamentally asking what the hell was going on within Republicanism. There had always been attempts by the UVF,*

*for as long as I remember, to try and understand what was going on
with the Provos. In some cases it was done through relationship with
priests, and I'm certain that from 1989 onwards the relationship
with priests and then eventually other clergymen substantially
intensified, but that was never taken on its own. There were little
soirées in Dublin and places like that where, as a community
worker, one could suggest something more visionary . . . that hadn't
previously ever been suggested, so there were those type of little
things going on.*

*There would be many people within the UVF who had always felt
that the only way to carry out a campaign was incisively and with
stealth and absolute precision. They didn't always have their way
and the emotion and anger and opportunities sometimes mitigate
against that, but they seemed to have their way and there was a dili-
gent attempt [made] to identify very expressly specific targets. It was
about trying to damage the Republican movement. For many years
Loyalism simply believed that a Catholic, any Catholic, would do.
The UVF, in fairness to them, even though some of the statistics
don't indicate that their ideas always bore fruit, it's clear that they
felt that it was counter-productive, that sectarianism, wounding the
Nationalist community in order that it stop harbouring the IRA,
was absolutely counter-productive. So they became much more
incisive and I think it did create a huge fear factor in Republicans,
forcing them behind their steel doors, and really for the first time the
Republicans felt themselves being hounded.*

*. . . there was a single-mindedness that at times one felt the UVF
had lacked [in the past] and there are periods of course where that
wasn't the case . . . [but] one would have never expected that the
Republicans would have been screaming from the rooftops and
admitting weakness, but it was clear through, shall we say, conduits
and messages . . . that it was getting home because they were suing
for peace, but suing for peace in very pathetic and irrational terms
like 'You don't kill us and we won't kill you' and 'We're not fighting
ye', you know. That type of thing. 'You're not really the enemy',
which betrayed a huge misunderstanding about what the UVF may*

*or may not have been about from their point of view. The UVF were insulted by suggestions that in order to save their own skins they should make deals with the IRA and I think it [so] infuriated them the kill rate may well have gone up.*

It would be wrong to conclude from David Ervine's remarks that the UVF and its associated group, the Red Hand Commando, were the only Loyalist groups trying to kill Republicans. The UDA was doing exactly the same thing and from the spring of 1991 onwards the three groups – the UDA, UVF and Red Hand Commando – worked together, co-ordinating strategies, not least of which was the idea that killing Republicans could encourage the IRA to embrace peace more urgently. Given the history of bloody feuding between the UVF and the UDA, it was remarkable that they could come together in this way and a measure of the level of Protestant unease caused by the peace process. David Ervine claimed that it was the UVF's idea to create the Combined Loyalist Military Command (CLMC) to take on that task but, whatever the truth, the existence of the CLMC did ensure that when the peace process became serious, the hard men of Unionism were more or less singing from the same hymn sheet.

*. . . the UVF leadership, conscious of the need to have a very clear political understanding of (1) what was going on, and (2) what the hell they were going to do about what was going on, realised there was the need to ask, 'Right, what's the first item on the agenda?' Well, if you're going to move within Loyalism then you need to try and move on with all of Loyalism because to move separately is very, very dangerous and leaves you ripe for plucking. So the UVF leadership, not the PUP, were of a mind that the way to do that was through some kind of overarching process of interaction between the Loyalist paramilitaries. There's no doubt about it, that the creation of the Combined Loyalist Military Command was the UVF's baby, but that did not go down universally well within the UVF. I mean, there were a lot of UVF people who were very opposed and felt that*

*they didn't want to get into bed with people who they felt were dubious. That of course didn't mean every UDA person, but there were elements in the UDA who were strange animals, to say the least, on the basis that they were supposed to be defending their community, and yet were employed more in running nefarious businesses. That's not meant simplistically to be a criticism; it's meant to give an understanding of the backdrop against which the UVF leadership moved. Not only did it have the problem of the enemy, the IRA; it had the problem of the enemy within, in terms of the potential objectors within the UVF. It was one of those times where you watch [people's] status grow and when I had immense appreciation for the deftness of footwork which was practised at that time by the UVF leadership. The one single thing that Republicans did not want was a thinking Loyalism, and we saw that from their actions; they weren't ready for a ceasefire, they weren't ready for the moment for whatever reasons, at that time, but clearly they wanted to derail Loyalism.*

*. . . the UVF's theory about escalating the war to end the war came before the creation of the CLMC.*

Q.  *Would it have been a factor in terms of the CLMC?*

A. *Oh, big style, but you've got to remember where I think the dynamic was introduced was that we were all trying to understand what the Republicans meant by pan-Nationalism. That indicated there was a 'game on', [but] we needed to try and find out what the 'game on' was, and if there was going to be a 'game on' we needed to be playing in it and that therefore the creation of the Combined Loyalist Military Command was a requirement in order to make Loyalism able to move at all. The CLMC was an interesting vehicle because also set up around the CLMC was the Combined Loyalist Political Alliance. One, you could argue, was military and the other one was political. This was a discussion process between the UDP [the Ulster Democratic Party, the UDA's political wing] and the PUP, and indeed the UVF and the UDA attended it as well . . .*

Q. *What would have been the make-up of that?*

A. *It would have been two PUP, two UDP and the Military Commander of the UVF and the Military Commander of the UDA.*

Q. *And same sort of things on the table but more expressly about the political direction?*

A. *Yes, very clearly, yeah. I think we would have been talking about the same things, maybe from different directions, but were actually talking about the same things. There was only one show in town, what was going on in the Republican movement . . .*

Perhaps one reason why the two groups were able to work together is that they both began targeting Republicans in a serious way at around the same time. Indeed one could argue that the pathfinder in this regard was a thirty-three-year-old, self-described freelance Loyalist, a gunman from East Belfast called Michael Stone who had done much of his previous killing on behalf of the UDA as a roaming hitman. In March 1988, Stone attacked the funeral of three IRA members who had been shot dead by the SAS while on a bombing mission in Gibraltar, Britain's quaint colony and military garrison perched at the southern tip of Spain. Attacking the crowd of mourners inside Milltown cemetery in West Belfast with grenades and firing pistol shots at his pursuers, Stone killed three people, one of them an IRA member. He later said that his real targets had been the Sinn Fein President, Gerry Adams; the Derry IRA leader, Martin McGuinness, and Danny Morrison, the Provos' chief propagandist cum publicity officer. He also claimed to have stalked McGuinness once before, as well as the former Fermanagh–South Tyrone MP, Owen Carron, and the leading County Derry Republican, John Joe Davey. When he went to trial it emerged that he had killed three times before the Milltown attack; two of his victims were Catholics and a third a Sinn Fein member. Stone immediately acquired cult status among the Loyalist hardliners in Northern Ireland and, because of that, became something of a role model as well. It was not that Loyalists had never killed or tried to kill top Republicans before or that Stone was the first to come up with the idea. In 1984, the UDA came close to killing the Sinn Fein leader when they ambushed his car in the centre of Belfast and they tried again in 1988, although this time the security forces frustrated the attempt before it became serious.[46] Nor did the UDA need the then three-month-long talks between Sinn Fein and the SDLP to act as an incentive. But as the peace process gathered speed and diplomacy of this sort with Sinn Fein intensified and expanded beyond the SDLP, it became increasingly clear that the Provos were seeking a way out of conflict. Republican vulnerability to pressure from the Loyalists accordingly grew and so, therefore, did the killing.

It would be wrong to think that in the years of the peace process the UVF turned its guns exclusively against Republicans and spared Catholics from death. Nothing could be further from the truth. According to figures culled from *Lost Lives*, the exhaustive and widely respected record of Northern Ireland's victims of violence, 58 of the 115 people killed by the UVF between 1988 and the IRA ceasefire of 1994 – almost exactly half – were innocent, largely uninvolved Catholics chosen for death, like so many before, entirely randomly or by mistake. Some of the worst indiscriminate sectarian slaughter carried out by Loyalists during the entire Troubles, such the public-house killings at Greysteel in 1993 or at Loughinisland in 1994, took place during the peace-process years. But, equally, it was a significant break from past behaviour that so many of the remaining victims – perhaps a quarter of the total – were associated in one way or another with Republicanism. By contrast only 4 of the 44 people killed by the UVF between 1982 and 1987 were in that category.

Although the doorstep assassination of IRA activist Larry Marley at his home in Ardoyne, North Belfast, in April 1987 is sometimes thought of as marking the start of the UVF's more selective targeting campaign, it properly began more than eighteen months later at a lonely bungalow between Ardboe, a strongly

Republican village on the County Tyrone shore of Lough Neagh and the Loyalist town of Coagh further inland. On the night of 24 November 1988, twenty-eight-year-old Phelim McNally was playing traditional Irish music on an accordion in the kitchen of his brother's home on the Derrychin Road when one or more UVF gunmen fired bursts of automatic gunfire through a window killing him instantly. Phelim McNally was a member of a strong Republican family; one brother, Francie, was a Sinn Fein councillor in Cookstown while another, Lawrence, was in the IRA and would be killed in an SAS ambush some three years later. Ardboe was in the heart of one of the IRA's strongest Brigade areas, East Tyrone. The McNally killing is an appropriate start for any examination of the UVF's campaign during these years because it was also the first carried out by its Mid-Ulster units, which played by far the greatest role targeting Republicans. Although there is evidence of Belfast participation in some of the killings, the Mid-Ulster UVF was involved in half of the some twenty-six UVF operations against Republican targets that resulted in fatalities during these years. The operations took place in County Armagh, County Derry and most of all in County Tyrone. Between 1988 and August 1994, 86 people died violent deaths in the East Tyrone operational zone and the UVF was responsible for 40 of them, nearly half the slaughter.

The Mid-Ulster UVF was headquartered in Portadown, County Armagh, once described by the SDLP's Brid Rodgers as 'the citadel of Orangeism' and was dominated by two figures, both infamous for their violence. One was Robin Jackson,* dubbed 'The Jackal' by the tabloid media, who has been blamed for two of the UVF's worst atrocities: the 1974 bombing of Dublin and Monaghan and the Miami Showband massacre in 1975. The other was Billy Wright, the Mid-Ulster Commander during this time who went under the soubriquet 'King Rat', another a tabloid invention. Which of the two was more responsible for the Mid-Ulster violence is debatable. Wright got most of the public blame and notoriety and became a

---

* He died of natural causes in June 1998.

greatly hunted target for the IRA, which attempted to kill him five times.* The UVF prefer to credit Jackson but the claim must be set alongside the fact that Wright turned against the UVF ultimately and formed a rival group opposed to the peace process that feuded with its former colleagues.

The McNally killing might have been the starting point of the UVF's campaign but its origins in a bout of tit-for-tat retaliatory killings shows how much local conditions shaped the campaign and might even have inspired it, at least as far as County Tyrone was concerned. In April 1988, Edward Gibson, a binman who was also a soldier in the UDR, was shot dead by the IRA as he collected garbage in Ardboe. He was from Coagh and his death affected most of the village where inter-marriage over the years meant that many of its inhabitants were related. The McNally killing was thus an act of revenge and in response the IRA killed three Coagh Protestants, one of them a suspected local UVF member, the other two unfortunate innocents, and the spiral of violence gathered speed. It is possible that by the time the PUP and UVF leadership devised the selective killing campaign, it was already happening.

In February 1989 the UDA killed the Belfast solicitor Pat Finucane in his North Belfast home and claimed that he was an officer in the IRA. That allegation has been denied by his family, the RUC and the British government but he had two strikes against him: he was one of the Provisional IRA's regular lawyers and the go-to solicitor for the Belfast Brigade, and some of his brothers were deeply involved in the IRA. The following day, the UVF shot dead the Sinn Fein councillor and IRA veteran John Joe Davey as he returned to his home near Magherafelt in County Derry. Davey had been named under privilege in the British House of Commons by the DUP MP for Mid-Ulster, the Reverend William McCrea, as being involved in IRA murders. The next UVF victim in the area was a publican, Liam Ryan, who was shot dead at the doorway of his bar, the Battery Bar on the shores of Lough Neagh near Ardboe

---

* Wright was shot dead by INLA prisoners inside the Maze prison in December 1997.

in November 1989. The gunmen are thought to have made their way to the bar by boat and then escaped in a waiting getaway car. Ryan, a former United States Commander of the IRA, was the East Tyrone Brigade's Intelligence Officer. A year later, a Sinn Fein worker, Tommy Casey, was killed by the UVF in Cookstown, County Tyrone, in mistake for a former Tyrone Commander. In March the following year, the UVF struck its most deadly blow against the IRA to date when it shot up an IRA meeting taking place in a bar in Cappagh, County Tyrone, killing three of its members. The Tyrone Commander of the IRA was supposed to have been at the meeting but escaped death. However, in November the UVF caught up with the former Commander, Sean Anderson, near his home in Pomeroy.

The Republican reaction to these killings is an important part of the story, one that arguably amplified the effect of the Loyalist campaign and encouraged the UVF and the UDA to intensify it. The IRA had traditionally responded to Loyalist attacks such as these with disproportionate intensity. When Bernadette McAliskey and her husband were badly wounded by the UDA, for instance, the IRA retaliated by killing two high-level Unionist figures, the eighty-six-year-old former Stormont Speaker Sir Norman Stronge and his merchant banker son James (aged forty-eight) and burned their mansion near the Armagh–Monaghan border to the ground. But the peace process had changed priorities for the Sinn Fein and IRA leadership. Sensitive to accusations of sectarianism from the media and politicians south of the border, the Army Council had ordered an end to reprisal political assassinations and stipulated that Loyalist targets could be chosen solely on the basis of accurate intelligence. Only those who could be shown to have had direct involvement in such killings, such as Billy Wright, could be singled out for reprisal. In the wake of the attack on the IRA meeting in Cappagh, the Provo leadership ordered that the three victims' IRA membership should not be acknowledged, nor should they be given Republican funerals.[47] Similarly the Republican leadership refused to acknowledge the IRA ties of Sinn Fein figures, including councillors, assassinated by Loyalists. All this was partly done to stir sympathy in the South but another effect was to dampen pressure for retaliation. By the early 1990s it become open season on Republicans. Sinn Fein members and workers, councillors, IRA members, ex-IRA members and relatives of Republicans, including in one gruesome instance the heavily pregnant wife of a former IRA prisoner, were all targets.

The UVF campaign in Mid-Ulster indisputably shattered Republican morale. In these years a small industry grew up in County Tyrone and in Belfast devoted to making Republican homes secure against attack. Heavy grille doors would be installed in homes to deter intruders, often placed at the bottom of the staircase so that when the family retired to bed at night they could lock themselves upstairs, hopefully out of harm's way. The presence of such precautions was a sure sign that the house was a Republican one. In Tyrone the precautions could be even more elaborate. In one home visited by the author at the time there were a number of such doors downstairs preventing access from several directions, each one strengthened by heavy steel girders which could be lowered through holes in the floor of the master bedroom above last thing at night. Republicans lived in terror in such areas, fearful of strange cars driving past in the middle of the night and constantly on the outlook for a violent attack. Some moved home regularly. During one night-time visit made by the author to a Tyrone IRA member's home, the host's sleeping wife was having a nightmare upstairs. Her moans were clearly audible from the bottom of the staircase: 'Please don't shoot!' The impact of all this was captured by another local Republican interviewed by the author in 2000: 'As the killings grew, the demand grew to do something. People were afraid because it seemed the Loyalists had a free hand. People were afraid to be identified with Sinn Fein, not just the IRA. You could be shot for having the same name as a Republican or for being a Sinn Fein councillor. Meanwhile the IRA was doing nothing to protect people.'[48]

A key feature of the UVF campaign in Tyrone, and the wider Loyalist effort, is that the assault on Republicans was being paralleled by the British Army in two ways. In Tyrone, ambushes set by the SAS became an accepted way of taking on the IRA. Starting with the ambush in Loughgall, which wiped out the cream of the East Tyrone Brigade in May 1987, through to February 1992, when an IRA unit was similarly ambushed near Coalisland, the SAS killed twenty IRA activists. British Military Intelligence also gave the Loyalists a helping hand. In 1987, a British Army outfit known as the Force Research Unit (FRU) recruited and placed an agent at the top of the UDA's Intelligence Department in order to ensure that 'proper targeting of Provisional IRA members [took] place prior to any shootings'.[49] Brian Nelson worked for the FRU until 1990, when he was exposed during a British police inquiry into British military collusion with the UDA. Whether Nelson's recruitment was just a coincidence and unconnected to the wider Loyalist strategy – or whether the UDA was not alone in being infiltrated in this way by the British and that a similar agent or agents had been placed inside the UVF – are among the great unknowns from the Troubles. But there can be little doubt that the combined effect of the Loyalist assault was to sharpen the general Republican appetite for ending the conflict and, in the key area of Tyrone, to ensure that the expected Republican opposition to the peace process there would be minimal.

# 6

Those in the UVF and the PUP including David Ervine who had the task of trying to unravel the mysteries of the emerging peace process in the late 1980s and early 1990s had two main problems. The first was that the process was a bit like an iceberg; only the tip was visible above the waves while the rest, the bulk of the ice, was hidden from public view. The second problem was that it was difficult to judge the bona fides of those involved. The Provos were sending out mixed signals; one day Gerry Adams would talk of peace and the next day the IRA would commit an outrageous act of violence to balance the scales. Then there was the British government. A long and often difficult history of dealing with various administrations in Britain had taught Unionists to distrust their overlords in London and always to suspect the worst. If the Provos were genuine about seeking peace would British self-interest ensure that it would happen on Nationalist terms and at the expense of Unionism? Some Unionists, Ian Paisley being the prime example, had made a career out of predicting precisely this sort of betrayal and he always had a receptive audience. The peace process, he maintained, was a Republican plot to destroy Ulster, a view largely echoed, at least initially, by his mainstream rivals in the Ulster Unionists. The irony about this phase of the Troubles was that it was the hard men of Loyalism, the UVF and UDA, who had spent years slaughtering Catholics and sending bombs south of the border who had the more open minds about the matter and who took the time and trouble to investigate whether or not the peace process really presented the threat assumed by Paisley and others.

The process had its origins in the 1981 hunger strikes. Although the protest was best remembered for the deaths of ten IRA and INLA prisoners and the hostility provoked between Nationalist Ireland

and the British prime minister of the day, Margaret Thatcher, its significance lay in one of its unintended consequences. Thanks to the untimely death of Frank Maguire, the sitting Independent Republican MP for Fermanagh–South Tyrone, the hunger strikers' leader and former Maze O/C, Bobby Sands, was able to stand in the subsequent by-election and, to the delight of the Provos and the alarm of nearly everybody else, he won. By June, four prisoners had died and that month hunger strikers or their supporters stood in the Irish general election where they won two seats in the Dail. Local council elections in Northern Ireland meanwhile saw significant victories for candidates supporting the hunger strikers and then Owen Carron retained Bobby Sands's seat, giving the SF leadership a real, live MP to tour around the country. After these successes, going fully political seemed the logical next step for Sinn Fein even though it marked a real fork in the road for the Provisional movement. After all, one of the breaking points with the Officials in 1969–70 was the then Republican leadership's obsession with electoral politics to the exclusion of military methods. Elections equalled sell-out to the new Provisionals and it is against this yardstick that the U-turn of 1981–82 should be seen. The move was significant for another reason, the impact of which took several years to manifest publicly. Securing support at the hustings meant that the political leadership of Sinn Fein had been offered both an alternative to violence and the possibility of exercising real political influence and power in both parts of Ireland. But there was a downside for the IRA. As time wore on the contradictions between electoralism and violence grew, the reality that IRA violence often cost votes harder to deny. This brought closer the day when the Provo leadership would have to choose between one and the other.

In 1982, the new Northern Ireland secretary, James Prior, eager to leave a mark on British and Irish politics, launched an initiative aimed at creating a power-sharing government in Belfast. It was a cautious effort, based on the idea that powers could be transferred to local politicians slowly and gradually as trust between them grew. The first stage was the election of a new assembly to replace the old and long-suspended Stormont parliament and it offered Sinn Fein its first outing under its own name. Sinn Fein's performance stunned the political establishment. But winning 10 per cent of the vote and five seats in the Prior assembly was only one dividend. The other was that the SDLP, the moderate, constitutional and majority voice of Nationalism, was put under considerable threat. Some 40 per cent of Nationalists had plumped for Sinn Fein and the party's potential to overtake the SDLP was a prospect that worried in particular the government in Dublin. It was at this point that the soon-to-be leader of Sinn Fein, Gerry Adams, began discussions, first with a Redemptorist priest based in West Belfast, Father Alex Reid, and subsequently with Cardinal O Fiaich and other Catholic clerics, aimed at creating a political alternative to the IRA's armed struggle.

By 1986–87, in the wake of the Anglo-Irish Agreement, the initiative was ready to be launched. Essentially the proposal said that in return for a place for Sinn Fein at the negotiating table, the convening of a conference involving all the parties, Unionist and non-Unionist, and a British assurance of non-interference or 'neutrality', then the IRA would declare a ceasefire that implicitly, if the conference reached a settlement, could become a permanent one. As a prelude to this, Sinn Fein proposed the creation of a pan-Nationalist alliance with the SDLP in the North and Fianna Fail in the Republic, which could pressurise Britain into convening the all-Ireland conference and bring the IRA into ceasefire mode. Implicit in all this was that nothing would infringe the consent principle, that Irish unity could happen only with the consent of a majority of Northern Ireland's population. It was there, unspoken and unacknowledged, at the heart of the process.

Through Father Reid, Gerry Adams, who was by now MP for West Belfast, contacted the Fianna Fail leader and soon to be re-installed Taoiseach, Charles Haughey, and the new British Northern Ireland secretary, Tom King, to outline these ideas. In the case of Haughey, Father Reid ferried messages back and forth from Gerry Adams but when Adams sought direct, face-to-face contact, the first stage in constructing pan-Nationalism in effect, Haughey baulked. His colourful history included allegations that as a government minister after the violence of August 1969 he had provided guns to the nascent Provisionals and was thus to blame for the rise of the IRA. Terrified that meetings with Adams would be leaked and his career destroyed, Haughey suggested instead that the SDLP leader, John Hume, should take his place. And so, in 1988, the SDLP and Sinn Fein leaders met to discuss and debate their respective analyses of the political situation. When the subsequent series of meetings involving party delegations ended that autumn, Hume and Adams continued to meet secretly until, by chance or otherwise, their dialogue became public in April 1993.

If the world of Northern Unionism was suspicious about this Nationalist liaison then the Irish and British governments were downright sceptical. Right from the start, and all the way through to the end of the process many years later, the Provos' bona fides were a subject for debate and disagreement. One reason for this was that the IRA's violence continued apace and actually was intensified during 1988. Gerry Adams's words of peace were clashing with the reality on the ground. Tom King ended the dialogue with Father Reid when, in August 1987, the IRA was discovered reconnoitring his home in Somerset, in the West of England, presumably prior to an assassination attempt. The following year IRA violence soared, fuelled by hundreds of tonnes of recently imported modern weaponry supplied by Libya. Only when King was succeeded by Peter Brooke in 1989 did the process resume. If the British were doubtful, Haughey was worried. It was no accident that Haughey turned down Adams's request for direct contact in the wake of the Enniskillen bomb, the November 1987 botched IRA attack on the UDR that instead killed eleven Protestant civilians in a crowd that had gathered for a Remembrance Day service. Antipathy to the IRA soared in the Republic, adding to Haughey's nervousness.

There was one very good reason for this dissonance in the Provos. The IRA's leadership, the Army Council, was unaware of

Adams's discussions with Father Reid and Cardinal O Fiaich, much less the proposal they had constructed between them or the implied acceptance by Adams of the consent principle. But, in 1988, the Council did authorise peace negotiations, which would be based upon a British declaration of its intent to withdraw from Northern Ireland at some point in the future, even the far distant future. Traditional IRA policy said that if the British agreed to withdraw then they must do so without delay, in the lifetime of a British parliament, so that a successor administration could not renege. But in 1988, the IRA leadership agreed to modify this significantly and a secret decision was made to extend the period for withdrawal up to twenty or thirty years hence. Any consequent all-Ireland conference would, in the leadership's view, be convened to determine the future shape of a united Ireland, albeit one that might not come into being until the second or third decade of the new millennium. What the conference was not supposed to do was to discuss the shape of a new Northern Ireland, an arrangement that could only copper-fasten partition; equally, in the IRA's eyes, it could not happen unless Britain came up with the withdrawal pledge and a date by which British involvement in Irish affairs would finally cease.

As far as the Army Council was concerned, the talks between John Hume and Gerry Adams were supposed to be about drawing up a statement distilling all of this into an agreed statement – the so-called Hume–Adams Document – and then presenting it to the British and the Irish governments for their endorsement. Predictably, the talks stalled over the vital issue of a date for British withdrawal, with neither government at all inclined to go down a road that would be regarded as a victory for the IRA's violence and a rejection of a principle that had underpinned government policy in Northern Ireland for decades. The date was never agreed and the two governments went ahead with their own statement, preserving the consent principle. The outcome of the inter-governmental dialogue was fully consistent with the secret proposals put together by Father Reid and Gerry Adams but utterly in conflict with traditional, and current, IRA policy. But it was the governmental version that provided the basis for the rest of the peace process and ultimately the Good Friday Agreement. In doing so they were incorporating a blueprint agreed by the Sinn Fein president largely behind the backs of most in the IRA's top echelons. Adams and those around him were playing a dangerous game for huge stakes and it complicated enormously the task of those, like David Ervine, the UVF and the PUP, who were trying to make sense of it all.

Although much of this was played out behind closed doors, enough seeped into the public domain to suggest strongly that something serious was stirring in the undergrowth, that the Provos seemed to be seeking an end to the conflict. For instance while the 1988 Hume–Adams contacts were accompanied by indignant denials from Adams and Martin McGuinness, the hardline Northern Commander of the IRA, that a ceasefire was on the table, a few weeks before, Adams had told a Dublin magazine, 'There's no military solution, none whatsoever. Military solutions by either of the two main protagonists [in the North] only mean more tragedies. There can only be a political solution . . .'[50] While IRA violence continued, it was clear that its violence was becoming more of a liability and a burden, reflected not least in Sinn Fein's increasingly stagnant and disappointing electoral performances. One IRA unit in Fermanagh had been disbanded for killing a former police reservist visiting his relatives in County Donegal, one of several sectarian killings along the border. There were other signs of a scaling down: the IRA stopped firing volleys at paramilitary funerals, the policy of retaliation for Loyalist killings was refined and leaders, including Gerry Adams, became more vocal in their criticism of IRA activity, especially civilian killings, which harmed Sinn Fein's electoral prospects. Sinn Fein published a series of policy documents that all had 'peace' as a theme, in which elements of the Reid–Adams proposals figured prominently, such as pan-Nationalism or the all-Ireland conference. Sinn Fein councillors agreed to take an oath of office, abjuring the use of violence and both the party and the IRA began working the judicial system, notably in civil cases.

The task facing the Sinn Fein leadership was a tough one. They had to say and do what they could to convince the two governments they were ready to deliver peace on terms London and Dublin would find acceptable, while reassuring their grassroots and the IRA rank and file that they were not selling out. It all made reading the tea leaves extraordinarily difficult for the Loyalists, and when the British joined the game publicly an already complex and opaque story was further muddied. In an interview marking his first hundred days in office, Tom King's successor, Peter Brooke, conceded that the IRA could not be militarily defeated and that in the event of a ceasefire the British government would need to be 'imaginative and flexible' in its response. Twelve months later, in November 1990, Brooke took the diplomacy a step further with a statement declaring that the British had 'no selfish strategic or economic interest' in staying in Northern Ireland. This went a long way to meet one of the Reid–Adams conditions, British 'neutrality', for a ceasefire cum settlement. Clearly, the effort was getting serious.

The semaphor traffic around Sinn Fein intensified from 1990 onwards both in public and in secret. Just before Peter Brooke's neutrality speech, for example, the British intelligence agency MI5 re-opened the so-called 'pipeline' to the IRA, the secret conduit beween them that had been used fitfully from the first IRA ceasefire in 1972 onwards to send messages back and forth. The UVF and the PUP, along with their UDA partners in the CLMC, had by early 1992 created their own 'pipeline' to the two governments, to discover both how serious the peace overtures were and whether these threatened the Unionist position. The key moment for the UVF and PUP came in June 1992 when one of Gerry Adams's closest confidants, a former IRA prisoner called Jim Gibney, gave the annual Bodenstown address. Bodenstown cemetery in County Kildare holds the grave of Wolfe Tone, one of the leaders of the 1798 United Irishmen rebellion and widely regarded as the founding father of modern Irish Republicanism. For many years the keynote speech at Bodenstown had been used by the IRA leadership to enunciate military and political policy and 1992 was no exception.

The key sentence in Gibney's address read: 'We know and accept that the British government's departure must be preceded by a sustained period of peace and will arise out of negotiations involving the different shades of Irish Nationalism and Unionism.'[51] Gibney's remarks were remarkably candid, for they reflected the still-secret Reid–Adams proposals rather than the approach endorsed by the Army Council. The IRA leadership envisaged the all-Ireland conference happening as a result of a British declaration of withdrawal, not the other way round. In fact the Reid–Adams formulation contained no guarantee that British withdrawal would ever happen, merely that a period of political stability and amity between Unionists and Nationalists might create conditions favourable to unity by consent. Gibney's speech had not been cleared by the Army Council beforehand and when the IRA's Chief of Staff, Kevin McKenna, confronted Gerry Adams he was told that Gibney's speech had been written in haste and that the deviation from IRA policy was a clumsy mistake on his part. Two days later Gibney 'clarified' his speech, saying that before peace could happen the British would need to declare their long-term intention to withdraw. Unaware of the IRA's internal bickering, the UVF and the PUP took the Gibney speech at face value, judging it – correctly as it turned out – to be an accurate reflection of the Sinn Fein leadership's intentions. In fact, so delighted were some in the UVF/PUP camp that they could hardly believe what they were seeing.

Q. *How significantly did the Jim Gibney speech play in the deliberations of the UVF and PUP?*

A. *Big style. Huge . . . the discussions were about the question, 'Where does this stand up against everything we know about the IRA?' And that's exactly the point that I'm making, that the UVF Provo experts were struggling [to work out] what was going on within the Republican movement, but eventually we all came to the same conclusion: the game's on. And it was hard to believe at first, it really was, and for some [of us] very hard to believe, because it was like, you know, an abandonment of the whole* raison d'être *[of the IRA], which was something huge. I don't think anybody would suggest that an IRA ceasefire, one now that has held ten years, is of little significance; it's of huge significance, and the debate and discussion process and indeed the elite management processes [inside the Provos] that must have taken place to get to that point were such that we were saying, 'Good grief, you know, amazing', and we were amazed and fellas would be saying to you, 'Fuck, this is hard to believe', people who had been watching for a lifetime, and we all came to the same conclusion: the game was on and the Provos were playing . . .*

By the end of 1991, Charles Haughey's reign as Taoiseach was coming to a close. When an old scandal about the wiretapping of Dublin journalists by an earlier Haughey administration resurfaced, he resigned and in January 1991 was replaced by Albert Reynolds, a figure not known hitherto for his interest in Northern Ireland. Reynolds had inherited a peace process from Haughey that had slowed considerably and, with none of Haughey's Republican baggage to hold him back, he relaunched it. The dialogue between John Hume and Gerry Adams had continued in the background with both governments aware of what was being discussed. In April 1993 the secret talks became public knowledge when, by chance or otherwise, Adams was spotted entering Hume's home on the edge of the Bogside. The two men announced that despite protests from Unionists and the intense hostility of elements in the Dublin media, they would continue their dialogue.[52] Long before that, the UVF and the PUP had concluded that they needed to know much more and so they set out to rectify the deficit. The intelligence-gathering effort they launched involved dialogue with Nationalists, mostly Catholic priests known for their access to the IRA, the Irish government and with the Provos themselves. David Ervine and Billy Hutchinson, a former UVF prisoner who had been jailed for a double murder of Catholics in 1974, did most of the digging. Their diplomacy mirrored the Republicans' in striking ways; they had to tread carefully for fear of alienating their base and chose to employ intermediaries to talk for them, not least because of their status as independent witnesses.

*Well, there was a series of conduits, I mean it was done in a number of ways. We would have been talking to a few priests; I spoke to [them] on a fairly regular basis. One then would find oneself in Dublin as a community worker, touching base with people, trying to make sense and get an understanding of what the mood music was, what the attitudes were, and hopefully be able to assess what the government attitude was. So those things were going on; they were all genteel enough because they had to be, to be brash at all would have placed people in, I think, specific and serious danger, and not just from the other side but from our own side. 'What the fuck are they doing there?' would have been the question, you know. 'What's he doing talking to them?' I think people have got to remember that as time moved on the degree to which contacts had to be made intensified to the point where there was clear requirement to talk to church emissaries on both sides and even indeed as far up as the Archbishop. It was clear by that time there was a game on, [but] what was that game, what was it about? Was the integrity of Northern Ireland's position within the United Kingdom under threat or challenge? All Unionists at some point or another, if not constantly, believed that the British government was betraying them; people were very nervous about what the British government might be doing and that had to be seen against the backdrop of commentaries by Conservative Secretaries of State, constantly playing megaphone diplomacy with the Republicans, and in that respect, you know, the more that the game intensified, the greater the risks associated with trying to find out what the hell was going on . . . What you found was that you were painting almost by numbers. People were coming back and they were giving their little tuppence worth but it was not a process that you could . . . sit down and say in what sequence this happened and who said what where and how. It would be very*

428

*difficult. You've also got to remember that you were functioning on behalf of an illegal organisation so it was never documented, which is a tragedy, a lot of it was not documented, that is who went where and saw who and when and all of that, and it's a pity we didn't do that.*

In 1993, as the process accelerated, the UVF and the PUP recruited a Dublin-based trade unionist to be their contact, or 'touchstone' as Ervine called him, with the Reynolds government. On the face of it, Chris Hudson was an odd choice as a conduit. His father had been in the Old IRA, as the veterans of the 1919–21 Anglo-Irish War were called, and he had helped Eamon de Valera found Fianna Fail. His mother, the daughter of a mixed marriage, had fled Belfast in the 1920s with her family after a death threat from Loyalists while one of his closest friends, Fran O'Toole, the lead singer in the Miami Showband, had been killed by the UVF in 1975. But Hudson was an active member of the Peace Train organisation, which had been set up in 1989 to protest at repeated Provisional IRA bombings and bomb scares which closed the Belfast–Dublin railway line. Prominent in the Peace Train group leadership were activists in the Workers Party, the old Official IRA with which the UVF had such cordial relations inside Long Kesh. In addition, the UVF/PUP, either by themselves or in co-ordination with the UDA via the CLMC, used two other conduits, the Reverend Roy Magee, a Belfast-born Presbyterian minister who had a history of supporting Loyalist causes, and the Church of Ireland primate, Archbishop Robin Eames. All three mediated with both governments and the Loyalists were able to examine their reports for inconsistencies or to confirm their intelligence. Of the two governments, the UVF and the PUP found the Dublin government, first of Albert Reynolds and then his successor, Fine Gael leader John Bruton, the more helpful. That was hardly surprising since Dublin had a greater interest in securing a Loyalist ceasefire than the British since the UVF and the UDA were far more likely to bomb and kill in Dublin than in London. As far as any threat presented by the process was concerned, the test for the Loyalists was whether their views would be incorporated in the modified Hume–Adams Document that the British and Irish were working on during most of 1993. When the Downing Street Declaration was unveiled in December that year Article 5 outlined five pledges from the Irish government underpinning the principle of consent, much to the satisfaction of Ervine and his colleagues.

*I remember going to Dublin and a very senior UVF member was with me. We were both community workers, speaking on the platform in Dublin at a community affair and getting to know people and starting to talk to people and we met a guy . . . who had been a fairly outspoken advocate for peace in the Republic of Ireland, someone who we felt carried his own integrity. Whilst he could hardly be described as a rampant Loyalist, coming from an IRA background, his family had an IRA background, Old IRA background, in the Republic of Ireland, [and] it was clear that he wasn't a kindred spirit of ours, maybe [he] was someone with integrity who could be a touchstone with the Irish government. He was headhunted, the UVF headhunted him; there are those fools who think that he somehow ingratiated himself with the UVF and then did a great job [but] it's exactly the opposite way round. The UVF headhunted that man . . . We're talking 1993 here [and we did this] because I'm not so sure we fully understood the game, and we had many, many concerns, one being the attitude of the British government. Since we weren't breaking a whole lot of Delph with the British government . . . we felt it was a safe option to guarantee that you never ever, ever satisfied yourself with one answer and that therefore there had to be other sources and other touchstones that you could touch to assess the veracity of the information that was coming in to you. So the Irish government became vital and Chris Hudson was actually headhunted by the leadership of the UVF for a specific role in mediating with the Irish government and was tested in late 1993 in terms of insertion of material provided by Loyalism for the Downing Street Declaration. The six key principles that were included* verbatim in the Downing Street Declaration was our indicator very clearly that we were being heard, that not only was the conduit in place but it was open and working.

Q. *What type of things were being sent back and forward?*

A. *Well, I think that from our own point of view it was probably a mixture of 'What is happening?' and 'This better not be happening'. I would say that's the simplistic way to put it, but it would be pretty accurate. 'What's going on? What really is happening here? What's the outcome going to be? What about the principle of consent? Where are the democratic imperatives?' Those types of things, plus: 'I hope to fuck this is all above board and honourable, because you see if you play games here, this is deadly, this is very dangerous.' It was a hard time, I mean, it was heady days in some respects and sometimes I look back on them and wonder why I'm not more grey, but I have to say I'm delighted to have taken part in it and delighted to have had the experience. I learned a lot, but, you know, the relationship between the UVF and the Irish government was hardly going to be particularly cordial, but the conduit worked. It was created by the UVF, the UVF forced its way in . . . to take part in the game and if the game was about peace and stability, why shouldn't they? Indeed you could argue that governments should have been trying to encourage them into that position, but they were not, absolutely not.*

*The Irish government embraced it, I have to say, much more readily than the British. In terms of understanding the need for the conduit and understanding the need for integrity and honour in the use of the conduit, I think the Irish were much more attuned to that . . . you could argue that they saw the UVF as dangerous and wanted to mediate and defuse whatever difficulties there may have been but the British government would have seen the UVF as less dangerous because it was not likely to be expressly damaging the, the British exchequer.*

*. . . there had been already a conduit, the Reverend Roy Magee, who was our conduit to Robin Eames and also was partially used to*

*test out the Irish government to check constantly to see was he get-*
*ting the same feedback . . . Robin Eames also became important in*
*both jurisdictions in terms of talking directly to the senior people,*
*but again it was all about the remeasuring and measuring and*
*remeasuring of what we already had been told . . . [The UVF] was*
*never satisfied with the answers that it got back unless it got a series*
*of answers that all concurred from different touchstones, and even*
*then there was a risk of being wrong. It was a very nervous time;*
*you could be lied to, you could be getting shafted, and they were very*
*conscious of that, but in the main they operated a very simple copper-*
*fastening process. It came down to Chris Hudson's integrity, it came*
*down to Robin Eames's integrity and [having] someone who could*
*call the truth if in the event you were shafted, someone [who] would*
*stand up and say, 'No, this is shameful and ridiculous, this did not*
*happen or this was said or that was said.' It was all the UVF had,*
*but it was relatively comfortable, I think, in that the UVF had done*
*everything that it could to get to the nitty-gritty and it was then a*
*question of: 'Well, OK, and if this is true and if this is right, what is*
*our fallback position, what is, what is our capacity for redress apart*
*from violence?'*

*At that stage the UVF was not offering a ceasefire. It was trying*
*to understand what the fuck was going on in terms of the constitu-*
*tional position of Northern Ireland within the United Kingdom and*
*what deals were being made with the IRA . . . The bit that worried*
*us all to our backbone was what is the position of the British adminis-*
*tration and the British were about as helpful as a fart in a spacesuit*
*in terms of our explorations and deliberations; indeed the Irish*
*government were much more forthcoming. The IRA, remember, has*
*diametrically opposed desires for the outcome of the political struggle*
*in Northern Ireland than does the UVF. None of us trusted the*
*British government because we had the debacle of the Anglo-Irish*
*Agreement, which was clearly a steamroller of the democratic rights*
*of the Unionist community. They'd done it before, and one could*
*imagine they could do it again. I remember in separate conversa-*
*tions with two Taoisigh, or whatever you call them . . . [John]*

*Bruton and [Albert] Reynolds, and as far as they were concerned, without the principle of consent nothing was possible, and they meant it, and at least one believed that they meant it, and that was important, absolutely vital. Their assertion [was] that central to anything would be the principle of consent, and we were getting that similarly from Robin Eames directly from the British prime minister, and, and though it turned out to be that was the case, we didn't know whether to believe or trust them. But when you're getting it from two separate Taoiseachs and you're getting it from a British prime minister and you have, if you like, whistleblowers in the event of dishonour, then I think it was all we could get. It all had to fit . . . it all did fit and that's why there was confusion in the UVF. We didn't believe the Provos were going there; we didn't see the Provos pulling their people to that position, and we struggled with that, but eventually you had to take it on face value. If it walks like a duck, looks like a duck, quacks like a duck, it's a fucking duck, and we knew the game was absolutely, absolutely on.*

*The Downing Street Declaration was another indicator of the game being on, but eight months for the Provos to respond to the Downing Street Declaration was a serious confusion, and I remember, about April of 1994, big questions about whether the Provos were going for it or not, whether it was really going to happen or not, and shortly thereafter there were rumours of ceasefire from the end of April 1994 and that ceasefire didn't come till August, and the UVF leadership was watching and listening and all of a sudden then you started to see that there was the odd Unionist politician who started to know a wee bit about it. Now whether we were ahead of them, I think we were. I think we were way ahead of them.*

*I can remember going down to Armagh to meet [Archbishop] Robin Eames along with military people from the UDA, UVF and Red Hand [Commando] . . . They had built a relationship with him in the first instance through Roy Magee, then with him directly about his bona fides as a monitor, in other words: 'If this all goes belly up maybe you can just tell the truth here.' I refuse to think of it as a confidence-builder, but a barrier-diminisher. One of the most fundamental issues for the UVF was a single issue, it was the principle of consent, that was a simple requirement, also that . . . Northern Ireland be a separate [unit] for the principle of consent, that it wasn't going to be exercised on an island-wide basis and it wasn't a United Kingdom or British Isles-wide basis; it was expressly the people of Northern Ireland. There are some people who chastise us for having the audacity to discuss the issue [but] for me it's the epitome of democracy. Others say, 'Well, what happens if they outbreed you?' Well, I think we needed to be dealing with very straightforward democratic concepts, and there is no greater democratic concept than self-determination by the people of Northern Ireland. And that principle of consent was enshrined not only in legislation in the United Kingdom parliament, but legislation in the Republic of Ireland's parliament. Forget about Articles 2 and 3; for me the insertion into Irish government legislation of the principle of consent for Northern Ireland was fundamental, absolutely fundamental. The UVF got what it wanted; the UVF effectively got what it wanted . . .*

*I think released prisoners were important, some very important [in all this]; they were coming out [of jail] with attitudes that were more liberal, and I think they had an effect on the ground in the communities that they came from. But then there were others who had a direct role or relationship with the [UVF] leadership, and they were significant. I think one of them in particular was hugely significant and a second one was slightly less so; the first one was Gusty Spence, and the second was Billy Hutchinson. Billy Hutchinson was in a role, a very unofficial role in liaison across the wall [with Republicans], which was of significance . . . I think the [UVF] leadership would probably have felt bolstered [by all this], felt confirmed in the direction that they were travelling, because it was travelling, it was an exploration, it was a process of exploration, it had all the hallmarks of horror, but behind that horror was a clear search to find out what was going on . . . There was confusion on many occasions; the UVF had its own Provo experts, and then you*

434

*had the political analysis, and very often the political analysis was at absolute variance with what anybody believed the Provos would or would not do. They were very intense discussions and quite brilliant discussions . . . but you could have the UVF Provo experts saying, 'Well, this doesn't add up, they're not going there', and the political analysis we were getting and the feedback we were getting was saying, 'They are going somewhere and it is to a better place, potentially a better place. The question for us is what price did they get for it, and is the dealing between the British and the Provos detrimental to Unionism?' So when the UVF finally arrived at a position in 1994 it was a relatively comfortable position; it knew it had no choice because the game was on, and the game was going on with or without them, and indeed the IRA wanted the game to go on most definitely without Loyalists.*

The sixteen or so months between the April 1993 disclosure that John Hume and Gerry Adams had 'resumed' their meetings and the IRA ceasefire of August 1994, have to be among the most turbulent in recent Irish history. Again, some of the events were played out in public but much happened in secret; extraordinary acts of violence at times seemed to doom the peace process to failure but each time the process was dragged back from the edge.

As if to reassure its grassroots that there would be no sell-out, the IRA launched a bombing blitz in the spring of 1993 within days of the Hume–Adams meeting in Derry. A huge truck bomb in Bishopsgate in the City of London devastated the financial district while many of the targets in Northern Ireland seemed designed to provoke Loyalist anger; the Glengall Street headquarters of the Official Unionist Party was blitzed by a 1000-pound lorry bomb and the centres of the predominantly Protestant towns of Portadown, Newtownards and Magherafelt were badly shattered. As the British and Irish governments wrestled with the Hume–Adams dialogue, important gestures were made by Dublin to the Provos. Irish Taoiseach Albert Reynolds made a secret offer to lift the ban on Sinn Fein appearing on the Irish electronic media while the Irish president, Mary Robinson, travelled to West Belfast to shake hands with Gerry Adams, albeit well out of the view of the TV cameras. In September, the IRA called an unofficial seven-day ceasefire to mark the presence of a delegation of influential Irish-Americans who were in Ireland on a peace-process fact-finding mission. The move was intended to impress the Americans and through them to recruit the Clinton White House to the Nationalist side of the peace debate. The Sinn Fein leadership had expanded the notion of pan-Nationalism to incorporate Irish America in the hope that the combined pressure would persuade the British to move positively.

Also in September, John Hume and Gerry Adams suspended their talks, saying that they had reached sufficient agreement to create the basis for progress and were forwarding a report on their deliberations to Dublin. In fact no such report existed; the ploy seemed calculated to add pressure on the governments to move in their direction. Their statement was the trigger for an upsurge in Loyalist violence. Over the next month or so attacks by the UVF, the UDA or the Red Hand Commando averaged one a day. Under pressure from their grassroots to retaliate, the IRA decided to strike at the leadership of the UDA. A bomb was placed inside a fish shop in the floor below the UDA's headquarters, timed to explode as the Loyalist leadership was holding its weekly meeting. The IRA's intelligence was faulty and so was the plan. The bomb exploded prematurely, killing one of the IRA team and nine Protestant shoppers, four of them women and two schoolgirls. The UDA leadership had not been meeting at the time. The Loyalists struck back and within a week had killed twelve Catholic civilians. The worst single incident was in Greysteel, County Derry, on Hallowe'en weekend, where the UDA machine-gunned customers in the Rising Sun Bar, killing six Catholics and one Protestant. As if to reinforce the impression that events were spiralling out of control, a consignment of weapons bound from Poland for the UVF was intercepted on a cargo ship in Teesport, England. Its cargo included nearly two tonnes of high explosives.

This was the background to the unveiling of the Downing Street Declaration (DSD) in mid-December, 1993. Stripped of a date for British withdrawal at the insistence of both British premier John Major and his Irish counterpart Albert Reynolds, the DSD was not what the IRA Army Council had been hoping for. Instead the document restated the principle of consent in terms that could have come straight out of Father Reid's playbook and offered Sinn Fein a place at the conference table if the IRA ended its violence. Meanwhile the Irish government broadly hinted that it would alter its constitutional claim to Northern Ireland to reflect the need for consent, a significant concession to Unionists. The British were staying and Northern Ireland, that is the Unionist majority in effect, would be a separate unit in the exercise of Irish self-determination, just as Father Reid had envisaged and the UVF/PUP had demanded.[53] Not surprisingly the IRA Army Council rejected the document but Adams persuaded his military colleagues to keep the judgement secret and to ask for 'clarification' of the document instead, a move that helped tie the IRA into a process that would lead eventually to the Good Friday Agreement and the fulfilment of the Reid–Adams blueprint. With the exception of Paisley's DUP, mainstream Unionists reacted with equanimity to the Downing Street Declaration while the UVF said it did not feel threatened and would not support any 'publicity stunt' organised by Paisley.

In the wake of the DSD, Sinn Fein became the target for a stream of government-supplied 'goodies' designed to make retreat from the process by the IRA costly enough to give it pause for thought. The media ban on Sinn Fein in the South was lifted by Albert Reynolds in January 1994 and the next month Gerry Adams was granted a forty-eight-hour visa to visit New York, during which he was fêted as a media star cum statesman by Irish America. The British government's anger at the move served only to strengthen Adams's hand in his dealings with the Army Council. The violence continued apace in the background, with both Republicans and Loyalists killing freely. The former INLA leader Dominic McGlinchey was shot dead by unknown assailants; Loyalist attacks on the SDLP intensified, as did the killing of Catholics and people associated with Republicanism, and in April members of the UVF's sister organisation, the Red Hand Commando, brutally beat and shot dead a Protestant woman, Margaret Wright, who had wandered into an illegal drinking club where she was mistaken for a Catholic.

According to David Ervine, a Loyalist ceasefire was tentatively planned by the CLMC for July and the intention was twofold: first to pre-empt the IRA ceasefire if possible and second to ensure that the Loyalist groups were not left behind when the IRA cessation came. But then the Republican violence ramped up, followed closely by that of the Loyalists. In mid-June, an INLA gunman sprayed shots into a group of men standing near the PUP's offices on the Shankill Road, killing the UVF's Shankill Commander, Trevor King, and two other UVF men. The next day the UVF struck out wildly, killing one Catholic and two Protestants mistaken for Catholics. But worse was to follow twenty-four hours later when UVF gunmen sprayed customers in the Heights Bar in Loughinisland, County Down, as they were watching a World Cup football game between Ireland and Italy, killing six Catholics and wounding five more. On 10 July 1994, two days before the 12th, the IRA fired forty shots at the home in Magherafelt, County Derry, of DUP MP the Reverend William McCrea, two of whose relatives, Leslie Dallas and Derek Ferguson, had been shot dead by the IRA, which claimed both had been active in the Mid-Ulster UVF. The following day, 11 July, the IRA killed Ray Smallwood, a key UDA member of the CLMC's peace team, and at the end of the month two South Belfast UDA men were also shot dead. Ervine was close by when Smallwood was shot and tried to help him, but to no effect. These killings, and that of Dublin gangster Martin Cahill, long suspected of colluding with Northern Loyalists against the IRA, were regarded by some as score settling by the IRA prior to their ceasefire. Smallwood had tried to kill Bernadette McAliskey and her husband Michael back in 1981, while the two UDA men had killed the wife of a South Belfast Sinn Fein councillor. But the UVF and the PUP took a darker view, suspecting that the aim was to ensure that when the IRA called its ceasefire, Republicans would have sole possession of the mantle of peace.

*Well, I think there were moments of horror for all of us, because you thought you had understood what was going on and then all of a sudden something would happen and you're devastated by it and [you're] trying to make sense of it. But it was clear that when the dust settled [that] the game was still on, and it was about touch-stoning all the time to see what state the game was in, or the preparations for the game, and that therefore anger and emotion was something that you knew you didn't have the luxury for. We were all very angry and very emotional; the Shankill bombing was devastating, an unbelievably devastating set of circumstances which had its knock-on effects . . . as well which were horrific. In that respect you were derailed . . . but you had to come back to the reality of what was going on, and the game was still on, and you either played it or you rebelled and tried to destroy the game, [but] the game looked very powerful to us . . .*

*It became clear to Loyalists that around April of 1994 something was really on the go and . . . the IRA were going to move, we thought, to a ceasefire. The indicators were that the IRA was going to cause a lot of mayhem in the Loyalist community, [settling] old scores, that type of stuff, a big bang, and then a ceasefire, so to everyone who would listen, people like me and others were dispatched to say, 'This is a bad idea, a bad, bad, bad idea', and Loyalism would react very badly. You need to do a chronology of it almost because my memory isn't great, but I can remember things began to happen that hadn't . . . really happened in a long time, like a bomb in the Berlin Arms, I think it was, and a bomb in the Grove Tavern, things the IRA hadn't done in a very long time . . . We had then the murder of Ray Smallwood and the murders of Joe Bratty and [Raymond] Elder and there were many who perceived that they were expressly about making sure that Loyalism was agitated. Where one gets a little confused is the shooting of Trevor King, Colin Craig and Davy*

*Hamilton, because it was suggested that was INLA rather than the IRA who was responsible. Could they be working in cahoots? I don't know, I don't think any of us knew for sure, but certainly around that time there was clear tension, and why wouldn't there be, within the Loyalist community, great anger within the Loyalist community, notwithstanding the fact that we'd had the aftermath of the Shankill bomb, Greysteel. All of that, I suppose, culminated for many in Loughinisland . . . it just seemed to us that somebody wanted to keep the Loyalist pot boiling. Our history had always been that one action will beget another action, there's no question about that . . . but where I started this conversation was about Loyalists calling a ceasefire first, and that was destroyed by the murderous campaigns of Republicanism, and I have to say to you that there are those who believe it was nothing short of a miracle that six weeks after the IRA ceasefire, a Loyalist ceasefire was called. The IRA were on their way to a ceasefire and were clearly doing things that were expressly about derailing Loyalism, and it brought me to the conclusion . . . that Gerry Adams was meant to swan the world stage as a peacemaker, as Loyalists rumbled on in violence. What a horror that would have been and what a tragedy that would have been, but again I empha-sise a point that I made . . . before. Loyalists forced their way into the frame as far as a ceasefire was concerned by analysing and by getting out and finding out what was happening. That consultation process prior to the IRA ceasefire [meant] we'd a fair idea things were on their way and we had expressly believed that they were likely to come around April, but many things happened between April and the IRA's declaration in August, that were really awful and very, very hard to deal with . . .*

*[After the killing of Trevor King, there was] nervousness piled on top of more nervousness. Had we got it right, were we right about our assessments about where this was going? We were very nervous about that. The mood of our own community massively enhanced the degree of nervousness, because our community were dismayed [by the IRA cessation]. I think James Molyneaux described it as more or less the worst thing that ever happened, and I'm saying to*

*myself, 'People alive, that's good news!' but I understood the complexities in the minds of the people in the Unionist community. Was there a secret, surreptitious deal done by Republicans? But we had done our homework as far as we could, but the Unionist politicians had not done their homework. I think many of them were oblivious, absolutely oblivious to what was coming. Not all of them, [but] many of them.*

Q. *When you say not all ... ?*

A. *I think elements of the Ulster Unionist Party were relatively well tuned in to what was coming up.*

Q. *On an individual basis?*

A. *Yeah, I think Ken Maginnis was relatively well tuned in, I think that [Reg] Empey, [Michael and Chris] McGimpsey were a little nucleus around [James] Molyneaux, they seemed to have an idea. One just saw the DUP cower, cowed if you like, fearful of what was happening. I remember meetings with Ulster Unionists and, shortly after the IRA ceasefire, they were keen that Loyalism should respond, unlike elements of the Democratic Unionist Party who were keen that Loyalism should not respond.*

*I think there were those who believed it was pretty damn close to being in the bag, that the Loyalist ceasefire could be achieved, but you couldn't achieve that just moments after the IRA ceasefire. We hadn't been involved in the game between the government and the IRA. Why should we rush? The IRA took eight months to respond to the Downing Street Declaration, and meanwhile back at the ranch Loyalism was getting chided for not responding within days of the IRA. I remember Bruce Morrison,\* the American, saying: 'The government will now have to move to crush the Loyalists.' That's the way it was all meant to be. Of course the Loyalists were ahead of the game, the Loyalists had analysed, assessed and knew that it had to come but you could not do it with undue haste. It would have been*

---

\* Former US Congressman and member of Americans for a New Irish Agenda.

*madness and it would have been detrimental in our own commu-
nity and detrimental to the organisations. They needed the time
and space to watch and see how the IRA ceasefire was likely to
develop, what the political atmosphere around it was like, the mood
music in the community. There were attempts by us to try and build
up a bit of confidence in the Unionist community around that time
and again that was all about our capacity to respond, and eventually
we did respond six weeks later.*

On 31 August 1994 the IRA finally announced a ceasefire that
came into effect at midnight, following a day of flag-waving caval-
cades through Republican areas of the city organised by Sinn Fein
and intended to convey the impression that a great victory had been
won. But there were differences with past IRA ceasefires that
marked this one out as significantly unusual, that perhaps made
the street celebrations a little premature. The ceasefires of 1972 and
1975 had been predicated on secret talks with the British but this
cessation was attached to nothing more concrete than 'the potential of the current situation', as the IRA described the position post-
Downing Street Declaration.[54] While in prior cessations the IRA
leadership played the more prominent role, this time the centre
stage would be occupied by its political wing, Sinn Fein. In other
ceasefires the IRA was seeking a commitment from Britain for a
withdrawal date from Northern Ireland but in this ceasefire that
issue had been consigned to the back burner and instead Sinn Fein
was seeking admittance to political talks that inevitably would leave
the essence of the constitutional status quo largely untouched.

Reaction to the IRA statement was nothing if not predictable.
While the Irish government and the SDLP gave it an unequivocal
welcome, Unionist leaders chose not to read the ceasefire positively,
focusing instead on the use of the word 'complete' instead of the
adjective 'permanent' in the IRA's description of its action. The
British premier, John Major, had 'no option' except to reject the
IRA's bona fides because it had not gone far enough in this regard,
protested the Ulster Unionist leader, James Molyneaux. His DUP

counterpart, Ian Paisley, declared, 'I don't see in the document any renunciation of violence; I hear the salute to murderers.'

The Loyalist paramilitary response was a study in contrasts. The CLMC, which included the UDA, said, '[We] wish to make it clear that we will not be dancing to the Pan-Nationalist tune . . . Is our constitution being tampered with or is it not? What deals have been done?' Scepticism, fear and suspicion ran through the statement but the UVF's reaction was mixed. Within a day of the ceasefire, graffiti appeared on a Shankill Road gable wall which reflected both the UVF/PUP analysis of the peace process and their need to cope with the Loyalist anxiety generated by the ceasefire. Past IRA ceasefires usually signalled British treachery, at least in Loyalist minds and a *Belfast Telegraph* poll showing that 56 per cent of people believed there had been a secret deal with the IRA demonstrated that it was no different this time. So the UVF slogan was designed to calm and reassure: 'On behalf of the Loyalist people on the Shankill Road, we accept the unconditional surrender of the IRA.' But it was clear that not everyone in the UVF believed the message from their own leadership. Although the ceasefire had been well telegraphed in the preceding days, the UVF went out to kill a Catholic just a few hours before the IRA announcement. Using sledgehammers to break into a house in Antrim, the UVF kidnapped thirty-seven-year-old Sean McDermott, a Catholic building worker who was later found dead in his car, killed by two shotgun blasts to the head. Three days after the IRA announcement, the UVF planted a bomb outside Sinn Fein's headquarters, a small device was placed on the Belfast–Dublin train, much to Chris Hudson's anger, and an attempt was made to assassinate a Republican on the Falls Road.

As Gerry Adams flew off to the United States to an ecstatic reception, this time on a regular and unrestricted visitor's visa, the UVF's fears that Adams would attempt to claim all the credit for peace looked prescient. With the IRA declaration made, the spotlight turned on to the UVF and UDA. The first indication that a Loyalist ceasefire was on its way came when the CLMC distanced itself from Ian Paisley. In the wake of the IRA's ceasefire, Ian Paisley had sounded his customary alarm and offered to create a pan-Unionist forum. But this time the Loyalist paramilitaries shunned his offer, beginning a period of bitter rivalry and hostility between them. To stymie Paisley and accelerate the Loyalist journey towards a ceasefire, the CLMC hosted its own pan-Unionist conference in mid-September which the DUP refused to attend.

By October 1994, the UVF and UDA were ready to call their own cessation although there were telling differences in the approach favoured by the two groups. The UDA was most eager to make the move and wanted to announce it in the car park of the Maze prison, a clear sign that its prisoners, who at that point included the already notorious gunman Johnny Adair, played a dominant role in the decision-making process. The UVF and the PUP preferred a more formal, dignified affair which could generate valuable publicity and kudos for the Loyalists. The UVF got its way and from that as well as the nature of the event that was held, it is reasonable to suggest that within the internal counsels of the CLMC, David Ervine and his people held greater sway. The venue for the announcement was Fernhill House, which during the Home Rule crisis of 1912 had been the headquarters of the West Belfast UVF. To underscore the significance of the ceasefire and to suggest a deeper sincerity than the IRA had shown, Gusty Spence, the first paramilitary prisoner of the Troubles, wrote and read the ceasefire announcement. The words that attracted most media attention came at the start of the last but third paragraph: 'In all sincerity, we offer, to the loved ones of all innocent victims over the past twenty years, abject and true remorse.'

*When the Loyalist ceasefire came, it came with a rush. We were saying in the CLMC, 'Yes, we're working towards it', but the UDA wanted to call it virtually instantly. I think one suggestion by the UDA, and you can check this with the UVF leadership, was to drive up to Long Kesh car park and declare a ceasefire there. This was always one of the confusions with the UVF and the UDA, certainly in the media's mind. The UVF never placed its prisoners on the same plane as the UDA seemed to place theirs. Individually they placed their prisoners on a very high plane, but collectively the prisoners were an incarcerated battalion. They had no greater authority than any other battalion; they were entitled to an opinion, were certainly entitled to discussion and dialogue, but they weren't entitled to have such influence. People said [to the UDA], 'Hold on a minute, you can't do it that way . . . This needs to be vigorous, it needs to make a splash because it is coming on the back of the IRA ceasefire.' There had to be a splash in order to force our way into the frame. We were being left out of the frame, and that the Loyalist ceasefire was going to be called was brilliant, but how was it going to make serious headline news, how was it going to change the atmosphere and the mood within our whole society? In discussion, between the UDA, UVF, Red Hand, it became clear that, 'OK, maybe that's not a bad idea, how would you do that?' 'OK, we could . . . put all our people up on the platform.' So next was: 'Who wants to be on the platform?' All of the very reticent military people said, 'Well, it'll not be me, I'm not going anywhere near a camera.' In the main the UVF is still a bit like that. UVF personnel have never sought the cameras; the PUP who are very close to the UVF do, because we're involved expressly and directly in politics, but while other paramilitaries have sought the cameras, the UVF personnel have very, very rarely done that. It was clear that it needed to be of significance. I can't remember who came up with the idea of the alpha and omega, [but] Spence was effectively the first Loyalist prisoner as far as this phase of Northern Ireland's nightmare is concerned, and somebody came up with the idea of alpha and omega, the beginning and the end, which is quite significant, and if you look at the sentiment behind that, it's huge. I think it was quite brilliantly handled. One guy told me he was in a hotel room in Pakistan, he just happened to be watching – I think it was Sky or CNN or whatever – and, you know, flash, big news. You don't have to travel very far to know that Loyalism doesn't exist . . . in the minds of many people beyond these shores, and all of a sudden they did, and that was important for a number of reasons. They were heady days and interesting times and I actually think that the style and nature of the way it was approached, with the media briefed the evening before to be at . . . Fernhill House, and, you know, Fernhill House had its own significance as well, not just [because of] its relationship with the UVF, [but] . . . its relationship with fighting Ulstermen and Ulstermen prepared to say, 'Well, I'm not going to be bullied, I'm not going to be downtrodden, I'm going to stand up and do something about it' . . . and remember, this had never been done before, and I actually think it was done quite well, and it was the PUP and the UDP who took the platform and Gusty Spence who read out the statement. You could argue that Gusty Spence wrote the statement, which I think is fair enough, but only in draft form and then to be read and discussed . . . and then copper-fastened. I don't remember, although others may, the draft being adjusted, because it had some interesting, quite fundamental issues in it, like abject and true remorse to all of the innocent victims. And we're still waiting on the IRA saying that. Also it said that never again shall we allow our society to dissolve into bloody conflict . . . They were quite brilliant pieces. I mean, somebody needs to take it apart word for word and see what does it really mean, because those sentiments were real. I think they still are . . .*

Q. *Was there any opposition within the UVF that you sensed at that time towards the notion of ceasefire?*

A. *Yes, but not jumping up and down or breathing fire or threatening splits, no . . .*

Q. *Nervousness?*

A. *Nervousness . . . people who were the leaders were nervous, people like me who were analysts were nervous. People . . . had the right to be nervous, we'd never been there before, and . . . there's also parts of the jigsaw that you are always conscious are either in shadow or can't be seen at all and we admitted that . . . if all that we know is as we know it this could be OK, but then if it was 'if', it was a big risk, and I can remember one UVF leader saying, 'It is risky, but sure there are no guarantees in life', and . . . that phrase has been played in my head for a very long time, but played alongside it is: 'Well, we're at the crossroads', and the UVF has managed to maintain itself at the crossroads, I would say, very well. It's had discipline difficulties like many others, in fact less than many others, but nevertheless has sat solidly at the crossroads.*

The positive language notwithstanding, the UVF ceasefire was called on exactly the same terms as the IRA's: it was not final but was conditional on events and could be called off if it was felt necessary. In the months that followed, those circumstances evolved twice, the first time with the publication of the so-called *Frameworks* documents which outlined very ambitious, and for Unionists, provocative British and Irish ideas about Northern Ireland's possible future relationship with the government in Dublin, and the second was in February 1996 when the IRA's ceasefire broke down. In neither instance, however, did the UVF's nerve break. As things turned out, the *Framework* papers were much diluted down in the Good Friday Agreement while the IRA ceasefire was restored in the summer of 1997.

*. . . there was only one major issue for me . . . in calling a ceasefire the UVF signed up to nothing. The language used meant the UVF placed itself at the crossroads, interested in viewing down that street . . . but retaining the capacity to go in whatever direction it felt [was] required . . . The ceasefire meant, 'We're looking'; it didn't mean you've gone away, it didn't mean you've no weaponry, it didn't mean you haven't got the ability. I can remember Francie Molloy, the Sinn Fein councillor from Coalisland, saying, 'If things go wrong we can always go back to what we do best', and I can remember saying similar things, because it was actually true. You're sitting at the crossroads, you're having a juke down the road, you might sent a few scouts out, to find out what's up the road; if you don't like what's up the road, if up the road is dishonourable, you*

*come back and you retain the option to go in whatever direction is required. And that is where the UVF were. No, I think that we need to extrapolate that a little, that's where the UVF are. Journalists who play games with the existence of paramilitaries . . . need to waken up and smell the coffee, [and understand] that neither the IRA, the UVF nor the UDA signed up to anything; they signed up to the ceasefire for exploration. And [even] what came out of the exploration has not been signed up to. The Good Friday Agreement, for instance, is not signed up to by either the IRA or the UVF or the UDA or the Red Hand for that matter. In that respect I think we all need to think very carefully about what we think people's mindsets are, and if people's mindsets are confused, as they always have been in this society by the perceived distrust of the other, well then we're going nowhere. It's slow, it's laborious, it's tedious, it's painful; against that backdrop there's also a loss of discipline because the war isn't being fought and what do you do with your 'soldiers' when the war is not being fought? All those are nightmare management positions for leaderships to deal with . . . Some cope better than others . . . but it seems to me that the UVF was saying, 'Well, we'll have a look, let's explore, let's see . . .' And of course then, you know, we hit all kinds of shit when the* Framework for the Future *documents appeared, I think it was February 1995. That was a nightmare . . . because they were expressly green; they were Provo-pandering material, there's no question about that. But you had to outwork [the questions]: 'What is that for, what game is being played . . .?' Certainly, in those early days, you have to realise that the ceasefire was constantly, constantly under threat, and effectively under review, because we had the IRA's abandonment of a ceasefire again in 1996, never mind the nightmare of the* Framework *document, and Loyalism pulling itself apart and Unionism pulling itself apart, politically and intellectually, over what the future might hold, who is honourable, who is dishonourable. I've never known the British government to be considered honourable by the Unionist community . . . and where I think the UVF got this right was in this way . . . Our great leaders within Unionism accused British governments of being betrayers then demanded that the betrayer look after their interests, [whereas] the UVF was moving away from the betrayer looking after our interests and thinking, 'Well, fuck me, we need to do this, this has to be done by us, or people like us, insomuch as that we take responsibility for ourselves, that the judgement isn't going to be Robin Eames's for ever . . . we can't keep playing this third-party game, we've got to take responsibility', and I think that in many ways that was another brave step by the UVF. I can remember as well the* Framework *documents. We took those apart and put them together, and I mean took them apart and put them together again, through a process of conference and dialogue . . . and it was, I have to say, another interesting time and a time of great fear because those ceasefires were under strain and stress. And then of course the IRA detonated bombs in Canary Wharf that killed two people . . . it was very, very difficult against that backdrop and yet Loyalism held. And the same scumbags of journalists, and they're not all scumbags, but the same scumbag journalists who play the tittle-tattle were shocked beyond belief at Loyalism's capacity to hold . . . I think the Loyalist paramilitary leadership need serious appreciation for the way in which they held the line . . . there were . . . a few wobbly bits, you know, the beginnings of 'no claim, no blame', but in the main, and certainly the people that I was dealing with, were absolutely solid as a rock . . . It wasn't a question of 'Oh well, they've done this so we'll do that'; it was a question: 'What does all this mean, where is this going?' That required analysis, and they pulled in all the avenues for analysis and, and stayed their hand, thankfully, because it was, it was, it was serious enough . . .*

With the CLMC ceasefire came a new respectability for the UVF and the UDA. The ultimate mark of this was an invitation to visit the United States of America, made possible when the Clinton White House agreed to waive the visa ban on people such as Ervine, whose prison records normally disqualified them from entering the country. Eventually, David Ervine, Billy Hutchinson and their UDA equivalents would get to wine and dine in the White House, just like Gerry Adams, but Ervine's first trip to the States came only a month after the CLMC had suspended its violence. The expedition was a revelation to David Ervine, not least because of the insight he gained into how America's self-interest shaped foreign policy. Bill Clinton's interest in the peace process might have been shaped by the prospect of Irish-American votes but as far the mandarins of Washington were concerned, it was about fighting its own wars. Peace in Northern Ireland would free up British military resources for use against the United States's new, emerging enemy: militant Islam.

*. . . the Loyalist ceasefire was declared on 14 October 1994, and less than a month later we were invited to speak to people in the United States, in three cities – New York, Boston and Washington – and that was interesting; certainly, as one of the delegates, it was extremely interesting and very pleasurable. I had never been in America before, I had never been on a flight that length of time, I had never been picked up in a limousine and driven around, and I have no doubt people believed that we were being seduced, but leaving that element of it aside, it was vital. We were able to talk to the State Department, to the United Kingdom desk officer and when we simplistically accused the United States administration of being pro-Provo, he said, 'Well, you know the Provisional IRA don't have Buccaneer bombers, they don't have aircraft carriers, and we need to help sew up the British exchequer so that we can take on the next big battle in the world.' And we all looked at him, and he said, 'Islamic fundamentalism.' That was November 1994, and I was not alone, there are witnesses. We came away, I think, a little annoyed with ourselves. We went with a view that somehow or other all Irish-Americans were rampant Provos, and came back chastened because that's not the case, far from it. But I found them . . . very pro-United Kingdom, even many of the Irish-Americans. You've also got to remember that it was also a case of Gerry Adams got his visa, so we had to get ours, and there is an element of legitimacy in that. Clinton gave Adams his visa when Adams could not achieve legitimacy*

*from anywhere else; he couldn't get it from Unionism at all, and he couldn't get it from the British, so the Americans provided that legitimacy which fuelled the belief in Adams's constituency that what he was advocating was of value. And it wasn't dissimilar for Loyalism; [it] was in many ways an indication of legitimacy [or] an indicator that the path that one had chosen was being recognised. For too long anyway the American understanding of Northern Ireland was minimalist to say the least, and in the words of a UVF Commander, 'Maybe part of the job was if you can't convince, confuse', and I think we did because they began to realise . . . the complexity of Northern Ireland. It is not as simple as many outsiders perceive, and certainly the vast array of Irish Americans were quite simplistic in their views . . .*

The IRA ceasefire broke down in February 1996 largely because of the growing influence of IRA leaders who had been critical of Gerry Adams's peace strategy for some time. The principal detractor was the IRA's Quarter Master General, Michael McKevitt, whose views carried great weight in the IRA's Southern Command and around the crucial border areas of South Armagh and Louth. His influence was all the greater because he had played a key role in arranging the Libyan arms shipments to the IRA and his marriage to Bernadette Sands, the sister of the hunger-strike icon Bobby Sands, during the peace-process years added to his pedigree. McKevitt's critique of the Adams strategy had been legitimised by the British government's stand on IRA decommissioning, refusing to allow Sinn Fein into political talks until the IRA had started destroying its weapons, and ending the ceasefire over this issue was the first stage in his plan to topple Gerry Adams.

Nor was it surprising that division and discord were also visited on the Loyalist paramilitaries in the wake of their ceasefires and at around the very same time. By embracing the peace process, the UVF and the UDA were way ahead of their own people, sometimes dangerously so. At best Unionism was evenly split on whether the IRA was genuine or whether the British could be trusted and those politicians, such as Molyneaux's successor David Trimble, who share the Loyalist analysis of the IRA, were constantly under challenge and threat. Inevitably the ceasefire was opposed inside the UVF and the UDA but in the UVF's case there was an early conviction that the hand of Ian Paisley's DUP was helping to stir the pot.

The central figure in the drama was forty-six-year-old Billy Wright, the organisation's Mid-Ulster Commander who lived in Portadown, County Armagh, possibly the staunchest of Loyalist towns in Northern Ireland. A member of the UVF's youth wing, the Young Citizen Vounteers, at the age of fifteen, Wright had served time in jail for a paramilitary hijacking and arms offences but afterwards became an evangelical gospel preacher in County Armagh. In the mid-1980s he returned to the UVF's ranks and was in charge during its 'escalate the war to end the war' phase when the UVF set out to kill Republicans. The irony of Wright's break with the mainstream UVF was that he and his Mid-Ulster colleagues had killed more Republicans than most and by so doing strengthened Ervine and the peace party in the UVF. Estimates of the number killed during his watch go upwards from twenty and his men were the first, and only, paramilitaries ever to kill a journalist, Martin O'Hagan, who had offended Wright by renaming his UVF 'Brat Pack' in Mid-Ulster the 'Rat Pack' and Wright himself, 'King Rat', although Wright later grew to like the soubriquet.

The spat came to a head during mid-summer 1996 over a stand-off that had by that point become a semi-permanent feature of Northern Ireland's political architecture. For decades Orangemen had marched along the Garvaghy Road in Portadown en route to a church service. But over the years the area had become mostly Catholic and the marches turned into an occasion for communal strife and conflict. As the peace process gathered strength, a Nationalist demand to ban the march became something of a litmus test for overall British sincerity. In 1995, Catholic residents blocked the marchers and Orangemen refused to be re-routed, a stance that led to a violent confrontation with the RUC. The march was eventually allowed through with Nationalists asserting that there had been an agreement that any parade the following year could happen only after the Orangemen had consulted local residents. The Orangemen's protest had spread, however; there were riots and road blockades across Northern Ireland and the seaport of Larne had been closed off by protesters. Two senior Unionists, Ian Paisley and soon-to-be Ulster Unionist leader David Trimble had turned up at Drumcree to show solidarity, a sure sign of where majority Unionist sentiment lay.

In 1996, it was the same story but more of it. At first the RUC banned the Orange march but after an outburst of Protestant violence, the police reversed course and pushed the march through, notwithstanding Nationalist anger. What changed the police mind was not just the rioting and roadblocking that had broken out all over Northern Ireland but the threat presented by Wright's UVF teams. The UVF leadership in Belfast had ordered Wright to withdraw from Drumcree but he refused and in a calculated act of defiance Wright's men picked a random Catholic target, a taxi driver called Michael McGoldrick, and shot him dead. Wright had so arranged the McGoldrick shooting, according to David Ervine, to make it appear that his incipient rebellion had support in the UVF's Belfast base. A handgun was shipped up from the Shankill UVF's dumps but as it turned out the weapon had no forensic history and so the ploy failed. Wright was expelled from the UVF and a threat made to kill him if he persisted in his defiance. Wright took up the challenge and formed the Loyalist Volunteer Force (LVF), made up of disaffected Mid-Ulster UVF men. The hatred between Billy Wright and the UVF leadership was of a special intensity. Each side accused the other of working for the British and worse. Ironically it was not the UVF that finally claimed Billy Wright's life, but prisoners from the INLA wings of the Maze prison who, in December 1997, managed to get near Wright, then serving a prison term for threatening to kill a woman in Portadown, and shot him dead. Just how the INLA was able to gain access to Wright is currently the subject of a British government investigation.

*There are a number of reasons to dismiss Billy Wright's version of why he and the UVF parted company. Billy Wright was a Commander in an area of Northern Ireland that had lost the greatest number of weapons and the greatest number of men over a seven- or eight-year period, yet not one single inquiry was ordered by Billy Wright's leadership into why they were losing so much. That was one reason. Another, which I have no doubt heightened the first, was that Billy Wright was involved heavily with drugs. There is a notorious story about a dance hall in Northern Ireland, where, on one side of the hall, the Irish National Liberation Army sold certain types of drugs and, on the other side, Billy Wright's UVF members sold a different type of drugs. This is where they'd carved up a drugs market; these were diametrically opposed, absolutely violent enemies of each other, who could function together in that respect. As I understand it, Billy Wright was requested to attend an inquiry and the history of inquiries within the UVF is that one is absolutely safe attending one; there would be no likelihood of summary justice or being manhandled or beaten or harshly dealt with during it. I'm aware of three separate occasions when Billy Wright refused to attend a UVF inquiry. Now there will be many people around the world will say, 'Sure, Billy Wright's entitled to go there or not to go', [but] Billy Wright joined the Ulster Volunteer Force, Billy Wright accepted the rules, regulations and procedures of the Ulster Volunteer Force, accepted the leadership of the Ulster Volunteer Force, and was duty bound as a member of that organisation to fulfil his responsibility, to honour the codes that were laid down. He chose not to do that and for that reason he and his cohorts were expelled, not for any other reason, although there were issues that were undoubtedly adding to the annoyances that the UVF was suffering from Billy Wright. Not least of all [was] his relationship with some constitutional Unionists who were encouraging him, if you like, to destabilise the UVF peace ship . . . I personally believe with all that is in me . . . that he was an agent of some outside force or other. Why were no inquiries requested into the number of men or weapons that were lost? Why could he function – it would seem with impunity – selling drugs openly in a public place, when Northern Ireland was effectively living in a police state because of the Troubles?*

*It's absolutely not the case that Billy Wright's people were [always] opposed to the peace process. I can remember sitting at home – the IRA ceasefire must have been about two weeks old, that would have taken us into mid-September 1994 – and I can remember my door being rapped, it was a Saturday night, strangely enough, and he and another man were there. I brought them in, and Billy Wright launched into a great tirade about how important it was for the Loyalists to call a ceasefire: 'We need our people to be going to university, we need to be getting funding off governments to help with university places', and all the rest of it . . . You couldn't knock down the logic of it, but the ceasefire was not my gift, the ceasefire was not agreed – far from it. You had three paramilitary organisations involved in the Loyalist ceasefire. They each had to assess the IRA's motives and the role of the British government . . . those issues were the largest determining factors in whether there would be a ceasefire or not and yet Billy Wright was at my door demanding that there be a ceasefire. You could argue that a similar situation happened and I think it was in February of 1995 when the* Framework for the Future *document were published [and] Billy Wright was demanding the end to the ceasefire. Billy Wright's knee-jerk reaction was: 'Ah, end the ceasefire, end the ceasefire.' There was a headline in the* Belfast Telegraph *shortly thereafter and again in* The Sunday Times *on the same weekend heralding this coming UVF ceasefire and I have no doubt that the journalists were talking to Billy Wright, so if that was a man who was opposed to the peace process, I'll eat my hat. The same Billy Wright who met the Irish government in secret, by the way, unknown to the leadership of the UVF, seeking funding for whatever purpose . . .*

At the same time that Wright was expelled from the UVF, the UDA threw out one of its own alleged dissidents, Alec Kerr. Death threats were issued to both men by the CLMC but soon, Ervine alleged, the UDA began to play 'footsie' with Wright, which encouraged him to set up the LVF.

*... it was the UDA who forced it, and I think the UVF leadership were very uncomfortable at the suggestion that they were going to put a death threat on Billy Wright. They wanted him to go away and leave them alone, that's effectively what it was; they wanted him to go away and leave them alone. Of course Billy Wright being Billy Wright was never going to do that, but shortly after the UVF and UDA jointly said they were going to kill Alec Kerr and Billy Wright if they didn't behave themselves, the UDA was playing footsie with Billy Wright, and there was never a chance that Alec Kerr was going to get killed. So I don't know for sure what was going on at that time, but I feel fairly certain that the UVF leadership were trying to keep the peace with the UDA, and clearly the UVF had the wherewithal to kill Billy Wright and never tried to; they had no intentions of killing Billy Wright, none, at least that's what it seems to me ... It played right into the hands of Billy Wright and the constitutional Unionists, of which Billy Wright was clearly an emissary.*

*It was fairly common knowledge that Billy Wright was involved in drugs, and I watched these constitutional politicians who would have been aware of Billy Wright's involvement in drugs describe his only crime as loyalty, that people were trying to drive him out of the country that he loved ... He was the first ever public terrorist; he was the first ever TV terrorist. He's been somewhat overshadowed by Osama Bin Laden of late, but in Northern Ireland terms he was the first ever public terrorist and politicians, it would seem, for their own purposes, could align themselves perfectly well to people who described themselves as being a very effective terrorist. Now, within the ranks of the UVF, it is debatable whether or not he was as effective a terrorist as he suggested ...*

*He certainly achieved support within the UVF, [but] thankfully I don't think it was widespread, I think that there were a number of people who were probably nervous because the leadership of the*

*UVF in their mind had gone down the wrong road. [The type of people who joined him] hadn't been heard of for a long time, and certainly when the war was on hadn't been heard of, and then all of a sudden they're back again, and they in the main were the type of people that Billy Wright took with him, or seemed to take with him. I think there was a risk of a major challenge, but they weren't clever enough for it. I think the attempt came with the murder of Michael McGoldrick when a weapon was taken from Belfast and offered to Billy Wright . . . and I think that not only was it meant to suggest that it was the UVF [who killed McGoldrick] but that the weapon was a Belfast weapon. However, it seemed that they picked a weapon that had no forensics; had the weapon any forensics that were related to the Shankill it would have given the illusion that the degree of support that Wright had was larger than was the case. I would never know about battalion sizes – it's a logistical issue that the UVF would never talk about – but certainly the first battalion of the UVF has to be a large battalion. I can't imagine it's a small battalion. How many men did they lose? Five? How many men went to the LVF and Billy Wright, maybe five? Five? As far as I'm aware, it was a very small number. One of the people who went Billy Wright's direction was quite highly placed in Belfast, and you could argue was close to the leadership, and I would have to assume that that was more of an ego [thing] . . .*

Q. *Jackie Mahood,\* I assume you're talking about?*

A. *Yeah, absolutely. I wouldn't doubt it was him provided the weapon. I can remember he was the liaison between the leadership and Billy Wright . . . Shortly thereafter Jackie Mahood met his demise within the UVF, but I was there that Sunday [a UVF leadership meeting] when Jackie Mahood was overselling Billy Wright's power and strength and I think that there was purpose in that. I think that he was sympathetic to Billy Wright and I think there was*

---

\* A UVF leader and member of the PUP talks team who was shot by the UVF in November 1997 after he resigned from the organisation.

*scheming going on at that time. I think that there were questions about Mahood, but as I understand it there was actually a situation where a man, Jackson, was accused of a robbery and had his hands broken [and] put out of the country without the capacity to wipe his own ass. Events then became clearer, that it may not have been this lad who was involved in the robbery but Jackie Mahood. There was a figure of twenty thousand pounds spoken about, but I don't think that that was alone the issue that saw the demise of Jackie Mahood . . . he's the type of man that always struck me that if there wasn't a problem he'll create one, couldn't leave things alone, and Billy Wright was very like that. They were kindred spirits and I think that a number of factors forced a microscope to be focused on the name Jackie Mahood. Now I don't function in the higher echelons of the UVF, no matter what anybody thinks, so what I say to you is in my understanding. It can't be definitive because I wasn't party to or privy to all of the information, but the bits and pieces that I do know, I can't imagine I'd be refuted on.*

*When you talk to me about dissident Loyalism, these are the people who got stopped with drugs and no charges are proffered, these are the people who walk about like larger-than-life cardboard cut-out characters breaking every law known to man including murder and not being charged with them. These are the type of people who got found with police officers, sitting having private chats, one-to-one private chats. There's a whole host of areas where you have to question the engine that was so-called Loyalist dissent. I have questioned the so-called leader of Loyalist dissent and accused him clearly and, by the way, before his death, of being an agent of the Crown. Of that I have absolutely no doubt . . .*

The three or four years that followed Billy Wright's death were violent, confusing ones for Loyalism. The UVF and the LVF, now in the hands of Billy Wright's deputy, Mark Fulton, would feud bloodily in 2000. There would also be fighting between the UVF and the Shankill UDA, led by Johnny Adair, a muscled veteran gunman motivated, his critics would allege, by criminal greed as much as by politics, once described by an associate as having 'a lethal combination of ego and adrenalin'.[55] The UDA and the LVF, which called a ceasefire in 1998, resumed killing, sharing the cover names 'Orange Volunteers' and 'Red Hand Defenders' to hide responsibility for violence and to escape government sanctions. But each group would in turn be 'delisted' by the British government, their ceasefires officially declared over and their political wings obliged to forfeit the privileges and rights such a status brought, albeit briefly in most instances. By 2002, however, a calm of the sort brought by exhaustion was restored between the UDA and the UVF with the forced exile of Adair, although violence would again flare up between the UVF and Billy Wright's group in 2005 after which the LVF formally 'stood down'. Some twenty people were killed during this turbulent time, most of them rival Loyalists but some, like eighteen-year-old Bernadette Martin, a Catholic killed by the LVF in Lurgan, County Armagh, guilty merely of dating a Protestant boyfriend.

By the time Billy Wright was killed, the peace process had been put back on the rails. The IRA had renewed its ceasefire in July 1997, almost coinciding with the election of British and Irish governments that were more favourably disposed towards the peace process than their predecessors – one led by Tony Blair, the other by Bertie Ahern – and Sinn Fein was readmitted to the process. Political talks resumed at Stormont in mid-September with all the parties present except Ian Paisley's DUP and Bob McCartney's small UK Unionists who boycotted them in protest at Sinn Fein's presence. The road to the Good Friday Agreement had been opened up.

The UVF and the UDA had been talking to the British on an 'exploratory' basis since December 1974 and attended meetings at Stormont as a joint delegation from the CLMC. Those were difficult days for David Ervine. He and Billy Hutchinson were part of a UVF/PUP team that included two allies of Billy Wright, then in the early stages of his revolt against the UVF leadership. One was Jackie Mahood, the North Belfast UVF leader whose presence at the talks forced Ervine to resign briefly from the PUP team. The other was

Lindsay Robb,* from Lurgan, a member of Wright's 'Rat Pack' in Mid-Ulster, who was suspected of leaking the PUP's secrets to Ian Paisley's DUP and helping to sow dissension in UVF ranks on behalf of Wright. Within a year, Robb was beginning a ten-year jail term for smuggling weapons from Scotland and eighteen months later Wright was back in jail. By late 1997, with Billy Wright safely dead, the UVF and the PUP were preparing their approach at the inter-party talks that, thanks to Sinn Fein's return, were about to take a serious turn.

The structure and shape of the talks conformed broadly to the all-Ireland conference envisaged by Father Reid and Gerry Adams back in the late 1980s. Chaired by the former US Senate leader George Mitchell, the two governments and most of the North's parties, even the tiny Women's Coalition, were involved and committed, in theory at least, to reaching and abiding by an agreement that would determine 'the future of Ireland', as one of Father Reid's documents put it.[56] The agenda was split into three strands, one devoted to internal Northern Ireland arrangements, another dealing with North–South relations and a third, the least controversial, considered the East–West relationship as it was called, between the island of Ireland and Britain. The UVF and the PUP found themselves in a curious position, at one with the Ulster Unionists on the issues dear to both their hearts, such as the consent principle, but on the same side as their Republican enemies on the question of prisoner releases, which they both favoured, and paramilitary decommissioning, which they together opposed. Only on the conditions for prisoner releases did the UVF differ from the other two paramilitary groups, the UDA eager to swap guns for prisoners, Sinn Fein seeking a speedy release date and the UVF/PUP pushing for a deal that wouldn't alarm mainstream Unionist opinion. The PUP, which brought the UVF and Red Hand Commando leaderships into the negotiating room, also held something of a sword

---

* Robb, who was convicted of gun-running in 1995, was stabbed to death in a Glasgow street in 2006.

over David Trimble's head on issues such as North–South relations. If Ervine and his colleagues withheld their approval, Trimble
could find himself dangerously isolated. With Ian Paisley and Bob
McCartney roaring 'traitor' at Trimble from outside the conference
rooms, that gave Ervine's team not a little leverage.

*. . . our agenda was simple: 'Northern Ireland shall remain part of
the United Kingdom for as long as it is the wish of the greater number of people so to do.' It's called the principle of consent, and again
us Neanderthals, the scumbags, the gangsters as we're called on a
constant basis, were way ahead of the game. From our point of view
the issue fundamentally was about adhering to democratic principles.
Way back into the 1980s we issued papers like* Sharing Responsibility in Northern Ireland, *advocating proportional representation
and positions in government as of right for both sections of our
society . . . [but] the issue of Strand Two was the nightmare for us.
It's all very well having accountability within Northern Ireland, but
. . . does your accountability collapse when you have a relationship
with the Irish government? We were very conscious that all the
soundings from the Republicans, the Irish government and the
SDLP were: 'Oh aye, more or less a road to a united Ireland and
that's the way it's going to be and we'll create these hawser wires to
link Dublin to Belfast and meanwhile back at the ranch it'll be a
one millimetre piece of string between Belfast and London.' Those
were the issues that were very much on our mind, and again we
attacked them only on the basis of the principle of consent, that the
process of accountability had to be such that there was clear consent
by the people of Northern Ireland. Some people have argued, including people in the UVF, that this was a weakness because 'What happens if they outbreed us?' Well, the difficulty with that of course is
that you can't be an à-la-carte democrat . . . There were a number
of things that the UVF was interested in achieving. First and foremost was the principle of consent, and secondly was the absence of
violence in that the threat from the Republican movement had to
end, the war needed to be over . . . but again really it's back to the*

*principle of consent, and every single argument that we have relates back to that principle, including the Provos' capacity to frighten our community . . . either democracy rules or it doesn't. If democracy doesn't rule you've got a war on your hands, it's as simple as that, I think that's still the UVF's position . . .*

*There were a number of difficulties that we had, and one of them was our association with the Ulster Democratic Party [the UDA's political wing]. Two members of the UDP were very capable people, one spectacularly capable. A number of others were more military connected than they were, and they were a nightmare. When for instance the British government wanted to play games with decommissioning, they were actually prepared to trade prisoners for weapons. That was unbelievable; we were shocked to our foundations at the notion that they would trade prisoners for weapons. 'What would you trade next?' This was not about prisoners and it wasn't about weapons, it was about consolidating Northern Ireland's position within the United Kingdom, and by this time of course the relationship between the UDP and the Progressive Unionist Party, whilst never fully comfortable, was now fairly polluted. We were polite at best, and we didn't know what games they were playing behind closed doors, and you could argue, in fairness to them, they didn't know for sure what we were playing behind our closed doors, but the difference between us is that we were operating from a series of documents that had been created as far back as 1978, 1982, 1985, 1989, updated in 1992. We had a core political process and I think that we stuck to it as tight as we could. Prisoners weren't part of the issue; prisoners were part of the issue in terms of the making of peace – there's no question about that – but they certainly weren't high on our agenda.*

*Another nightmare concerned the preferential treatent given to the Women's Coalition. They were highly intelligent and capable people. I have a great admiration for them, which I didn't think I'd ever have. I didn't know them, but I learned to appreciate the talent that they had, no question about that, but I was finding that even though they had no paramilitary organisation to worry about, the*

*Women's Coalition were getting documents before we were. A document would be circulated inside this so-called equal negotiation process and we would only find out about it a day later. We went absolutely bonkers, we were angry, we were frustrated; we had to have a special meeting to decide whether to stay in the talks because of this treatment. When we voiced our anger, Gary McMichael, who was the leader of the Ulster Democratic Party, said, 'Well, everything is all right with us.'*

*Cross-border relationships became the make-or-break issue for us. You've got to remember that Sinn Fein would not talk about Strand One, although they were doing so privately with the Irish government and the Irish government was probably building an understanding of how far they could go in that. A lot of this was done by proxy, the Irish government virtually dealing with the Unionists on behalf of Sinn Fein and the British government dealing with Sinn Fein on behalf of the Unionists in many respects, so there was a lot of it unseen and a lot of it unknown, and it was only when you had a formalised mass draft [of the Agreement] that you began to realise that shifts had taken place. The mechanisms for the election of ministers was something the Nationalists were hell bent on achieving. We had previously had arguments about whether you should have executive authority or whether should we operate in the form of committees but all that was kicked into touch, because clearly we couldn't get agreement until you could close the gaps on the cross-border stuff. Even up until the last day, the mechanisms and the role that the cross-border secretariat would play vis-à-vis the Northern Ireland parliament was of major concern. Initially the creation of the secretariat was to be in the hands of Westminster and Dail Eireann. But . . . if our partner in this North–South stuff is going to be Dail Eireann then there had to be an equal partnership between Belfast and Dail Eireann and therefore Westminster would have to butt out. We needed as much control of that secretariat as the Irish, and there was also the dream by the Irish that they would create this massive and very proactive secretariat that would plan agendas; these would be civil servants, these wouldn't be politicians.*

*I remember having blazing rows with the Irish on the last day or, or the last evening, and I think it was [Bertie] Ahern who accepted and acknowledged that we would not go with what was suggested. Now we were a small party, and if we didn't go, Trimble couldn't go. It was as simple as that. If we'd have said no, Trimble would have had to have jumped back . . .*

*At times there was a way of ensuring that the UVF leadership were aware of what was going on inside Castle Buildings at Stormont. When we moved to an intensified period, effectively the last week we had two offices, and I can remember counting fifty-three people in the two offices. Let's be open and honest with everybody because I don't think there's any point in telling lies. A substantial number of those people were members of the Ulster Volunteer Force, the Red Hand Commando, let's not kid ourselves, because whilst the Progressive Unionist Party in fairness to the UVF had always been given a substantial degree of latitude in where it could go and how far it could go, as far as relating the understanding of the UVF's position in relation to Northern Ireland's constitution, it would be foolish to have left ourselves having to run back and forward to the UVF. So they were there, they sat round and read the documents just as much as we did, and we did it together, and I can remember people being dispatched from Castle Buildings in Stormont up to Long Kesh where a special visit was arranged at night to try and explain to the prisoners . . . what the position was and where the UVF leadership and the PUP leadership was on the issue of prisoners. The prisoners were more interested in the major deal, and that that explanation had to be given as well . . . there was a constancy of relationship that meant we virtually slept together, and that would be not putting it too dramatically.*

*The prisoners issue was a piece of the required material for an agreement, so let's not kid ourselves that we believed that without prisoners you could get nothing. That's not true. You could have gotten things without prisoners, but we believed prisoners needed to be part of it. Clearly the Republicans did, and I remember . . . we'd talked to the British and they thought that three years was probably the best that they could come up with, that over a period of three years all the political prisoners would be released, and we felt that was too long. The British government acknowledged that they understood that and the very best they could move to was two years. Gerry Kelly came and rapped the PUP's door, much to the chagrin of the assembled Ulster Volunteer Force members, and I went outside and spoke to him. He said, 'Look, we've got the Brits on the run here, we can get the prisoners down to a year', and my answer very simply was: 'A year, no. This has to be a sellable deal, two years is as short as it needs to be.' Now some prisoners would probably say, 'Davy Ervine could have got a better deal for us', but it wasn't about prisoners; you also had to have a sellable commodity, and I can remember coming back into the room and the attitude among the UVF was the same: 'It was as good as you could go for; it was as good as it dared be.' Having given my initial response to Kelly, I then went looking for him and I found Adams instead, and I related what was clearly by that time the expressed view of the assembled PUP, UVF and Red Hand, and made it clear that the Progressive Unionist Party was happy to go for two years because we felt that any more was to push the boat out.*

On 25 March 1998, George Mitchell set a deadline of two weeks for final agreement that was due to expire at midnight on Thursday, 9 April. The deal that was eventually agreed exceeded Mitchell's deadline by eighteen hours, in the early evening of the next day, Good Friday – but few complained. As the UVF and PUP had intended, the principle of consent ran like a thread through the document and was reflected both in the Agreement's opening statement of constitutional principles and in the commitment of the Irish government to redraft the claim to Northern Ireland, Articles 2 and 3, contained in the constitution, Bunreacht na hEireann, in such a way as to reflect this new reality. A power-sharing executive, drawn from a new assembly, would be chosen in proportion to major party strength; the assembly would have devolved legislative powers and would have to subject major decisions to the cross-community principle, meaning they would require a majority of both Unionists and Nationalists for approval. And there would be a new North–South Ministerial Council to oversee cross-border matters. The UVF/PUP approach to this was also the one followed. The Council would be in the hands of politicians, not government bureaucrats, and all decisions needed the approval of the assembly and, courtesy of the cross-community rule, of a majority of Unionist members. Unionists thus effectively exercised a veto over the one mechanism in the Good Friday Agreement that could edge Northern Ireland towards Irish unity. The UVF/PUP approach to prisoner release was also adopted and paramilitary inmates would be freed by June 2000, two years later. So too was the joint UVF–IRA stance on decommissioning. Both groups favoured 'rust' as the ultimate answer and the Good Friday Agreement obligingly long-fingered the issue in a way acceptable to the major paramilitaries.

The Good Friday Agreement was in all these ways a triumph for the UVF and PUP and for David Ervine, by this stage the dominant spokesman for the Loyalist paramilitaries. They had got most of what they had sought out of the negotiations and by so doing vindicated the positive view they had taken in the early days of the peace process. The IRA and Sinn Fein had de facto accepted the consent principle, had agreed to disavow the use of violence and once the Good Friday Agreement was endorsed by referenda on both sides of the border, they could return to violence only in defiance of the wishes of all the Irish people, North and South. The UVF and PUP had helped diminish the power of Irish Republicanism in a most significant way. But the fudge on paramilitary disarming would doom the Agreement to years of delay and crisis, destroy the Ulster Unionist leader David Trimble and pave the way for a final outcome that David Ervine could never have foreseen and would surely have deplored. But as the PUP and UVF settled down in the final hours of the talks to consider the final drafts, there were no such thoughts.

*Well, we got a larger room, and a number of copies of the last draft and we went through it word by word, line by line, and I have to say that I probably played a fairly substantial role in this asking: 'Well, what does that mean?' 'What do you think that means?' 'What do you think that paragraph means?' 'What is the effect of this or that paragraph?' We talked about it all for quite a long time and then the draft was closed and we agreed that this was probably as good as it could get. We then had a long and interesting wait for the Ulster Unionists.*

# 7

On the face of it, the Good Friday Agreement seemed to be a good deal for the Unionists of Northern Ireland. Republicans had settled for something they had long condemned as an SDLP sell-out: a resolution that accepted the existence of Northern Ireland and the principle of consent. Sinn Fein and the IRA had actually gone farther than the SDLP had ever dared, facilitating the incorporation of the principle into the Irish constitution via a special amendment. The IRA's war, while technically still in place, had effectively been ended since the political costs of resuming would now be enormous. The Unionists had a veto over decisions in the Assembly and in the new cross-border body and while so did Nationalists, the reality was that the Unionists could halt any perceived erosion of the link to Britain if and when they thought it necessary. And the arrangements for the new assembly and executive meant that while power would have to be shared with former enemies, a Unionist hand would invariably exert the heaviest pressure on the tiller of state. Compared to what might have happened at other times in the Troubles, Unionists were entitled to feel quite pleased with the result. They hadn't won back the Northern Ireland of the 1960s but the union had arguably been placed on a sounder basis than ever. Even so, there were features of the deal that many Unionists found unsettling and disturbing and these made the outcome of the referendum held shortly afterwards anything but a certainty. Of all the aspects that worried Unionists, the release of paramilitary prisoners was probably the hardest to take, followed closely by the prospect of IRA leaders such as Martin McGuinness and Gerry Kelly exercising power as government ministers. And then there was still the IRA. Was it genuine or again playing tricks? There was no sign that the IRA was about to go away and its refusal to decommission, made plain during the referendum campaign, suggested that the IRA would stay in the game, its mere existence a threat, no matter what fine words the Good Friday Agreement used about the rejection of violence. As it was the result was actually a comfortable win for the 'Yes' campaign, its magnitude evidence that most Protestants and Unionists had decided to err on the side of peace. At the count in South Belfast, PUP and UVF jeers directed at Ian Paisley and the 'No' camp were the loudest and heartiest of the 'Yes' campaigners. At the same time nearly 250,000 had voted 'No'. That and the many loose ends that still had to be tied, not least of them how and when the IRA would start decommissioning its weapons, meant that there was a lot of travelling still to do and many opportunities for the settlement to crash. The concerns were acutely felt within the UVF and the PUP after the deal had been agreed and these account for the UVF's own gyrations, including feuds with the rival LVF which more than once would disqualify the UVF's ceasefire of October 1994.

*I mean, who knew what value the ceasefires had? 'Were the Provos genuine?' 'Was there a sell-out by the Brits even though we had worked bloody hard to be pretty certain there wasn't?' 'Was there some dirty work afoot?' You know, all of that. It was all playing on your mind, it was a whole series of mixed feelings. The most dominant feeling would have been a sense of euphoria that the thing that nobody believed could be done was done. I would argue that the vast majority of nightmares that came after the signing of the Good Friday Agreement came because governments were prepared to work with people outside the agreement rather than inside. But I don't think any agreement you make could ever be perfect and wouldn't need changes or adjustments to it, but in the main I was quite elated, elated and exhausted, as I imagine most others were.*

*. . . there would have been quite a number in the PUP who were relatively happy but the shit had yet to hit the fan . . . in other words, what was it going to be like within our own community, what would the responses be? Would people think we were being too soft on the other side? You've got to remember there were a large number of people within the Unionist community who thought that talking to the enemy was tantamount to surrender, never mind making a deal with them, so*

*you knew that the knives were being sharpened. We need to document an historic fact, that as far as I'm aware there were only two people who signed the Good Friday Agreement, one was the prime minister of the United Kingdom, the other was the prime minister of the Republic of Ireland. When we talk about signing the Agreement we mean, I suppose, signing up to or acknowledging its rightness. I think the UVF leadership would have been the most nervous of all because they had the hard work to do. It's all very well going into a pub or a club or a church and somebody saying, 'I don't agree with your signing of that agreement', but back at the ranch it's a fundamentally different issue when you knock about with people that carry guns . . .*

*I think essentially the constitutional question was the big issue. Something that has unnerved many Unionists is the determination that society can't function without a weighted majority, and yet the determination of whether Northern Ireland shall remain part of the United Kingdom would be made on a basis of 50 per cent plus. So you had one methodology of deciding what you can do on a day–to-day basis where the barrier was set very, very high, to getting the most single important issue that will ever face anybody on the island of Ireland, it was 50 per cent plus one. That was very unnerving for the UVF and so was the suggestion of Irish culture and dance being held higher than . . . our culture. There were many arguments about to unfold within Unionism, those for and those against, and if a mistake was made by pro-Agreement Unionists including myself, it was that maybe we were too dismissive of those who were nervous . . .*

*Maybe I come at this from a different angle. I've done a bit of time in jail, I've been arrested, I've seen my mates' brains blown out, standing beside them on the pavement as the blood runs down the street; I've seen some horrific things, experienced some terrible circumstances, and maybe I look at things differently. There's no such things as guarantees in life; the shell at the end has to be cracked before you can do very much with the egg, you know, and yeah, there was always a possibility that no matter how well you analysed or how many touchstones you visited, that there was cheating or shafting or whatever . . . all those things were possible. The question was, 'Were they likely, were they*

*going to happen?' And I think the fruit is there for all to see. I mean,
structured violence has ended . . .*

While David Ervine had felt elated by the Good Friday Agreement,
the negotiations and their outcome also represented something of a
personal triumph. He had emerged as an articulate if sometimes
wordy spokesman for Loyalism, as far from the image the UVF
normally conjured in the public mind as it was possible to be, and had
earned a reputation as a shrewd and capable negotiator. For years
Loyalism had served up a series of public faces to explain or justify its
existence to the world, each one a case study in antediluvian Unionism or addiction to sectarian violence and hatred. There were excep-
tions to be sure, the UDA's John McMichael being one, but David
Ervine did the impossible: he managed to make the UVF's view of the
world sound reasonable and he was very good on television. It is often
said that Unionism suffers from an inferiority complex in relation to
Nationalism. The Catholics have brighter, more articulate and charismatic politicians than the Unionists and if that is true then Ervine was
evidence that it didn't always have to be that way. The reward came
during the assembly elections held right after the Good Friday Agreement when Ervine was elected in East Belfast, reaching the quota, and
his PUP colleague, Billy Hutchinson, won in North Belfast, the first
time candidates with such explicit links to Loyalist paramilitarism had
tasted success at such a level. In sharp contrast, the UDA's political
wing, the Ulster Democratic Party, fared miserably, coming well
behind the Women's Coalition, which wasn't even a real party. Within
three years the UDP had given up, choosing to dissolve rather than
remain the political wing of an organisation that had moved against
the Good Friday Agreement and was racked with conflict over crimi-
nality, violence and corruption. Hutchinson lost his seat in 2003 and
the PUP's vote more than halved, and while Ervine survived in East
Belfast, the result was a bad one for the UVF – punished for being too
moderate and a consequence of the rise of Sinn Fein and the accompanying surge in support for Ian Paisley's DUP. By then Ervine had
assumed the formal leadership of the PUP, and it is a comment on the

profile he had that when he was elected leader in April 2002, the *Belfast Telegraph* reported it in this way: 'David Ervine was today taking up the post that many people thought he has held all along . . .'[57]

. . . *what we'd seen was a cultural change within the Unionist community. The Unionist community did not elect people who were former paramilitarists, it had never happened before, and Billy Hutchinson and myself were both former paramilitarists and it was a bit of a mould-breaker, in that respect, I suppose. You got carried away with that because you were only as good as your last election and the mood has changed since. We don't vote [in Northern Ireland] for what we want, we vote against what we don't want, so the perceived political bulwark against that which you don't want is the one that's trawling in all the votes. That rather tells us that you can have all the agreements in the world but unless you're very mindful of the needs of the broader public the broader public will rebel. The Sinn Fein rise in electoral terms is, you could argue, skilful work by Sinn Fein, but undoubtedly some of it, and I would argue quite a lot of it, is about: 'Well, who winds up the Unionists most, the SDLP or Sinn Fein?' 'Well, Sinn Fein winds the Unionists up, so that's what I like so.' And similarly on the Unionist side, the DUP are seen as the great bulwark against Sinn Fein and that attracts Unionist votes . . . The mood music of hatred and bitterness still exists: don't be soft on the other side, if you're soft or if you're perceived soft on the other side, there's a price to pay for it, and we've seen that in, in recent elections . . .*

*We and the UDP were structured in different ways with subtly different relationships between the paramilitary organisations to which we were close. It would seem that the UDP did not have any latitude. It went to the table virtually as a representative of the UDA and at every turn had to report back to and get permission from the UDA, at least that's how it seemed. I think that was very damaging for the UDP, I mean, Gary McMichael and Davy Adams in particular, very talented people, very able people, but every time there was a wobble they had a nightmare from an organisation that was structured completely differently than the UVF. The UVF, like the IRA, like the British military system and like all military systems, is an elitist process; it's not a democracy. Whereas the UDA was structured differently, in six regions within Northern Ireland and each regional leader as important as the others, so you had, if you like, a six-headed discussion process. You could argue . . . that, with the UVF, you were dealing with a one-headed discussion process and that made a fundamental difference. Also we were trusted or trusted more by the UVF than was the case in the UDA–UDP set-up . . .*

It would take another eight years before the Good Friday Agreement would be fully implemented. The years between 1998 and 2007 saw an endless series of political crises, each one seemingly more bewilderingly complex than the one before and at several critical moments the Agreement was suspended until obstacles could be removed. At the start David Trimble and John Hume led Northern Ireland's two major parties, Unionist and Nationalist, but at the end, in May 2007, Ian Paisley's DUP and Sinn Fein had replaced them and formed the first, stable power-sharing government. If there was one issue responsible for that reversal, it was paramilitary decommissioning, the longest untied thread of the Good Friday Agreement. Ironically the PUP and UVF found themselves in the same camp as Sinn Fein and the IRA, arguing that forcing the issue could cause internal instability and wreck the peace. The IRA began decommissioning in 2001, in the wake of the 9/11 attacks, but it did so grudgingly and with no transparency and this, along with excursions by the IRA that were regular and serious enough to cause Unionists to question its bona fides, fuelled the conflict between the Good Friday parties. It helped that there were voices in the Loyalist paramilitary world raising the same objection as the IRA.

*The UVF has a major difficulty over decommissioning, every paramilitary organisation has, because it's your* raison d'être *being given away. But the UVF has a major problem in that its existence is about challenging violent Nationalism . . . if you don't trust the other side and the other side hasn't divested itself of the wherewithal to challenge the state militarily, then Loyalism is trapped, because its very existence is about challenging violent Nationalism. Now if violent Nationalism is clearly a partner in the democratic process, well, that changes the ballgame, but we're not at that point yet, and that will be an issue that will confront the UVF when that time comes. I've always been an advocator of a four-letter word, and that was 'rust'. I believed decommissioning was a red herring but has grown now into a cause célèbre and had to be addressed, [but] it was massively out of sequence. If you march people along a democratic path even though the weapons are still there, the more that you march people along that path the less relevant the weapons become. It takes on a totally different hue. That's been my argument for a long time, it hasn't really changed. However, the IRA have made a cross for their own back. The Progressive Unionist Party's argument was: 'Tell us the war's over.'*

David Ervine did not live long enough to see the UVF decommission its guns but, in June 2009, it happened in much the same way as outlined in his interviews with Boston College, that it wouldn't be possible until the IRA had finished destroying its arsenals and declared its war against Britain over. Nor did he live to see Sinn Fein and the DUP take office together in May 2007 although he was alive when the St Andrews Agreement, which made that possible, was reached. His last interview with Boston College took place in October 2004, just after inter-party talks at Leeds Castle when it first became apparent that Ian Paisley and the DUP could make a deal with Sinn Fein. The talks came to grief but the IRA's robbery of the Northern Bank that December and the Sinn Fein cover-up of Robert McCartney's murder in January 2005 set the scene for final IRA decommissioning and its declaration that its violence had ended, both of which heralded the DUP–Sinn Fein pact. Ervine's optimism, while delayed, was finally fulfilled.

*. . . the Good Friday Agreement . . . merely creates the space within which one can explore the possibility of ending the hurt and the bitterness. It has been cackhandedly implemented, I think, or failed to be*

*implemented in some cases. Rather than get upset about it I think we have to recognise that all of us are in uncharted waters, we've never been here before, nobody has got ever this close to putting stability, peace and the sanctity of life as high on the agenda as we have them today. It's not been easy but then nobody told us it was going to be easy. We've had a suspension of our political institutions . . . But slowly and surely, incrementally, I think we're getting to the, the narrowest part of the funnel. We've all been thrown in at the top and in some ways because of gravity and many other reasons we're being pushed into the neck of the funnel and there's nowhere else to go. It is now really down to intent. I fancy that as we speak the issue of intent is to be clarified on all sides, instead of suspension of the institutions continuing that we will have a restoration of them. I'd be extremely confident about what 2005 can deliver us in terms of stable government and the beginning of a process that will make the people believe that the war is over . . . and I would be extremely confident, extremely confident that the people of Northern Ireland will see peace.*

*My sense is that, that the UVF will, or I hope will, graciously wither on the vine. The* raison d'être *hopefully will change for Loyalism, but the friendships won't disappear, the camaraderie is not likely to go away and the sense of fellowship will remain. I would have thought that the UVF is quite capable of being positive to the changes that are taking place at the moment. It won't be easy, but I believe . . . they will become something different. I think that they will go through a status change. I sincerely hope that many of them will traverse the relatively short journey from the UVF to the PUP. The Progressive Unionist Party is going through somewhat of a torrid time. It's like the little welding company that knows there's about to be a global upturn in the economy but has a serious and deep requirement to make sure its cash flow continues long enough for it to take advantage of the opportunity. The Progressive Unionist Party's socialist philosophies might well be the process by which the needs of a deeply underprivileged people begin to be delivered . . .*

*I think there are a number of regrets that I would have but I'm not inclined to make apologies for them. What I am inclined to say is that at times people like me have too simplistically been reasonable . . . and I'm minded of a George Bernard Shaw quote: 'The reasonable man attempts to adapt himself to the world, the unreasonable man attempts to adapt the world to himself, therefore all change is created by the unreasonable man.'*

\* \* \*

By the end of 2006, David Ervine, now the sole PUP member of the Northern Ireland Assembly, had joined the Ulster Unionist Assembly group at the invitation of its new leader, Reg Empey. The move gave the UUP an extra ministerial post in the event of a power-sharing government at the expense of Sinn Fein but the ploy was controversial. The UVF's ceasefire was still delisted by the two governments and for a large section of the UUP this liaison with a group responsible for some of the most horrid killings of the Troubles was a step too far. But in a way it was the circle completing a full turn. By Gusty Spence's account the UVF had come into being at the initiative of members of that party's ruling Ulster Council back in 1965 and many of the UVF's early members had been active in Unionist constituency politics, especially in the Court ward on the Shankill. Like the UVF of 1912, the UVF of Gusty Spence and Bo McClelland had a credible claim to a distinct relationship with the Unionist Party and in a way David Ervine acknowledged this when he sought shelter under the UUP's umbrella.

Whether the deal might have seen Ervine given a post in a future power-sharing government or was the first stage in the PUP's absorption by the UUP was a piece of conjecture destined never to be tested. In the event the move was stopped by the Assembly speaker and when the UUP suffered dramatic reversals at the 2007 Assembly election any immediate gain from such an alliance evaporated. By that stage in his life, Ervine and his wife Jeanette had taken to retreating at weekends to a caravan in Groomsport, a popular Protestant resort on the shores of Belfast Lough, midway between Bangor and Donaghadee, and a welcome escape from the busy life of a constituency politician. On the first weekend of 2007, the caravan was being repaired so the couple stayed at home in Braniel on the eastern fringes of the city, within sight of the Castlereagh hills, and on the Saturday Ervine went to watch his favourite football team, Glentoran, thump Armagh City eight goals to nil. That night the couple went for a walk. Jeanette Ervine took up the story: 'It was quite hilly and David complained on the way back, "I haven't the breath I was born with," he said but everything seemed normal. We watched TV, shared a bottle of wine and then went to bed. He awoke and disturbed me, went to the bathroom and when he came back he sat at the edge of the bed. "I'm not feeling well," he said. "I'm feeling very ill." He complained of a burning sensation inside but when I touched him he was freezing and his colour was awful.' Jeanette Ervine phoned for an ambulance and her husband was taken to Dundonald Hospital in East Belfast where at first he seemed to be making a recovery, chatting to the nurses and offering to raise their complaints about the Health Service in the Assembly. But later he deteriorated badly. His heart attack had triggered a stroke and he was transferred across Belfast to the Royal Victorial Hospital right in the heart of the Falls Road for specialist care. But the two blows had been fatal and on Monday, 8 January 2007, David Ervine died. He was just fifty-three.

David Ervine's death and funeral happened at one of those frequent moments in the peace process when the entire enterprise balanced on a knife edge of failure or success. Previous crises had been weathered somehow but this one came with very few throws in the game left to play. If it faltered and failed this time, it might be very difficult to reconstruct it. The endless crises in the near decade-long process had acted like grit in a glacier, scratching away the surface of politics in Northern Ireland, with the IRA's undecommissioned stockpiles of arms and explosives playing the role of the ice-embedded gravel. David Trimble, the Ulster Unionist leader, was a major casualty and so was the SDLP, the dominant voice of Northern Nationalism for so long. The DUP had destroyed Trimble and his party, skilfully exploiting Protestant suspicions about the Provos' bona fides, while Sinn Fein had eclipsed the SDLP by playing on Catholic resentment at the Unionists' reluctance to have Republicans in government. With the extremes triumphant in each community it seemed as if the Good

Friday Agreement was doomed. But both the DUP and Sinn Fein harboured ambitious leaderships. They had each plotted and schemed the downfall of their rivals, they had succeeded brilliantly and now they dominated their respective communities, seemingly beyond challenge. The IRA's moves, completing the destruction of its weaponry and formally ending its war against Britain, changed the game for some in the DUP, offering its leader, Ian Paisley, an extraordinary way to end his life in politics, as first minister of Northern Ireland and the leader of Unionism. For Sinn Fein, sharing power with the DUP might be distasteful but there was a bigger picture to consider, the boost this could give to the party's electoral fortunes in the South. It was not inconceivable the party could some day soon be in government in both jurisdictions.

Both parties had good reason to want to play. Some two years of delicate negotiations had produced a deal at St Andrews in Scotland in October 2006 which could see a new executive in power by mid-2007 with Ian Paisley and Martin McGuinness holding down the top jobs. The sticking point hitherto had been Sinn Fein's recognition of the new policing arrangements and the judicial system. Would the Republicans say yes to the Police Service of Northern Ireland (PSNI) before or only after power-sharing was up and running or should SF be kept on ice, as some hardliners in the DUP favoured, for months or even a year while its commitment to the PSNI was tested? St Andrews had been convened to resolve this issue but it had only partly succeeded. The deal set a date for elections to a new assembly and a deadline for the new executive to take office but as the New Year dawned there were signs of unrest in both parties' grassroots. One opinion poll found less than half the DUP's activists in favour of sharing power with Sinn Fein and in response Paisley was beginning to move away from the St Andrews commitments. Sinn Fein's imminent acceptance of the police service was likewise unsettling for some in the ranks, especially in the IRA, and some key stalwarts had decided the time had finally come to leave, their departure boosting the ranks of dissident groups.

David Ervine's death came just as this set of difficulties was gaining strength and not surprisingly his funeral became a metaphor for

Northern Ireland's possible future, one in which Loyalist and Republican could sit down and share responsibility for governing their people. And so the plaudits for Ervine the UVF bomber turned peacemaker flowed in from across the spectrum. Irish prime minister Bertie Ahern called him 'a courageous politician'; his British counterpart Tony Blair said he had 'played a major part . . . in trying to bring peace to Ulster'; George Mitchell, the former US Senate leader who chaired the Good Friday talks, said Ervine's legacy was that 'he has led Loyalism out of the Dark Ages' while the Ulster Unionist leader, Reg Empey, called him 'a unique, charismatic and uncharacteristically spin-free politician'.

His funeral at the East Belfast Methodist Mission on the Newtownards Road, not far from where he was born and reared, was as politically eclectic as it was possible to be in Northern Ireland. The British Secretary of State Peter Hain shared pews with former Taoiseach Albert Reynolds, the Republic's Foreign Minister Dermot Ahern, the PSNI Chief Constable Sir Hugh Orde and a host of Unionist and Nationalist politicians, Catholic clerics and Protestant ministers and community workers from both sides of Belfast's sectarian divide. The UVF turned out in force, as did the PUP. The UVF longtime Chief of Staff, John 'Bunter' Graham, the UVF's Brigade Command staff and scores of UVF activists were there, as were Gusty Spence, Billy Hutchinson and other PUP leaders.

Just before the hearse was due to arrive, as the crowds of UVF veterans gathered outside the church to greet it, a car drew up and out stepped the Sinn Fein leader, Gerry Adams, accompanied by the former SF Mayor of Belfast, Alex Maskey. Some of those present remember it being an eerie moment, Adams walking into the church past men who a few years earlier would gladly have shot him or worse. After the service the cameras caught Adams giving Jeanette Ervine a comforting hug, as she stood at the door of the church thanking mourners. The photograph of the IRA leader commiserating with the widow of a UVF man seemed to symbolise the possibilities ahead.

'It was no surprise that he came,' she told the author. 'Tom Hartley had been in touch and asked if he could come over. David had worked in Belfast City Council and the Assembly with these people; he engaged with them. Tom Hartley had made a programme about the Battle of the Somme with David so he was welcome. Jim Gibney also asked to come over, so we had Tom Hartley and Gibney to the house, and there were UVF people there and that opened the way for Gerry Adams to come. I didn't know he was coming but he was welcome. We talked briefly and later he actually rang me at home to express his condolences. I thought it was brave of Gerry Adams to come. I told him that and he said he had come out of respect for David.'[58]

# CHRONOLOGY

| 1170 | First English invasion of Ireland led by Strongbow. |
|---|---|
| 1541 | English Tudor monarch, Henry VII declares himself King of Ireland. |
| 1558–1603 | Six of Ulster's nine counties 'planted' with English and Scots settlers. |
| 1690 | King William of Orange defeats Stuart King James II at Battle of the Boyne. |
| 1795 | Orange Order founded after battle between Catholic Defenders and Protestant 'Peep O'Day Boys'. |
| 1798 | United Irishmen Rebellion put down. |
| 1801 | Act of Union unites Ireland and England creating United Kingdom. |
| 1867 | Fenian Rising defeated. |
| 1916 | Easter Rising put down. |
| 1919 | Sinn Fein wins 75 of 105 Irish seats at Westminster and forms First Dail in Dublin. |
| 1921–23 | IRA wages armed campaign to force British withdrawal and Irish independence. Anglo-Irish Treaty negotiated. Irish Civil War begins. Michael Collins killed. IRA defeated. Northern Ireland state and the new Free State consolidated. |
| 1926 | Eamon de Valera forms Fianna Fail. |
| 1932 | De Valera forms first Fianna Fail government. |
| 1938 | Anti-treaty remnants of Second Dail elected in 1921 pass on their powers to the IRA Army Council. |
| 1939 | IRA declares war on Britain with bombing campaign in English cities. |
| 1942 | Belfast IRA leader Tom Williams hanged. Gerry Adams senior jailed. |
| 1948 | Brendan Hughes and Gerry Adams junior born. IRA General Army Order No. 8 promulgated. Forbids military action against Southern security forces. |
| 1953 | David Ervine born. |

**1956**   IRA begins Border Campaign in Northern Ireland.

**1959**   Eamon de Valera retires as Taoiseach and succeeded by
Sean Lemass.

**1962**   Border Campaign abandoned in failure.
Cathal Goulding becomes IRA Chief of Staff.

**1963**   Terence O'Neill becomes prime minister of Northern Ireland.
Roy Johnston and Tony Coughlan join Republican Movement.

**1964**   Divis Street riots in Belfast over display of Irish flag.

**1966**   UVF re-formed in Belfast and kills Catholics.
*deaths* 3

**1967**   Northern Ireland Civil Rights Association (NICRA) formed.
Unionist prime minister Terence O'Neill meets Irish Taoiseach
Jack Lynch at Stormont – Loyalist demonstrators marshalled
by Ian Paisley throw snowballs at his car.

**1968**   First civil rights marches in Northern Ireland.

**1969**   Riots in Derry and deaths in Belfast.
*deaths* 18   Brendan Hughes joins D Company of Belfast IRA.
*total* 21   British Army sent to Northern Ireland.
IRA splits into Official and Provisional wings.
Provisional IRA Convention held; Sean MacStiofain becomes
first Chief of Staff.

**1970**   Sinn Fein splits after majority vote to drop abstentionism;
*deaths* 28   dissidents walk and give their allegiance to new 'Provisional' IRA.
*total* 49   Ian Paisley elected to Westminster parliament.
Siege of St Matthew's; Falls curfew boosts Provisionals.
IRA commercial bombing campaign begins.
Billy McKee is Belfast Commander.
Adams heads IRA in Ballymurphy and choreographs
Ballymurphy riots, defying McKee.

**1971**   IRA campaign intensifies.
*deaths* 180   First British soldier shot dead and Provo commercial bombing
*total* 229   campaign begins in Belfast.
Brendan Hughes become O/C of D Company; Gerry Adams on
Second Belfast Battalion staff and then Commander;
Adams on Belfast Brigade staff.
Internment without trial introduced.
IRA campaign mushrooms.

**1972**
*deaths* 496
*total* 725

Bloody Sunday in Derry.
Stormont parliament prorogued and Direct Rule from London imposed.
Adams interned but at insistence of Ivor Bell is released to take part in ceasefire talks with British.
Adams becomes Adjutant of Belfast Brigade.
Special-category status granted to IRA prisoners.
Ceasefire breaks down at urging of Belfast Brigade.
Adams introduces Armalite rifle to IRA.
IRA kills nine in 'Bloody Friday' bombings.
David Ervine joins UVF.
Operation Motorman puts IRA under pressure.
Adams becomes Belfast Brigade Commander; Brendan Hughes is the Operations Officer.
Four Square Laundry operation.
'Unknowns' cell formed by Adams.
Belfast Brigade begins to 'disappear' double agents starting with Joe Linskey and including Jean McConville.
Breton Nationalists introduce IRA to Libyans.

**1973**
*deaths* 263
*total* 988

London bombings carried out by Belfast Brigade.
Adams and Hughes arrested and interned.
Hughes escapes from Long Kesh and becomes Belfast Commander.

**1974**
*deaths* 303
*total* 1291

Power-sharing Sunningdale deal brought down by Ulster Workers' Council general strike assisted by UDA and UVF and mainstream Loyalist politicians.
Brendan Hughes re-arrested.
David Ervine arrested while on bombing mission.

**1975**
*deaths* 267
*total* 1558

IRA ceasefire called, IRA leadership believes British wish to disengage.
Lengthy talks with British.
Adams, Hughes and Ivor Bell lead Long Kesh dissidents against Billy McKee and David Morley leadership and oppose ceasefire.
Loyalist killings of Catholics surge and IRA responds with sectarian assassinations.
IRA ceasefire peters out.

**1976**
*deaths* 308
*total* 1866

New British security policy introduced.
RUC put in charge of security operations, internment phased out, juryless courts set up, IRA to be treated as criminals in jail.
Prison protest to restore political status by IRA inmates in new H-blocks begins.

**1977**
*deaths* 116
*total* 1982

Police interrogation centres begin to process scores of IRA suspects.
Adams released from jail and eventually reappointed as Belfast Brigade Commander.
Brendan Hughes becomes IRA Commander in jail.
Adams becomes Adjutant-General and joins Army Council.
Long War speech at Bodenstown in June.
Northern Command set up and Revolutionary Council established.
Cellular restructuring of IRA starts.

**1978**
*deaths* 88
*total* 2070

Adams loses his rank as Chief of Staff when he is arrested in the wake of La Mon bombing.
Martin McGuinness becomes IRA Chief of Staff.
Adams cleared and released – he becomes Adjutant-General, second in command to McGuinness.
British Army document, *Northern Ireland – Future Terrorist Trends*, leaked to IRA; names Adams and Bell as architects of IRA restructuring.

**1979**
*deaths* 125
*total* 2195

Margaret Thatcher becomes British prime minister.
Lord Mountbatten killed in IRA bombing.
18 British soldiers killed in ambush on border.

**1980**
*deaths* 86
*total* 2281

First IRA prison hunger strike begins with Brendan Hughes leading the protest.
Northern IRA leaders negotiate secret deal to end fast with Britain's MI6.
Hunger strike ends with no significant concessions; IRA leadership tries to disguise defeat

**1981**
*deaths* 117
*total* 2398

Second jail hunger strike starts.
IRA prison leader Bobby Sands elected MP for Fermanagh–South Tyrone.
When Sands dies Owen Carron is elected in his place.
Two IRA prisoners elected to the Dail in Dublin.
Hunger strike ends with ten deaths.
Brendan Hughes moves to non-IRA blocks.
Sinn Fein adopts 'Armalite and ballot box' strategy and agrees to contest elections.

**1982**
*deaths* 112
*total* 2510

Army Council allows Adams and McGuinness to stand in elections to new NI Assembly but McGuinness forced to quit as Chief of Staff while Adams stands down as Adjutant-General, the last time he holds rank in the IRA.
Ivor Bell becomes new Chief of Staff.

Sinn Fein wins 10 per cent of the vote in Assembly elections, causing political sensation.
New Sinn Fein leadership dominated by Adams allies.
Peace process begins with talks between Gerry Adams and Father Alex Reid.

**1983**
*deaths* 87
*total* 2597

Gerry Adams elected MP for West Belfast; Sinn Fein tops 100,000 votes in British general election.
Adams succeeds Ruairi O Bradaigh as President of Sinn Fein as old guard is vanquished.
Ivor Bell forced to quit as Chief of Staff after he is arrested. Kevin McKenna succeeds him.
Major IRA jail escape: 38 inmates break out of Long Kesh/Maze.

**1984**
*deaths* 72
*total* 2669

Libyan Intelligence Service negotiates arms and cash deal with IRA Army Council.
Failure of rebellion against Adams leadership by Ivor Bell and Belfast Brigade staff over resources devoted to elections fails.
Army Council plans Irish 'Tet' offensive.

**1985**
*deaths* 58
*total* 2727

Anglo-Irish Agreement signed giving Dublin a consultative say in Northern Ireland's affairs.
Libyan arms shipments begin.
Adams publicly seeks talks with SDLP leader John Hume.
He also calls for a united Nationalist approach to North.

**1986**
*deaths* 66
*total* 2793

Father Reid first approaches Charles Haughey for peace talks on behalf of Gerry Adams.
IRA drops abstentionism and lifts ban on taking seats in the Dail at first General Army Convention held since 1970. Sinn Fein follow suit at ard-fheis – number of delegates nearly doubles for this one meeting.
McGuinness briefs IRA Executive and IRA field commanders about large arms shipments, saying more is on the way.
Brendan Hughes is released from jail and rejoins IRA.

**1987**
*deaths* 106
*total* 2899

Charles Haughey becomes Taoiseach after Fianna Fail returns to power.
East Tyrone IRA unit wiped out in SAS ambush at Loughgall.
*Eksund* intercepted off Brittany coast with 150 tonnes of Libyan weaponry, betrayed by IRA informer.

**1988**
*deaths* 105
*total* 3004

Hume–Adams talks begin but conclude with no agreement.
Secret contacts between Hume and Adams resume immediately afterwards.
IRA attempt to kill British Foreign Secretary Sir Geoffrey Howe in Brussels apparently betrayed.

Gibraltar bombing ends with three IRA deaths amidst suspicion of betrayal.

Republican leaders deny IRA ceasefire on the agenda of SDLP talks.

**1989**
*deaths* 81
*total* 3085

Sinn Fein criticism of botched IRA operations intensifies. Major IRA informer Joe Fenton killed before he can be fully interrogated. Brendan Hughes, then in charge of spy-catcher unit, suspects Fenton was killed to protect other spies.

New NI Secretary Peter Brooke raises possibility of talks with Sinn Fein.

**1990**
*deaths* 84
*total* 3169

Peter Brooke said Britain had 'no selfish strategic or economic interest' in staying in NI.

Martin McGuinness proposes formal Christmas ceasefire, the first official cessation since 1975.

**1991**
*deaths* 102
*total* 3271

Margaret Thatcher resigns as British prime minister.

First drafts of joint government declaration on NI, otherwise known as Hume–Adams Document, drafted.

**1992**
*deaths* 91
*total* 3362

Hume–Adams Document agreed but leaves blank a date for British withdrawal.

**1993**
*deaths* 90
*total* 3452

Hume–Adams contacts publicly revealed for first time.

Irish prime minister Albert Reynolds negotiates separate document with British, called Downing Street Declaration.

Shankill bomb kills nine Protestants and one IRA man.

Loyalist violence claims 16 lives.

**1994**
*deaths* 69
*total* 3521

IRA Army Council votes 5–1 with one abstention for four-month ceasefire.

Army Council extends ceasefire until April 1995.

**1995**
*deaths* 9
*total* 3530

British harden demand for IRA decommissioning before Sinn Fein gets into talks.

US politician George Mitchell heads decommissioning inquiry. Martin McGuinness suggests voluntary self-decommissioning.

**1996**
*deaths* 22
*total* 3552

Army Council votes 7–0 to end ceasefire.

Huge truck bomb kills two and causes £100 million sterling damage at Canary Wharf, London.

IRA campaign confined to England.

Adams survives IRA Convention when dissidents fail to capture Army Council but suffers setbacks.

**1997**
*deaths* 21
*total* 3573

British general election called; Tony Blair becomes British prime minister and Bertie Ahern is the new Irish Taoiseach.

Four days before controversial Garvaghy Orange march Army Council votes 7–0 for second ceasefire.

IRA Executive and Army Council clash over ceasefire decision; dissidents defeated at Convention; Real IRA formed.

All-party talks start at Stormont. Sinn Fein attend and subscribe to Mitchell principles of non-violence.

**1998**
*deaths* 57
*total* 3630

Good Friday Agreement negotiated.

IRA Convention lifts abstentionist ban on taking seats in Stormont parliament.

After two attempts, Sinn Fein ard-fheis endorses Good Friday Agreement and lifts ban on taking seats at Stormont.

**1999**
*deaths* 6
*total* 3636

Army Council agrees to locate the bodies of 'disappeared'.

Eamon Molloy's body returned but not that of Jean McConville.

Power-sharing government set up, Martin McGuinness and Bairbre de Brun are the two Sinn Fein ministers, for Education and Health respectively.

**2000**
*deaths* 19
*total* 3655

Army Council agrees in principle to initiate a process to put all its weapons 'beyond use' and in the interim agrees to international inspection of two arms dumps.

Last IRA and Loyalist paramilitary prisoners released.

**2001**
*deaths* 16
*total* 3671

IRA agrees on methods to decommission IRA weapons.

11 September attacks in New York and Washington kill nearly 3,000 and Bush administration declares war on terrorism.

IRA decommissions unspecified amount of weaponry.

Police Service of Northern Ireland replaces RUC.

Assembly and Executive restored; David Trimble is first minister, Mark Durkan of the SDLP is his deputy.

**2002**
*deaths* 10
*total* 3681

Sinn Fein win five seats to Irish parliament; party has three seats at Westminster.

Assembly and Executive suspended by NI Secretary John Reid.

**2003**
*deaths* 11
*total* 3692

Freddie Scappaticci, former head of IRA's internal security unit exposed as a British agent.

Remains of Jean McConville discovered on County Down beach.

Postponed Assembly election takes place with Sinn Fein and DUP emerging as largest parties.

**2004**
*deaths* 3
*total* 3695

Adams denies on Irish TV that he was ever an IRA member.

Irish Justice minister Michael McDowell alleges Sinn Fein funded by IRA.

Sinn Fein's Bairbre de Brun wins John Hume's seat in European parliament.

Joe Cahill dies.

Talks aimed at reaching a settlement begin at Leeds Castle, Kent.

Political talks aimed at restoring power-sharing government founder over demand for photographs of IRA decommissioning.

£26.5 million stolen from Northern Bank cash centre in Belfast.

**2005**
*deaths* 8
*total* 3703

Irish Taoiseach Bertie Ahern says Sinn Fein leaders knew of planned Northern Bank robbery while they were in peace talks with him.

Belfast man Robert McCartney beaten and stabbed to death by IRA gang.

Independent Monitoring Commission says leading Sinn Fein figures also serve in key IRA leadership positions.

Former IRA prison public relations officer Richard O'Rawe publishes account of hunger strike alleging IRA leadership sabotaged deal to ensure election of Owen Carron.

White House decides not to invite NI politicians to St Patrick's Day celebrations, in snub of Sinn Fein leader Gerry Adams.

Adams calls on IRA to pursue goals through only political means.

IRA statement announces end to armed campaign against Britain; IRA ex-prisoner Seanna Walsh reads statement on DVD.

IRA completes weapons decommissioning, witnessed by two clerics.

**2006**
*deaths* 6
(*to 12/10*)
*total* 3709

British and Irish governments restore Assembly and set 24 November deadline for final deal.

Conference at St Andrews, Scotland, agrees outline deal for restoration of Assembly and Executive.

Sinn Fein to recognise PSNI.

Ian Paisley becomes first minister and Martin McGuinness his deputy.

**2007**

David Ervine dies after heart attack and stroke.

**2008**

Brendan Hughes dies in hospital.

# NOTES

BRENDAN HUGHES

### 1

1　David McKittrick, Seamus Kelters, Brian Feeney, and Chris Thornton, *Lost Lives*, pp. 38–9.
2　Scarman Report, paragraph 1.23.
3　McKittrick et al., *Lost Lives*, pp. 34–5.

### 2

4　Tim Pat Coogan, *Ireland in the Twentieth Century*, pp. 299–300.
5　Michael Farrell, *Northern Ireland: The Orange State*, p. 91.
6　Ibid., p. 92.
7　David Sharrock and Mark Devenport, *Man of War, Man of Peace? The Unauthorised Biography of Gerry Adams*, pp. 5–21.
8　Peter McDermott, *Northern Divisions: The Old IRA and the Belfast Pogroms, 1920–1922*, pp. 99–103; Dorothy McArdle, *The Irish Republic*, p. 478.
9　http://buckalecrobinson.rushlightmagazine.com

### 3

10　Ed Moloney, *A Secret History of the IRA*, pp. 52–60.
11　Ibid., pp. 70–73.
12　McKittrick et al., *Lost Lives*, pp. 67–8.
13　*The Sunday Times*, 24 May 2009.
14　McKittrick et al., *Lost Lives*, p. 1983.
15　Ibid., pp. 64–5.
16　Moloney, *A Secret History*, p. 103.

### 4

17　Moloney, *A Secret History*, pp. 72–3.
18　http://www.pbs.org/wgbh/pages/frontline/shows/ira/readings/america.htm
19　McKittrick et al., *Lost Lives*, p. 332.
20　Ibid., pp. 269–70.
21　Ibid., pp. 270–71.
22　Ibid., p. 271.
23　Ibid., pp. 348–9.

5

24   http://cain.ulst.ac.uk/publicrecords/1972/index.html#210672
25   Peter Taylor, *Provos: The IRA and Sinn Fein*, pp. 143–4.
26   Sidney Elliott and W. D. Flackes, *Northern Ireland: A Political Directory, 1968–1999*, p. 184.
27   http://www.amnesty.org/en/news-and-updates/news/perus-ex-president-convicted-landmark-case-20090407
28   Author's meeting with Linskey family members, May 2009.
29   Gerry Adams, *Before the Dawn: An Autobiography*, p. 213.
30   *Operation Banner: An Analysis of Military Operations in Northern Ireland*, paragraph 308.
31   Ibid.
32   http://hansard.millbanksystems.com/written_answers/1994/mar/15/military-reaction-force
33   *Washington Post*, 5 October 2008.
34   McKittrick et al., *Lost Lives*, p. 274.
35   PSNI Ombudsman report, August 2006.
36   *The Sunday Times*, 26 November 2000.
37   *Belfast News Letter*, 4 June 1973.
38   Father Denis Faul, Letter to the *Guardian*, [undated], June 1973.
39   'Long Kesh Camp staff reply to allegations', *Irish News*, 25 June 1973.
40   *Irish Times*, 12 June 1973.
41   *Irish News*, 5 June 1973.
42   *Irish Times*, 5 June 1973.
43   Interview with Anthony McIntyre, former IRA internee, 22 July 2009.
44   http://cain.ulst.ac.uk/sutton
45   Correspondence from Dr Peter Hughes, Archivist, Sisters of Nazareth, Hammersmith, London, 9 May 2009.
46   *Sunday Mirror*, 7 October 2001.
47   Frances Reilly, *Suffer the Little Children*.
48   Interview with former Sinn Fein activist, April 2009.
49   Redacted copy of inquest documents in death of Patrick Crawford, Public Records Office of Northern Ireland, released 1 July 2009.
50   Telephone interview, 15 July 2009.
51   Hansard, 11 January 2005, column 197.
52   Telephone interview, 16 July 2009.

6

53   Adams, *Before the Dawn*, pp. 231–2.
54   John McGuffin, *Internment*, chapter 8.
55   Ibid.
56   Robert W. White, *Provisional Irish Republicans: An Oral and Interpretative History*, p. 219.
57   Ibid., pp. 221–4.

58   McKittrick et al., *Lost Lives*, p. 445.
59   Ibid., pp. 487.


7

60   Kevin Kelley, *The Longest War: Northern Ireland and the IRA*, p. 265.
61   *An Phoblacht–Republican News*, 11 May 2000.
62   Padraig O'Malley, *Biting at the Grave*, p. 21.
63   *An Phoblacht–Republican News*, 11 May 2000.
64   David Beresford, *Ten Men Dead: The Story of the 1981 Irish Hunger Strike*.
65   'Scenario for establishing a socialist republic', *An Phoblacht–Republican News*, 19 April 1980.


8

66   *An Phoblacht–Republican News*, 31 October 1981.
67   See Moloney, *A Secret History*, 2nd edn, chapters 8 and 9.
68   Hansard, 26 March 2002, column 715.
69   http://www.parliament.the-stationery-office.com/pa/cm199798/cmselect/cmniaf/316ii/nis208.htm
70   Ibid.
71   *Independent*, 30 April 1997.
72   *Irish Independent*, 31 March 2002.
73   Adams, *Before the Dawn* (US edn), pp. 212–13.
74   The information in this section about the IRA's Security Department is taken from Ed Moloney and Anthony McIntyre, *The Security Department: IRA Counter Intelligence in a 30-year War Against the British* (unpublished).


9

75   Tim Pat Coogan, *Michael Collins: A Biography*, p. 70.
76   *The Pensive Quill* (http://the pensivequill.am), 5 March 2009.
77   *Irish News*, 18 February 2008.
78   Ibid.
79   Telephone interview, 20 July 2009.
80   Telephone interview, 21 July 2009.
81   *An Phoblacht–Republican News*, 21 February 2008.
82   *Daily Mail*, 20 February 2008.
83   Interview, Belfast, May 2009.
84   Telephone interview, 21 July 2009.

DAVID ERVINE

### 1

1   http://cain.ulst.ac.uk/events/bfriday/events.htm
2   *Irish Times*, 22 July 1972.
3   *Daily Telegraph*, 21 July 2002.
4   *Irish Times*, 26 July 1972.
5   *Irish Times*, 29 July 1972.

### 2

6   *Daily Ireland*, 27 June 2006.
7   *Murder in Ballymacarrett: The Untold Story.*
8   *The Lagan Enclave.*
9   *Murder in Ballymacarrett*, p. 60.
10  Ibid., p. 37.
11  *The Sunday Times*, 24 May 2009.

### 3

12  David Miller, *Queen's Rebels*, pp. 1–13.
13  Michael Hopkinson, *The Irish War of Independence.*
14  *Principles of Loyalism*, Progressive Unionist Party internal discussion paper, 1 November 2002.
15  Sarah Nelson, *Ulster's Uncertain Defenders.*
16  *Independent*, 18 October 1994.
17  Ed Moloney, *Paisley: From Demagogue to Democrat?*, p. 146.
18  Ibid., p. 231.
19  McKittrick et al., *Lost Lives*, p. 556.
20  *Principles of Loyalism.*
21  McKittrick et al., *Lost Lives*, pp. 1474–5.
22  Information culled from McKittrick et al., *Lost Lives.*
23  Ibid., pp. 441–2.

### 4

24  http://cain.ulst.ac.uk/publicrecords/1973/prem15_1689_1.jpg
25  http://www.irishecho.com/search/searchstory.cfm?id=8371&issueid=174
26  Peter Taylor, *Loyalists*, pp. 122–4.
27  Ibid., pp. 138–40.
28  Ibid., p. 141.
29  *Irish Times*, 20 March 1975.
30  Ibid., 17 March 1975.
31  Ibid., 18 March 1975.
32  Ibid., 29 October 1975.

33  McKittrick et al., *Lost Lives*, p. 922.
34  Ibid.


5
35  McKittrick et al., *Lost Lives*, p. 1475.
36  *Irish Times*, 9 August 1977.
37  Ibid., 25 November 1977.
38  Ibid., 2 December 1981.
39  *Principles of Loyalism.*
40  *Irish Times*, 18 July 1977.
41  Ibid., 12 November 1977.
42  *Principles of Loyalism.*
43  Moloney, *Paisley*, p. 303.
44  McKittrick et al., *Lost Lives*, p. 1475.
45  *Belfast Telegraph*, 15 September 2006.
46  Moloney, *A Secret History*, p. 578.
47  Ibid., chapter 11.
48  Interview with Tyrone Republican, April 2000.
49  *Sunday Telegraph*, 29 March 1998.


6
50  *Irish Times*, 11 January 1988.
51  Moloney, *A Secret History*, p. 400.
52  First joint Hume–Adams statement, 24 April 1993.
53  Moloney, *A Secret History*, Appendix 8.
54  IRA statement on ceasefire, 31 August 1994.
55  *Guardian*, 28 September 2002.
56  Moloney, *A Secret History*, Appendix 8.


7
57  *Belfast Telegraph*, 13 April 2002.
58  Interview with Jeanette Ervine, 21 May 2009.

# BIBLIOGRAPHY

Adams, Gerry, *Before the Dawn: An Autobiography*, London: Heinemann, 1996, and New York: William Morrow, 1997

Beresford, David, *Ten Men Dead: The Story of the 1981 Irish Hunger Strike*, London: Grafton Books, 1987

Coogan, Tim Pat, *Michael Collins: A Biography*, London: Hutchinson, 1990

—, *Michael Collins: The Man Who Made Ireland*, London: Palgrave Macmillan, 2002

—, *Ireland in the Twentieth Century*, London: Palgrave Macmillan, 2004

Deutsch, Richard, and Vivien Magowan, *Northern Ireland 1968–73: A Chronology of Events*, Belfast: Blackstaff Press, 1974

Dillon, Martin, *The Dirty War*, London: Hutchinson, 1988

—, *The Shankill Butchers: A Case Study in Mass Murder*, London: Hutchinson, 1989

Elliott, Sidney, and W. D. Flackes, *Northern Ireland: A Political Directory, 1968–1999*, Belfast: Blackstaff Press, 1999

Farrell, Michael, *Northern Ireland: The Orange State*, London: Pluto Press, 1976

Holland, Jack, *The American Connection: US Guns, Money and Influence in Northern Ireland*, Dublin: Poolbeg Press, 1989

Hopkinson, Michael, *The Irish War of Independence*, Dublin: Gill and Macmillan, 2004

Kelley, Kevin, *The Longest War: Northern Ireland and the IRA*, Dingle, Co. Kerry: Brandon Books, 1983

McArdle, Dorothy, *The Irish Republic*, Dublin: Wolfhound Press, 1999

McDermott, Peter, *Northern Divisions: The Old IRA and the Belfast Pogroms 1920–1922*, Belfast: Beyond the Pale, 2001

McDonald, Henry, and Jim Cusack, *UVF: The Endgame*, Dublin: Poolbeg, 2008

McGuffin, John, *Internment*, Dublin: Anvil Books, 1973

McKittrick, David, Seamus Kelters, Brian Feeney, and Chris Thornton, *Lost Lives*, Edinburgh: Mainstream Publishing, 1999

Miller, David W., *Queen's Rebels: Ulster Loyalism in Historical Perspective*, Dublin: Gill and Macmillan, 1978

Moloney, Ed, *A Secret History of the IRA*, Harmondsworth: Penguin, 2007

—, *Paisley: From Demagogue to Democrat?*, Dublin: Poolbeg Press, 2008

Moloney, Ed, and Anthony McIntyre, *The Security Department: IRA Counter Intelligence in a 30-year War Against the British*, Georgetown University, Washington DC, April 2006; unpublished

Nelson, Sarah, *Ulster's Uncertain Defenders*, Belfast: Appletree Press, 1984

O'Malley, Padraig, *Biting at the Grave: The Irish Hunger Strikes and the Politics of Despair*, Boston: Beacon Press, 1990

O'Rawe, Richard, *Blanketmen: An Untold Story of the H-Block Hunger Strike*, Dublin: New Island, 2005

Reilly, Frances, *Suffer the Little Children*, London: Orion Books, 2009

Sharrock, David, and Mark Devenport, *Man of War, Man of Peace? The Unauthorised Biography of Gerry Adams*, London: Macmillan, 1997

Stewart, A. T. Q., *The Ulster Crisis: Resistance to Home Rule 1912–1914*, London: Faber and Faber, 1967

Taylor, Peter, *Provos: The IRA and Sinn Fein*, London: Bloomsbury, 1998

—, *Loyalists*, London: Bloomsbury, 2000

White, Robert W., *Provisional Irish Republicans: An Oral and Interpretative History*, Santa Barbara, Ca.: Greenwood Press, 1993

—, *Ruairi O Bradaigh: The Life and Politics of an Irish Revolutionary*, Bloomington, In.: Indiana University Press, 2006

PAMPHLETS, AND POLITICAL AND OFFICIAL PUBLICATIONS

*Common Sense* (UDA, 1987)

Hansard

Inquest documents in death of Patrick Crawford [redacted], Public Records Office of Northern Ireland

*The Lagan Enclave*, Ballymacarrett Research Group, 1987

*Murder in Ballymacarrett: The Untold Story*, East Belfast Historical and Cultural Society, 2003

*Operation Banner: An Analysis of Military Operations in Northern Ireland*, London: Ministry of Defence, July 2006

*Principles of Loyalism*, Progressive Unionist Party internal discussion paper, 1 November 2002

PSNI Ombudsman report, August 2006

Scarman Report

*Sharing Responsibility* (PUP, 1979)

WEBSITES

http://www.amnesty.org/en/news-and-updates/news/perus-ex-president-convicted-landmark-case-20090407

http://buckalecrobinson.rushlightmagazine.com

http://cain.ulst.ac.uk/events/bfriday/events.htm

http://cain.ulst.ac.uk/publicrecords/1972/index.html#210672

http://cain.ulst.ac.uk/publicrecords/1973/prem15_1689_1.jpg

http://cain.ulst.ac.uk/sutton
http://hansard.millbanksystems.com/written_answers/1994/mar/15/military-reaction-force
http://www.irishecho.com/search/searchstory.cfm?id=8371&issueid=174
http://www.parliament.the-stationery-office.com/pa/cm199798/cmselect/cmniaf/316ii/nis208.htm
http://thepensivequill.am
http://www.pbs.org/wgbh/pages/frontline/shows/ira/readings/america.htm

NEWSPAPERS AND MAGAZINES

*Belfast News Letter*
*Belfast Telegraph*
*Combat* (UVF magazine; later the *Purple Standard*)
*Daily Ireland*
*Daily Mail*
*Daily Telegraph*
*Guardian*
*Independent*
*Irish Independent*
*Irish News*
*Irish Times*
*An Phoblacht–Republican News*
*Sunday Mirror*
*The Sunday Times*
*Washington Post*

# INDEX

ED MOLONEY was born in England. A former Northern Ireland editor of the *Irish Times* and *Sunday Tribune*, he was named Irish Journalist of the Year in 1999. Apart from *A Secret History of the IRA*, he has written a biography of Ian Paisley. He now lives and works in New York.

Professor Thomas E. Hachey and Dr Robert K. O'Neill are the General Editors of the Boston College Center for Irish Programs IRA/UVF project, of which *Voices from the Grave* is the inaugural publication.

∾